The Evolving Presidency

Fifth Edition

CQ Press, an imprint of SAGE, is the leading publisher of books, periodicals, and electronic products on American government and international affairs. CQ Press consistently ranks among the top commercial publishers in terms of quality, as evidenced by the numerous awards its products have won over the years. CQ Press owes its existence to Nelson Poynter, former publisher of the *St. Petersburg Times,* and his wife Henrietta, with whom he founded Congressional Quarterly in 1945. Poynter established CQ with the mission of promoting democracy through education and in 1975 founded the Modern Media Institute, renamed The Poynter Institute for Media Studies after his death. The Poynter Institute (*www.poynter .org*) is a nonprofit organization dedicated to training journalists and media leaders.

In 2008, CQ Press was acquired by SAGE, a leading international publisher of journals, books, and electronic media for academic, educational, and professional markets. Since 1965, SAGE has helped inform and educate a global community of scholars, practitioners, researchers, and students spanning a wide range of subject areas, including business, humanities, social sciences, and science, technology, and medicine. A privately owned corporation, SAGE has offices in Los Angeles, Boston, London, New Delhi, and Singapore, in addition to the Washington DC office of CQ Press.

The Evolving Presidency

Landmark Documents,
1787–2015

Fifth Edition

Michael Nelson, Editor

Rhodes College

Los Angeles | London | New Delhi
Singapore | Washington DC | Boston

Los Angeles | London | New Delhi
Singapore | Washington DC | Boston

FOR INFORMATION:

CQ Press

An Imprint of SAGE Publications, Inc.

2455 Teller Road

Thousand Oaks, California 91320

E-mail: order@sagepub.com

SAGE Publications Ltd.

1 Oliver's Yard

55 City Road

London EC1Y 1SP

United Kingdom

SAGE Publications India Pvt. Ltd.

B 1/I 1 Mohan Cooperative Industrial Area

Mathura Road, New Delhi 110 044

India

SAGE Publications Asia-Pacific Pte. Ltd.

3 Church Street

#10-04 Samsung Hub

Singapore 049483

Printed in the United States of America

ISBN 978-1-4833-6856-6

This book is printed on acid-free paper.

Acquisitions Editor: Sarah Calabi

Editorial Assistant: Raquel Christie

Production Editor: Veronica Stapleton Hooper

Copy Editor: Terri Lee Paulsen

Typesetter: C&M Digitals (P) Ltd.

Proofreader: Alison Syring

Cover Designer: Scott Van Atta

Marketing Manager: Amy Whitaker

Certified Chain of Custody
Promoting Sustainable Forestry
www.sfiprogram.org
SFI-01268

SFI label applies to text stock

16 17 18 19 10 9 8 7 6 5 4 3 2

To my sons, Michael and Sam,
and my grandson, Mc Clain

❧ ❧

May our sons be like plants
growing strong from their earliest days.
(Psalm 144:12)

SAGE was founded in 1965 by Sara Miller McCune to support the dissemination of usable knowledge by publishing innovative and high-quality research and teaching content. Today, we publish more than 750 journals, including those of more than 300 learned societies, more than 800 new books per year, and a growing range of library products including archives, data, case studies, reports, conference highlights, and video. SAGE remains majority-owned by our founder, and after Sara's lifetime will become owned by a charitable trust that secures our continued independence.

Los Angeles | London | New Delhi | Singapore | Washington DC | Boston

Contents

Contents

Preface

A User's Guide to *The Evolving Presidency*

S OMETIMES NEW wine actually does fit into old wineskins. E-mail and text-messaging seem to have restored the lost art of note writing, to the astonishment and delight of the parents of college students. Political websites offer a newfangled way for like-minded activists to find each other and hold old-fashioned meetings. In classrooms, the Web's vast store of information has revived interest in primary and documentary sources, which for so long relegated to textbook summaries important historical texts, such as what James Monroe actually said in announcing his famous doctrine, or how the Supreme Court reasoned in its decision ordering Richard Nixon to turn over the Watergate tapes. But, as many students have found from experience, the Web's very abundance of information can be overwhelming.

This book is my effort to weave together for students of the presidency the virtues of primary and documentary sources with those of careful, reliable editing and close treatment of political and historical context. The documentary record of the presidency is rich and varied, ranging from laws and Supreme Court decisions to speeches and letters. This edition contains fifty-nine documents (four more than in the previous edition), including additions that reflect historically significant recent events, such as Barack Obama's 2015 State of the Union address and the Supreme Court's 2014 decision in *National Labor Relations Board v. Noel Canning et al.* It also fills gaps in the previous edition with the inclusion of excerpts from James Madison's Notes of the Federal Convention, George Mason's Objections to This Constitution of Government, Abraham Lincoln's 1861 Message to Congress in Special Session, Lord Bryce's Why Great Men Are Not Chosen President, Franklin D. Roosevelt's Executive Order on Japanese American Internment, the Truman Doctrine, and Lyndon B. Johnson's Equality of Result address.

The emphasis in this edition is still on the founding and the modern presidency, although Thomas Jefferson is represented by two documents, Andrew Jackson by two, and Abraham Lincoln by five. Many documents are printed in full; others have been edited both to highlight those sections that have proven to be of enduring importance and to preserve the flavor of the original. All of the documents are preceded by essays that place them in political and historical context. I have included a URL with each edited document, when available, for access to the complete, unedited text. Because of the ever-changing nature of the Web, however, readers should not assume that documents will always be available at the listed sites. Typing a phrase from the document into an Internet search engine is a good alternate strategy.

Students and professors will find that *The Evolving Presidency* fits well in a course on the American presidency or American political development. The table of contents is chronological, but courses that are organized into topical units such as the president and the Constitution, the president and Congress, and presidential elections will benefit from the Topical Guide on pages xv–xviii.

The Topical Guide shows that a course unit on, say, the president and the bureaucracy can draw profitably on some or all of the following documents in this book: the Constitution (1787); The Federalist Papers, Nos. 69 through 73 (1788); James Madison's Defense of the President's Removal Power (1789); Andrew Jackson's First Message to Congress (1829); the Articles of Impeachment against Andrew Johnson (1868); the Pendleton Act (1883); *Myers v. United States* (1926); *Humphrey's Executor v. United States* (1935); Report of the Brownlow Committee (1937); the Cuban Missile Crisis (1962); Walter F. Mondale's Memo to Jimmy Carter on the Role of the Vice President (1976); George W. Bush's Signing Statement for the Defense Supplemental Appropriations Act (2005); and *National Labor Relations Board v. Noel Canning et al.* (2014). Some of these documents could be used in other units as well, providing ample flexibility for course use. The *Canning* case, for example, would fit well in units on the president and the Constitution, the president and Congress, the president and the courts, or the president and domestic policy.

Librarians and researchers will find *The Evolving Presidency* to be a one-stop guide to the most important documents concerning the highest office in the land. A majority of presidents are represented in this book, several of them more than once. Ten Supreme Court decisions that have shaped the presidency are included. So are documents bearing on vital events in American history, such as the debate on the Constitution, the Civil War, the Great Depression, the civil rights movement, the Watergate scandal, and the war on terror.

Words generally serve me well, but they are inadequate to express my thanks to those involved in the publication of this book. I especially thank Charisse Kiino, the director of CQ Press's College division, who recognized the book's possibilities at an early stage and advised me well at every step on the way to completion, and Sarah Calabi, CQ Press's always perceptive and encouraging political science acquisitions editor, as well as Catherine Forrest, managing editor; Terri Lee Paulsen, copy editor; and Raquel Christie, editorial assistant; all of whom worked on the book with grace and skill. I also thank David Barrett (Villanova University), Brad Clark (Fort Lewis College), Albert Cover (SUNY Stonybrook), David Crockett (Trinity University), Matthew Dickinson (Middlebury College), Gary Donato (Bentley University), David Greenberg (Rutgers University), Timothy S. Huebner (Rhodes College), Ronald Lee (Rockford University), David Lewis (Vanderbilt University), Lauri McNown (University of Colorado), Andrew Moore (Saint Anselm College), Stephen K. Shaw (Northwest Nazarene University), Brooks D. Simpson (Arizona State University), Robert Speel (Penn State Erie), and Barry Tadlock (Ohio University) for their helpful comments on the previous editions of the book.

Topical Guide to the Documents

	Constitution & history	Pres. elect.	Pres. & public	W.H. staff	Pres. & burrcy	Pres. & Congress	Pres. & courts	Pres. & dom. pol.	Pres. & econ. pol.	Pres. & nat'l sec.
1. James Madison's Notes of the Federal Convention	×	×	×							
2. The Constitution	×	×			×	×	×	×	×	×
3. Anti-Federalist Essays: George Mason's "Objections to This Constitution of Government" and Cato's "Letter No. 4"	×			×		×				
4. *The Federalist Papers*, Nos. 69–73	×	×		×	×	×				×
5. George Washington's First Inaugural Address	×		×							
6. James Madison's Defense of the President's Removal Power	×				×	×				
7. The Pacificus-Helvidius Letters	×					×				×
8. George Washington's Farewell Address	×		×							×
9. Thomas Jefferson's First Inaugural Address		×	×							
10. Thomas Jefferson's Letter to the Vermont Legislature	×	×								
11. The Monroe Doctrine	×					×				×
12. The Tennessee General Assembly's Protest against the Caucus System		×						×		
13. Andrew Jackson's First Message to Congress	×	×	×		×					

(Continued)

	1	2	3	4	5	6	7	8
30. Report of the Brownlow Committee					×			×
31. Franklin D. Roosevelt's Executive Order on Japanese American Internment	×				×			×
32. The Truman Doctrine	×			×				×
33. *Youngstown Sheet & Tube Co. v. Sawyer*	×		×	×				×
34. Dwight D. Eisenhower's Little Rock Executive Order	×	×	×					×
35. John F. Kennedy's Inaugural Address							×	
36. The Cuban Missile Crisis: John F. Kennedy's Letter to Soviet Premier Nikita Khrushchev	×		×		×	×		×
37. Lyndon B. Johnson's "Great Society" Speech	×	×		×			×	
38. Lyndon B. Johnson's Gulf of Tonkin Message	×			×				×
39. Lyndon B. Johnson's "Equality of Result" Speech	×	×					×	
40. Richard Nixon's China Trip Announcement	×						×	×
41. The McGovern–Fraser Commission Report					×			
42. The War Powers Resolution	×			×				×
43. Proposed Articles of Impeachment against Richard Nixon	×			×		×	×	
44. *United States v. Nixon*	×	×				×		×
45. Gerald R. Ford's Pardon of Richard Nixon	×	×					×	

(Continued)

Topical Guide to the Documents (Continued)

James Madison's Notes of the Federal Convention*

(1787)

"LADIES AND GENTLEMEN, the presi*dents* of the United States."

A typographical error, right? Not if certain delegates to the Constitutional Convention had had their way. The question of whether the national executive should be unitary—a person—or plural—a group of people—occasioned the convention's first serious debate about the nature of the executive in the new plan of government the delegates were creating.

The convention came into being because on February 21, 1787, the Confederation Congress passed a resolution calling for "a Convention of delegates who shall have been appointed by the several states to be held in Philadelphia for the sole and express purpose of revising the Articles of Confederation." The government that had been created by the Articles in 1781 was widely regarded as having a number of weaknesses, including insufficient powers and the absence of an executive branch.

The convention met from May 25 to September 17, 1787. The delegates went far beyond their charter, drafting an entirely new plan of government that, if approved by nine of the thirteen states, would replace the Articles.

The presidency is the Constitution's most original feature. Yet although Virginia delegate James Madison often is referred to as "the father of the Constitution," his paternity does not extend to the executive branch. As Madison readily admitted, his views about the executive were vague and variable. Like most of the delegates, he feared both executive power and executive weakness, regarding the former as the seed of tyranny and the latter as the wellspring of anarchy.

In advance of the convention, Madison helped to write the Virginia Plan, a draft for an entirely new government that was presented to the delegates by his state's governor, Edmund Randolph, on May 29. The plan included a provision for a "National Executive," as well as a "National Legislature" and a "National Judiciary," but it said nothing about whether the executive would be unitary or plural. The convention accepted the Virginia Plan as its working document, and then reconstituted itself as a Committee of the Whole House to review it thoroughly.

The debate on the executive began on June 1, when Pennsylvania delegate James Wilson "moved that the Executive consist of a single person." In his daily

*Go to *http://avalon.law.yale.edu/subject_menus/debcont.asp*.

notes on the convention, Madison recorded "a considerable pause" in the debate as the delegates considered the magnitude of the decision Wilson was asking them to make.

Concern that a unitary executive would be "the foetus of monarchy," in Randolph's phrase, prompted some convention members to propose alternatives. Randolph favored "three members of the Executive to be drawn from different portions of the Country." Roger Sherman of Connecticut urged leaving the decision to the legislature, which at different times might prefer that "a person or persons" execute its decisions, depending on circumstances. Massachusetts delegate Elbridge Gerry wanted to attach a council to any executive the convention decided to create "in order to give weight & inspire confidence."

In the end, Wilson's argument that a unitary executive would give "most energy dispatch and responsibility to the office" prevailed. A plural executive could not lead, act promptly in time of crisis, or be held accountable, he contended. Seven state delegations voted in favor of Wilson's motion, with only three opposed. Madison records that Virginia delegate George Washington, the most esteemed person in the country, voted aye. Washington and his fellow delegates knew that if a new plan of government were adopted, the first unitary executive would be him.

⁂ ⁂ ⁂

Tuesday, May 29

. . . Resolutions proposed by Mr. [Edmund] Randolph [of Virginia] in Convention . . .

7. Resd. that a National Executive be instituted; to be chosen by the National Legislature for the term of——— years, to receive punctually at stated times, a fixed compensation for the services rendered, in which no increase or diminution shall be made so as to affect the Magistracy, existing at the time of increase or diminution, and to be ineligible a second time; and that besides a general authority to execute the National laws, it ought to enjoy the Executive rights vested in Congress by the Confederation. . . .

He concluded with an exhortation, not to suffer the present opportunity of establishing general peace, harmony, happiness and liberty in the U. S. to pass away unimproved.

It was then Resolved—That the House will tomorrow resolve itself into a Committee of the Whole House to consider of the state of the American Union.—and that the propositions moved by Mr. Randolph be referred to the said Committee.

Adjourned. . . .

Friday, June 1

. . . The Committee of the whole proceeded to Resolution 7. "that a national Executive be instituted, to be chosen by the national Legislature-for the term of———years &c to be ineligible thereafter, to possess the executive powers of Congress &c."

Mr. {Charles Cotesworth} PIN{C}KNEY {of South Carolina} was for a vigorous Executive but was afraid the Executive powers of the existing Congress might extend to peace & war &c., which would render the Executive a monarchy, of the worst kind, to wit an elective one.

Mr. {James} WILSON {of Pennsylvania} moved that the Executive consist of a single person.

Mr. C{harles} PIN{C}KNEY {of South Carolina} seconded the motion, so as to read "that a National Ex. to consist of a single person, be instituted.

A considerable pause ensuing and the Chairman asking if he should put the question, Docr. {Benjamin} FRANKLIN {of Pennsylvania} observed that it was a point of great importance and wished that the gentlemen would deliver their sentiments on it before the question was put.

Mr. {John} RUTL{E}DGE of {South Carolina} animadverted on the shyness of gentlemen on this and other subjects. He said it looked as if they supposed themselves precluded by having frankly disclosed their opinions from afterwards changing them, which he did not take to be at all the case. He said he was for vesting the Executive power in a single person, tho' he was not for giving him the power of war and peace. A single man would feel the greatest responsibility and administer the public affairs best.

Mr. {Roger} SHERMAN {of Connecticut} said he considered the Executive magistracy as nothing more than an institution for carrying the will of the Legislature into effect, that the person or persons ought to be appointed by and accountable to the Legislature only, which was the depositary of the supreme will of the Society. As they were the best judges of the business which ought to be done by the Executive department, and consequently of the number necessary from time to time for doing it, he wished the number might not be fixed but that the legislature should be at liberty to appoint one or more as experience might dictate.

Mr. WILSON preferred a single magistrate, as giving most energy dispatch and responsibility to the office. He did not consider the Prerogatives of the British Monarch as a proper guide in defining the Executive powers. Some of these prerogatives were of Legislative nature. Among others that of war & peace &c. The only powers he conceived strictly Executive were those of executing the laws, and appointing officers, not appertaining to and appointed by the Legislature.

Mr. {Elbridge} GERRY {of Massachusetts} favored the policy of annexing a Council to the Executive in order to give weight & inspire confidence.

Mr. RANDOLPH strenuously opposed a unity in the Executive magistracy. He regarded it as the foetus of monarchy. We had he said no motive to be governed by the British Governmt. as our prototype. He did not mean however to throw censure on that Excellent fabric. If we were in a situation to copy it he did not know that he should be opposed to it; but the fixt genius of the people of America required a different form of Government. He could not see why the great requisites for the Executive department, vigor, despatch & responsibility could not be found in three men, as well as in one man. The Executive ought to be independent. It ought therefore in order to support its independence to consist of more than one.

Mr. WILSON said that unity in the Executive instead of being the fetus of monarchy would be the best safeguard against tyranny. He repeated that he was not governed by the British Model which was inapplicable to the situation of this Country; the extent of which was so great, and the manners so republican, that nothing but a great confederated Republic would do for it.

Mr. Wilson's motion for a single magistrate was postponed by common consent, the Committee seeming unprepared for any decision on it; and the first part of the clause agreed to, viz-"that a National Executive be instituted."

Saturday, June 2

. . . Mr. RUTL[E]DGE & Mr. C. PIN[C]KNEY moved that the blank for the no. of persons in the Executive be filled with the words "one person." He supposed the reasons to be so obvious & conclusive in favor of one that no member would oppose the motion.

Mr. RANDOLPH opposed it with great earnestness, declaring that he should not do justice to the Country which sent him if he were silently to suffer the establishmt. of a Unity in the Executive department. He felt an opposition to it which he believed he should continue to feel as long as he lived. He urged 1. that the permanent temper of the people was adverse to the very semblance of Monarchy. 2. that a unity was unnecessary a plurality being equally competent to all the objects of the department. 3. that the necessary confidence would never be reposed in a single Magistrate. 4. that the appointments would generally be in favor of some inhabitant near the center of the Community, and consequently the remote parts would not be on an equal footing. He was in favor of three members of the Executive to be drawn from different portions of the Country.

Mr. [Pierce] BUTLER [of South Carolina] contended strongly for a single magistrate as most likely to answer the purpose of the remote parts. If one man should be appointed he would be responsible to the whole, and would be impartial to its interests. If three or more should be taken from as many districts, there would be a constant struggle for local advantages. In Military matters this would be particularly mischievous. He said his opinion on this point had been formed under the opportunity he had had of seeing the manner in which a plurality of military heads distracted Holland when threatened with invasion by the imperial troops. One man was for directing the force to the defence of this part, another to that part of the Country, just as he happened to be swayed by prejudice or interest.

The motion was then postpd. the Committee rose & the House Adjd. . . .

Monday, June 4

The Question was resumed on motion of **Mr. PIN[C]KNEY** 2ded. by **WILSON**, "shall the blank for the number of the Executive be filled with a single person?"

Mr. WILSON was in favor of the motion. It had been opposed by the gentleman from Virga. [**Mr. Randolph**] but the arguments used had not convinced him. He observed that the objections of Mr. R. were levelled not so much agst. the measure itself, as agst. its unpopularity. If he could suppose that it would occasion a rejection of the plan of which it should form a part, though the part was an important one, yet he would give it up rather than lose the whole. On examination he could see no evidence of the alledged antipathy of the people. On the contrary he was persuaded that it does not exist. All know that a single magistrate is not a King. One fact has great weight with him. All the 13 States tho agreeing in scarce any other instance, agree in placing a single magistrate at the head of the Governt. The idea of three heads has taken place in none. The degree of power is indeed different; but there are no co-ordinate heads. In addition to his former reasons for preferring a unity, he would mention another. The tranquility not less than the vigor of the Govt. he thought would be favored by it. Among three equal members, he foresaw nothing but uncontrouled, continued, & violent animosities; which would not only interrupt the public administration; but diffuse their poison thro' the other branches of Govt., thro' the States, and at length thro' the people at large. If the members were to be unequal in power the principle of the opposition to the unity was given up. If equal, then making them an odd number would not be a remedy. In Courts of Justice there are two sides only to a question. In the Legislative & Executive departmts. questions have commonly many sides. Each member therefore might espouse a separate one & no two agree.

Mr. SHERMAN. This matter is of great importance and ought to be well considered before it is determined. Mr. Wilson he said had observed that in each State a single magistrate was placed at the head of the Govt. It was so he admitted, and properly so, and he wished the same policy to prevail in the federal Govt. But then it should be also remarked that in all the States there was a Council of advice, without which the first magistrate could not act. A council he thought necessary to make the establishment acceptable to the people. Even in G. B. the King has a Council; and though he appoints it himself, its advice has its weight with him, and attracts the Confidence of the people.

Mr. [Hugh] WILLIAMSON [of North Carolina] asks **Mr. WILSON** whether he means to annex a Council.

Mr. WILSON means to have no Council, which oftener serves to cover, than prevent malpractices.

Mr. GERRY was at a loss to discover the policy of three members for the Executive. It Wd. be extremely inconvenient in many instances, particularly in military matters, whether relating to the militia, an army, or a navy. It would be a general with three heads.

On the question for a single Executive it was agreed to Massts. ay. Cont. ay. N. Y. no.
Pena. ay. Del. no. Maryd. no. Virg. ay. [Mr. R[andolph]. & Mr.[John] Blair no-Docr.
[James]Mc.C[lur]g. Mr. [James] M[adison]. & Gen [George] W[ashington]. ay. Col.
[George] Mason being no, but not in house, Mr. [George] Wythe ay but gone home].
N. C. ay. S. C. ay. Georgia ay.

⤙ 2 ⤚

The Constitution*

(1787)

THE PRESIDENCY was the Constitutional Convention's most creative act. In designing Congress and the Supreme Court, the delegates were guided by long experience with legislatures and courts. But when it came to the executive, they were in a quandary. The executives with which they were familiar were either too powerful, like the British king, or too weak, like the state governors. Similarly, their study of history provided no example of an effective and accountable republican executive.

In the course of inventing the presidency, the Convention considered a number of proposals. The ideas ranged from Connecticut delegate Roger Sherman's suggestion of a committee-style executive that would be elected by Congress for the sole purpose of "carrying the will of the Legislature into effect," to New York delegate Alexander Hamilton's plan for a one-person "Governor" chosen by electors and granted vast powers and lifetime tenure. Hamilton's plan was considered too extreme, but other delegates—notably James Wilson and Gouverneur Morris, both of Pennsylvania—nevertheless succeeded in persuading the convention to create a strong presidency. The near-certain knowledge that George Washington, who presided over the convention, would be the first president was a source of reassurance to many delegates.

Most of what the Constitution says about the presidency is in Article II. It provides that the president is elected by an Electoral College to a four-year term and is empowered, among other things, to recommend legislation to Congress; to appoint, with the Senate's advice and consent, judges and executive officials; to command the army and navy; to negotiate treaties; and to issue pardons. Congress may impeach and remove a president for committing acts of "Treason, Bribery, or other high Crimes and Misdemeanors."

Other provisions of Article II include qualifications for president, the presidential oath, and a restriction on the ability of Congress to change the salary of an

---

*Go to *www.law.ou.edu/hist/constitution*.

incumbent president. The Constitution also created the vice presidency and charged the vice president (originally, the second-place finisher in the presidential election) to serve as president of the Senate and successor to the president should the office become vacant. Article I, which deals with Congress, is the source of the president's power to veto congressional legislation.

The proposed Constitution was ratified by the ninth state (New Hampshire) on June 21, 1788, and took effect on March 4, 1789. In subsequent years, several constitutional amendments were added to the document that deal with the presidency and vice presidency. The Twelfth Amendment (1804) adapted the Electoral College to the rise of political parties by requiring electors to cast separate ballots for president and vice president. The Twentieth Amendment (1933) advanced the start of the president's term from March 4 to January 20. The Twenty-second Amendment (1951) imposed a two-term limit on the president. (The framers had felt strongly that there should be no limit on presidential reeligibility.) The Twenty-fifth Amendment (1967) charged the president, with confirmation by Congress, to appoint a vice president when the vice presidency becomes vacant. It also created procedures to govern situations of presidential disability. Other constitutional amendments have affected the circumstances under which presidents are elected, such as the Twenty-third Amendment (1961), which granted the District of Columbia the right to participate in presidential elections, and the Twenty-fourth Amendment (1964), which barred the poll tax from all federal elections. Except for the two-term limit, none of these changes altered the fundamental design of the presidency invented by the Convention in 1787.

Article I

SECTION 1. All legislative Powers herein granted shall be vested in a Congress of the United States, which shall consist of a Senate and House of Representatives.

SECTION 2. . . . The House of Representatives shall chuse their Speaker and other Officers; and shall have the sole Power of Impeachment.

SECTION 3. . . . The Vice President of the United States shall be President of the Senate, but shall have no Vote, unless they be equally divided.

The Senate shall chuse their other Officers, and also a President pro tempore, in the Absence of the Vice President, or when he shall exercise the Office of President of the United States.

The Senate shall have the sole Power to try all Impeachments. When sitting for that Purpose, they shall be on Oath or Affirmation. When the President of the United States is tried, the Chief Justice shall preside: And no Person shall be convicted without the Concurrence of two thirds of the Members present.

Judgment in Cases of Impeachment shall not extend further than to removal from Office, and disqualification to hold and enjoy any Office of honor, Trust or Profit under the United States: but the Party convicted shall nevertheless be liable and subject to Indictment, Trial, Judgment and Punishment, according to Law. . . .

SECTION 6. . . . No Senator or Representative shall, during the Time for which he was elected, be appointed to any civil Office under the Authority of the United States, which shall have been created, or the Emoluments whereof shall have been encreased during such time; and no Person holding any Office under the United States, shall be a Member of either House during his Continuance in Office.

SECTION 7. . . . Every Bill which shall have passed the House of Representatives and the Senate, shall, before it become a Law, be presented to the President of the United States; If he approve he shall sign it, but if not he shall return it, with his Objections to that House in which it shall have originated, who shall enter the Objections at large on their Journal, and proceed to reconsider it. If after such Reconsideration two thirds of that House shall agree to pass the Bill, it shall be sent, together with the Objections, to the other House, by which it shall likewise be reconsidered, and if approved by two thirds of that House, it shall become a Law. But in all such Cases the Votes of both Houses shall be determined by yeas and Nays, and the Names of the Persons voting for and against the Bill shall be entered on the Journal of each House respectively. If any Bill shall not be returned by the President within ten Days (Sundays excepted) after it shall have been presented to him, the Same shall be a Law, in like Manner as if he had signed it, unless the Congress by their Adjournment prevent its Return, in which Case it shall not be a Law.

Every Order, Resolution, or Vote to which the Concurrence of the Senate and House of Representatives may be necessary (except on a question of Adjournment) shall be presented to the President of the United States; and before the Same shall take Effect, shall be approved by him, or being disapproved by him, shall be repassed by two thirds of the Senate and House of Representatives, according to the Rules and Limitations prescribed in the Case of a Bill. . . .

Article II

SECTION 1. The executive Power shall be vested in a President of the United States of America. He shall hold his Office during the Term of four Years, and, together with the Vice President, chosen for the same Term, be elected, as follows.

Each State shall appoint, in such Manner as the Legislature thereof may direct, a Number of Electors, equal to the whole Number of Senators and Representatives to which the State may be entitled in the Congress: but no Senator or Representative, or Person holding an Office of Trust or Profit under the United States, shall be appointed an Elector.

[The Electors shall meet in their respective States, and vote by Ballot for two Persons, of whom one at least shall not be an Inhabitant of the same State with themselves. And they shall make a List of all the Persons voted for, and of the Number of Votes for each; which List they shall sign and certify, and transmit sealed to the Seat of the Government of the United States, directed to the President of the Senate. The President of the Senate shall, in the Presence of the Senate and House of Representatives, open all the Certificates, and the Votes shall then be counted. The Person having the greatest Number of Votes shall be the President, if such Number be a Majority of the whole Number of Electors appointed; and if there be more than one who have such Majority, and have an equal Number of Votes, then the House of Representatives shall immediately chuse by Ballot one of them for President; and if no Person have a Majority, then from the five highest on the list the said House shall in like Manner chuse the President. But in chusing the President, the Votes shall be taken by States, the Representation from each State having one Vote; a quorum for this Purpose shall consist of a Member or Members from two thirds of the States, and a Majority of all the States shall be necessary to a Choice. In every Case, after the Choice of the President, the Person having the greatest Number of Votes of the Electors shall be the Vice President. But if there should remain two or more who have equal Votes, the Senate shall chuse from them by Ballot the Vice President. [superseded by Amendment XII]

The Congress may determine the Time of chusing the Electors, and the Day on which they shall give their Votes; which Day shall be the same throughout the United States.

No Person except a natural born Citizen, or a Citizen of the United States, at the time of the Adoption of this Constitution, shall be eligible to the Office of President; neither shall any Person be eligible to that Office who shall not have attained to the Age of thirty five Years, and been fourteen Years a Resident within the United States.

In Case of the Removal of the President from Office, or of his Death, Resignation, or Inability to discharge the Powers and Duties of the said Office, the Same shall devolve on the Vice President, and the Congress may by Law provide for the Case of Removal, Death, Resignation or Inability, both of the President and Vice President, declaring what Officer shall then act as President, and such Officer shall act accordingly, until the Disability be removed, or a President shall be elected.

The President shall, at stated Times, receive for his Services, a Compensation, which shall neither be encreased nor diminished during the Period for which he shall have been elected, and he shall not receive within that Period any other Emolument from the United States, or any of them.

Before he enter on the Execution of his Office, he shall take the following Oath or Affirmation:—"I do solemnly swear (or affirm) that I will faithfully execute the Office of President of the United States, and will to the best of my Ability, preserve, protect and defend the Constitution of the United States."

SECTION 2. The President shall be Commander in Chief of the Army and Navy of the United States, and of the Militia of the several States, when called into the actual Service of the United States; he may require the Opinion, in writing, of the principal Officer in each of the executive Departments, upon any Subject relating to the Duties of their respective Offices, and he shall have Power to grant Reprieves and Pardons for Offenses against the United States, except in Cases of Impeachment.

He shall have Power, by and with the Advice and Consent of the Senate, to make Treaties, provided two thirds of the Senators present concur; and he shall nominate, and by and with the Advice and Consent of the Senate, shall appoint Ambassadors, other public Ministers and Consuls, Judges of the supreme Court, and all other Officers of the United States, whose Appointments are not herein otherwise provided for, and which shall be established by Law: but the Congress may by Law vest the

Appointment of such inferior Officers, as they think proper, in the President alone, in the Courts of Law, or in the Heads of Departments.

The President shall have Power to fill up all Vacancies that may happen during the Recess of the Senate, by granting Commissions which shall expire at the End of their next Session.

SECTION 3. He shall from time to time give to the Congress Information of the State of the Union, and recommend to their Consideration such Measures as he shall judge necessary and expedient; he may, on extraordinary Occasions, convene both Houses, or either of them, and in Case of Disagreement between them, with Respect to the Time of Adjournment, he may adjourn them to such Time as he shall think proper; he shall receive Ambassadors and other public Ministers; he shall take Care that the Laws be faithfully executed, and shall Commission all the Officers of the United States.

SECTION 4. The President, Vice President and all Civil Officers of the United States, shall be removed from office on Impeachment for, and Conviction of, Treason, Bribery, or other high Crimes and Misdemeanors.

Article III

SECTION 1. The judicial Power of the United States, shall be vested in one supreme Court, and in such inferior Courts as the Congress may from time to time ordain and establish. . . .

Amendment XII
(Ratified June 15, 1804)

The Electors shall meet in their respective states and vote by ballot for President and Vice-President, one of whom, at least, shall not be an inhabitant of the same state with themselves; they shall name in their ballots the person voted for as President, and in distinct ballots the person voted for as Vice-President, and they shall make distinct lists of all persons voted for as President, and of all persons voted for as Vice-President, and of the number of votes for each, which lists they shall sign and certify, and transmit sealed to the seat of the government of the United States, directed to the President of the Senate;—The President of the Senate shall, in the presence of the Senate and House of Representatives, open all the certificates and the votes shall then be counted;—The person having the greatest number of votes for President, shall be the President, if such number be a majority of the whole number of Electors appointed; and if no person have such majority, then from the persons having the highest numbers not exceeding three on the list of those voted for as President, the House of Representatives shall choose immediately, by ballot, the President. But in choosing the President, the votes shall be taken by states, the representation from each state having one vote; a quorum for this purpose shall consist of a member or members from two-thirds of the states, and a majority of all the states shall be necessary to a choice. [And if the House of Representatives shall not choose a President whenever the right of choice shall devolve upon them, before the fourth day of March next following, then the Vice-President shall act as President, as in the case of the death or other constitutional disability of the President—]* The person having the greatest number of votes as Vice-President, shall be the Vice-President, if such number be a majority of the whole number of Electors appointed, and if no person have a majority, then from the two highest numbers on the list, the Senate shall choose the Vice-President; a quorum for the purpose shall consist of two-thirds of the whole number of Senators, and a majority of the whole number shall be necessary to a choice. But no person constitutionally ineligible to the office of President shall be eligible to that of Vice-President of the United States. . . .

Amendment XX
(Ratified January 23, 1933)

SECTION 1. The terms of the President and Vice President shall end at noon on the 20th day of January, and the terms of Senators and Representatives at noon on the 3d day of January, of the years in which such terms would have ended if this article had not been ratified; and the terms of their successors shall then begin. . . .

SECTION 3. If, at the time fixed for the beginning of the term of the President, the President elect shall have died, the Vice President elect shall become President. If a President shall not have been chosen before the time fixed for the beginning of his term, or if the President elect shall have failed to qualify, then the Vice President elect shall act as President until a President shall have qualified; and the Congress may by law provide for the case wherein neither a President elect nor a Vice President elect shall have qualified, declaring who shall then act as President, or the manner in which one who is to act shall be selected, and such person shall act accordingly until a President or Vice President shall have qualified.

SECTION 4. The Congress may by law provide for the case of the death of any of the persons from whom the House of Representatives may choose a President whenever the right of choice shall have devolved upon them, and for the case of the death of any of the persons from whom the Senate may choose a Vice President whenever the right of choice shall have devolved upon them.

SECTION 5. Sections 1 and 2 shall take effect on the 15th day of October following the ratification of this article.

SECTION 6. This article shall be inoperative unless it shall have been ratified as an amendment to the Constitution by the legislatures of three-fourths of the several States within seven years from the date of its submission. . . .

Amendment XXII
(Ratified February 27, 1951)

SECTION 1. No person shall be elected to the office of the President more than twice, and no person who has held the office of President, or acted as President, for more than two years of a term to which some other person was elected President shall be elected to the office of the President more than once. But this Article shall not apply to any person holding the office of President when this Article was proposed by the Congress, and shall not prevent any person who may be holding the office of President, or acting as President, during the term within which this Article becomes operative from holding the office of President or acting as President during the remainder of such term.

SECTION 2. This Article shall be inoperative unless it shall have been ratified as an amendment to the Constitution by the legislatures of three-fourths of the several States within seven years from the date of its submission to the States by the Congress.

Amendment XXIII
(Ratified March 29, 1961)

SECTION 1. The District constituting the seat of Government of the United States shall appoint in such manner as the Congress may direct:

A number of electors of President and Vice President equal to the whole number of Senators and Representatives in Congress to which the District would be entitled if it were a State, but in no event more than the least populous State; they shall be in addition to those appointed by the States, but they shall be considered, for the purposes of the election of President and Vice President, to be electors appointed by a State; and they shall meet in the District and perform such duties as provided by the twelfth article of amendment.

SECTION 2. The Congress shall have power to enforce this article by appropriate legislation.

Amendment XXIV
(Ratified January 23, 1964)

SECTION 1. The right of citizens of the United States to vote in any primary or other election for President or Vice President, for electors for President or Vice President, or for Senator or Representative in Congress, shall not be denied or abridged by the United States or any State by reason of failure to pay any poll tax or other tax.

SECTION 2. The Congress shall have power to enforce this article by appropriate legislation.

Amendment XXV
(Ratified February 10, 1967)

SECTION 1. In case of the removal of the President from office or of his death or resignation, the Vice President shall become President.

SECTION 2. Whenever there is a vacancy in the office of the Vice President, the President shall nominate a Vice President who shall take office upon confirmation by a majority vote of both Houses of Congress.

SECTION 3. Whenever the President transmits to the President pro tempore of the Senate and the Speaker of the House of Representatives his written declaration that he is unable to discharge the powers and duties of his office, and until he transmits to them a written declaration to the contrary, such powers and duties shall be discharged by the Vice President as Acting President.

SECTION 4. Whenever the Vice President and a majority of either the principal officers of the executive departments or of such other body as Congress may by law provide, transmit to the President pro tempore of the Senate and the Speaker of the House of Representatives their written declaration that the President is unable to discharge the powers and duties of his office, the Vice President shall immediately assume the powers and duties of the office as Acting President.

Thereafter, when the President transmits to the President pro tempore of the Senate and the Speaker of the House of Representatives his written declaration that no inability exists, he shall resume the powers and duties of his office unless the Vice President and a majority of either the principal officers of the executive department or of such other body as Congress may by law provide, transmit within four days to the President pro tempore of the Senate and the Speaker of the House of Representatives their written declaration that the President is unable to discharge the powers and duties of his office. Thereupon Congress shall decide the issue, assembling within forty-eight hours for that purpose if not in session. If the Congress, within twenty-one days after receipt of the latter written declaration, or, if Congress is not in session, within twenty-one days after Congress is required to assemble, determines by two-thirds vote of both houses that the President is unable to discharge the powers and duties of his office, the Vice President shall continue to discharge the same as Acting President; otherwise, the President shall resume the powers and duties of his office.

❧ 3 ❧

Anti-Federalist Essays: George Mason's Objections to This Constitution of Government and Cato's Letter No. 4[*]

(1787)

ARTICLE II POSED a political problem for those who were trying to persuade the states to ratify the Constitution. The presidency was the most obvious and important innovation in the proposed plan of government, and its unitary

---

[*]Go to *http://www.gunstonhall.org/library/archives/manuscripts/objections.html* and *http://press-pubs .uchicago.edu/founders/documents/a2_1_1s6.html.*

nature and strong powers roused fears of the most horrifying political specter that many Americans could imagine: a powerful monarchy like the one they had overthrown in the Revolutionary War. Opponents of the Constitution—the so-called Anti-Federalists—effectively exploited these fears.

Two of the first Anti-Federalist writers to publish their objections to the Constitution were George Mason, a Virginia delegate to the Constitutional Convention who refused to sign the document, and "Cato," who is believed to have been either Gov. George Clinton of New York or Abraham Yates Jr., a New York delegate who left midway through the convention in silent protest. Mason's use of his real name was unusual at the time. Pseudonymous political writings, often under a name from Roman antiquity, were more customary. "Brutus," "Marcus," "Agrippa," and the well-known "Publius," the listed author of *The Federalist Papers,* were among the writers who contributed to the ratification debate, along with "The Federal Farmer" and "The Republican."

Mason published his objections to the proposed Constitution in October 1787 as the opening salvo in his campaign to persuade Virginia to vote against ratification. Although best known for objecting to the absence of a bill of rights in the document, Mason also disliked certain features of the presidency. In the absence of a "Constitutional Council" chosen by the House of Representatives, he claimed, the president "would be unsupported by proper information and advice, and will generally be directed by minions and favorites." Mason also criticized the president's unilateral pardon power, the exclusion of the House from treaty making, and the vice presidency for "dangerously blending the executive and legislative powers." So opposed was Mason to the Constitution that his major doubt was whether the government it created would degenerate into "a monarchy, or a corrupt, tyrannical aristocracy."

In his fourth (November 8) letter, Cato attacked the president as a monarch in disguise: surrounded by a royal court, "oppressing his fellow-citizens and raising himself to permanent grandeur on the ruins of his country." Some of Cato's warnings now seem farfetched. For example, he charged that the Constitution required that only one election ever be held. But other of his cautions were prescient, especially his concern that the national capital, and the president in particular, could become insulated from the rest of the country.

Mason's and Cato's identification of the presidency with monarchy was echoed by many other Anti-Federalists. At the Virginia ratifying convention, Gov. Patrick Henry charged: "This Constitution is said to have beautiful features, but when I come to examine these features, Sir, they appear to me to be horridly frightful: Among other deformities, it has an awful squinting; it squints toward monarchy: And does this not raise indignation in the breast of every American?" Narrowly rejecting his, Cato's, and Mason's concerns, the Virginia convention ratified the document by a vote of 89–79.

George Mason, Objections to This Constitution of Government

There is no Declaration of Rights, and the laws of the general government being paramount to the laws and constitution of the several States, the Declarations of Rights in the separate States are no security. Nor are the people secured even in the enjoyment of the benefit of the common law. . . .

The President of the United States has no Constitutional Council, a thing unknown in any safe and regular government. He will therefore be unsupported by proper information and advice, and will generally be directed by minions and favorites; or he will become a tool to the Senate—or a Council of State will grow out of the principal officers of the great departments; the worst and most dangerous of all ingredients for such a Council in a free country; From this fatal defect has arisen the improper power of the Senate in the appointment of public officers, and the alarming dependence and connection between that branch of the legislature and the supreme Executive.

Hence also sprang that unnecessary officer the Vice-President, who for want of other employment is made president of the Senate, thereby dangerously blending the executive and legislative powers, besides always giving to some one of the States an unnecessary and unjust pre-eminence over the others.

The President of the United States has the unrestrained power of granting pardons for treason, which may be sometimes exercised to screen from punishment those whom he had secretly instigated to commit the crime, and thereby prevent a discovery of his own guilt.

By declaring all treaties supreme laws of the land, the Executive and the Senate have, in many cases, an exclusive power of legislation; which might have been avoided by proper distinctions with respect to treaties, and requiring the assent of the House of Representatives, where it could be done with safety. . . .

This government will set out a moderate aristocracy: it is at present impossible to foresee whether it will, in its operation, produce a monarchy, or a corrupt, tyrannical aristocracy; it will most probably vibrate some years between the two, and then terminate in the one or the other. . . .

᠅ ᠅ ᠅

Cato, Letter No. 4

To the Citizens of the State of New York.

. . . I shall begin with observations on the executive branch of this new system; and though it is not the first in order, as arranged therein, yet being the *chief*, is perhaps entitled by the rules of rank to the first consideration. The executive power as described in the 2d article, consists of a president and vice-president, who are to hold their offices during the term of four years; the same article has marked the manner and time of their election, and established the qualifications of the president; it also provides against the removal, death, or inability of the president and vice-president—regulates the salary, of the president, delineates his duties and powers; and, lastly, declares the causes for which the president and vice-president shall be removed from office.

Notwithstanding, the great learning and abilities of the gentlemen who composed the convention, it may be here remarked with deference, that the construction of the first paragraph of the first section of the second article is vague and inexplicit, and leaves the mind in doubt as to the election of a president and vice-president, after the expiration of the election for the first term of four years; in every other case, the election of these great officers is expressly provided for; but there is no explicit provision for their election in case of expiration of their offices, subsequent to the election which is to set this political machine in motion, no certain and express terms as in your state constitution, that *statedly* once in every four years, and as often as these offices shall become vacant, by expiration or otherwise, as is therein expressed, an election shall be held as follows, &c., this inexplicitness perhaps may lead to an establishment for life.

It is remarked by Mon[t]esquieu, in treating of republics, that in all magistracies, the greatness of the power must be compensated by the brevity of the duration, and that a longer time than a year would be dangerous. It is, therefore, obvious to the least intelligent mind to account why great power in the hands of a magistrate, and that power connected with considerable duration, may be dangerous to the liberties of a republic, the deposit of vast trusts in the hands of a single magistrate, enables him in their exercise to create a numerous train of dependents; this tempts his ambition, which in a republican magistrate is also remarked, to be pernicious, and the duration of his office for any considerable time favors his views, gives him the means and time to perfect and execute his designs, he therefore fancies that he may be great and glorious by oppressing his fellow citizens, and raising himself to permanent grandeur on the ruins of his country. And here it may be necessary to compare the vast and important powers of the president, together with his continuance in office, with the foregoing doctrine— his eminent magisterial situation will attach many adherents to him, and he will be surrounded by expectants and courtiers, his power of nomination and influence on all appointments, the strong posts in each state comprised within his superintendence, and garrisoned by troops under his direction, his control over the army, militia, and navy, the unrestrained power of granting pardons for treason, which may be used to screen from punishment those whom he had secretly instigated to commit the crime, and thereby prevent a discovery of his own guilt, his duration in office for four years: these, and various other principles evidently prove the truth of the position, that if the president is possessed of ambition, he has power and time sufficient to ruin his country.

Though the president, during the sitting of the legislature, is assisted by the senate, yet he is without a constitutional council in their recess; he will therefore be unsupported by proper information and advice, and will generally be directed by minions and favorites, or a council of state will grow out of the principal officers of the great departments, the most dangerous council in a free country.

The ten miles square, which is to become the seat of government, will of course be the place of residence for the president and the great officers of state; the same observations of a great man will apply to the court of a president possessing the powers of a monarch, that is observed of that of a *monarch—ambition with idleness—baseness with pride—the thirst of riches without labor—aversion to truth—flattery—treason—perfidy—violation of engagements—contempt of civil duties—hope from the magistrate's weakness: but above all the perpetual ridicule of virtue*—these, he remarks, are the characteristics by which the courts in all ages have been distinguished.

The language and the manners of this court will be what distinguishes them from the rest of the community, not what assimilates them to it; and in being remarked for a behavior that shows they are not *meanly-born,* and in adulation to people of fortune and power.

The establishment of a vice-president is as unnecessary as it is dangerous. This officer, for want of other employment, is made president of the senate, thereby blending the executive and legislative powers, besides always giving to some one state, from which he is to come, an unjust pre-eminence.

It is a maxim in republics that the representative of the people should be of their immediate choice; but by the manner in which the president is chosen, he arrives to this office at the fourth or fifth hand, nor does the highest vote, in the way he is elected, determine the choice, for it is only necessary that he should be taken from the highest of five, who may have a plurality of votes.

Compare your past opinions and sentiments with the present proposed establishment, and you will find, that if you adopt it, that it will lead you into a system which you heretofore reprobated as odious. Every American Whig, not long since, bore his emphatic testimony against a monarchical government, though limited, because of the dangerous inequality that it created among citizens as relative to their rights and property; and wherein does this president, invested with his powers and prerogatives, essentially differ from the king of Great Britain (save as to name, the creation of nobility, and some immaterial incidents, the offspring of absurdity and locality). The direct prerogatives of the president, as springing from his political character, are among the following: It is necessary, in order to distinguish him from the rest of the community, and enable him to keep, and maintain his court, that the compensation for his services, or in other words, his revenue, should be such as to enable him to appear with the splendor of a prince; he has the power of receiving ambassadors from, and a great influence on their appointments to foreign courts; as also to make treaties, leagues, and alliances with foreign states, assisted by the Senate, which when made become the supreme law of the land: he is a constituent part of the legislative power, for every bill which shall pass the House of Representatives and Senate is to be presented to him for approbation: if he approves of it he is to sign it, if he disapproves he is to return it with objections, which in many cases will amount to a complete negative; and in this view he will have a great share in the power of making peace, coining money, etc., and all the various objects of legislation, expressed or implied in this Constitution: for though it may be asserted that the king of Great Britain has the express power of making peace or war, yet he never thinks it prudent to do so without the advice of his Parliament, from whom he is to derive his support, and therefore these powers, in both president and king, are substantially the same: he is the generalissimo of the nation, and of course has the command and control of the army, navy and militia; he is the general conservator of the peace of the union—he may pardon all offences, except in cases of impeachment, and the principal fountain of all offices and employments. Will not the exercise of these powers therefore tend either to the establishment of a vile and arbitrary aristocracy or monarchy? The safety of the people in a republic depends on the share or proportion they have in the government; but experience ought to teach you, that when a man is at the head of an elective government invested with great powers, and interested in his re-election, in what circle appointments will be made; by which means an *imperfect aristocracy* bordering on monarchy may be established.

You must, however, my countrymen, beware that the advocates of this new system do not deceive you by a fallacious resemblance between it and your own state government which you so much prize; and, if you examine, you will perceive that the chief magistrate of this state is your immediate choice, controlled and checked by a just and full representation of the people, divested of the prerogative of influencing war and peace, making treaties, receiving and sending embassies, and commanding standing armies and navies, which belong to the power of the confederation, and will be convinced that this government is no more like a true picture of your own than an Angel of Darkness resembles an Angel of Light.

❧ 4 ❧

The Federalist Papers, Nos. 69–73[*]

(1788)

PROPONENTS OF THE Constitution at the state ratifying conventions—the Federalists—answered "Cato," George Mason, and other Anti-Federalist opponents by stressing both the virtues of the presidency and the restraints that the Constitution places on the office. In doing so they leaned heavily on the explanations and defenses of the Constitution that Alexander Hamilton and John Jay, two New Yorkers, and James Madison, a Virginian, were advancing in a series of eighty-five newspaper articles. These articles, gathered together in late 1788 in a book called *The Federalist Papers,* appeared under the pseudonym "Publius" in several New York newspapers between October 27, 1787, and May 28, 1788. They were widely reprinted around the country.

Hamilton wrote Nos. 69–77, the articles that deal with the presidency. No. 69, which appeared on March 14, 1788, squarely addressed the Anti-Federalist charge that the presidency was a disguised monarchy. Hamilton argued that in contrast to the British king, who secures his office by inheritance and serves for life, the president is freely elected for a limited term. The king rules without restriction; the president, Hamilton continued, can be impeached and removed from office. The king has an absolute veto over laws passed by the legislature; the president's veto can be overridden.

[*]Go to *http://thomas.loc.gov/home/histdox/fedpapers.html.*

The king can declare war and raise an army; the president can do neither. The king can create offices and appoint people to fill them; the president cannot create offices and can fill those that Congress creates only after securing the Senate's approval.

Federalist Nos. 70–73 were published during the week that followed. Less defensive in tone than No. 69, these essays described what Hamilton regarded as the chief virtue of the presidency. He called this virtue "energy," a quality essential for the defense of the nation and the steady administration of the laws. *Federalist* No. 70 described the unitary design of the executive as the office's first source of energy. Unity, Hamilton argued, imbues the presidency with a host of desirable qualities: "decision, activity, secrecy, and dispatch," along with "vigor and expedition."

Hamilton outlined the second source of executive energy in *Federalist* No. 71: duration. The four-year term is long enough for the president to withstand "every sudden breeze of passion, or . . . every transient impulse" that "ambitious" and "avaricious" demagogues may ignite in the people. Duration also allows the president to resist undue pressure from Congress or, as Hamilton put it, from "the humors of the legislature." Although long enough "to contribute to the firmness of the Executive," the president's term is not so long as to "justify any alarm for the public liberty."

As a corollary to duration, the president's eligibility for reelection is the subject of *Federalist* No. 72. From the president's perspective, Hamilton, argued, "the desire for reward is one of the strongest incentives of human conduct," so much so that even a leader greedy for money or power will be motivated to serve the country well in order to win another term. From the nation's perspective, Hamilton asked, why forbid the voters to keep an experienced president in office when "experience is the parent of wisdom"? Noting that one consequence of a one-term limit would be to create a steady supply of former presidents, he wondered: "Would it promote the peace of the community, or the stability of the government to have half a dozen men who had credit enough to be raised to the seat of the supreme magistracy, wandering among the people like discontented ghosts, and sighing for a place which they were destined never more to possess?"

In *Federalist* No. 73, Hamilton defined the third ingredient of energy in the executive—"adequate provision for its support"—and then launched a long discussion of energy's fourth ingredient: "competent powers." By "adequate provision" Hamilton meant the president's salary, which under the Constitution may neither be raised nor lowered while a president is in office. As a result, Congress cannot "reduce him by famine, or tempt him by largesses, to surrender at discretion his judgment to their inclination." By "competent powers" Hamilton meant the powers of the president that are enumerated in Article I (the veto, discussed in No. 73) and especially Article II (commander in chief, appointer of judicial and executive officials, and so on, discussed later in Nos. 74–77).

Federalist No. 69

To the People of the State of New-York.

I proceed now to trace the real characters of the proposed executive, as they are marked out in the plan of the convention. This will serve to place in a strong light the unfairness of the representations which have been made in regard to it.

The first thing which strikes our attention is that the executive authority, with few exceptions, is to be vested in a single magistrate. This will scarcely, however, be considered as a point upon which any comparison can be grounded; for if, in this particular, there be a resemblance to the king of Great Britain, there is not less a resemblance to the Grand Seignior, to the khan of Tartary, to the Man of the Seven Mountains, or to the governor of New York.

That magistrate is to be elected for *four* years; and is to be re-eligible as often as the people of the United States shall think him worthy of their confidence. In these circumstances there is a total dissimilitude between *him* and a king of Great Britain, who is an *hereditary* monarch, possessing the crown as a patrimony descendible to his heirs forever; but there is a close analogy between *him* and a governor of New York, who is elected for *three* years, and is re-eligible without limitation or intermission. If we consider how much less time would be requisite for establishing a dangerous influence in a single State than for establishing a like influence throughout the United States, we must conclude that a duration of *four* years for the Chief Magistrate of the Union is a degree of permanency far less to be dreaded in that office, than a duration of *three* years for a corresponding office in a single State.

The President of the United States would be liable to be impeached, tried, and, upon conviction of treason, bribery, or other high crimes or misdemeanors, removed from office; and would afterwards be liable to prosecution and punishment in the ordinary course of law. The person of the King of Great Britain is sacred and inviolable; there is no constitutional tribunal to which he is amenable; no punishment to which he can be subjected without involving the crisis of a national revolution. In this delicate and important circumstance of personal responsibility, the President of Confederated America would stand upon no better ground than a governor of New York, and upon worse ground than the governors of Maryland and Delaware.

The President of the United States is to have power to return a bill, which shall have passed the two branches of the legislature, for reconsideration; but the bill so returned is not to become a law unless, upon that reconsideration, it be approved by two thirds of both houses. The king of Great Britain, on his part, has an absolute negative upon the acts of the two houses of Parliament. The disuse of that power for a considerable time past does not affect the reality of its existence and is to be ascribed wholly to the crown's having found the means of substituting influence to authority, or the art of gaining a majority in one or the other of the two houses, to the necessity of exerting a prerogative which could seldom be exerted without hazarding some degree of national agitation. The qualified negative of the President differs widely from this absolute negative of the British sovereign and tallies exactly with the revisionary authority of the council of revision of this State, of which the governor is a constituent part. In this respect the power of the President would exceed that of the governor of New York, because the former would possess, singly, what the latter shares with the chancellor and judges; but it would be precisely the same with that of the governor of Massachusetts, whose constitution, as to this article, seems to have been the original from which the convention have copied.

The President is to be the "commander-in-chief of the army and navy of the United States, and of the militia of the several States, when called into the actual service of the United States. He is to have power to grant reprieves and pardons for offenses against the United States, *except in cases of impeachment;* to recommend to the consideration of Congress such measures as he shall judge necessary and expedient; to convene, on extraordinary occasions, both houses of the legislature, or either of them, and, in case of disagreement between them *with respect to the time of adjournment,* to adjourn them to such time as he shall think proper; to take care that the laws be faithfully executed; and to commission all officers of the United States." In most of these particulars, the power of the President will resemble equally that of the king of Great Britain and of the governor of New York. The most material points of difference are these:—*First.* The President will have only the occasional command of such part of the militia of the nation as by legislative provision may be called into the actual service of the Union. The king of Great Britain and the governor of New York have at all times the entire command of all the militia within their several jurisdictions. In this article, therefore, the power of the President would be inferior to that of either the monarch or the governor. *Second.* The President is to be commander-in-chief of the army and navy of the United States. In this respect his authority would be nominally the same with that of the king of Great Britain, but in substance much inferior to it. It would amount to nothing more than the supreme command and direction of the military and naval forces, as first general and admiral of the Confederacy; while that of the British king extends to the *declaring* of war and to the *raising* and *regulating* of fleets and armies—all which, by the Constitution under consideration, would appertain to the legislature.[1] The governor of New York, on the other hand, is by the constitution of the State vested only with the command of its militia and navy. But the constitutions of several of the States expressly declare their governors to be commanders-in-chief, as well of the army as navy; and it may well be a question whether those of New Hampshire and Massachusetts, in particular, do not, in this instance, confer larger powers upon their respective governors than could be claimed by a President of the United States. *Third.* The power of the President, in respect to pardons, would extend to all cases, *except those of impeachment.* The governor of New York may pardon in all cases, even in those of impeachment, except for treason and murder. Is not the power of the governor, in this article, on a calculation of political consequences, greater than that of the President? All conspiracies and plots against the government which have not been matured into actual treason may be screened from punishment of every kind by the interposition of the prerogative of pardoning. If a governor of New York, therefore, should be at the head of any such conspiracy, until the design had been ripened into actual hostility he could insure his accomplices and adherents an entire impunity. A President of the Union, on the other hand, though he may even pardon treason, when prosecuted in the ordinary course of law, could shelter no offender, in any degree, from the effects of impeachment and conviction. Would not the prospect of a total indemnity for all the preliminary steps be a greater temptation to undertake and persevere in an enterprise against the public liberty, than the mere prospect of an exemption from death and confiscation, if the final execution of the design, upon an actual appeal to arms, should miscarry? Would this last expectation have any influence at all, when the probability was computed that the person who was to afford that exemption might himself be involved in the consequences of the measure, and might be incapacitated by his agency in it from affording the desired impunity? The better to judge of this matter, it will be necessary to recollect that, by the proposed Constitution, the offense of treason is limited "to levying war upon the United States, and adhering to their enemies, giving them aid and comfort"; and that by the laws of New York it is confined within similar bounds. *Fourth.* The President can only adjourn the national legislature in the single case of disagreement about the time of adjournment. The British monarch may prorogue or even dissolve the Parliament. The governor of New York may also prorogue the legislature of this State for a limited time; a power which, in certain situations, may be employed to very important purposes.

The President is to have power, with the advice and consent of the Senate, to make treaties, provided two thirds of the senators present concur. The king of Great Britain is the sole and absolute representative of the nation in all foreign transactions. He can of his own accord make treaties of peace, commerce, alliance, and of every other description. It has been insinuated that his authority in this respect is not conclusive, and that his conventions with foreign powers are subject to the revision, and stand in need of the ratification, of Parliament. But I believe this doctrine was never heard of until it was broached upon the present occasion. Every jurist[2] of that kingdom, and every other man acquainted with its Constitution knows, as an established fact, that the prerogative of making treaties exists in the crown in its utmost plenitude; and that the compacts entered into by the royal authority have the most complete legal validity and perfection, independent of any other sanctions. The Parliament, it is true, is sometimes seen employing itself in altering the existing laws to conform them to the stipulations in a new treaty; and this may have possibly given birth to the imagination that its co-operation was necessary to the obligatory efficacy of the treaty. But this parliamentary interposition proceeds from a different cause: from the necessity of adjusting a most artificial and intricate system of revenue and commercial laws, to the changes made in them by the operation of the treaty; and of adapting new provisions and precautions to the new state of things, to keep the machine from running into disorder. In this respect, therefore, there is no comparison between the intended power of the President and the actual power of the British sovereign. The one can perform alone what the other can only do with the concurrence of a branch of the legislature. It must be admitted that in this instance the power of the federal executive would exceed that of any State executive. But this arises naturally from the exclusive possession by the Union of that part of the sovereign power which relates to treaties. If the Confederacy were to be dissolved, it would become a question whether the executives of the several States were not solely invested with that delicate and important prerogative.

The President is also to be authorized to receive ambassadors and other public ministers. This, though it has been a rich theme of declamation, is more a matter of dignity than of authority. It is a circumstance which will be without consequence in the administration of the government; and it was far more convenient that it should be arranged in this manner than that there should be a necessity of convening the legislature, or one of its branches, upon every arrival of a foreign minister, though it were merely to take the place of a departed predecessor.

The President is to nominate, and, *with the advice and consent of the Senate,* to appoint ambassadors and other public ministers, judges of the Supreme Court, and in general all officers of the United States established by law, and whose appointments are not otherwise provided for by the Constitution. The king of Great Britain is emphatically and truly styled the fountain of honor. He not only appoints to all offices, but can create offices. He can confer titles of nobility at pleasure, and has the disposal of an immense number of church preferments. There is evidently a great inferiority in the power of the President, in this particular, to that of the British king; nor is it equal to that of the governor of New York, if we are to interpret the meaning of the constitution of the State by the practice which has obtained under it. The power of appointment is with us lodged in a council, composed of the governor and four members of the Senate, chosen by the Assembly. The governor *claims,* and has frequently *exercised,* the right of nomination, and is *entitled* to a casting vote in the appointment. If he really has the right of nominating, his authority is in this respect equal to that of the President, and exceeds it in the article of the casting vote. In the national government, if the Senate should be divided, no appointment could be made; in the government of New York, if the council should be divided, the governor can turn the scale and confirm his own nomination.[3] If we compare the publicity which must necessarily attend the mode of appointment by the President and an entire branch of the national legislature, with the privacy in the mode of appointment by the governor of New York, closeted in a secret apartment with at most four, and frequently with only two persons; and if we at the same time consider how much more easy it must be to influence the small number of which council of appointment consists than the considerable number of which the national Senate would consist, we cannot hesitate to pronounce that the power of the chief magistrate of this State, in the disposition of offices, must, in practice, be greatly superior to that of the Chief Magistrate of the Union.

Hence it appears that, except as to the concurrent authority of the President in the article of treaties, it would be difficult to determine whether that magistrate would, in the aggregate, possess more or less power than the governor of New York. And it appears yet more unequivocally that there is no pretense for the parallel which has been attempted between him and the king of Great Britain. But to render the contrast in this respect still more striking, it may be of use to throw the principal circumstances of dissimilitude into a closer group.

The President of the United States would be an officer elected by the people for *four* years; the king of Great Britain is a perpetual and *hereditary* prince. The one would be amenable to personal punishment and disgrace; the person of the other is sacred and inviolable. The one would have a qualified negative upon the acts of the legislative body; the other has an *absolute* negative. The one would have a right to command the military and naval forces of the nation; the other, in addition to this right, possesses that of *declaring* war, and of *raising* and *regulating* fleets and armies by his own authority. The one would have a concurrent power with a branch of the legislature in the formation of treaties; the other is the *sole possessor* of the power of making treaties. The one would have a like concurrent authority in appointing to offices; the other is the sole author of all appointments. The one can confer no privileges whatever; the other can make denizens of aliens, noblemen of commoners; can erect corporations with all the rights incident to corporate bodies. The one can prescribe no rules concerning the commerce or currency of the nation; the other is in several respects the arbiter of commerce, and in this capacity can establish markets and fairs, can regulate weights and measures, can lay embargoes for a limited time, can coin money, can authorize or prohibit the circulation of foreign coin. The one has no particle of spiritual jurisdiction; the other is the supreme head and governor of the national church. What answer shall we give to those who would persuade us that things so unlike resemble each other? The same that ought to be given to those who tell us that a government, the whole power of which would be in the hands of the elective and periodical servants of the people, is an aristocracy, a monarchy, and a despotism.

NOTES

1. A writer in a Pennsylvania paper, under the signature of Tamony, has asserted that the king of Great Britain owes his prerogative as commander-in-chief to an annual mutiny bill. The truth is, on the contrary, that his prerogative in this respect is immemorial, and was only disputed "contrary to all reason and precedent," as Blackstone, vol. i, page 262, expresses it, by the Long Parliament of Charles I; but by the statute the 13th of Charles II, chap. 6, it was declared to be in the king alone, for that the sole supreme government and command of the militia with his majesty's realms and dominions, and of all forces by sea and land, and of all forts and places of strength, ever was and is the undoubted right of his Majesty and his royal predecessors, kings and queens of England, and that both or either house of Parliament cannot nor ought to pretend to the same.

2. Vide *Blackstone's Commentaries*, Vol. I, p. 257.

3. Candor, however, demands an acknowledgment that I do not think the claim of the governor to a right of nomination well founded. Yet it is always justifiable to reason from the practice of a government till its propriety has been constitutionally questioned. And independent of this claim, when we take into view the other considerations and pursue them through all their consequences, we shall be inclined to draw much the same conclusion.

Federalist No. 70

To the People of the State of New-York.

There is an idea, which is not without its advocates, that a vigorous executive is inconsistent with the genius of republican government. The enlightened well-wishers to this species of government must at least hope that the supposition is destitute of foundation; since they can never admit its truth, without at the same time admitting the condemnation of their own principles. Energy in the executive is a leading character in the definition of good government. It is essential to the protection of the community against foreign attacks; it is not less essential to the steady administration of

the laws; to the protection of property against those irregular and high-handed combinations which sometimes interrupt the ordinary course of justice; to the security of
liberty against the enterprises and assaults of ambition, of faction, and of anarchy.
Every man the least conversant in Roman history knows how often that republic was
obliged to take refuge in the absolute power of a single man, under the formidable
title of dictator, as well against the intrigues of ambitious individuals who aspired to
the tyranny, and the seditions of whole classes of the community whose conduct
threatened the existence of all government, as against the invasions of external enemies who menaced the conquest and destruction of Rome.

There can be no need, however, to multiply arguments or examples on this head. A
feeble executive implies a feeble execution of the government. A feeble execution is
but another phrase for a bad execution; and a government ill executed, whatever it
may be in theory, must be, in practice, a bad government.

Taking it for granted, therefore, that all men of sense will agree in the necessity of
an energetic executive, it will only remain to inquire, what are the ingredients which
constitute this energy? How far can they be combined with those other ingredients
which constitute safety in the republican sense? And how far does this combination
characterize the plan which has been reported by the convention?

The ingredients which constitute energy in the executive are unity; duration; an
adequate provision for its support; and competent powers.

The ingredients which constitute safety in the republican sense are a due dependence on the people, and a due responsibility.

Those politicians and statesmen who have been the most celebrated for the sound-
ness of their principles and for the justness of their views have declared in favor of a
single executive and a numerous legislature. They have, with great propriety, considered energy as the most necessary qualification of the former, and have regarded this as
most applicable to power in a single hand; while they have, with equal propriety, considered the latter as best adapted to deliberation and wisdom, and best calculated to
conciliate the confidence of the people and to secure their privileges and interests.

That unity is conducive to energy will not be disputed. Decision, activity, secrecy,
and dispatch will generally characterize the proceedings of one man in a much more
eminent degree than the proceedings of any greater number; and in proportion as the
number is increased, these qualities will be diminished.

This unity may be destroyed in two ways: either by vesting the power in two or
more magistrates of equal dignity and authority, or by vesting it ostensibly in one
man, subject in whole or in part to the control and cooperation of others, in the capacity of counselors to him. Of the first, the two consuls of Rome may serve as an example; of the last, we shall find examples in the constitutions of several of the States.
New York and New Jersey, if I recollect right, are the only States which have intrusted
the executive authority wholly to single men.[1] Both these methods of destroying the
unity of the executive have their partisans; but the votaries of an executive council are
the most numerous. They are both liable, if not equal, to similar objections, and may
in most lights be examined in conjunction.

The experience of other nations will afford little instruction on this head. As far,
however, as it teaches anything, it teaches us not to be enamored of plurality in the

executive. We have seen that the Achaeans, on an experiment of two Praetors, were induced to abolish one. The Roman history records many instances of mischiefs to the republic from the dissensions between the consuls, and between the military tribunes, who were at times substituted for the consuls. But it gives us no specimens of any peculiar advantages derived to the state from the circumstance of the plurality of those magistrates. That the dissensions between them were not more frequent or more fatal is matter of astonishment, until we advert to the singular position in which the republic was almost continually placed, and to the prudent policy pointed out by the circumstances of the state, and pursued by the consuls, of making a division of the government between them. The patricians engaged in a perpetual struggle with the plebeians for the preservation of their ancient authorities and dignities; the consuls, who were generally chosen out of the former body, were commonly united by the personal interest they had in the defense of privileges of their order. In addition to this motive of union, after the arms of the republic had considerably expanded the bounds of its empire, it became an established custom with the consuls to divide the administration between themselves by lot—one of them remaining at Rome to govern the city and its environs, the other taking command in the more distant provinces. This expedient must no doubt have had great influence in preventing those collisions and rivalships which might otherwise have embroiled the peace of the republic.

But quitting the dim light of historical research, and attaching ourselves purely to the dictates of reason and good sense, we shall discover much greater cause to reject than to approve the idea of plurality in the executive, under any modification whatever.

Whenever two or more persons are engaged in any common enterprise or pursuit, there is always danger of difference of opinion. If it be a public trust or office in which they are clothed with equal dignity and authority, there is peculiar danger of personal emulation and even animosity. From either, and especially from all these causes, the most bitter dissensions are apt to spring. Whenever these happen, they lessen the respectability, weaken the authority, and distract the plans and operations of those whom they divide. If they should unfortunately assail the supreme executive magistracy of a country, consisting of a plurality of persons, they might impede or frustrate the most important measures of the government in the most critical emergencies of the state. And what is still worse, they might split the community into the most violent and irreconcilable factions, adhering differently to the different individuals who composed the magistracy.

Men often oppose a thing merely because they have had no agency in planning it, or because it may have been planned by those whom they dislike. But if they have been consulted, and have happened to disapprove, opposition then becomes, in their estimation, an indispensable duty of self-love. They seem to think themselves bound in honor, and by all the motives of personal infallibility, to defeat the success of what has been resolved upon contrary to their sentiments. Men of upright, benevolent tempers have too many opportunities of remarking, with horror, to what desperate lengths this disposition is sometimes carried, and how often the great interests of society are sacrificed to the vanity, to the conceit, and to the obstinacy of individuals, who have credit enough to make their passions and their caprices interesting to mankind. Perhaps the question now before the public may, in its consequences, afford melancholy proofs of the effects of this despicable frailty, or rather detestable vice, in the human character.

Upon the principles of a free government, inconveniences from the source just mentioned must necessarily be submitted to in the formation of the legislature; but it is unnecessary, and therefore unwise, to introduce them into the constitution of the executive. It is here too that they may be most pernicious. In the legislature, promptitude of decision is oftener an evil than a benefit. The differences of opinion, and the jarring of parties in that department of the government, though they may sometimes obstruct salutary plans, yet often promote deliberation and circumspection, and serve to check excesses in the majority. When a resolution too is once taken, the opposition must be at an end. That resolution is a law, and resistance to it punishable. But no favorable circumstances palliate or atone for the disadvantages of dissension in the executive department. Here they are pure and unmixed. There is no point at which they cease to operate. They serve to embarrass and weaken the execution of the plan or measure to which they relate, from the first step to the final conclusion of it. They constantly counteract those qualities in the executive which are the most necessary ingredients in its composition, vigor and expedition, and this without any counterbalancing good. In the conduct of war, in which the energy of the executive is the bulwark of the national security, everything would be to be apprehended from its plurality.

It must be confessed that these observations apply with principal weight to the first case supposed—that is, to a plurality of magistrates of equal dignity and authority, a scheme, the advocates for which are not likely to form a numerous sect; but they apply, though not with equal yet with considerable weight to the project of a council, whose concurrence is made constitutionally necessary to the operations of the ostensible executive. An artful cabal in that council would be able to distract and to enervate the whole system of administration. If no such cabal should exist, the mere diversity of views and opinions would alone be sufficient to tincture the exercise of the executive authority with a spirit of habitual feebleness and dilatoriness.

But one of the weightiest objections to a plurality in the executive, and which lies as much against the last as the first plan, is that it tends to conceal faults and destroy responsibility. Responsibility is of two kinds—to censure and to punishment. The first is the more important of the two, especially in an elective office. Men in public trust will much oftener act in such a manner as to render them unworthy of being any longer trusted, than in such a manner as to make them obnoxious to legal punishment. But the multiplication of the executive adds to the difficulty of detection in either case. It often becomes impossible, amidst mutual accusations, to determine on whom the blame or the punishment of a pernicious measure, or series of pernicious measures, ought really to fall. It is shifted from one to another with so much dexterity, and under such plausible appearances, that the public opinion is left in suspense about the real author. The circumstances which may have led to any national miscarriage or misfortune are sometimes so complicated that where there are a number of actors who may have had different degrees and kinds of agency, though we may clearly see upon the whole that there has been mismanagement, yet it may be impracticable to pronounce to whose account the evil which may have been incurred is truly chargeable.

"I was overruled by my council. The council were so divided in their opinions that it was impossible to obtain any better resolution on the point." These and similar pretexts are constantly at hand, whether true or false. And who is there that will either take the trouble or incur the odium of a strict scrutiny into the secret springs of the transaction? Should there be found a citizen zealous enough to undertake the unpromising task, if there happened to be a collusion between the parties concerned, how easy it is to clothe the circumstances with so much ambiguity as to render it uncertain what was the precise conduct of any of those parties.

In the single instance in which the governor of this State is coupled with a council—that is, in the appointment to offices, we have seen the mischiefs of it in the view now under consideration. Scandalous appointments to important offices have been made. Some cases, indeed, have been so flagrant that *all parties* have agreed in the impropriety of the thing. When inquiry has been made, the blame has been laid by the governor on the members of the council, who, on their part, have charged it upon his nomination; while the people remain altogether at a loss to determine by whose influence their interests have been committed to hands so unqualified and so manifestly improper. In tenderness to individuals, I forbear to descend to particulars.

It is evident from these considerations that the plurality of the executive tends to deprive the people of the two greatest securities they can have for the faithful exercise of any delegated power; *first,* the restraints of public opinion, which lose their efficacy as well, on account of the division of the censure attendant on bad measures among a number, as on account of the uncertainty on whom it ought to fall; and, *second,* the opportunity of discovering with facility and clearness the misconduct of the persons they trust, in order either to their removal from office or to their actual punishment in cases which admit of it.

In England, the king is a perpetual magistrate; and it is a maxim which has obtained for the sake of the public peace that he is unaccountable for his administration, and his person sacred. Nothing, therefore, can be wiser in that kingdom than to annex to the king a constitutional council, who may be responsible to the nation for the advice they give. Without this, there would be no responsibility whatever in the executive department—an idea inadmissible in a free government. But even there the king is not bound by the resolutions of his council, though they are answerable for the advice they give. He is the absolute master of his own conduct in the exercise of his office and may observe or disregard the counsel given to him at his sole discretion.

But in a republic where every magistrate ought to be personally responsible for his behavior in office, the reason which in the British Constitution dictates the propriety of a council not only ceases to apply, but turns against the institution. In the monarchy of Great Britain, it furnishes a substitute for the prohibited responsibility of the Chief Magistrate, which serves in some degree as a hostage to the national justice for his good behavior. In the American republic, it would serve to destroy, or would greatly diminish, the intended and necessary responsibility of the Chief Magistrate himself.

The idea of a council to the executive, which has so generally obtained in the State constitutions, has been derived from that maxim of republican jealousy which considers power as safer in the hands of a number of men than of a single man. If the maxim should be admitted to be applicable to the case, I should contend that the advantage on that side would not counterbalance the numerous disadvantages on the opposite side. But I do not think the rule at all applicable to the executive power. I clearly concur in opinion, in this particular, with a writer whom the celebrated Junius pronounces to be "deep, solid, and ingenious," that "the executive power is more easily confined when it is one"[2] that it is far more safe there should be a single object for the jealousy and watchfulness of the people; and, in a word, that all multiplication of the executive is rather dangerous than friendly to liberty.

A little consideration will satisfy us that the species of security sought for in the multiplication of the executive is unattainable. Numbers must be so great as to render combination difficult, or they are rather a source of danger than of security. The united credit and influence of several individuals must be more formidable to liberty than the credit and influence of either of them separately. When power, therefore, is placed in the hands of so small a number of men as to admit of their interests and views being easily combined in a common enterprise, by an artful leader, it becomes more liable to abuse, and more dangerous when abused, than if it be lodged in the hands of one man, who, from the very circumstance of his being alone, will be more narrowly watched and more readily suspected, and who cannot unite so great a mass of influence as when he is associated with others. The decemvirs of Rome, whose name denotes their number,[3] were more to be dreaded in their usurpation than any *one* of them would have been. No person would think of proposing an executive much more numerous than that body; from six to a dozen have been suggested for the number of the council. The extreme of these numbers is not too great for an easy combination; and from such a combination America would have more to fear than from the ambition of any single individual. A council to a magistrate, who is himself responsible for what he does, are generally nothing better than a clog upon his good intentions, are often the instruments and accomplices of his bad, and are almost always a cloak to his faults.

I forbear to dwell upon the subject of expense; though it be evident that if the council should be numerous enough to answer the principal end aimed at by the institution, the salaries of the members, who must be drawn from their homes to reside at the seat of government, would form an item in the catalogue of public expenditures too serious to be incurred for an object of equivocal utility.

I will only add that, prior to the appearance of the Constitution, I rarely met with an intelligent man from any of the States who did not admit, as the result of experience, that the UNITY of the executive of this State was one of the best of the distinguishing features of our Constitution.

NOTES

1. New York has no council except for the single purpose of appointing to offices; New Jersey has a council whom the governor may consult. But I think, from the terms of the Constitution, their resolutions do not bind him.

2. De Lolme.

3. Ten.

Federalist No. 71

To the People of the State of New York:

DURATION in office has been mentioned as the second requisite to the energy of the Executive authority. This has relation to two objects: to the personal firmness of the executive magistrate, in the employment of his constitutional powers; and to the stability of the system of administration which may have been adopted under his auspices. With regard to the first, it must be evident, that the longer the duration in office, the greater will be the probability of obtaining so important an advantage. It is a general principle of human nature, that a man will be interested in whatever he possesses, in proportion to the firmness or precariousness of the tenure by which he holds it; will be less attached to what he holds by a momentary or uncertain title, than to what he enjoys by a durable or certain title; and, of course, will be willing to risk more for the sake of the one, than for the sake of the other. This remark is not less applicable to a political privilege, or honor, or trust, than to any article of ordinary property. The inference from it is, that a man acting in the capacity of chief magistrate, under a consciousness that in a very short time he MUST lay down his office, will be apt to feel himself too little interested in it to hazard any material censure or perplexity, from the independent exertion of his powers, or from encountering the ill-humors, however transient, which may happen to prevail, either in a considerable part of the society itself, or even in a predominant faction in the legislative body. If the case should only be, that he MIGHT lay it down, unless continued by a new choice, and if he should be desirous of being continued, his wishes, conspiring with his fears, would tend still more powerfully to corrupt his integrity, or debase his fortitude. In either case, feebleness and irresolution must be the characteristics of the station.

There are some who would be inclined to regard the servile pliancy of the Executive to a prevailing current, either in the community or in the legislature, as its best recommendation. But such men entertain very crude notions, as well of the purposes for which government was instituted, as of the true means by which the public happiness may be promoted. The republican principle demands that the deliberate sense of the community should govern the conduct of those to whom they intrust the management of their affairs; but it does not require an unqualified complaisance to every sudden breeze of passion, or to every transient impulse which the people may receive from the arts of men, who flatter their prejudices to betray their interests. It is a just observation, that the people commonly INTEND the PUBLIC GOOD. This often applies to their very errors. But their good sense would despise the adulator who should pretend that they always REASON RIGHT about the MEANS of promoting it. They know from experience that they sometimes err; and the wonder is that they so seldom err as they do, beset, as they continually are, by the wiles of parasites and sycophants, by the snares of the ambitious, the avaricious, the desperate, by the artifices of men who possess their confidence more than they deserve it, and of those who seek to possess rather than to deserve it. When occasions present themselves, in which the interests of the people are at variance with their inclinations, it is the duty of the persons whom they have appointed to be the guardians of those interests, to withstand the temporary delusion, in order to give them time and opportunity for more cool and sedate reflection. Instances might be cited in which a conduct of this kind has saved the people from very fatal consequences of their own mistakes, and has procured lasting monuments of their gratitude to the men who had courage and magnanimity enough to serve them at the peril of their displeasure.

But however inclined we might be to insist upon an unbounded complaisance in the Executive to the inclinations of the people, we can with no propriety contend for a like complaisance to the humors of the legislature. The latter may sometimes stand in opposition to the former, and at other times the people may be entirely neutral. In either supposition, it is certainly desirable that the Executive should be in a situation to dare to act his own opinion with vigor and decision.

The same rule which teaches the propriety of a partition between the various branches of power, teaches us likewise that this partition ought to be so contrived as to render the one independent of the other. To what purpose separate the executive or the judiciary from the legislative, if both the executive and the judiciary are so constituted as to be at the absolute devotion of the legislative? Such a separation must be merely nominal, and incapable of producing the ends for which it was established. It is one thing to be subordinate to the laws, and another to be dependent on the legislative body. The first comports with, the last violates, the fundamental principles of good government; and, whatever may be the forms of the Constitution, unites all power in the same hands. The tendency of the legislative authority to absorb every other, has been fully displayed and illustrated by examples in some preceding numbers. In governments purely republican, this tendency is almost irresistible. The representatives of the people, in a popular assembly, seem sometimes to fancy that they are the people themselves, and betray strong symptoms of impatience and disgust at the least sign of opposition from any other quarter; as if the exercise of its rights, by either the executive or judiciary, were a breach of their privilege and an outrage to their dignity. They often appear disposed to exert an imperious control over the other departments; and as they commonly have the people on their side, they always act with such momentum as to make it very difficult for the other members of the government to maintain the balance of the Constitution.

It may perhaps be asked, how the shortness of the duration in office can affect the independence of the Executive on the legislature, unless the one were possessed of the power of appointing or displacing the other. One answer to this inquiry may be drawn from the principle already remarked that is, from the slender interest a man is apt to take in a short-lived advantage, and the little inducement it affords him to expose himself, on account of it, to any considerable inconvenience or hazard. Another answer, perhaps more obvious, though not more conclusive, will result from the consideration of the influence of the legislative body over the people; which might be employed to prevent the re-election of a man who, by an upright resistance to any sinister project of that body, should have made himself obnoxious to its resentment.

It may be asked also, whether a duration of four years would answer the end proposed; and if it would not, whether a less period, which would at least be recommended by greater security against ambitious designs, would not, for that reason, be preferable to a longer period, which was, at the same time, too short for the purpose of inspiring the desired firmness and independence of the magistrate.

It cannot be affirmed, that a duration of four years, or any other limited duration, would completely answer the end proposed; but it would contribute towards it in a degree which would have a material influence upon the spirit and character of the government. Between the commencement and termination of such a period, there would always be a considerable interval, in which the prospect of annihilation would be sufficiently remote, not to have an improper effect upon the conduct of a man indued with a tolerable portion of fortitude; and in which he might reasonably promise himself, that there would be time enough before it arrived, to make the community sensible of the propriety of the measures he might incline to pursue. Though it be probable that, as he approached the moment when the public were, by a new election, to signify their sense of his conduct, his confidence, and with it his firmness, would decline; yet both the one and the other would derive support from the opportunities which his previous continuance in the station had afforded him, of establishing himself in the esteem and good-will of his constituents. He might, then, hazard with safety, in proportion to the proofs he had given of his wisdom and integrity, and to the title he had acquired to the respect and attachment of his fellow-citizens. As, on the one hand, a duration of four years will contribute to the firmness of the Executive in a sufficient degree to render it a very valuable ingredient in the composition; so, on the other, it is not enough to justify any alarm for the public liberty. If a British House of Commons, from the most feeble beginnings, FROM THE MERE POWER OF ASSENTING OR DISAGREEING TO THE IMPOSITION OF A NEW TAX, have, by rapid strides, reduced the prerogatives of the crown and the privileges of the nobility within the limits they conceived to be compatible with the principles of a free government, while they raised themselves to the rank and consequence of a coequal branch of the legislature; if they have been able, in one instance, to abolish both the royalty and the aristocracy, and to overturn all the ancient establishments, as well in the Church as State; if they have been able, on a recent occasion, to make the monarch tremble at the prospect of an innovation[1] attempted by them, what would be to be feared from an elective magistrate of four years' duration, with the confined authorities of a President of the United States? What, but that he might be unequal to the task which the Constitution assigns him? I shall only add, that if his duration be such as to leave a doubt of his firmness, that doubt is inconsistent with a jealousy of his encroachments.

NOTE

1. This was the case with respect to Mr. Fox's India bill, which was carried in the House of Commons, and rejected in the House of Lords, to the entire satisfaction, as it is said, of the people.

Federalist No. 72

To the People of the State of New York:

The administration of government, in its largest sense, comprehends all the operations of the body politic, whether legislative, executive, or judiciary; but in its most usual, and perhaps its most precise signification. it is limited to executive details, and falls peculiarly within the province of the executive department. The actual conduct of foreign negotiations, the preparatory plans of finance, the application and disbursement of the public moneys in conformity to the general appropriations of the legislature, the arrangement of the army and navy, the directions of the operations of war, these, and other matters of a like nature, constitute what seems to be most properly understood by the administration of government. The persons, therefore, to whose immediate management these different matters are committed, ought to be considered as the assistants or deputies of the chief magistrate, and on this account, they ought to derive their offices from his appointment, at least from his nomination, and ought to be subject to his superintendence. This view of the subject will at once suggest to us the intimate connection between the duration of the executive magistrate in office and the stability of the system of administration. To reverse and undo what has been done by a predecessor, is very often considered by a successor as the best proof he can give of his own capacity and desert; and in addition to this propensity, where the alteration has been the result of public choice, the person substituted is warranted in supposing that the dismission of his predecessor has proceeded from a dislike to his measures; and that the less he resembles him, the more he will recommend himself to the favor of his constituents. These considerations, and the influence of personal confidences and attachments, would be likely to induce every new President to promote a change of men to fill the subordinate stations; and these causes together could not fail to occasion a disgraceful and ruinous mutability in the administration of the government.

With a positive duration of considerable extent, I connect the circumstance of re-eligibility. The first is necessary to give to the officer himself the inclination and the resolution to act his part well, and to the community time and leisure to observe the tendency of his measures, and thence to form an experimental estimate of their merits. The last is necessary to enable the people, when they see reason to approve of his conduct, to continue him in his station, in order to prolong the utility of his talents and virtues, and to secure to the government the advantage of permanency in a wise system of administration.

Nothing appears more plausible at first sight, nor more ill-founded upon close inspection, than a scheme which in relation to the present point has had some respectable advocates, I mean that of continuing the chief magistrate in office for a certain time, and then excluding him from it, either for a limited period or forever after. This exclusion, whether temporary or perpetual, would have nearly the same effects, and these effects would be for the most part rather pernicious than salutary.

One ill effect of the exclusion would be a diminution of the inducements to good behavior. There are few men who would not feel much less zeal in the discharge of a duty when they were conscious that the advantages of the station with which it was connected must be relinquished at a determinate period, than when they were permitted to entertain a hope of OBTAINING, by MERITING, a continuance of them. This position will not be disputed so long as it is admitted that the desire of reward is one of the strongest incentives of human conduct; or that the best security for the fidelity of mankind is to make their interests coincide with their duty. Even the love of fame, the ruling passion of the noblest minds, which would prompt a man to plan and undertake extensive and arduous enterprises for the public benefit, requiring considerable time to mature and perfect them, if he could flatter himself with the prospect of being allowed to finish what he had begun, would, on the contrary, deter him from the undertaking, when he foresaw that he must quit the scene before he could accomplish the work, and must commit that, together with his own reputation, to hands which might be unequal or unfriendly to the task. The most to be expected from the generality of men, in such a situation, is the negative merit of not doing harm, instead of the positive merit of doing good.

Another ill effect of the exclusion would be the temptation to sordid views, to peculation, and, in some instances, to usurpation. An avaricious man, who might happen to fill the office, looking forward to a time when he must at all events yield up the emoluments he enjoyed, would feel a propensity, not easy to be resisted by such a man, to make the best use of the opportunity he enjoyed while it lasted, and might not scruple to have recourse to the most corrupt expedients to make the harvest as abundant as it was transitory; though the same man, probably, with a different prospect before him, might content himself with the regular perquisites of his situation, and might even be unwilling to risk the consequences of an abuse of his opportunities. His avarice might be a guard upon his avarice. Add to this that the same man might be vain or ambitious, as well as avaricious. And if he could expect to prolong his honors by his good conduct, he might hesitate to sacrifice his appetite for them to his appetite for gain. But with the prospect before him of approaching an inevitable annihilation, his avarice would be likely to get the victory over his caution, his vanity, or his ambition.

An ambitious man, too, when he found himself seated on the summit of his country's honors, when he looked forward to the time at which he must descend from the exalted eminence for ever, and reflected that no exertion of merit on his part could save him from the unwelcome reverse; such a man, in such a situation, would be much more violently tempted to embrace a favorable conjuncture for attempting the prolongation of his power, at every personal hazard, than if he had the probability of answering the same end by doing his duty.

Would it promote the peace of the community, or the stability of the government to have half a dozen men who had had credit enough to be raised to the seat of the supreme magistracy, wandering among the people like discontented ghosts, and sighing for a place which they were destined never more to possess?

A third ill effect of the exclusion would be, the depriving the community of the advantage of the experience gained by the chief magistrate in the exercise of his office. That experience is the parent of wisdom, is an adage the truth of which is recognized by the wisest as well as the simplest of mankind. What more desirable or more essential than this quality in the governors of nations? Where more desirable or more essential than in the first magistrate of a nation? Can it be wise to put this desirable and essential quality under the ban of the Constitution, and to declare that the moment it is acquired, its possessor shall be compelled to abandon the station in which it was acquired, and to which it is adapted? This, nevertheless, is the precise import of all those regulations which exclude men from serving their country, by the choice of their fellow citizens, after they have by a course of service fitted themselves for doing it with a greater degree of utility.

A fourth ill effect of the exclusion would be the banishing men from stations in which, in certain emergencies of the state, their presence might be of the greatest moment to the public interest or safety. There is no nation which has not, at one period or another, experienced an absolute necessity of the services of particular men in particular situations; perhaps it would not be too strong to say, to the preservation of its political existence. How unwise, therefore, must be every such self-denying ordinance as serves to prohibit a nation from making use of its own citizens in the manner best suited to its exigencies and circumstances. Without supposing the personal essentiality of the man, it is evident that a change of the chief magistrate, at the breaking out of a war, or at any similar crisis, for another, even of equal merit, would at all times be detrimental to the community, inasmuch as it would substitute inexperience to experience, and would tend to unhinge and set afloat the already settled train of the administration.

A fifth ill effect of the exclusion would be, that it would operate as a constitutional interdiction of stability in the administration. By NECESSITATING a change of men, in the first office of the nation, it would necessitate a mutability of measures. It is not generally to be expected, that men will vary and measures remain uniform. The contrary is the usual course of things. And we need not be apprehensive that there will be too much stability, while there is even the option of changing; nor need we desire to prohibit the people from continuing their confidence where they think it may be safely placed, and where, by constancy on their part, they may obviate the fatal inconveniences of fluctuating councils and a variable policy.

These are some of the disadvantages which would flow from the principle of exclusion. They apply most forcibly to the scheme of a perpetual exclusion; but when we consider that even a partial exclusion would always render the readmission of the person a remote and precarious object, the observations which have been made will apply nearly as fully to one case as to the other.

What are the advantages promised to counterbalance these disadvantages? They are represented to be: 1st, greater independence in the magistrate; 2d, greater security to the people. Unless the exclusion be perpetual, there will be no pretense to infer the first advantage. But even in that case, may he have no object beyond his present station, to which he may sacrifice his independence? May he have no connections, no friends, for whom he may sacrifice it? May he not be less willing by a firm conduct, to make personal enemies, when he acts under the impression that a time is fast approaching, on the arrival of which he not only MAY, but MUST, be exposed to their resentments, upon an equal, perhaps upon an inferior, footing? It is not an easy point to determine whether his independence would be most promoted or impaired by such an arrangement.

As to the second supposed advantage, there is still greater reason to entertain doubts concerning it. If the exclusion were to be perpetual, a man of irregular ambition, of whom alone there could be reason in any case to entertain apprehension, would, with infinite reluctance, yield to the necessity of taking his leave forever of a post in which his passion for power and pre-eminence had acquired the force of habit. And if he had been fortunate or adroit enough to conciliate the good-will of the people, he might induce them to consider as a very odious and unjustifiable restraint upon themselves, a provision which was calculated to debar them of the right of giving a fresh proof of their attachment to a favorite. There may be conceived circumstances in which this disgust of the people, seconding the thwarted ambition of such a favorite, might occasion greater danger to liberty, than could ever reasonably be dreaded from the possibility of a perpetuation in office, by the voluntary suffrages of the community, exercising a constitutional privilege.

There is an excess of refinement in the idea of disabling the people to continue in office men who had entitled themselves, in their opinion, to approbation and confidence; the advantages of which are at best speculative and equivocal, and are overbalanced by disadvantages far more certain and decisive.

Federalist No. 73

To the People of the State of New York:

THE third ingredient towards constituting the vigor of the executive authority, is an adequate provision for its support. It is evident that, without proper attention to this article, the separation of the executive from the legislative department would be merely nominal and nugatory. The legislature, with a discretionary power over the salary and emoluments of the Chief Magistrate, could render him as obsequious to their will as they might think proper to make him. They might, in most cases, either reduce him by famine, or tempt him by largesses, to surrender at discretion his judgment to their inclinations. These expressions, taken in all the latitude of the terms, would no doubt convey more than is intended. There are men who could neither be distressed nor won into a sacrifice of their duty; but this stern virtue is the growth of few soils; and in the main it will be found that a power over a man's support is a power over his will. If it were necessary to confirm so plain a truth by facts, examples would not be wanting, even in this country, of the intimidation or seduction of the Executive by the terrors or allurements of the pecuniary arrangements of the legislative body.

It is not easy, therefore, to commend too highly the judicious attention which has been paid to this subject in the proposed Constitution. It is there provided that "The President of the United States shall, at stated times, receive for his services a compensation WHICH SHALL NEITHER BE INCREASED NOR DIMINISHED DURING THE PERIOD FOR WHICH HE SHALL HAVE BEEN ELECTED; and he SHALL NOT RECEIVE WITHIN THAT PERIOD ANY OTHER EMOLUMENT from the United States, or any of them." It is impossible to imagine any provision which would have been more eligible than this. The legislature, on the appointment of a President, is once for all to declare what shall be the compensation for his services during the time for which he shall have been elected. This done, they will have no power to alter it, either by increase or diminution, till a new period of service by a new election commences. They can neither weaken his fortitude by operating on his necessities, nor corrupt his integrity by appealing to his avarice. Neither the Union, nor any of its members, will be at liberty to give, nor will he be at liberty to receive, any other emolument than that which may have been determined by the first act. He can, of course, have no pecuniary inducement to renounce or desert the independence intended for him by the Constitution.

The last of the requisites to energy, which have been enumerated, are competent powers. Let us proceed to consider those which are proposed to be vested in the President of the United States.

The first thing that offers itself to our observation, is the qualified negative of the President upon the acts or resolutions of the two houses of the legislature; or, in other words, his power of returning all bills with objections, to have the effect of preventing their becoming laws, unless they should afterwards be ratified by two thirds of each of the component members of the legislative body.

The propensity of the legislative department to intrude upon the rights, and to absorb the powers, of the other departments, has been already suggested and repeated; the insufficiency of a mere parchment delineation of the boundaries of each, has also been remarked upon; and the necessity of furnishing each with constitutional arms for its own defense, has been inferred and proved. From these clear and indubitable principles results the propriety of a negative, either absolute or qualified, in the Executive, upon the acts of the legislative branches. Without the one or the other, the former would be absolutely unable to defend himself against the depredations of the latter. He might gradually be stripped of his authorities by successive resolutions, or annihilated by a single vote. And in the one mode or the other, the legislative and executive powers might speedily come to be blended in the same hands. If even no propensity had ever discovered itself in the legislative body to invade the rights of the Executive, the rules of just reasoning and theoretic propriety would of themselves teach us, that the one ought not to be left to the mercy of the other, but ought to possess a constitutional and effectual power of self defense.

But the power in question has a further use. It not only serves as a shield to the Executive, but it furnishes an additional security against the enaction of improper laws. It establishes a salutary check upon the legislative body, calculated to guard the community against the effects of faction, precipitancy, or of any impulse unfriendly to the public good, which may happen to influence a majority of that body.

The propriety of a negative has, upon some occasions, been combated by an observation, that it was not to be presumed a single man would possess more virtue and wisdom than a number of men; and that unless this presumption should be entertained, it would be improper to give the executive magistrate any species of control over the legislative body.

But this observation, when examined, will appear rather specious than solid. The propriety of the thing does not turn upon the supposition of superior wisdom or virtue in the Executive, but upon the supposition that the legislature will not be infallible; that the love of power may sometimes betray it into a disposition to encroach upon the rights of other members of the government; that a spirit of faction may sometimes pervert its deliberations; that impressions of the moment may sometimes hurry it into measures which itself, on maturer reflection, would condemn. The primary inducement to conferring the power in question upon the Executive is, to enable him to defend himself; the secondary one is to increase the chances in favor of the community against the passing of bad laws, through haste, inadvertence, or design. The oftener the measure is brought under examination, the greater the diversity in the situations of those who are to examine it, the less must be the danger of those errors which flow from want of due deliberation, or of those missteps which proceed from the contagion of some common passion or interest. It is far less probable, that culpable views of any kind should infect all the parts of the government at the same moment and in relation to the same object, than that they should by turns govern and mislead every one of them.

It may perhaps be said that the power of preventing bad laws includes that of preventing good ones; and may be used to the one purpose as well as to the other. But this objection will have little weight with those who can properly estimate the mischiefs of that inconstancy and mutability in the laws, which form the greatest blemish in the character and genius of our governments. They will consider every institution calculated to restrain the excess of law-making, and to keep things in the same state in which they happen to be at any given period, as much more likely to do good than harm; because it is favorable to greater stability in the system of legislation. The injury which may possibly be done by defeating a few good laws, will be amply compensated by the advantage of preventing a number of bad ones.

Nor is this all. The superior weight and influence of the legislative body in a free government, and the hazard to the Executive in a trial of strength with that body, afford a satisfactory security that the negative would generally be employed with great caution; and there would oftener be room for a charge of timidity than of rashness in the exercise of it. A king of Great Britain, with all his train of sovereign attributes, and with all the influence he draws from a thousand sources, would, at this day, hesitate to put a negative upon the joint resolutions of the two houses of Parliament. He would not fail to exert the utmost resources of that influence to strangle a measure disagreeable to him, in its progress to the throne, to avoid being reduced to the dilemma of permitting it to take effect, or of risking the displeasure of the nation by an opposition to the sense of the legislative body. Nor is it probable, that he would ultimately venture to exert his prerogatives, but in a case of manifest propriety, or extreme necessity. All well-informed men in that kingdom will accede to the justness of this remark. A very considerable period has elapsed since the negative of the crown has been exercised.

If a magistrate so powerful and so well fortified as a British monarch, would have scruples about the exercise of the power under consideration, how much greater caution may be reasonably expected in a President of the United States, clothed for the short period of four years with the executive authority of a government wholly and purely republican?

It is evident that there would be greater danger of his not using his power when necessary, than of his using it too often, or too much. An argument, indeed, against its expediency, has been drawn from this very source. It has been represented, on this account, as a power odious in appearance, useless in practice. But it will not follow, that because it might be rarely exercised, it would never be exercised. In the case for which it is chiefly designed, that of an immediate attack upon the constitutional rights of the Executive, or in a case in which the public good was evidently and palpably sacrificed, a man of tolerable firmness would avail himself of his constitutional means of defense, and would listen to the admonitions of duty and responsibility. In the former supposition, his fortitude would be stimulated by his immediate interest in the power of his office; in the latter, by the probability of the sanction of his constituents, who, though they would naturally incline to the legislative body in a doubtful case, would hardly suffer their partiality to delude them in a very plain case. I speak now with an eye to a magistrate possessing only a common share of firmness. There are men who, under any circumstances, will have the courage to do their duty at every hazard.

But the convention have pursued a mean in this business, which will both facilitate the exercise of the power vested in this respect in the executive magistrate, and make its efficacy to depend on the sense of a considerable part of the legislative body. Instead of an absolute negative, it is proposed to give the Executive the qualified negative already described. This is a power which would be much more readily exercised than the other. A man who might be afraid to defeat a law by his single VETO, might not scruple to return it for reconsideration; subject to being finally rejected only in the event of more than one third of each house concurring in the sufficiency of his objections. He would be encouraged by the reflection, that if his opposition should prevail, it would embark in it a very respectable proportion of the legislative body, whose influence would be united with his in supporting the propriety of his conduct in the public opinion. A direct and categorical negative has something in the appearance of it more harsh, and more apt to irritate, than the mere suggestion of argumentative objections to be approved or disapproved by those to whom they are addressed. In proportion as it would be less apt to offend, it would be more apt to be exercised; and for this very reason, it may in practice be found more effectual. It is to be hoped that it will not often happen that improper views will govern so large a proportion as two thirds of both branches of the legislature at the same time; and this, too, in spite of the counterposing weight of the Executive. It is at any rate far less probable that this should be the case, than that such views should taint the resolutions and conduct of a bare majority. A power of this nature in the Executive, will often have a silent and unperceived, though forcible, operation. When men, engaged in unjustifiable pursuits, are aware that obstructions may come from a quarter which they cannot control, they will often be restrained by the bare apprehension of opposition, from doing what they would with eagerness rush into, if no such external impediments were to be feared.

This qualified negative, as has been elsewhere remarked, is in this State vested in a council, consisting of the governor, with the chancellor and judges of the Supreme Court, or any two of them. It has been freely employed upon a variety of occasions, and frequently with success. And its utility has become so apparent, that persons who, in compiling the Constitution, were violent opposers of it, have from experience become its declared admirers.[1]

I have in another place remarked, that the convention, in the formation of this part of their plan, had departed from the model of the constitution of this State, in favor of that of Massachusetts. Two strong reasons may be imagined for this preference. One is that the judges, who are to be the interpreters of the law, might receive an improper bias, from having given a previous opinion in their revisionary capacities; the other is that by being often associated with the Executive, they might be induced to embark too far in the political views of that magistrate, and thus a dangerous combination might by degrees be cemented between the executive and judiciary departments. It is impossible to keep the judges too distinct from every other avocation than that of expounding the laws. It is peculiarly dangerous to place them in a situation to be either corrupted or influenced by the Executive.

NOTE

1. Mr. Abraham Yates, a warm opponent of the plan of the convention is of this number.

❧ 5 ❧

George Washington's First Inaugural Address*
(1789)

T HE CONSTITUTION makes no provision for presidential inaugurations. It requires only that the new president take the oath stated in Article II: "I do solemnly swear (or affirm) that I will faithfully execute the Office of President of the United States, and will to the best of my Ability preserve, protect and defend the Constitution of the United States." Tradition is the wellspring of every other aspect of inaugural ceremonies. The 1789 inauguration of George Washington as the first president began many of these traditions, such as swearing the oath with left hand on an open Bible and right hand raised to heaven, adding the words "so help me God," delivering an inaugural address, and holding a public celebration afterward.

Washington was elected president on February 4, 1789. The election was organized by the outgoing Congress, which existed under the Articles of Confederation. On September 13, 1788, ten weeks after declaring that the Constitution was ratified, Congress had passed a resolution calling on each state to appoint presidential electors on the first Wednesday in January 1789, which fell on the seventh. When these electors convened in their state capitals on the first Wednesday in February (February 4), they voted unanimously for Washington. They also elected John Adams of Massachusetts as vice president.

Although Congress had set March 4 as the day the government created by the Constitution would begin, not enough newly elected legislators arrived on time in New York City (still the capital) to constitute a quorum. As a result, the electoral votes for president were not opened by Congress, and Washington was not declared elected, until April 6. The president-elect waited at Mount Vernon, his Virginia home, until he was officially informed by messenger of his election on April 14. Washington then proceeded slowly northward to New York by coach. He was greeted by ecstatic crowds, pealing church bells, and cannon salutes at every stop along the way. On April 30 Washington arrived in New York to be sworn in as president.

*Go to *www.law.ou.edu/hist/wash1.html.*

Washington took the constitutional oath of office on the outdoor balcony of New York's Federal Hall before an exuberant crowd. The first president then went inside to the Senate chamber to deliver the first inaugural address.

Washington's address sounded two themes that have echoed in the inaugural addresses of most of his successors. First, he paid "homage to the Great Author of every public and private good," noting the benign workings of "providential agency" in the birth of the United States and urging Congress and the American people to earn "the propitious smiles of Heaven" by acting with justice and magnanimity. Second, Washington spoke of national unity and dedication to the Constitution. What he did not do was equally precedent setting, namely, use the inaugural address as an occasion to exercise his constitutional power to make "recommendation of particular measures" to Congress.

The final event of the first presidential inauguration was a public fireworks display. After it was over, the president walked to his new home.

※ ※ ※

Fellow-Citizens of the Senate and of the House of Representatives:

Among the vicissitudes incident to life no event could have filled me with greater anxieties than that of which the notification was transmitted by your order, and received on the 14th day of the present month. On the one hand, I was summoned by my country, whose voice I can never hear but with veneration and love, from a retreat which I had chosen with the fondest predilection, and, in my flattering hopes, with an immutable decision, as the asylum of my declining years—a retreat which was rendered every day more necessary as well as more dear to me by the addition of habit to inclination, and of frequent interruptions in my health to the gradual waste committed on it by time. On the other hand, the magnitude and difficulty of the trust to which the voice of my country called me, being sufficient to awaken in the wisest and most experienced of her citizens a distrustful scrutiny into his qualifications, could not but overwhelm with despondence one who (inheriting inferior endowments from nature and unpracticed in the duties of civil administration) ought to be peculiarly conscious of his own deficiencies. In this conflict of emotions all I dare aver is that it has been my faithful study to collect my duty from a just appreciation of every circumstance by which it might be affected. All I dare hope is that if, in executing this task, I have been too much swayed by a grateful remembrance of former instances, or by an affectionate sensibility to this transcendent proof of the confidence of my fellow-citizens, and have thence too little consulted my incapacity as well as disinclination for the weighty and untried cares before me, my error will be palliated by the motives which mislead me, and its consequences be judged by my country with some share of the partiality in which they originated.

Such being the impressions under which I have, in obedience to the public summons, repaired to the present station, it would be peculiarly improper to omit in this first official act my fervent supplications to that Almighty Being who rules over the universe who presides in the councils of nations, and whose providential aids can supply every human defect, that His benediction may consecrate to the liberties and happiness of the people of the United States a Government instituted by themselves for these essential purposes, and may enable every instrument employed in its administration to execute with success the functions allotted to his charge. In tendering this homage to the Great Author of every public and private good, I assure myself that it expresses your sentiments not less than my own, nor those of my fellow-citizens at large less than either. No people can be bound to acknowledge and adore the Invisible Hand which conducts the affairs of men more than those of the United States. Every step by which they have advanced to the character of an independent nation seems to have been distinguished by some token of providential agency; and in the important revolution just accomplished in the system of their united government the tranquil deliberations and voluntary consent of so many distinct communities from which the event has resulted can not be compared with the means by which most governments have been established without some return of pious gratitude, along with an humble anticipation of the future blessings which the past seem to presage. These reflections, arising out of the present crisis, have forced themselves too strongly on my mind to be suppressed. You will join with me, I trust, in thinking that there are none under the influence of which the proceedings of a new and free government can more auspiciously commence.

By the article establishing the executive department it is made the duty of the President "to recommend to your consideration such measures as he shall judge necessary and expedient." The circumstances under which I now meet you will acquit me from entering into that subject further than to refer to the great constitutional charter under which you are assembled, and which, in defining your powers, designates the objects to which your attention is to be given. It will be more consistent with those circumstances, and far more congenial with the feelings which actuate me, to substitute, in place of a recommendation of particular measures, the tribute that is due to the talents, the rectitude, and the patriotism which adorn the characters selected to devise and adopt them. In these honorable qualifications I behold the surest pledges that as on one side no local prejudices or attachments, no separate views nor party animosities, will misdirect the comprehensive and equal eye which ought to watch over this great assemblage of communities and interests, so, on another, that the foundation of our national policy will be laid in the pure and immutable principles of private morality, and the preeminence of free government be exemplified by all the attributes which can win the affections of its citizens and command the respect of the world. I dwell on this prospect with every satisfaction which an ardent love for my country can inspire, since there is no truth more thoroughly established than that there exists in the economy and course of nature an indissoluble union between virtue and happiness; between duty and advantage; between the genuine maxims of an honest and magnanimous policy and the solid rewards of public prosperity and felicity; since we ought to be no less persuaded that the propitious smiles of Heaven can never be expected on a nation that disregards the eternal rules of order and right which Heaven itself has ordained; and since the preservation of the sacred fire of liberty and the destiny of the republican model of government are justly considered, perhaps, as deeply, as finally, staked on the experiment intrusted to the hands of the American people.

Besides the ordinary objects submitted to your care, it will remain with your judgement to decide how far an exercise of the occasional power delegated by the fifth article of the Constitution is rendered expedient at the present juncture by the nature of objections which have been urged against the system, or by the degree of inquietude which has given birth to them. Instead of undertaking particular recommendations on this subject, in which I could be guided by no lights derived from official opportunities, I shall again give way to my entire confidence in your discernment and pursuit of the public good; for I assure myself that whilst you carefully avoid every alteration which might endanger the benefits of an united and effective government, or which ought to await the future lessons of experience, a reverence for the characteristic rights of freemen and a regard for the public harmony will sufficiently influence your deliberations on the question how far the former can be impregnably fortified or the latter be safely and advantageously promoted.

To the foregoing observations I have one to add, which will be most properly addressed to the House of Representatives. It concerns myself, and will therefore be as brief as possible. When I was first honored with a call into the service of my country, then on the eve of an arduous struggle for its liberties, the light in which I contemplated my duty required that I should renounce every pecuniary compensation. From this resolution I have in no instance departed; and being still under the impressions which produced it, I must decline as inapplicable to myself any share in the personal emoluments which may be indispensably included in a permanent provision for the executive department, and must accordingly pray that the pecuniary estimates for the station in which I am placed may during my continuance in it be limited to such actual expenditures as the public good may be thought to require.

Having thus imparted to you my sentiments as they have been awakened by the occasion which brings us together, I shall take my present leave; but not without resorting once more to the benign Parent of the Human Race in humble supplication that, since He has been pleased to favor the American people with opportunities for deliberating in perfect tranquility, and dispositions for deciding with unparalleled unanimity on a form of government for the security of their union and the advancement of their happiness, so His divine blessing may be equally conspicuous in the enlarged views, the temperate consultations, and the wise measures on which the success of this Government must depend.

⊷ 6 ⊷

James Madison's Defense of the President's Removal Power

(1789)

GEORGE WASHINGTON was not the only one trying to sort out the ambiguities in the Constitution once the new government was under way. The First Congress was involved in this process as well. One prominent example: although the Constitution said that presidential appointments to the executive branch required the "Advice and Consent of the Senate," it was silent concerning the removal power (that is, the power to fire an executive official). When enacting the laws that created the first three departments—state (or foreign affairs), Treasury, and war—Congress had to address this constitutional silence. In doing so, legislators implicitly addressed a larger issue: who should control the executive branch?

Rep. James Madison of Virginia believed strongly that the president is the chief executive. On May 19, 1789, he introduced a resolution stating that "there should be established for the aid of the chief magistrate in executing the duties of his office the following departments, to wit: a department for foreign affairs . . . Treasury . . . [and] war." The House of Representatives signaled its initial reluctance to recognize the executive nature of the departments by voting to strike the phrase "for the aid of the chief magistrate in executing the duties of his office" from Madison's resolution. A month later, when the state department bill came before the House, this reluctance was made manifest in the debate over a provision that the secretary of state "shall be removed from office by the President of the United States," acting alone.

Several positions emerged in the debate. Rep. Roger Sherman of Connecticut, who, like Madison, had been a prominent participant in the Constitutional Convention, argued that Congress had the power to assign the removal power in any way it saw fit. Rep. William Smith of South Carolina interpreted the Constitution to mean that the only appropriate process for removing an executive official was impeachment. Others argued that because the Constitution required the Senate's consent for appointments, it must also require the Senate's consent for removals. Much to Madison's dismay, they were able to cite *Federalist* No. 77 in defense of their argument. Of the Senate, Hamilton had written, "The consent of that body would be necessary to displace as well as to appoint."

On June 17 Madison attacked all of these positions and defended the president's exclusive power of removal. He agreed that the Constitution's appointment provision, taken by itself, was ambiguous. "But there is another part of the constitution . . . ," Madison argued; "it is that part which declares that the executive power shall be vested in a president of the United States." How could presidents be held accountable for executing the laws if they lacked the authority to remove officials who were impeding their efforts?

One week later, the House voted 29–22 to enact the state department bill, including Madison's presidential removal clause. On July 14 the Senate split 10–10 on a motion to strike that clause from the bill. Vice President John Adams broke the tie in favor of presidential removal, which President Washington favored. The Senate approved the entire bill on July 18 by a 10–9 vote, and Washington signed it into law nine days later.

The state department bill established a precedent: every department's principal officers are removable by the president alone. When Andrew Johnson became president in 1865, Congress changed its mind and enacted the Tenure of Office Act, which required the president to secure the Senate's approval to remove an official. Even after Congress repealed that act in the late nineteenth century, however, the creation of independent regulatory agencies like the Federal Trade Commission reopened the removal question. (See Document 23, p. 116.)

☙ ☙ ☙

. . . Several constructions have been put upon the constitution relative to the point in question. The gentleman from Connecticut (Mr. SHERMAN) has advanced a doctrine which was not touched upon before. He seems to think (if I understood him rightly) that the power of displacing from office is subject to legislative discretion; because it is having a right to create, it may limit or modify as it thinks proper. I shall not say but at first view this doctrine may seem to have some plausibility. But when I consider, that the constitution clearly intended to maintain a marked distinction between the legislative, executive, and judicial powers of Government; and when I consider, that if the Legislature has a power, such as contended for, they may subject and transfer at discretion powers from one department of our Government to another; they may, on that principle, exclude the President altogether from exercising any authority in the removal of officers; they may give it to the Senate alone, or the President and Senate combined; they may vest it in the whole Congress; or they may reserve it to be exercised by this House. When I consider the consequences of this doctrine, and compare them with the true principles of the constitution, I own that I cannot subscribe to it.

Another doctrine, which has found very respectable friends, has been particularly advocated by the gentleman from South Carolina, (Mr. SMITH). It is this: when an officer is appointed by the President and Senate, he can only be displaced for malfeasance in his office by impeachment. I think this would give a stability to the executive department, so far as it may be described by the heads of departments, which is more incompatible with the genius of republican Governments in general, and this constitution in particular, than any doctrine which has yet been proposed. The danger to liberty, the danger of mal-administration, has not been found to lie so much in the facility of introducing improper persons into office, as in the difficulty of displacing those who are unworthy of the public trust. If it is said, that an officer once appointed shall not be displaced without the formality required by impeachment, I shall be glad to know what security we have for the faithful administration of the Government? Every individual, in the long chain which extends from the highest to the lowest link of the Executive Magistracy, would find a security in his situation which would relax his fidelity and promptitude in the discharge of his duty.

The doctrine, however, which seems to stand most in opposition to the principles I contend for, is, that the power to annul an appointment is, in the nature of things, incidental to the power which makes the appointment. I agree that if nothing more was said in the constitution than that the President, by and with the advice and consent of the Senate, should appoint to office, there would be great force in saying that the power of removal resulted by a natural implication from the power of appointing.

But there is another part of the constitution, no less explicit than the one on which the gentleman's doctrine is founded; it is that part which declares that the executive power shall be vested in a President of the United States. The association of the Senate with the President in exercising that particular function, is an exception to this general rule; and exception to general rules, I conceive, are ever to be taken strictly. But there is another part of the constitution which inclines, in my judgment, to favor the construction I put upon it; the President is required to take care that the laws be faithfully executed. If the duty to see the laws faithfully executed be required at the hands of the Executive Magistrate, it would seem that it was generally intended he should have that species of power which is necessary to accomplish that end. Now, if the officer when once appointed is not to depend upon the President for his official existence, but upon a distinct body (for where there are two negatives required, either can prevent the removal), I confess I do not see how the President can take care that the laws be faithfully executed. It is true, by circuitous operation, he may obtain an impeachment, and even without this it is possible he may obtain the concurrence of the Senate for the purpose of displacing an officer; but would this give that species of control to the Executive Magistrate which seems to be required by the constitution? I own, if my opinion was not contrary to that entertained by what I suppose to be the minority on this question, I should be doubtful of being mistaken, when I discovered how inconsistent that construction would make the constitution with itself. I can hardly bring myself to imagine the wisdom of the convention who framed the constitution contemplated such incongruity.

There is another maxim which ought to direct us in expounding the constitution, and is of great importance. It is laid down, in most of the constitutions or bills of rights in the republics of America; it is to be found in the political writings of the most celebrated civilians, and is every where held as essential to the preservation of liberty, that the three great departments of Government be kept separate and distinct; and if in any case they are blended, it is in order to admit a partial qualification, in order more effectually to guard against an entire consolidation. I think, therefore, when we review the several parts of this constitution, when it says that the legislative powers shall be vested in a Congress of the United States under certain exceptions, and the executive power vested in the President with certain exceptions, we must suppose they were intended to be kept separate in all cases in which they are not blended, and ought, consequently, to expound the constitution so as to blend them as little as possible.

Every thing relative to the merits of the question as distinguished from a constitutional question, seems to turn on the danger of such a power vested in the President alone. But when I consider the checks under which he lies in the exercise of this power, I own to you I feel no apprehensions but what arise from the dangers incidental to the power itself; for dangers will be incidental to it, vest it where you please. I will not reiterate what was said before with respect to the mode of election, and the extreme improbability that any citizen will be selected from the mass of citizens who is not highly distinguished by his abilities and worth; in this alone we have no small security for the faithful exercise of this power. But, throwing that out of the question, let us consider the restraints he will feel after he is placed in that elevated station. It is to be remarked, that the power in this case will not consist so much in continuing a bad man in office, as in the danger of displacing a good one. Perhaps the great danger, as has been observed, of abuse in the executive power, lies in the improper continuance of bad men in office. But the power we contend for will not enable him to do this; for if an unworthy man be continued in office by an unworthy President, the House of Representatives can at any time impeach him, and the Senate can remove him, whether the President chooses or not. The danger then consists merely in this: the President can displace from office a man whose merits require that he should be continued in it. What will be the motives which the President can feel for such abuse of his power, and the restraints that operate to prevent it? In the first place, he will be impeachable by this House, before the Senate, for such an act of mal-administration; for I contend that the wanton removal of meritorious officers would subject him to impeachment and removal from his own high trust. But what can be his motives for displacing a worthy man? It must be that he may fill the place with an unworthy creature of his own. Can he accomplish this end? No; he can place no man in the vacancy whom the Senate shall not approve. . . .

But let us not consider the question on one side only; there are dangers to be contemplated on the other. Vest this power in the Senate jointly with the President, and you abolish at once that great principle of unity and responsibility in the executive department, which was intended for the security of liberty and the public good. If the President should possess alone the power of removal from office, those who are employed in the execution of the law will be in their proper situation, and the chain of dependence be preserved; the lowest officers, the middle grade, and the highest, will depend, as they ought, on the President, and the President on the community. The chain of dependence therefore terminates in the supreme body, namely, in the people, who will possess, besides, in aid of their original power, the decisive engine of impeachment. . . .

⊷ 7 ⊷

The Pacificus-Helvidius Letters*

(1793)

GEORGE WASHINGTON hoped to preserve unity within the new government, but a rift developed between Secretary of the Treasury Alexander Hamilton and Secretary of State Thomas Jefferson, along with their political allies in Congress. This division emerged during Washington's first term when Jefferson opposed several of Hamilton's proposals to involve the federal government in the nation's economy. It was aggravated during the first year of Washington's second term when the president issued the Neutrality Proclamation of 1793, declaring

*Go to *http://www.claremont.org/basicpage/the-pacificus-helvidius-debates/#.VN-KwdbOypo.*

that the United States would not take sides in the war between England and France. Jefferson had urged Washington to support France, which had helped the Americans to win the Revolutionary War against England.

Hamilton, a partisan of England, defended the proclamation in a series of newspaper articles written under the pseudonym "Pacificus." As a member of the administration, Jefferson was unwilling to attack the president's proclamation in public; instead, he recruited Rep. James Madison of Virginia to answer Hamilton as "Helvidius." "For God's sake, my dear Sir," Jefferson urged Madison, "take up your pen, select the most striking heresies, and cut him to pieces in the face of the public."

The opening letters in the exchange between Hamilton (Pacificus) and Madison (Helvidius), so recently allied as the coauthors of *The Federalist Papers,* were published in the *Gazette of the United States,* a Philadelphia newspaper, during the summer of 1793. The debate focused less on the merits of Washington's policy than on whether the president has the constitutional power to issue a proclamation of neutrality without securing Congress's support.

Hamilton, arguing for a broad construction of presidential power, emphasized the difference between the vesting clauses of Article I and Article II of the Constitution. Article I begins: "All legislative Powers herein granted shall be vested in a Congress of the United States." The opening sentence of Article II omits the words "herein granted" and states: "The executive Power shall be vested in a President of the United States of America." From this difference, Hamilton concluded that although the powers of Congress are limited to those enumerated in the remainder of Article I, the "executive Power" enjoyed by the president extends beyond the list of specific powers granted in Article II to include any other powers that may be construed as executive in nature, including the power to declare American neutrality.

Madison refused to accept Hamilton's characterization of neutrality as a "natural" executive power. Because it is an aspect of the treaty-making and war-making powers, Madison argued, neutrality is, if anything, essentially legislative. Madison even echoed the rhetoric of his erstwhile Anti-Federalist opponents during the fight to ratify the Constitution, finding "royal prerogatives" lurking in Hamilton's argument.

🐜 🐜 🐜

Pacificus No. 1

As attempts are making very dangerous to the peace, and it is to be feared not very friendly to the constitution of the U[nited] States—it becomes the duty of those who wish well to both to endeavor to prevent their success. The objections which have been raised against the Proclamation of Neutrality lately issued by the President have been urged in a spirit of acrimony and invective, which demonstrates, that more was in view than merely a free discussion of an important public measure; that the discussion covers a design of weakening the confidence of the People in the author of the measure; in order to remove or lessen a powerful obstacle to the success of an opposition to the Government, which however it may change its form, according to circumstances, seems still to be adhered to and pursued with persevering Industry.

This Reflection adds to the motives connected with the measure itself to recommend endeavours by proper explanations to place it in a just light. Such explanations at least cannot but be satisfactory to those who may not have leisure or opportunity for pursuing themselves an investigation of the subject, and who may wish to perceive that the policy of the Government is not inconsistent with its obligations or its honor. . . .

The inquiry then is—what department of the Government of the U[nited] States is the prop[er] one to make a declaration of Neutrality in the cases in which the engagements [of] the Nation permit and its interests require such a declaration.

A correct and well informed mind will discern at once that it can belong neit[her] to the Legislative nor Judicial Department and of course must belong to the Executive.

The Legislative Department is not the *organ* of intercourse between the U[nited] States and foreign Nations. It is charged neither with *making* nor *interpreting* Treaties. It is therefore not naturally that Organ of the Government which is to pronounce the existing condition of the Nation, with regard to foreign Powers, or to admonish the Citizens of their obligations and duties as rounded upon that condition of things. Still less is it charged with enforcing the execution and observance of these obligations and those duties.

It is equally obvious that the act in question is foreign to the Judiciary Department of the Government. The province of that Department is to decide litigations in particular cases. It is indeed charged with the interpretation of treaties; but it exercises this function only in the litigated cases; that is where contending parties bring before it a specific controversy. It has no concern with pronouncing upon the external political relations of Treaties between Government and Government. This position is too plain to need being insisted upon.

It must then of necessity belong to the Executive Department to exercise the function in Question—when a proper case for the exercise of it occurs.

It appears to be connected with that department in various capacities, as the *organ* of intercourse between the Nation and foreign Nations—as the interpreter of the National Treaties in those cases in which the Judiciary is not competent, that is in the cases between Government and Government—as that Power, which is charged with the Execution of the Laws, of which Treaties form a part—as that Power which is charged with the command and application of the Public Force.

This view of the subject is so natural and obvious—so analogous to general theory and practice—that no doubt can be entertained of its justness, unless such doubt can be deduced from particular provisions of the Constitution of the U[nited] States.

Let us see then if cause for such doubt is to be found in that constitution.

The second Article of the Constitution of the U[nited] States, section 1st, establishes this general Proposition, that "The executive power shall be vested in a President of the United States of America."

The same article in a succeeding Section proceeds to designate particular cases of Executive Power. It declares among other things that the President shall be Commander in Chief of the army and navy of the U[nited] States and of the Militia of the several states when called into the actual service of the U[nited] States, that he shall have power by and with the advice of the senate to make treaties; that it shall be his duty to receive ambassadors and other public Ministers and to take care that the laws be faithfully executed.

It would not consist with the rules of sound construction to consider this enumeration of particular authorities as derogating from the more comprehensive grant, contained in the general clause, further than as it may be coupled with express restrictions or qualifications; as in regard to the cooperation of the Senate in the appointment of Officers and the making of treaties; which are qualifica[tions] of the general executive powers of appointing officers and making treaties: Because the difficulty of a complete and perfect specification of all the cases of Executive authority would naturally dictate the use of general terms—and would render it improbable that a specification of certain particulars was design[e]d as a substitute for those terms, when antecedently used. The different mode of expression employed in the constitution in regard to the two powers the Legislative and the Executive serves to conform this inference. In the article which grants the legislative powers of the Governt. The expressions are—"All Legislative powers herein granted shall be vested in a Congress of the U[nited] States" in that which grants the Executive Power the expressions are, as already quoted "The Executive Po[wer] shall be vested in a President of the U[nited] States of America."

The enumeration ought rather therefore to be considered as intended by way of greater caution, to specify and regulate the principal articles implied in the definition of Executive Power; leaving the rest to flow from the general grant of that power, interpreted in conformity to other parts [of] the constitution and to the principles of free government.

The general doctrine then of our constitution is, that the executive power of the Nation is vested in the President; subject only to the *exceptions* and *qu{a}lifications* which are expressed in the instrument.

Two of these have been already noticed—the participation of the Senate in the appointment of Officers and the making of Treaties. A third remains to be mentioned[:] the right of the Legislature "to declare war and grant letters of marque and reprisal."

With these exceptions the executive power of the Union is completely lodged in the President. This mode of construing the Constitution has indeed been recognized by Congress in formal acts, upon full consideration and debate. The power of removal from office is an important instance.

And since upon general principles for reasons already given, the issuing of a proclamation of neutrality is merely an Executive Act; since also the general Executive Power of the Union is vested in the President, the conclusion is, that the step, which has been taken by him, is liable to no just exception on the score of authority. It may be observed that this Inference w[ould] be Just if the power of declaring war had [not] been vested in the Legislature, but that [this] power naturally includes the right of judg[ing] whether the Nation is under obligations to m[ake] war or not.

The answer to this is, that however true it may be, that th[e] right of the Legislature to declare wa[r] includes the right of judging whether the N[ation] be under obligations to make War or not—it will not follow that the Executive is in any case excluded from a similar right of Judgment, in the execution of its own functions.

If the Legislature have a right to make war on the one hand—it is on the other the duty of the Executive to preserve Peace till war is declared; and in fulfilling that duty, it must necessarily possess a right of judging what is the nature of the obligations which the treaties of the Country impose on the Government; and when in pursuance of this right it has concluded that there is nothing in them inconsistent with a *state* of neutrality, it becomes both its province and its duty to enforce the laws incident to that state of the Nation. The Executive is charged with the execution of all laws, the laws of Nations as well as the Municipal law, which recognises and adopts those laws. It is consequently bound, by faithfully executing the laws of neutrality, when that is the state of the Nation, to avoid giving a cause of war to foreign Powers. . . .

In this distribution of powers the wisdom of our constitution is manifested. It is the province and duty of the Executive to preserve to the Nation the blessings of peace. The Legislature alone can interrupt those blessings, by placing the Nation in a state of War.

But though it has been thought advisable to vindicate the authority of the Executive on this broad and comprehensive ground—it was not absolutely necessary to do so. That clause of the constitution which makes it his duty to "take care that the laws be faithfully executed" might alone have been relied upon, and this simple process of argument pursued.

The President is the constitutional Executor of the laws. Our Treaties and the laws of Nations form a part of the law of the land. He who is to execute the laws must first judge for himself of their meaning. In order to the observance of that conduct, which the laws of nations combined with our treaties prescribed to this country, in reference to the present War in Europe, it was necessary for the President to judge for himself whether there was any thing in our treaties incompatible with an adherence to neutrality. Having judged that there was not, he had a right, and if in his opinion the interests of the Nation required it, it was his duty, as Executor of the laws, to proclaim the neutrality of the Nation, to exhort all persons to observe it, and to warn them of the penalties which would attend its non observance.

The Proclamation has been represented as enacting some new law. This is a view of it entirely erroneous. It only proclaims a fact with regard to the existing state of the Nation, informs the citizens of what the laws previously established require of them in that state, & warns them that these laws will be put in execution against the Infractors of them.

Helvidius No. 1

Several pieces with the signature of PACIFICUS were lately published, which have been read with singular pleasure and applause, by the foreigners and degenerate citizens among us, who hate our republican government and the French revolution; whilst the publication seems to have been too little regarded, or too much despised by the steady friends to both.

Had the doctrines inculcated by the writer, with the natural consequences from them, been nakedly presented to the public, this treatment might have been proper.

Their true character would then have struck every eye, and been rejected by the feelings of every heart. But they offer themselves to the reader in the dress of an elaborate dissertation; they are mingled with a few truths that may serve them as a passport to credulity; and they are introduced with professions of anxiety for the preservation of peace, for the welfare of the government, and for the respect due to the present head of the executive, that may prove a snare to patriotism.

In these disguises they have appeared to claim the attention I propose to bestow on them; with a view to show, from the publication itself, that under colour of vindicating an important public act, of a chief magistrate, who enjoys the confidence and love of his country, principles are advanced [by Pacificus] which strike at the vitals of its constitution, as well as at its honor and true interest. . . .

If we consult for a moment, the nature and operation of the two powers to declare war and make treaties, it will be impossible not to see that they can never fall within a proper definition of executive powers. The natural province of the executive magistrate is to execute laws, as that of the legislature is to make laws. All his acts therefore, properly executive, must pre-suppose the existence of the laws to be executed. A treaty is not an execution of laws: it does not pre-suppose the existence of laws. It is, on the contrary, to have itself the force of a *law,* and to be carried into *execution,* like all *other laws,* by the *executive magistrate.* To say then that the power of making treaties which are confessedly laws, belongs naturally to the department which is to execute laws, is to say, that the executive department naturally includes a legislative power. In theory, this is an absurdity—in practice a tyranny.

The power to declare war is subject to similar reasoning. A declaration that there shall be war, is not an execution of laws: it does not suppose pre-existing laws to be executed: it is not in any respect, an act merely executive. It is, on the contrary, one of the most deliberative acts that can be performed; and when performed, has the effect of *repealing* all the *laws* operating in a state of peace, so far as they are inconsistent with a state of war: and of *enacting* as a *rule for the executive,* a *new code* adapted to the relation between the society and its foreign enemy. In like manner a conclusion of peace *annuls* all the *laws* peculiar to a state of war, and *revives* the general *laws* incident to a state of peace.

These remarks will be strengthened by adding that treaties, particularly treaties of peace, have sometimes the effect of changing not only the external laws of the society, but operate also on the internal code, which is purely municipal, and to which the legislative authority of the country is of itself competent and compleat.

From the view of the subject it must be evident, that although the executive may be a convenient organ of preliminary communications with foreign governments, on the subjects of treaty or war; and the proper agent for carrying into execution the final determinations of the competent authority; yet it can have no pretensions from the nature of the powers in question compared with the nature of the executive trust, to that essential agency which gives validity to such determinations.

It must be further evident that, if these powers be not in their nature purely legislative, they partake so much more of that, than of any other quality, that under a constitution leaving them to result to their most natural department, the legislature would be without a rival in its claim.

Another important inference to be noted is, that the posers of making war and treaty being substantially of a legislative, not an executive nature, the rule of interpreting exceptions strictly, must narrow instead of enlarging executive pretensions on these subjects. . . .

In the general distribution of powers, we find that of declaring war expressly vested in the Congress, where every other legislative power is declared to be vested, and without any other qualification than what is common to every other legislative act. The constitutional idea of this power would seem then clearly to be, that it is of a legislative and not an executive nature. . . .

The power of treaties is vested jointly in the President and in the Senate, which is a branch of the legislature. From this arrangement merely, there can be no interference that would necessarily exclude the power from the executive class: since the senate is joined with the President in another power, that of appointing to offices, which as far as relate to executive offices at least, is considered as of an executive nature. Yet on the other hand, there are sufficient indications that the power of treaties is regarded by the constitution as materially different from mere executive power, and as having more affinity to the legislative than to the executive character.

One circumstance indicating this, is the constitutional regulation under which the senate give their consent in the case of treaties. In all other cases the consent of the body is expressed by a majority of voices. In this particular case, a concurrence of two thirds at least is made necessary, as a substitute or compensation for the other branch of the legislature, which on certain occasions, could not be conveniently a party to the transaction.

But the conclusive circumstance is, that treaties when formed according to the constitutional mode, are confessedly to have the force and operation of *laws,* and are to be a rule for the courts in controversies between man and man, as much as any *other laws.* They are even emphatically declared by the constitution to be "the supreme law of the land."

So far the argument from the constitution is precisely in opposition to the [Pacificus] doctrine. As little will be gained in its favour from a comparison of the two powers, with those particularly vested in the President alone.

As there are but few it will be most satisfactory to review them one by one.

"The President shall be commander in chief of the army and navy of the United States, and of the militia when called into the actual service of the United States."

There can be no relation worth examining between this power and the general power of making treaties. And instead of being analogous to the power of declaring war, it affords a striking illustration of the incompatibility of the two powers in the same hands. Those who are to conduct a war cannot in the nature of things, be proper or safe judges, whether a war ought to be commenced, continued, or concluded. They are barred from the latter functions by a great principle in free government, analogous to that which separates the sword from the purse, of the power of executing from the power of enacting laws. . . .

"He shall take care that the laws shall be faithfully executed and shall commission all officers of the United States." To see the laws faithfully executed constitutes the essence of the executive authority. But what relation has it to the power of making treaties and war, that is, of determining what the laws shall be with regard to other nations? No other certainly than what subsists between the posers of executing and enacting laws; no other consequently, than what forbids a coalition of the powers in the same department.

I pass over the few other specified functions assigned to the President, such as that of convening of the legislature, &c. &c. which cannot be drawn into the present question.

It may be proper however to take notice of the power of removal from office, which appears to have been adjudged to the President by the laws establishing the executive departments; and which the writer has endeavoured to press into his service. To justify any favourable inference from this case, it must be shewn, that the powers of war and treaties are of a kindred nature to the power of removal, or at least are equally within a grant of executive power. Nothing of this sort has been attempted, nor probably will be attempted. Nothing can in truth be clearer, than that no analogy, or shade of analogy, can be traced between a power in the supreme officer responsible for the faithful execution of the laws, to displace a subaltern officer employed in the execution of the laws; and a power to make treaties, and to declare war, such as these have been found to be in their nature, their operation, and their consequences.

Thus it appears that by whatever standard we try this doctrine, it must be condemned as no less vicious in theory than it would be dangerous in practice. It is countenanced neither by the writers on law; nor by the nature of the powers themselves; nor by any general arrangements or particular expressions, or plausible analogies, to be found in the constitution.

Whence then can the writer have borrowed it?

There is but one answer to this question.

The power of making treaties and the power of declaring war, are *royal prerogatives* in the *British government.* . . .

⊰ 8 ⊱

George Washington's Farewell Address*

(1796)

GEORGE WASHINGTON had hoped to retire from public life at the end of his first term as president. He even asked James Madison to draft a farewell address in 1792. But Washington was prevailed on to stand for reelection. The president's advisers, along with many of the new nation's other leaders, were convinced that his retirement would unleash partisan warfare and place the fragile, four-year-old Constitution in jeopardy.

---

*Go to *http://avalon.law.yale.edu/18th_century/washing.asp.*

In 1796 Washington resolved to step down when his second term ended in March 1797. Weaving together Madison's earlier draft, a new draft by Alexander Hamilton, and his own words and ideas, Washington addressed a letter to his "Friends and Citizens" and released it to the *Daily American Advertiser,* a newspaper in the then-capital city of Philadelphia, where it was published on September 19, 1796. Newspapers around the country reprinted what soon came to be known as the "farewell address," even though Washington never delivered it before an audience. News of Washington's retirement inspired a national outpouring of thanks and tributes. By announcing his decision three months before the presidential election, Washington accomplished two objectives: he forestalled any effort to reelect him, and he shortened the length (and reduced the divisiveness) of the campaign to succeed him.

Washington had intentionally set several important precedents for his presidential successors. As Documents 4 (p. 18), 5 (p. 40), and 6 (p. 43) show, he invented the inaugural address; formed the heads of the departments into a cabinet; established the principle of presidential leadership of the executive branch, including the right to remove officials without consulting the Senate; and asserted the president's primacy in foreign policy. The precedent that no president should serve more than two terms, however, was one that Washington did not intend. In truth, as he said in the farewell address, his main reason for leaving office was personal. He longed for "the shade of retirement" after many years of service to his country.

In one area of presidential leadership Washington's effort to establish a precedent was notably unsuccessful. Although he had tried to govern in a nonpartisan style, his eight years in office were marked by growing differences between the pro-British, pro-national government, pro-business Federalist Party, led by Secretary of the Treasury Hamilton, and the pro-French, pro-local government, pro-agriculture Democratic-Republican Party, led by Secretary of State Thomas Jefferson.

In the farewell address, Washington discussed his service as president in characteristically modest terms and then looked ahead to the future of the nation he had helped to found. He was especially concerned about threats to national unity and dwelled at length on two such threats: the "Spirit of Party" that motivated citizens and their leaders to concentrate on what divided rather than what united them, and the inclination among Americans to choose sides in disputes between European powers, especially Great Britain and France. He offered the Neutrality Proclamation of 1793 (see Document 6) as "the index of my plan" to "steer clear of permanent alliances with any portion of the world." Washington concluded by urging Americans to cultivate "religion and morality" because these would foster "peace and harmony" within the United States and between the United States and the nations of the world.

Washington intended the farewell address not only to mark his retirement from the presidency but also to "terminate the career of my public life." In 1798, however, he was called back to service by his successor as president, John Adams. Fears of a French invasion in the aftermath of a diplomatic imbroglio prompted Adams to appoint Washington to take command of the army. The invasion never occurred. Washington died in 1799.

❧ ❧ ❧

Friends and Citizens:

The period for a new election of a citizen to administer the executive government of the United States being not far distant, and the time actually arrived when your thoughts must be employed in designating the person who is to be clothed with that important trust, it appears to me proper, especially as it may conduce to a more distinct expression of the public voice, that I should now apprise you of the resolution I have formed, to decline being considered among the number of those out of whom a choice is to be made.

I beg you, at the same time, to do me the justice to be assured that this resolution has not been taken without a strict regard to all the considerations appertaining to the relation which binds a dutiful citizen to his country; and that in withdrawing the tender of service, which silence in my situation might imply, I am influenced by no diminution of zeal for your future interest, no deficiency of grateful respect for your past kindness, but am supported by a full conviction that the step is compatible with both.

The acceptance of, and continuance hitherto in, the office to which your suffrages have twice called me have been a uniform sacrifice of inclination to the opinion of duty and to a deference for what appeared to be your desire. I constantly hoped that it would have been much earlier in my power, consistently with motives which I was not at liberty to disregard, to return to that retirement from which I had been reluctantly drawn. The strength of my inclination to do this, previous to the last election, had even led to the preparation of an address to declare it to you; but mature reflection on the then perplexed and critical posture of our affairs with foreign nations, and the unanimous advice of persons entitled to my confidence, impelled me to abandon the idea.

I rejoice that the state of your concerns, external as well as internal, no longer renders the pursuit of inclination incompatible with the sentiment of duty or propriety, and am persuaded, whatever partiality may be retained for my services, that, in the present circumstances of our country, you will not disapprove my determination to retire.

The impressions with which I first undertook the arduous trust were explained on the proper occasion. In the discharge of this trust, I will only say that I have, with good intentions, contributed towards the organization and administration of the government the best exertions of which a very fallible judgment was capable. Not unconscious in the outset of the inferiority of my qualifications, experience in my own eyes, perhaps still more in the eyes of others, has strengthened the motives to diffidence of myself; and every day the increasing weight of years admonishes me more and more that the shade of retirement is as necessary to me as it will be welcome. Satisfied that if any circumstances have given peculiar value to my services, they were temporary,

I have the consolation to believe that, while choice and prudence invite me to quit the political scene, patriotism does not forbid it. . . .

Here, perhaps, I ought to stop. But a solicitude for your welfare, which cannot end but with my life, and the apprehension of danger, natural to that solicitude, urge me, on an occasion like the present, to offer to your solemn contemplation, and to recommend to your frequent review, some sentiments which are the result of much reflection, of no inconsiderable observation, and which appear to me all-important to the permanency of your felicity as a people. These will be offered to you with the more freedom, as you can only see in them the disinterested warnings of a parting friend, who can possibly have no personal motive to bias his counsel. Nor can I forget, as an encouragement to it, your indulgent reception of my sentiments on a former and not dissimilar occasion.

Interwoven as is the love of liberty with every ligament of your hearts, no recommendation of mine is necessary to fortify or confirm the attachment.

The unity of government which constitutes you one people is also now dear to you. It is justly so, for it is a main pillar in the edifice of your real independence, the support of your tranquility at home, your peace abroad; of your safety; of your prosperity; of that very liberty which you so highly prize.

But as it is easy to foresee that, from different causes and from different quarters, much pains will be taken, many artifices employed to weaken in your minds the conviction of this truth; as this is the point in your political fortress against which the batteries of internal and external enemies will be most constantly and actively (though often covertly and insidiously) directed, it is of infinite moment that you should properly estimate the immense value of your national union to your collective and individual happiness; that you should cherish a cordial, habitual, and immovable attachment to it; accustoming yourselves to think and speak of it as of the palladium of your political safety and prosperity; watching for its preservation with jealous anxiety; discountenancing whatever may suggest even a suspicion that it can in any event be abandoned; and indignantly frowning upon the first dawning of every attempt to alienate any portion of our country from the rest, or to enfeeble the sacred ties which now link together the various parts. . . .

While, then, every part of our country thus feels an immediate and particular interest in union, all the parts combined cannot fail to find in the united mass of means and efforts greater strength, greater resource, proportionably greater security from external danger, a less frequent interruption of their peace by foreign nations; and, what is of inestimable value, they must derive from union an exemption from those broils and wars between themselves, which so frequently afflict neighboring countries not tied together by the same governments, which their own rival ships alone would be sufficient to produce, but which opposite foreign alliances, attachments, and intrigues would stimulate and embitter.

Hence, likewise, they will avoid the necessity of those overgrown military establishments which, under any form of government, are inauspicious to liberty, and which are to be regarded as particularly hostile to republican liberty. In this sense it is that your union ought to be considered as a main prop of your liberty, and that the love of the one ought to endear to you the preservation of the other.

These considerations speak a persuasive language to every reflecting and virtuous mind, and exhibit the continuance of the Union as a primary object of patriotic desire. Is there a doubt whether a common government can embrace so large a sphere? Let experience solve it. To listen to mere speculation in such a case were criminal. We are authorized to hope that a proper organization of the whole with the auxiliary agency of governments for the respective subdivisions, will afford a happy issue to the experiment. It is well worth a fair and full experiment. With such powerful and obvious motives to union, affecting all parts of our country, while experience shall not have demonstrated its impracticability, there will always be reason to distrust the patriotism of those who in any quarter may endeavor to weaken its bands.

In contemplating the causes which may disturb our Union, it occurs as matter of serious concern that any ground should have been furnished for characterizing parties by geographical discriminations, Northern and Southern, Atlantic and Western; whence designing men may endeavor to excite a belief that there is a real difference of local interests and views. One of the expedients of party to acquire influence within particular districts is to misrepresent the opinions and aims of other districts. You cannot shield yourselves too much against the jealousies and heartburnings which spring from these misrepresentations; they tend to render alien to each other those who ought to be bound together by fraternal affection. . . .

Let me now take a more comprehensive view, and warn you in the most solemn manner against the baneful effects of the spirit of party generally.

This spirit, unfortunately, is inseparable from our nature, having its root in the strongest passions of the human mind. It exists under different shapes in all governments, more or less stifled, controlled, or repressed; but, in those of the popular form, it is seen in its greatest rankness, and is truly their worst enemy.

The alternate domination of one faction over another, sharpened by the spirit of revenge, natural to party dissension, which in different ages and countries has perpetrated the most horrid enormities, is itself a frightful despotism. But this leads at length to a more formal and permanent despotism. The disorders and miseries which result gradually incline the minds of men to seek security and repose in the absolute power of an individual; and sooner or later the chief of some prevailing faction, more able or more fortunate than his competitors, turns this disposition to the purposes of his own elevation, on the ruins of public liberty.

Without looking forward to an extremity of this kind (which nevertheless ought not to be entirely out of sight), the common and continual mischiefs of the spirit of party are sufficient to make it the interest and duty of a wise people to discourage and restrain it.

It serves always to distract the public councils and enfeeble the public administration. It agitates the community with ill-founded jealousies and false alarms, kindles the animosity of one part against another, foments occasionally riot and insurrection. It opens the door to foreign influence and corruption, which finds a facilitated access to the government itself through the channels of party passions. Thus the policy and the will of one country are subjected to the policy and will of another.

There is an opinion that parties in free countries are useful checks upon the administration of the government and serve to keep alive the spirit of liberty. This within certain limits is probably true; and in governments of a monarchical cast, patriotism may look with indulgence, if not with favor, upon the spirit of party. But in those of the popular character, in governments purely elective, it is a spirit not to be encouraged. From their natural tendency, it is certain there will always be enough of that spirit for every salutary purpose. And there being constant danger of excess, the effort ought to be by force of public opinion, to mitigate and assuage it. A fire not to be quenched, it demands a uniform vigilance to prevent its bursting into a flame, lest, instead of warming, it should consume.

It is important, likewise, that the habits of thinking in a free country should inspire caution in those entrusted with its administration, to confine themselves within their respective constitutional spheres, avoiding in the exercise of the powers of one department to encroach upon another. The spirit of encroachment tends to consolidate the powers of all the departments in one, and thus to create, whatever the form of government, a real despotism. A just estimate of that love of power, and proneness to abuse it, which predominates in the human heart, is sufficient to satisfy us of the truth of this position. The necessity of reciprocal checks in the exercise of political power, by dividing and distributing it into different depositaries, and constituting each the guardian of the public weal against invasions by the others, has been evinced by experiments ancient and modern; some of them in our country and under our own eyes. To preserve them must be as necessary as to institute them. If, in the opinion of the people, the distribution or modification of the constitutional powers be in any particular wrong, let it be corrected by an amendment in the way which the Constitution designates. But let there be no change by usurpation; for though this, in one instance, may be the instrument of good, it is the customary weapon by which free governments are destroyed. The precedent must always greatly overbalance in permanent evil any partial or transient benefit, which the use can at any time yield.

Of all the dispositions and habits which lead to political prosperity, religion and morality are indispensable supports. In vain would that man claim the tribute of patriotism, who should labor to subvert these great pillars of human happiness, these firmest props of the duties of men and citizens. The mere politician, equally with the pious man, ought to respect and to cherish them. A volume could not trace all their connections with private and public felicity. Let it simply be asked: Where is the security for property, for reputation, for life, if the sense of religious obligation desert the oaths which are the instruments of investigation in courts of justice? And let us with caution indulge the supposition that morality can be maintained without religion. Whatever may be conceded to the influence of refined education on minds of peculiar structure, reason and experience both forbid us to expect that national morality can prevail in exclusion of religious principle.

It is substantially true that virtue or morality is a necessary spring of popular government. The rule, indeed, extends with more or less force to every species of free government. Who that is a sincere friend to it can look with indifference upon attempts to shake the foundation of the fabric?

Promote then, as an object of primary importance, institutions for the general diffusion of knowledge. In proportion as the structure of a government gives force to public opinion, it is essential that public opinion should be enlightened.

As a very important source of strength and security, cherish public credit. One method of preserving it is to use it as sparingly as possible, avoiding occasions of expense by cultivating peace, but remembering also that timely disbursements to prepare for danger frequently prevent much greater disbursements to repel it, avoiding likewise the accumulation of debt, not only by shunning occasions of expense, but by vigorous exertion in time of peace to discharge the debts which unavoidable wars may have occasioned, not ungenerously throwing upon posterity the burden which we ourselves ought to bear. The execution of these maxims belongs to your representatives, but it is necessary that public opinion should co-operate. To facilitate to them the performance of their duty, it is essential that you should practically bear in mind that towards the payment of debts there must be revenue; that to have revenue there must be taxes; that no taxes can be devised which are not more or less inconvenient and unpleasant; that the intrinsic embarrassment, inseparable from the selection of the proper objects (which is always a choice of difficulties), ought to be a decisive motive for a candid construction of the conduct of the government in making it, and for a spirit of acquiescence in the measures for obtaining revenue, which the public exigencies may at any time dictate.

Observe good faith and justice towards all nations; cultivate peace and harmony with all. Religion and morality enjoin this conduct; and can it be, that good policy does not equally enjoin it? It will be worthy of a free, enlightened, and at no distant period, a great nation, to give to mankind the magnanimous and too novel example of a people always guided by an exalted justice and benevolence.

Who can doubt that, in the course of time and things, the fruits of such a plan would richly repay any temporary advantages which might be lost by a steady adherence to it? Can it be that Providence has not connected the permanent felicity of a nation with its virtue? The experiment, at least, is recommended by every sentiment which ennobles human nature. Alas it is rendered impossible by its vices?

In the execution of such a plan, nothing is more essential than that permanent, inveterate antipathies against particular nations, and passionate attachments for others, should be excluded; and that, in place of them, just and amicable feelings towards all should be cultivated. The nation which indulges towards another a habitual hatred or a habitual fondness is in some degree a slave. It is a slave to its animosity or to its affection, either of which is sufficient to lead it astray from its duty and its interest. Antipathy in one nation against another disposes each more readily to offer insult and injury, to lay hold of slight causes of umbrage, and to be haughty and intractable, when accidental or trifling occasions of dispute occur. Hence, frequent collisions, obstinate, envenomed, and bloody contests. The nation, prompted by ill-will and resentment, sometimes impels to war the government, contrary to the best calculations of policy. The government sometimes participates in the national propensity, and adopts through passion what reason would reject; at other times it makes the animosity of the nation subservient to projects of hostility instigated by pride, ambition, and other sinister and pernicious motives. The peace often, sometimes perhaps the liberty, of nations, has been the victim. . . .

The great rule of conduct for us in regard to foreign nations is in extending our commercial relations, to have with them as little political connection as possible. So far as we have already formed engagements, let them be fulfilled with perfect good faith. Here let us stop. Europe has a set of primary interests which to us have none; or a very remote relation. Hence she must be engaged in frequent controversies, the causes of which are essentially foreign to our concerns. Hence, therefore, it must be unwise in us to implicate ourselves by artificial ties in the ordinary vicissitudes of her politics, or the ordinary combinations and collisions of her friendships or enmities.

Our detached and distant situation invites and enables us to pursue a different course. If we remain one people under an efficient government, the period is not far off when we may defy material injury from external annoyance; when we may take such an attitude as will cause the neutrality we may at any time resolve upon to be scrupulously respected; when belligerent nations, under the impossibility of making acquisitions upon us, will not lightly hazard the giving us provocation; when we may choose peace or war, as our interest, guided by justice, shall counsel.

Why forego the advantages of so peculiar a situation? Why quit our own to stand upon foreign ground? Why, by interweaving our destiny with that of any part of Europe, entangle our peace and prosperity in the toils of European ambition, rivalship, interest, humor or caprice?

It is our true policy to steer clear of permanent alliances with any portion of the foreign world; so far, I mean, as we are now at liberty to do it; for let me not be understood as capable of patronizing infidelity to existing engagements. I hold the maxim no less applicable to public than to private affairs, that honesty is always the best policy. I repeat it, therefore, let those engagements be observed in their genuine sense. But, in my opinion, it is unnecessary and would be unwise to extend them. . . .

How far in the discharge of my official duties I have been guided by the principles which have been delineated, the public records and other evidences of my conduct must witness to you and to the world. To myself, the assurance of my own conscience is, that I have at least believed myself to be guided by them.

In relation to the still subsisting war in Europe, my proclamation of the twenty-second of April, 1793, is the index of my plan. Sanctioned by your approving voice, and by that of your representatives in both houses of Congress, the spirit of that measure has continually governed me, uninfluenced by any attempts to deter or divert me from it.

After deliberate examination, with the aid of the best lights I could obtain, I was well satisfied that our country, under all the circumstances of the case, had a right to take, and was bound in duty and interest to take, a neutral position. Having taken it, I determined, as far as should depend upon me, to maintain it, with moderation, perseverance, and firmness. . . .

Though, in reviewing the incidents of my administration, I am unconscious of intentional error, I am nevertheless too sensible of my defects not to think it probable that I may have committed many errors. Whatever they may be, I fervently beseech the Almighty to avert or mitigate the evils to which they may tend. I shall also carry with me the hope that my country will never cease to view them with indulgence; and that, after forty five years of my life dedicated to its service with an upright zeal, the faults of incompetent abilities will be consigned to oblivion, as myself must soon be to the mansions of rest.

Relying on its kindness in this as in other things, and actuated by that fervent love towards it, which is so natural to a man who views in it the native soil of himself and his progenitors for several generations, I anticipate with pleasing expectation that retreat in which I promise myself to realize, without alloy, the sweet enjoyment of partaking, in the midst of my fellow-citizens, the benign influence of good laws under a free government, the ever-favorite object of my heart, and the happy reward, as I trust, of our mutual cares, labors, and dangers.

Geo. Washington.

❧ 9 ❧

Thomas Jefferson's First Inaugural Address
(1801)

AS THE DEBATE between Pacificus and Helvidius illustrated (see Document 6, p. 43), strong factional disagreements existed even within George Washington's avowedly nonpartisan administration. Washington's announcement in 1796 that he would retire from the presidency the following year loosed these spirits of partisanship into the larger political system. The Federalist Party, which won the election of 1796, passed laws such as the Alien and Sedition Acts of 1798 to stifle public criticism of the government and thereby undermine the opposition Democratic-Republican Party. In response, the Democratic-Republican–dominated legislatures of Kentucky and Virginia passed resolutions that denied the federal government's right to impose its laws on resisting states.

In 1800, in a rematch of the 1796 presidential election, Thomas Jefferson of Virginia, the Democratic-Republican candidate, defeated President John Adams of Massachusetts, the Federalist nominee. But the very act of tallying the votes aggravated partisan tensions. Under the Constitution, electors did not vote separately for president and vice president. Instead, each cast two votes for president, with the candidate who received the largest majority of electoral votes elected as president and the runner-up as vice president. The anomalous consequence of this system in 1800 was that when all seventy-three Democratic-Republican electors cast their two votes for both Jefferson and Aaron Burr of New York, the party's vice-presidential nominee, the result was recorded as a tie vote for president between Jefferson and Burr.

Constitutionally, the House of Representatives is charged to choose the president if the Electoral College fails to elect someone, with each state delegation casting one vote and support from a majority of states needed for victory. Federalist mischief-makers, who still dominated the House, delayed Jefferson's election through six days and thirty-six ballots. Burr tacitly encouraged them. Finally, on February 17, 1801, partly at the behest of Federalist leader Alexander Hamilton, who feared for both the reputation of his party and the stability of the still-fragile constitutional government he had worked so hard to create, the House chose Jefferson.

Under the circumstances, Jefferson's inaugural address on March 4, 1801, was uniquely significant. It marked the first peaceful transfer of power from one political party to another in the new nation, and one of the first in the world. It also was the first inauguration to take place in the new capital city of Washington.

In addition to the occasion itself, Jefferson's address was significant because of what he said. Resisting the temptation to proclaim a partisan triumph, the new president insisted that "every difference of opinion is not a difference of principle. We have called by different names brethren of the same principle. We are all republicans, we are all federalists." Jefferson did not eschew all differences with his partisan opponents, however. Later in the address he stated his minimalist and distinctly un-Federalist political philosophy: "a wise and frugal Government, which shall restrain men from injuring one another, shall leave them otherwise free to regulate their own pursuits of industry and improvement, and shall not take from the mouth of labor the bread it has earned. This is the sum of good government."

As president, Jefferson worked to undo some Federalist policies—he persuaded Congress to repeal the Alien and Sedition Acts, for example—but he preserved many others. His administration is best remembered for the Louisiana Purchase of 1803, a remarkable assertion of presidential power that nearly doubled the size of the United States by acquiring French territory west of the Mississippi River.

In 1804 Congress passed and the states ratified the Twelfth Amendment, which separated the voting for president and vice president. (See Document 1, p. 1.) The amendment preserved the Electoral College but ensured that the confusion of the 1800 election could not recur.

🐎 🐎 🐎

Friends and Fellow-Citizens:

Called upon to undertake the duties of the first executive office of our country, I avail myself of the presence of that portion of my fellow-citizens which is here assembled to express my grateful thanks for the favor with which they have been pleased to look toward me, to declare a sincere consciousness that the task is above my talents, and that I approach it with those anxious and awful presentiments which the greatness of the charge and the weakness of my powers so justly inspire. A rising nation, spread over a wide and fruitful land, traversing all the seas with the rich productions of their industry, engaged in commerce with nations who feel power and forget right, advancing rapidly to destinies beyond the reach of mortal eye—when I contemplate these transcendent objects, and see the honor, the happiness, and the hopes of this beloved country committed to the issue and the auspices of this day, I shrink from the contemplation, and humble myself before the magnitude of the undertaking. Utterly, indeed, should I despair did not the presence of many whom I here see remind me that in the other high authorities provided by our Constitution I shall find resources of wisdom, of virtue, and of zeal on which to rely under all difficulties. To you, then, gentlemen, who are charged with the sovereign functions of legislation, and to those associated with you, I look with encouragement for that guidance and support which may enable us to steer with safety the vessel in which we are all embarked amidst the conflicting elements of a troubled world.

During the contest of opinion through which we have passed the animation of discussions and of exertions has sometimes worn an aspect which might impose on strangers unused to think freely and to speak and to write what they think; but this being now decided by the voice of the nation, announced according to the rules of the Constitution, all will, of course, arrange themselves under the will of the law, and unite in common efforts for the common good. All, too, will bear in mind this sacred principle, that though the will of the majority is in all cases to prevail, that will to be rightful must be reasonable; that the minority possess their equal rights, which equal law must protect, and to violate would be oppression. Let us, then, fellow-citizens, unite with one heart and one mind. Let us restore to social intercourse that harmony and affection without which liberty and even life itself are but dreary things. And let us reflect that, having banished from our land that religious intolerance under which mankind so long bled and suffered, we have yet gained little if we countenance a political intolerance as despotic, as wicked, and capable of as bitter and bloody persecutions. During the throes and convulsions of the ancient world, during the agonizing spasms of infuriated man, seeking through blood and slaughter his long-lost liberty, it was not wonderful that the agitation of the billows should reach even this distant and peaceful shore; that this should be more felt and feared by some and less by others, and should divide opinions as to measures of safety. But every difference of opinion is not a difference of principle. We have called by different names brethren of the same principle. We are all republicans, we are all federalists. If there be any among us who would wish to dissolve this Union or to change its republican form, let them stand undisturbed as monuments of the safety with which error of opinion may be tolerated where reason is left free to combat it. I know, indeed, that some honest men fear that a republican government can not be strong, that this Government is not strong enough; but would the honest patriot, in the full tide of successful experiment, abandon a government which has so far kept us free and firm on the theoretic and visionary fear that this Government, the world's best hope, may by possibility want energy to preserve itself? I trust not. I believe this, on the contrary, the strongest Government on earth. I believe it the only one where every man, at the call of the law, would fly to the standard of the law, and would meet invasions of the public order as his own personal concern. Sometimes it is said that man can not be trusted with the government of himself. Can he, then, be trusted with the government of others? Or have we found angels in the forms of kings to govern him? Let history answer this question.

Let us, then, with courage and confidence pursue our own federal and republican principles, our attachment to union and representative government. Kindly separated by nature and a wide ocean from the exterminating havoc of one quarter of the globe; too high-minded to endure the degradations of the others; possessing a chosen country, with room enough for our descendants to the thousandth and thousandth generation; entertaining a due sense of our equal right to the use of our faculties, to the acquisitions of our own industry, to honor and confidence from our fellow-citizens, resulting not from birth, but from our actions and their sense of them; enlightened by a benign religion, professed, indeed, and practiced in various forms, yet all of them inculcating honesty, truth, temperance, gratitude, and the love of man; acknowledging and adoring an overruling Providence, which by all its dispensations proves that it delights in the happiness of man here and his greater happiness hereafter—with all these blessings, what more is necessary to make us a happy and a prosperous people? Still one thing more, fellow-citizens—a wise and frugal Government, which shall restrain men from injuring one another, shall leave them otherwise free to regulate their own pursuits of industry and improvement, and shall not take from the mouth of labor the bread it has earned. This is the sum of good government, and this is necessary to close the circle of our felicities.

About to enter, fellow-citizens, on the exercise of duties which comprehend everything dear and valuable to you, it is proper you should understand what I deem the essential principles of our Government, and consequently those which ought to shape its Administration. I will compress them within the narrowest compass they will bear, stating the general principle, but not all its limitations. Equal and exact justice to all men, of whatever state or persuasion, religious or political; peace, commerce, and honest friendship with all nations, entangling alliances with none; the support of the State governments in all their rights, as the most competent administrations for our domestic concerns and the surest bulwarks against antirepublican tendencies; the preservation of the General Government in its whole constitutional vigor, as the sheet anchor of our peace at home and safety abroad; a jealous care of the right of election by the people—a mild and safe corrective of abuses which are lopped by the sword of revolution where peaceable remedies are unprovided; absolute acquiescence in the decisions of the majority, the vital principle of republics, from which is not appeal but to force, the vital principle and immediate parent of despotism; a well-disciplined militia, our best reliance in peace and for the first moments of war, till regulars may relieve them; the supremacy of the civil over the military authority; economy in the public expense, that labor may be lightly burthened; the honest payment of our debts and sacred preservation of the public faith; encouragement of agriculture, and of commerce as its handmaid; the diffusion of information and arraignment of all abuses at the bar of the public reason; freedom of religion; freedom of the press, and freedom of person under the protection of the habeas corpus, and trial by juries impartially selected. These principles form the bright constellation which has gone before us and guided our steps through an age of revolution and reformation. The wisdom of our sages and blood of our heroes have been devoted to their attainment. They should be the creed of our political faith, the text of civic instruction, the touchstone by which to try the services of those we trust; and should we wander from them in moments of error or of alarm, let us hasten to retrace our steps and to regain the road which alone leads to peace, liberty, and safety.

I repair, then, fellow-citizens, to the post you have assigned me. With experience enough in subordinate offices to have seen the difficulties of this the greatest of all, I have learnt to expect that it will rarely fall to the lot of imperfect man to retire from this station with the reputation and the favor which bring him into it. Without pretensions to that high confidence you reposed in our first and greatest revolutionary character, whose preëminent services had entitled him to the first place in his country's love and destined for him the fairest page in the volume of faithful history, I ask so much confidence only as may give firmness and effect to the legal administration of your affairs. I shall often go wrong through defect of judgment. When right, I shall often be thought wrong by those whose positions will not command a view of the whole ground. I ask your indulgence for my own errors, which will never be intentional, and your support against the errors of others, who may condemn what they would not if seen in all its parts. The approbation implied by your suffrage is a great consolation to me for the past, and my future solicitude will be to retain the good opinion of those who have bestowed it in advance, to conciliate that of others by doing them all the good in my power, and to be instrumental to the happiness and freedom of all.

Relying, then, on the patronage of your good will, I advance with obedience to the work, ready to retire from it whenever you become sensible how much better choice it is in your power to make. And may that Infinite Power which rules the destinies of the universe lead our councils to what is best, and give them a favorable issue for your peace and prosperity.

❧ IO ❧

Thomas Jefferson's Letter to the Vermont Legislature*

(1807)

T HOMAS JEFFERSON did not attend the Constitutional Convention of 1787. Like John Adams, who was the American minister to Great Britain, Jefferson was representing his country abroad at the time, as minister to France.

Although Jefferson generally admired both the delegates to the convention (an "assembly of demigods," he observed from Paris, only half ironically) and the plan

*Go to *http://teachingamericanhistory.org/library/document/letter-to-the-legislature-of-vermont/*.

of government that they produced, he objected strongly to the absence of a term limit on the president. "Their President seems like a bad edition of a Polish king," Jefferson lamented in a letter to Adams on November 13, 1787. "He may be reelected from 4. years to 4. years for life. . . . Once in office, and possessing the military force of the union, without either the aid or check of a council, he would not be easily dethroned, even if the people could be induced to withdraw their votes from him. I wish that at the end of the 4. years they had made him for ever ineligible a second time."

As president, Jefferson managed to temper his objections to presidential reeligibility enough to run for a second term in 1804. He was reelected easily, by a margin of 162 electoral votes to 14 electoral votes for the Federalist candidate, Charles Cotesworth Pinckney of South Carolina.

Still, Jefferson's expediency on the term-limit issue extended only so far. In 1806 and 1807, six state legislatures petitioned him to stand for a third term. Undoubtedly, Jefferson would have been reelected if he had allowed his name to go forward. The Federalist Party was growing steadily weaker; the president's hold on the Democratic-Republican Party was strong; and his popularity, although not as great as in 1804, was more than sufficient to win a third term.

But two terms was Jefferson's limit. On December 10, 1807, in a letter to the legislature of Vermont, he stated his belief that no president should serve in office longer than eight years. Echoing his two-decade-old letter to Adams, Jefferson wrote, "If some termination to the services of the Chief Magistrate be not fixed by the Constitution, or supplied by practice, his office, nominally four years, will in fact become for life, and history shows how easily that degenerates into an inheritance." To strengthen his argument for a two-term tradition, Jefferson even invoked "the sound precedent set by an illustrious predecessor," George Washington. In truth, Washington had retired more for personal reasons than for reasons of state. As he confessed in his farewell address, Washington longed for "the shade of retirement." (See Document 8, p. 54.)

Jefferson's long-standing desire to impose a limit on presidential reeligibility stood in sharp contrast to the intention of the Constitution's framers, who believed that the president should always have an electoral incentive to do the best possible job and that the voters should always be free to reelect (or reject) the incumbent. Yet Jefferson won his argument in the court of history. No president even was nominated for a third term until 1940, when Franklin D. Roosevelt ran. Far from shattering the two-term tradition, Roosevelt's successful reelection campaigns in 1940 and 1944 triggered such a strong conservative backlash that the Twenty-second Amendment was enacted by Congress in 1947 and ratified by the states in 1951, forbidding third terms.

To the Legislature of Vermont.

Washington, December 10, 1807

I received in due season the *address* of the legislature of Vermont, bearing date the 5th of November, 1806, in which, with their approbation of the general course of my administration, they were so good as to express their desire that I would consent to be proposed again, to the public voice, on the expiration of my present term of office. Entertaining, as I do, for the legislature of Vermont those sentiments of high respect which would have prompted an immediate answer, I was certain, nevertheless, they would approve a delay which had for its object to avoid a premature agitation of the public mind, on a subject so interesting as the election of a chief magistrate.

That I should lay down my charge at a proper period, is as much a duty as to have borne it faithfully. If some termination to the services of the chief magistrate be not fixed by the Constitution, or supplied by practice, his office, nominally for years, will, in fact, become for life; and history shows how easily that degenerates into an inheritance. Believing that a representative government, responsible at short periods of election, is that which produces the greatest sum of happiness to mankind, I feel it a duty to do no act which shall essentially impair that principle; and I should unwillingly be the person who, disregarding the sound precedent set by an illustrious predecessor, should furnish the first example of prolongation beyond the second term of office.

Truth, also, requires me to add, that I am sensible of that decline which advancing years bring on; and feeling their physical, I ought not to doubt their mental effect. Happy if I am the first to perceive and to obey this admonition of nature, and to solicit a retreat from cares too great for the wearied faculties of age.

For the approbation which the legislature of Vermont has been pleased to express of the principles and measures pursued in the management of their affairs, I am sincerely thankful; and should I be so fortunate as to carry into retirement the equal approbation and good will of my fellow citizens generally, it will be the comfort of my future days, and will close a service of forty years with the only reward it ever wished.

❧ II ❧

The Monroe Doctrine*

(1823)

J AMES MONROE, a Democratic-Republican from Virginia who was elected president in 1816 and reelected without opposition in 1820, is best known for the doctrine that bears his name. Like most nineteenth-century presidents, Monroe faced an assertive Congress that dominated his administration in matters of

---

*Go to *http://www.law.ou.edu/ushistory/monrodoc.shtml*.

domestic policy. In foreign affairs, however, Monroe reinforced the constitutional authority of the president to take the initiative in establishing American policy.

The Monroe Doctrine was proclaimed, with the support of the British, in response to two foreign policy disputes in which the United States was involved during the early 1820s. The first was a Russian claim to exclusive trading rights in an area along the Pacific coast, from the Bering Strait south to an unspecified location on the shore of the Oregon territory. The other was a variety of rumored European plans, most involving France, to recolonize the newly independent nations of previously Spanish South America.

After frequent consultations with the cabinet and with former presidents James Madison and Thomas Jefferson during the fall of 1823, Monroe and Secretary of State John Quincy Adams resolved to declare the "new world" of the Americas off-limits to any attempts at colonization by the "old world" of Europe.

The Monroe Doctrine was included in Monroe's annual written message to Congress on December 2, 1823. Presidents from Jefferson to William Howard Taft, a century later, fulfilled their constitutional obligation to "give to the Congress Information of the State of the Union" in writing rather than in a speech, which was the practice followed by George Washington and John Adams, as well as by every president since Woodrow Wilson in 1913.

No consultation with Congress preceded the declaration of the Monroe Doctrine, and some legislators believed that the president had exceeded the powers of his office by unilaterally enunciating a major foreign policy on behalf of the entire government. Yet the doctrine stood as a fait accompli. Congress took no action either to affirm or to repudiate it. Public reaction around the country was generally positive.

The Monroe Doctrine had little immediate effect. As it turned out, European nations were not planning to recolonize South America. As for the Russians, they defied Monroe by continuing for a time their efforts in the Pacific Northwest. Nevertheless, the doctrine was widely understood, both at home and abroad, to be a bold assertion of American power and of presidential control of foreign policy.

Congress officially endorsed the Monroe Doctrine in 1899, and President Theodore Roosevelt expanded it in 1904. In his annual message to Congress, Roosevelt declared that the United States had the right to intervene if "chronic wrongdoing or impotence" in a country of the Western Hemisphere seemed to require such intervention. Protest from Latin America led to the withdrawal of the so-called Roosevelt Corollary in 1928.

The Monroe Doctrine has seldom been explicitly invoked in modern times. Even when Soviet nuclear missiles were installed in Cuba in 1962, President John F. Kennedy demanded their withdrawal on other diplomatic grounds. (See Document 36, p. 177.) Nevertheless, the United States has continued to regard Latin America as a sphere of influence, interfering both in its domestic politics and in its relations with other parts of the world when deemed useful to the national interest.

☙ ☙ ☙

Fellow Citizens of the Senate and House of Representatives:

. . . At the proposal of the Russian Imperial Government, made through the minister of the Emperor residing here, a full power and instructions have been transmitted to the minister of the United States at St. Petersburg [Russia] to arrange by amicable negotiation the respective rights and interests of the two nations on the northwest coast of this continent. A similar proposal had been made by His Imperial Majesty to the Government of Great Britain, which has likewise been acceded to. The Government of the United States has been desirous by this friendly proceeding of manifesting the great value which they have invariably attached to the friendship of the [Russian] Emperor and their solicitude to cultivate the best understanding with his Government. In the discussions to which this interest has given rise and in the arrangements by which they may terminate the occasion has been judged proper for asserting, as a principle in which the rights and interests of the United States are involved, that the American continents, by the free and independent condition which they have assumed and maintain, are henceforth not to be considered as subjects for future colonization by any European powers. . . .

In the wars of the European powers in matters relating to themselves we have never taken any part, nor does it comport with our policy to do so. It is only when our rights are invaded or seriously menaced that we resent injuries or make preparation for our defense. With the movements in this hemisphere we are of necessity more immediately connected, and by causes which must be obvious to all enlightened and impartial observers. The political system of the allied powers [of Europe] is essentially different in this respect from that of America. This difference proceeds from that which exists in their respective Governments; and to the defense of our own, which has been achieved by the loss of so much blood and treasure, and matured by the wisdom of their most enlightened citizens, and under which we have enjoyed unexampled felicity, this whole nation is devoted. We owe it, therefore, to candor and to the amicable relations existing between the United States and those powers to declare that we should consider any attempt on their part to extend their system to any portion of this hemisphere as dangerous to our peace and safety. With the existing colonies or dependencies of any European power we have not interfered and shall not interfere. But with the [South American] Governments who have declared their independence and maintained it, and whose independence we have, on great consideration and on just principles, acknowledged, we could not view any interposition for the purpose of oppressing them, or controlling in any other manner their destiny, by any European power in any other light than as the manifestation of an unfriendly disposition toward the United States. In the war between those new Governments and Spain we declared our neutrality at the time of their recognition, and to this we have adhered, and shall continue to adhere, provided no change shall occur which, in the judgment of the competent authorities of this Government, shall make a corresponding change on the part of the United States indispensable to their security. . . .

Our policy in regard to Europe, which was adopted at an early stage of the wars which have so long agitated that quarter of the globe, nevertheless remains the same, which is, not to interfere in the internal concerns of any of its powers; to consider the government de facto as the legitimate government for us; to cultivate friendly relations with it, and to preserve those relations by a frank, firm, and manly policy, meeting in all instances the just claims of every power, submitting to injuries from none. But in regard to those continents circumstances are eminently and conspicuously different. It is impossible that the allied powers should extend their political system to any portion of either continent without endangering our peace and happiness; nor can anyone believe that our southern brethren, if left to themselves, would adopt it of their own accord. It is equally impossible, therefore, that we should behold such interposition in any form with indifference. If we look to the comparative strength and resources of Spain and those new Governments, and their distance from each other, it must be obvious that she can never subdue them. It is still the true policy of the United States to leave the parties to themselves, in the hope that other powers will pursue the same course.

If we compare the present condition of our Union with its actual state at the close of our Revolution, the history of the world furnishes no example of a progress in improvement in all the important circumstances which constitute the happiness of a nation which bears any resemblance to it. At the first epoch our population did not exceed 3,000,000. By the last census it amounted to about 10,000,000, and, what is more extraordinary, it is almost altogether native, for the immigration from other countries has been inconsiderable. At the first epoch half the territory within our acknowledged limits was uninhabited and a wilderness. Since then new territory has been acquired of vast extent, comprising within it many rivers, particularly the Mississippi, the navigation of which to the ocean was of the highest importance to the original States. Over this territory our population has expanded in every direction, and new States have been established almost equal in number to those which formed the first bond of our Union. This expansion of our population and accession of new States to our Union have had the happiest effect on all its highest interests. That it has eminently augmented our resources and added to our strength and respectability as a power is admitted by all. But it is not in these important circumstances only that this happy effect is felt. It is manifest that by enlarging the basis of our system and increasing the number of States the system itself has been greatly strengthened in both its branches. Consolidation and disunion have thereby been rendered equally impracticable. Each Government, confiding in its own strength, has less to apprehend from the other, and in consequence each, enjoying a greater freedom of action, is rendered more efficient for all the purposes for which it was instituted. It is unnecessary to treat here of the vast improvement made in the system itself by the adoption of this Constitution and of its happy effect in elevating the character and in protecting the rights of the nation as well as of individuals. To what, then, do we owe these blessings? It is known to all that we derive them from the excellence of our institutions. Ought we not, then, to adopt every measure which may be necessary to perpetuate them?

✎ 12 ✎

The Tennessee General Assembly's
Protest against the Caucus System

(1823)

T HE PRESIDENTIAL SELECTION PROCESS underwent some wrenching changes during the four decades after the Constitution took effect. The delegates to the Constitutional Convention had explicitly rejected the simple expedient of having Congress elect the president, creating instead an Electoral College in which the candidate who received the most electoral votes became president and the runner-up became vice president. The early rise of political parties that nominated both presidential and vice-presidential candidates upset this arrangement, causing a tie vote for president between Thomas Jefferson and his running mate, Aaron Burr, in 1800 (see Document 9, p. 62) and prompting passage of the Twelfth Amendment in 1804 to separate the balloting for president and vice president.

The rise of political parties also meant that a mechanism had to be developed to nominate the candidates who would represent each party in the election. Beginning in 1796, the Federalist and Democratic-Republican delegations in Congress caucused separately every four years to choose their respective nominees. The Democratic-Republican caucus nominated Jefferson in 1796, 1800, and 1804; James Madison in 1808 and 1812; and James Monroe in 1816 and 1820. It also chose the party's vice-presidential candidates. The Federalist caucus nominated John Adams for president in 1796 and 1800, then fell into disuse as the party's fortunes in Congress drastically declined.

Almost from the beginning, "King Caucus," as its critics began to call it, was attacked by some as elitist and unrepresentative of the party rank and file. Any state or district that did not elect a party's candidate to Congress was, by definition, left out of that party's nominating process. The criticism intensified when voters had only the Democratic-Republican ticket to choose following the demise of the Federalist Party after the 1816 election. With just one party in the field, nomination by caucus was tantamount to election.

In late 1823 Tennessee felt particularly aggrieved by the caucus system because its home-state candidate for president, Gen. Andrew Jackson, seemed unlikely to be nominated. On November 1 the General Assembly published a resolution that condemned the caucus for, among other things, violating "the spirit of the Constitution," whose framers had rejected congressional election of the president. Other states registered protests of their own.

The Democratic-Republican caucus that took place in mid-February 1824 was a fiasco. Only 66 of 261 members of Congress attended. Their nominee, Secretary

72

of the Treasury William Crawford of Georgia, ran a distant third in the presidential election, trailing both Jackson and Secretary of State John Quincy Adams of Massachusetts. Because neither Jackson, who finished first, nor Adams received a majority of electoral votes, the House of Representatives was called on to choose the winner. In a very controversial decision, the House elected Adams.

The 1824 election marked the demise of King Caucus. By the 1830s political parties were nominating their candidates for president and vice president at national conventions. These conventions, consisting of delegates chosen by state and local party organizations all around the country, have been a feature of presidential elections ever since.

※ ※ ※

The General Assembly of the state of Tennessee has taken into consideration the practice which, on former occasions, has prevailed at the city of Washington, of members of the Congress of the United States meeting in caucus, and nominating persons to be voted for as President and Vice-President of the United States; and, upon the best view of the subject which this General Assembly has been able to take, it is believed that the practice of congressional nominations is a violation of the spirit of the Constitution of the United States.

That instrument provides that there shall be three separate and distinct departments of the government, and great care and caution seems to have been exercised by its framers to prevent any one department from exercising the smallest degree of influence over another; and such solicitude was felt on this subject, that, in the 2nd Section of the 2nd Article, it is expressly declared, "That no senator or representative, or person holding an office of trust or profit under the United States, shall be appointed an elector." From this provision, it is apparent that the Convention intended that the members of Congress should not be the principal and primary agents or actors in electing the President and Vice-President of the United States; so far from it, they are expressly disqualified from being placed in a situation to vote for these high officers.

Is there not more danger of undue influence to be apprehended when the members of Congress meet in caucus and mutually and solemnly pledge themselves to support the individuals who may have the highest number of votes in such meeting than there would be in permitting them to be eligible to the appointment of electors? In the latter case, a few characters rendered ineligible by the Constitution might succeed; but, in the former, a powerful combination of influential men is formed, who may fix upon the American people their highest officers against the consent of a clear majority of the people themselves; and this may be done by the very men whom the Constitution intended to prohibit from acting on the subject.

Upon an examination of the Constitution of the United States, there is but one case in which the members of Congress are permitted to act, which is in the event of a failure to make an election by the electoral college; and then the members of the House of Representatives vote by states. With what propriety the same men, who, in the year 1825, may be called on to discharge a constitutional duty, can, in the year 1824, go into a caucus and pledge themselves to support the men then nominated, cannot be discerned, especially when it might so happen that the persons thus nominated could not, under any circumstances, obtain a single vote from the state whose members stand pledged to support them. . . .

It has been said that the members of Congress in caucus only recommend to the people for whom to vote, and that such recommendation is not obligatory. This is true and clearly proves that it is a matter which does not belong to them—that, in recommending candidates, they go beyond the authority committed to them as members of Congress and thus transcend the trust delegated to them by their constituents. If their acts had any obligatory force, then the authority must be derived from some part of the Constitution of the United States and might be rightfully exercised; but when they say they only *recommend,* it is an admission, on their part, that they are acting without authority and are attempting, by a usurped influence, to effect an object not confided to them and not within their powers, even by implication.

It cannot be admitted that there is any weight in the argument drawn from the fact that both the [Federalist and Democratic-Republican] parties, heretofore contending for the superiority in the United States, have, in former times, resorted to this practice. The actions of public or private men, heated by party zeal and struggling for ascendency and power, ought not to be urged as precedents when circumstances have entirely changed. All political precedents are of doubtful authority and should never be permitted to pass unquestioned, unless made in good times and for laudable purposes. In palliation of the practice of resorting to caucus nominations in former times, it was said that each party must of necessity consult together in the best practicable way and select the most suitable persons from their respective parties so that the united efforts of all those composing it might be brought to bear upon their opponents. It is to be recollected that there is no danger of a departure from or violation of the Constitution, except when strong temptations are presented, and this will seldom occur, except when parties are arrayed against each other and their feelings violently excited.

The state of things, however, in the United States is entirely changed; it is no longer a selection made by members of Congress of different parties, but it is an election by the two houses of Congress, in which all the members must be permitted to attend and vote. It is not difficult to perceive that this practice may promote and place men in office who could not be elected were the constitutional mode pursued. It is placing the election of the President and Vice-President of the United States—an election in which all the states have an equal interest and equal rights—more in the power of a few of the most populous states than was contemplated by the Constitution. This practice is considered objectionable on other accounts: so long as Congress is considered as composed of the individuals on whom the election depends, the executive will is subjected to the control of that body, and it ceases, in some degree, to be a separate and independent branch of the government; and the expectation of executive patronage may have an unhappy influence on the deliberations of Congress.

Upon a review of the whole question, the following reasons which admit of much amplification and enlargement, more than has been urged in the foregoing, might be conclusively relied on to prove the impolicy and unconstitutionality of the congressional nominations of candidates for the presidency and vice-presidency of the United States: 1. A caucus nomination is against the spirit of the Constitution. 2. It is both inexpedient and impolitic. 3. Members of Congress may become the final electors and therefore ought not to prejudge the case by pledging themselves previously to support particular candidates. 4. It violates the equality intended to be secured by the Constitution to the weaker states. 5. Caucus nominations may, in time (by the interference of the states), acquire the force of precedents and become authoritative and, thereby, endanger the liberties of the American people.

This General Assembly, believing that the true spirit of the Constitution will be best preserved by leaving the election of President and Vice-President to the *people themselves,* through the medium of electors chosen by them, uninfluenced by any previous nomination made by members of Congress, have adopted the following resolutions:

1. *Resolved,* that the senators in Congress from this state be instructed, and our representatives be requested, to use their exertions to prevent a nomination being made during the next session of Congress, by the members thereof in caucus, of persons to fill the offices of President and Vice-President of the United States.

2. *Resolved,* that the General Assembly will, at its present session, divide the state into as many districts, in convenient form, as this state is entitled to electoral votes, for the purpose of choosing an elector in each to vote for the President and Vice-President of the United States.

3. *Resolved,* that the governor of this state transmit a copy of the foregoing preamble and resolutions to the executive of each of the United States, with a request that the same be laid before each of their respective legislatures.

4. *Resolved,* that the governor transmit a copy to each of the senators and representatives in Congress from this state.

❦ 13 ❦

Andrew Jackson's First Message to Congress

(1829)

ANDREW JACKSON MAY FAIRLY be described as the first "outsider" president. For one thing, he was the first to lack extensive experience in national affairs. Each of his four immediate predecessors had been secretary of state before becoming president. Jackson, only briefly a member of Congress, had made his reputation as the general who defeated the British in the Battle of New Orleans, the greatest American victory in the otherwise inconclusive War of 1812. Jackson was also a political outsider. He viewed the national government with suspicion, as a bastion of privilege for a ruling eastern commercial elite. A Tennessean, Jackson was the first president from west of the Appalachian Mountains. Each of the first six presidents had been from Virginia or Massachusetts.

In all of these ways, Jackson represented rising tendencies in the country that were broadening the base of the American political system. Settlement in the West (roughly the area between the Appalachians and the Mississippi River) had increased the number of states from thirteen in 1776 to twenty-four in 1828. Almost every state had abandoned the traditional requirement that to vote one must own property. And all but a few presidential electors now were selected by vote of the people, not the state legislatures.

The 1828 election was a rematch between Jackson and John Quincy Adams. In 1824, when Jackson won a plurality of electoral votes but not the constitutionally required majority, the House of Representatives had chosen Adams. Sullied by the circumstances of his election, Adams was an unpopular and politically ineffective president. Jackson easily defeated him in 1828 by an electoral vote majority of 178–83, becoming the first president of the recently formed Democratic Party. Jackson's majority consisted mainly of those whom he called "the humble members of society," especially the farmers, mechanics, and laborers of the South and West.

An outsider president elected by a coalition of outsider voters, Jackson used his first annual message to Congress, sent on December 8, 1829, to state officially his view that "the first principle of our system" is that "the majority is to govern." Among the proposals he offered in the message were direct popular election of the president, a single six-year presidential term, and restoration of power to the states. Jackson also announced his intention to give government jobs to the common people who had supported him in the election. He defended the policy, dubbed the "spoils system" by critics, on the grounds that it would foster "efficiency, . . . industry and integrity" in government. When spoils as the basis for appointments became unpopular after the Civil War, Congress created a merit-based civil service by passing the Pendleton Act in 1883 (see Document 21, p. 108).

🐎 🐎 🐎

Fellow Citizens of the Senate and of the House of Representatives:

It affords me pleasure to tender my friendly greetings to you on the occasion of your assembling at the Seat of Government, to enter upon the important duties to which you have been called by the voice of our countrymen. The task devolves on me, under a provision of the Constitution, to present to you, as the Federal Legislature of twenty-four sovereign States, and twelve millions of happy people, a view of our affairs; and to propose such measures as, in the discharge of my official functions, have suggested themselves as necessary to promote the objects of our Union.

In communicating with you for the first time, it is, to me, a source of unfeigned satisfaction, calling for mutual gratulation and devout thanks to a benign Providence, that we are at peace with all mankind; and that our country exhibits the most cheering evidence of general welfare and progressive improvement. Turning our eyes to other nations, our great desire is to see our brethren of the human race secured in the blessings enjoyed by ourselves, and advancing in knowledge, in freedom, and in social happiness. . . .

I consider it one of the most urgent of my duties to bring to your attention the propriety of amending that part of our Constitution which relates to the election of President and Vice President. Our system of government was, by its framers, deemed an experiment; and they, therefore, consistently provided a mode of remedying its defects.

To the People belongs the right of electing their Chief Magistrate: it was never designed that their choice should, in any case, be defeated, either by the intervention of electoral colleges, or by the agency confided, under certain contingencies, to the House of Representatives. Experience proves, that, in proportion as agents to execute the will of the People are multiplied, there is danger of their wishes being frustrated. Some may be unfaithful; all are liable to err. So far, therefore, as the People can, with convenience, speak, it is safer for them to express their own will. . . .

There are perhaps few men who can for any great length of time enjoy [appointed government] office and power, without being more or less under the influence of feelings unfavorable to the faithful discharge of their public duties. Their integrity may be proof against improper considerations immediately addressed to themselves; but they are apt to acquire a habit of looking with indifference upon the public interests, and of tolerating conduct from which an unpractised man would revolt. Office is considered as a species of property; and Government, rather as a means of promoting individual interests, than as an instrument created solely for the service of the People. Corruption in some, and, in others, a perversion of correct feelings and principles, divert Government from its legitimate ends, and make it an engine for the support of the few at the expense of the many. The duties of all public officers are, or, at least, admit of being made, so plain and simple, that men of intelligence may readily qualify themselves for their performance; and I cannot but believe that more is lost by the long continuance of men in office, than is generally to be gained by their experience. I submit therefore to your consideration, whether the efficiency of the Government would not be promoted, and official industry and integrity better secured, by a general extension of the law which limits appointments to four years.

In a country where offices are created solely for the benefit of the People, no one man has any more intrinsic right to official station than another. Offices were not established to give support to particular men, at the public expense. No individual wrong is therefore done by removal, since neither appointment to, nor continuance in, office, is a matter of right. The incumbent became an officer with a view to public benefits; and when these require his removal, they are not to be sacrificed to private interests. It is the People, and they alone, who have a right to complain, when a bad officer is substituted for a good one. He who is removed has the same means of obtaining a living, that are enjoyed by the millions who never held office. The proposed limitation would destroy the idea of property, now so generally connected with official station; and although individual distress may be sometimes produced, it would, by promoting that rotation which constitutes a leading principle in the republican creed, give healthful action to the system. . . .

[The] state of the finances exhibits the resources of the nation in an aspect highly flattering to its industry; and auspicious of the ability of Government, in a very short time, to extinguish the public debt. When this shall be done, our population will be relieved from a considerable portion of its present burthens; and will find, not only new motives to patriotic affection, but additional means for the display of individual enterprise. The fiscal power of the States will also be increased; and may be more extensively exerted in favor of education and other public objects; while ample means will remain in the Federal Government to promote the general weal, in all the modes permitted to its authority.

After the extinction of the public debt, it is not probable that any adjustment of the tariff, upon principles satisfactory to the People of the Union, will, until a remote period, if ever, leave the Government without a considerable surplus in the Treasury, beyond what may be required for its current service. . . . It appears to me that the most safe, just, and federal disposition which could be made of the surplus revenue, would be its apportionment among the several States according to their ratio of representation; and should this measure not be found warranted by the Constitution, that it would be expedient to propose to the States an amendment authorizing it. I regard an appeal to the source of power, in cases of real doubt, and where its exercise is deemed indispensable to the general welfare, as among the most sacred of all our obligations. Upon this country, more than any other, has, in the providence of God, been cast the special guardianship of the great principle of adherence to written constitutions. If it fail here, all hope in regard to it will be extinguished. That this was intended to be a Government of limited and specific, and not general powers, must be admitted by all; and it is our duty to preserve for it the character intended by its framers. If experience points out the necessity for an enlargement of these powers, let us apply for it to those for whose benefit it is to be exercised; and not undermine the whole system by a resort to overstrained constructions. The scheme has worked well. It has exceeded the hopes of those who devised it, and become an object of admiration to the world. We are responsible to our country, and to the glorious cause of self-government, for the preservation of so great a good. The great mass of legislation relating to our internal affairs, was intended to be left where the Federal Convention found it—in the State Governments. Nothing is clearer, in my view, than that we are chiefly indebted for the success of the Constitution under which we are now acting, to the watchful and auxiliary operation of the State authorities. This is not the reflection of a day, but belongs to the most deeply rooted convictions of my mind. I cannot, therefore, too strongly or too earnestly, for my own sense of its importance, warn you against all encroachments upon the legitimate sphere of State sovereignty. Sustained by its healthful and invigorating influence, the Federal system can never fall. . . .

I would suggest, also, an inquiry, whether the provisions of the act of Congress, authorizing the discharge of the persons of debtors to the Government, from imprisonment, may not, consistently with the public interest, be extended to the release of the debt, where the conduct of the debtor is wholly exempt from the imputation of fraud. Some more liberal policy than that which now prevails, in reference to this unfortunate class of citizens, is certainly due to them, and would prove beneficial to the country. The continuance of the liability, after the means to discharge it have been exhausted, can only serve to dispirit the debtor; or, where his resources are but partial, the want of power in the government to compromise and release the demand, instigates to fraud, as the only resource for securing a support to his family. He thus sinks into a state of apathy, and becomes a useless drone in society, or a vicious member of it, if not a feeling witness of the rigor and inhumanity of his country. All experience proves, that oppressive debt is the bane of enterprise; and it should be the care of a Republic not to exert a grinding power over misfortune and poverty. . . .

I now commend you, fellow-citizens, to the guidance of Almighty God, with a full reliance on his merciful providence for the maintenance of our free institutions; and with an earnest supplication, that, whatever errors it may be my lot to commit, in discharging the arduous duties which have devolved on me, will find a remedy in the harmony and wisdom of your counsels.

❧ 14 ❧
Andrew Jackson's Veto of the Bank Bill
(1832)

A NDREW JACKSON'S VETO of the bill Congress passed in 1832 to renew the Second Bank of the United States was politically important at the time and remains important as a precedent-setting assertion of presidential power.

Politically, Jackson regarded the bank as the leading institutional bastion of everything he opposed: favoritism for the eastern commercial and financial elite, excessive power for the federal government, and support for the new National Republican, or Whig, Party, turning vote-rich commercial states like New York and Pennsylvania against the Democrats. Indeed, bank president Nicholas Biddle, encouraged by Sen. Henry Clay of Kentucky, Jackson's opponent in the forthcoming 1832 presidential election, asked Congress to renew the bank's charter four years before the old charter was scheduled to expire. Clay thought that a veto by Jackson would be a good issue for the Whigs in the election. Despite Jackson's opposition, Congress acceded to Biddle's request.

All of Jackson's predecessors had used the veto sparingly. In forty years, presidents George Washington through John Quincy Adams had vetoed a total of nine bills, only three of them important. Federalist and Democratic-Republican presidents alike had believed that the veto should be reserved for legislation that was of doubtful constitutionality.

Jackson interpreted the veto power differently, grounding his view in a new and expansive conception of the presidency. The president, Jackson believed, was a truer representative of the people than Congress. He was their "tribune," the only person in the government who had been elected by the entire country and could claim to articulate the national interest. As a consequence, Jackson regarded the president's judgment that an act of Congress was unwise public policy as sufficient grounds for a veto.

On July 10, 1832, seven days after Congress voted to renew the charter of the national bank, Jackson sent his veto message to Capitol Hill. He took pains to explain his constitutional objections to the bank, refusing to defer to the Supreme Court on matters of constitutional interpretation. (In 1819 the Court had upheld the constitutionality of the nation's first national bank in *McCulloch v. Maryland*.) "The Congress, the executive, and the court must each for itself be guided by its own opinion of the Constitution," Jackson wrote. But he also made clear that he regarded his opinion that the bank was bad for the country as reason enough to cast a veto.

Congress failed to muster the two-thirds majority needed to override Jackson's veto of the bank bill. In the 1832 election, the president vanquished Clay by a margin of 219–49 in the Electoral College and 54 percent to 37 percent in the popular vote.

Both the veto and the theory of the presidency that underlay it established precedents that were of lasting significance. In the short term, Jackson's successors institutionalized his practice of vetoing bills on policy as well as constitutional grounds. In the long term, the attitude that the president is the people's main representative in government took hold widely and deeply in the American political system.

⁂ ⁂ ⁂

The bill "to modify and continue" the act entitled "An act to incorporate the subscribers to the Bank of the United States" was presented to me on the 4th July instant. Having considered it with that solemn regard to the principles of the Constitution which the day was calculated to inspire, and come to the conclusion that it ought not to become a law, I herewith return it to the Senate, in which it originated, with my objections.

A bank of the United States is in many respects convenient for the government and useful to the people. Entertaining this opinion, and deeply impressed with the belief that some of the powers and privileges possessed by the existing bank are unauthorized by the Constitution, subversive of the rights of the states, and dangerous to the liberties of the people, I felt it my duty at an early period of my administration to call the attention of Congress to the practicability of organizing an institution combining all its advantages and obviating these objections. I sincerely regret that in the act before me I can perceive none of those modifications of the bank charter which are necessary, in my opinion, to make it compatible with justice, with sound policy, or with the Constitution of our country.

The present corporate body, denominated the president, directors, and company of the Bank of the United States, will have existed at the time this act is intended to take effect twenty years. It enjoys an exclusive privilege of banking under the authority of the general government, a monopoly of its favor and support, and, as a necessary consequence, almost a monopoly of the foreign and domestic exchange. The powers, privileges, and favors bestowed upon it in the original charter, by increasing the value of the stock far above its par value, operated as a gratuity of many millions to the stockholders.

An apology may be found for the failure to guard against this result in the consideration that the effect of the original act of incorporation could not be certainly foreseen at the time of its passage. The act before me proposes another gratuity to the holders of the same stock, and in many cases to the same men, of at least 7 million more. This donation finds no apology in any uncertainty as to the effect of the act. On all hands it is conceded that its passage will increase at least 20 or 30 percent more the market price of the stock, subject to the payment of the annuity of 200,000 per year secured by the act, thus adding in a moment one-fourth to its par value. It is not our own citizens only who are to receive the bounty of our government. More than 8 million of the stock of this bank are held by foreigners. By this act the American republic proposes virtually to make them a present of some millions of dollars. For these gratuities to foreigners and to some of our own opulent citizens the act secures no equivalent whatever. They are the certain gains of the present stockholders under the operation of this act, after making full allowance for the payment of the bonus.

Every monopoly and all exclusive privileges are granted at the expense of the public, which ought to receive a fair equivalent. The many millions which this act proposes to bestow on the stockholders of the existing bank must come directly or indirectly out of the earnings of the American people. It is due to them, therefore, if their government sell monopolies and exclusive privileges, that they should at least exact for them as much as they are worth in open market. The value of the monopoly in this case may be correctly ascertained. The 28 million of stock would probably be at an advance of 50 percent and command in market at least 42 million, subject to the payment of the present bonus. The present value of the monopoly, therefore, is 17 million, and this the act proposes to sell for 3 million, payable in fifteen annual installments of 200,000 each. . . .

It is maintained by the advocates of the bank that its constitutionality in all its features ought to be considered as settled by precedent and by the decision of the Supreme Court. To this conclusion I cannot assent. Mere precedent is a dangerous source of authority and should not be regarded as deciding questions of constitutional power except where the acquiescence of the people and the states can be considered as well settled. So far from this being the case on this subject, an argument against the bank might be based on precedent. One Congress in 1791 decided in favor of a bank; another in 1811 decided against it. One Congress in 1815 decided against a bank; another in 1816 decided in its favor. Prior to the present Congress, therefore, the precedents drawn from that source were equal. If we resort to the states, the expressions of legislative, judicial, and executive opinions against the bank have been probably to those in its favor as four to one. There is nothing in precedent, therefore, which, if its authority were admitted, ought to weigh in favor of the act before me.

If the opinion of the Supreme Court covered the whole ground of this act, it ought not to control the coordinate authorities of this government. The Congress, the executive, and the court must each for itself be guided by its own opinion of the Constitution. Each public officer who takes an oath to support the Constitution swears that he will support it as he understands it and not as it is understood by others. It is as much the duty of the House of Representatives, of the Senate, and of the President to decide upon the constitutionality of any bill or resolution which may be presented to them for passage or approval as it is of the supreme judges when it may be brought before them for judicial decision. The opinion of the judges has no more authority over Congress than the opinion of Congress has over the judges, and on that point the President is independent of both. The authority of the Supreme Court must not, therefore, be permitted to control the Congress or the executive when acting in their legislative capacities, but to have only such influence as the force of their reasoning may deserve. . . .

It is to be regretted that the rich and powerful too often bend the acts of government to their selfish purposes. Distinctions in society will always exist under every just government. Equality of talents, of education, or of wealth cannot be produced by human institutions. In the full enjoyment of the gifts of Heaven and the fruits of superior industry, economy, and virtue, every man is equally entitled to protection by law; but when the laws undertake to add to these natural and just advantages artificial distinctions, to grant titles, gratuities, and exclusive privileges, to make the rich richer and the potent more powerful, the humble members of society—the farmers, mechanics, and laborers—who have neither the time nor the means of securing like favors to themselves, have a right to complain of the injustice of their government. There are no necessary evils in government. Its evils exist only in its abuses. If it would confine itself to equal protection, and, as Heaven does its rains, shower its favors alike on the high and the low, the rich and the poor, it would be an unqualified blessing. In the act before me there seems to be a wide and unnecessary departure from these just principles.

Nor is our government to be maintained or our Union preserved by invasions of the rights and powers of the several states. In thus attempting to make our general government strong, we make it weak. Its true strength consists in leaving individuals and states as much as possible to themselves—in making itself felt, not in its power, but in its beneficence; not in its control, but in its protection; not in binding the states more closely to the center, but leaving each to move unobstructed in its proper orbit.

Experience should teach us wisdom. Most of the difficulties our government now encounters and most of the dangers which impend over our Union have sprung from an abandonment of the legitimate objects of government by our national legislation and the adoption of such principles as are embodied in this act. Many of our rich men have not been content with equal protection and equal benefits but have besought us to make them richer by act of Congress. By attempting to gratify their desires, we have in the results of our legislation arrayed section against section, interest against interest, and man against man, in a fearful commotion which threatens to shake the foundations of our Union.

It is time to pause in our career to review our principles and, if possible, revive that devoted patriotism and spirit of compromise which distinguished the sages of the Revolution and the fathers of our Union. If we cannot at once, in justice to interests vested under improvident legislation, make our government what it ought to be, we can at least take a stand against all new grants of monopolies and exclusive privileges, against any prostitution of our government to the advancement of a few at the expense of the many, and in favor of compromise and gradual reform in our code of laws and system of political economy.

❧ 15 ❧

Abraham Lincoln's Message to Congress in Special Session

(1861)

DURING MUCH OF THE QUARTER-CENTURY that followed the presidency of Andrew Jackson, the rapidly expanding nation was torn by disagreement over the extension of slavery into new territories and states. In 1860, two years after his unsuccessful but widely admired campaign for U.S. senator from Illinois against Democratic incumbent Stephen A. Douglas, Abraham Lincoln was nominated for president by the recently formed Republican Party. Despite winning only 40 percent of the popular vote, Lincoln carried every free state (but no slave states) and triumphed over three opponents: Douglas, the nominee of the northern Democrats; Vice President John C. Breckinridge of Kentucky, who was nominated by southern Democrats; and Tennessean John Bell, the nominee of the newly formed Constitutional Union Party.

Although Lincoln pledged not to attack the rights of slave owners in the southern and border states, his opposition to extending slavery beyond its existing boundaries prompted seven Deep South states to secede from the United States on news of his election. On February 7, 1861 (nearly a month before Lincoln's inauguration), they formed the Confederate States of America. Before leaving office, President James Buchanan told Congress that although the southern states had no constitutional right to secede, he had no constitutional power to stop them. Lincoln disagreed strongly. He used his March 4 inaugural address to warn secessionists that they would not be allowed to leave the Union peacefully. "You have no oath registered in Heaven to destroy the government," he declared, "while I shall have the most solemn one 'to preserve, protect, and defend' it. You can forbear the assault; I can *not* shrink from the *defense* of it."

Ignoring Lincoln's warning, on March 5 rebel forces massed near Fort Sumter in Charleston, South Carolina. On April 12 they fired on the fort, which soon fell. On May 3 Lincoln issued a proclamation that called the various state militia into national service and asked for seventy-five thousand volunteers to assist in executing the national laws. Four more southern states seceded and joined the Confederacy. Border states, notably Kentucky and Maryland, seriously considered secession.

Although calling up the militia was clearly among the president's constitutional powers, other actions that Lincoln took during the spring of 1861 were not. As was the custom in this era, the outgoing Congress adjourned after the president's inauguration and the new one was not scheduled to convene until December. With Congress out of session, Lincoln unilaterally increased the size of the army and navy, ordered a blockade of southern ports, suspended the writ of habeas corpus (the constitutional guarantee against detention without legal cause) in certain militarily vital parts of the country, instructed the Treasury to pay $2 million to two secret agents to purchase military supplies, imposed new passport regulations on foreign visitors, and barred "treasonable correspondence" from being delivered by the post office.

Having set the Union war machine in motion, Lincoln called a special session of Congress on July 4. He greeted them with a written message defending all of his actions: those he "believed to be strictly legal," such as calling up the militia and imposing a blockade; those whose legality had been questioned but that he felt were within his constitutional authority, especially the suspension of habeas corpus; and those, "whether strictly legal or not," that he took in response to "what appeared to be a popular demand, and a public necessity," including his "large additions to the regular Army and Navy."

Lincoln wrote that he took actions beyond his legal authority "trusting, then as now, that Congress would readily ratify them." On August 5 it did so by a nearly unanimous vote, declaring that the president's actions after the attack on Fort Sumter were "in all respects legalized and made valid . . . as if they had been issued and done under the express authority and direction of the Congress of the United States."

🐾 🐾 🐾

Having been convened on an extraordinary occasion, as authorized by the Constitution, your attention is not called to any ordinary subject of legislation.

At the beginning of the present Presidential term, four months ago, the functions of the Federal Government were found to be generally suspended within the several States of South Carolina, Georgia, Alabama, Mississippi, Louisiana, and Florida, excepting only those of the Post Office Department.

Within these States, all the Forts, Arsenals, Dock-yards, Customhouses, and the like, including the movable and stationary property in, and about them, had been seized, and were held in open hostility to this Government, excepting only Forts Pickens, Taylor, and Jefferson, on, and near the Florida coast, and Fort Sumter, in Charleston harbor, South Carolina. The Forts thus seized had been put in improved condition; new ones had been built; and armed forces had been organized, and were organizing, all avowedly with the same hostile purpose.

The Forts remaining in the possession of the Federal government, in, and near, these States, were either besieged or menaced by warlike preparations; and especially Fort Sumter was nearly surrounded by well-protected hostile batteries, with guns equal in quality to the best of its own, and outnumbering the latter as perhaps ten to one. A disproportionate share, of the Federal muskets and rifles, had somehow found their way into these States, and had been seized, to be used against the government. Accumulations of the public revenue, lying within them, had been seized for the same object. The Navy was scattered in distant seas; leaving but a very small part of it within the immediate reach of the government. Officers of the Federal Army and Navy, had resigned in great numbers; and, of those resigning, a large proportion had taken up arms against the government. Simultaneously, and in connection, with all this, the purpose to sever the Federal Union, was openly avowed. In accordance with this purpose, an ordinance had been adopted in each of these States, declaring the States, respectively, to be separated from the National Union. A formula for instituting a combined government of these states had been promulgated; and this illegal organization, in the character of confederate States was already invoking recognition, aid, and intervention, from Foreign Powers.

Finding this condition of things, and believing it to be an imperative duty upon the incoming Executive, to prevent, if possible, the consummation of such attempt to destroy the Federal Union, a choice of means to that end became indispensable. This choice was made; and was declared in the Inaugural address. The policy chosen looked to the exhaustion of all peaceful measures, before a resort to any stronger ones. It sought only to hold the public places and property, not already wrested from the Government, and to collect the revenue; relying for the rest, on time, discussion, and the ballot-box. It promised a continuance of the mails, at government expense, to the very people who were resisting the government; and it gave repeated pledges against any disturbance to any of the people, or any of their rights. Of all that which a president might constitutionally, and justifiably, do in such a case, everything was foreborne, without which, it was believed possible to keep the government on foot.

On the 5th of March, (the present incumbent's first full day in office) a letter of Major Anderson, commanding at Fort Sumter, written on the 28th of February, and received at the War Department on the 4th of March, was, by that Department, placed in his hands. This letter expressed the professional opinion of the writer, that re-inforcements could not be thrown into that Fort within the time for his relief, rendered necessary by the limited supply of provisions, and with a view of holding possession of the same, with a force of less than twenty thousand good, and well-disciplined men. This opinion was concurred in by all the officers of his command; and their memoranda on the subject, were made enclosures of Major Anderson's letter. The whole was immediately laid before Lieutenant General Scott, who at once concurred with Major Anderson in opinion. On reflection, however, he took full time, consulting with other officers, both of the Army and the Navy; and, at the end of four days, came reluctantly, but decidedly, to the same conclusion as before. He also stated at the same time that no such sufficient force was then at the control of the Government, or could be raised, and brought to the ground, within the time when the provisions in the Fort would be exhausted. In a purely military point of view, this reduced the duty of the administration, in the case, to the mere matter of getting the garrison safely out of the Fort.

It was believed, however, that to so abandon that position, under the circumstances, would be utterly ruinous; that the necessity under which it was to be done, would not be fully understood—that, by many, it would be construed as a part of a voluntary policy—that, at home, it would discourage the friends of the Union, embolden its adversaries, and go far to insure to the latter, a recognition abroad— that, in fact, it would be our national destruction consummated. This could not be allowed. . . .

[T]he assault upon, and reduction of, Fort Sumter, was, in no sense, a matter of self defence on the part of the assailants. They well knew that the garrison in the Fort could, by no possibility, commit aggression upon them. They knew—they were expressly notified—that the giving of bread to the few brave and hungry men of the garrison, was all which would on that occasion be attempted, unless themselves, by resisting so much, should provoke more. They knew that this Government desired to keep the garrison in the Fort, not to assail them, but merely to maintain visible possession, and thus to preserve the Union from actual, and immediate dissolution—trusting, as hereinbefore stated, to time, discussion, and the ballot-box, for final adjustment; and they assailed, and reduced the Fort, for precisely the reverse object—to drive out the visible authority of the Federal Union, and thus force it to immediate dissolution.

That this was their object, the Executive well understood; and having said to them in the inaugural address, "You can have no conflict without being yourselves the aggressors," he took pains, not only to keep this declaration good, but also to keep the case so free from the power of ingenious sophistry, as that the world should not be able to misunderstand it. By the affair at Fort Sumter, with its surrounding circumstances, that point was reached. Then, and thereby, the assailants of the Government, began the conflict of arms, without a gun in sight, or in expectancy, to return their fire, save only the few in the Fort, sent to that harbor, years before, for their own protection, and still ready to give that protection, in whatever was lawful. In this act, discarding all else, they have forced upon the country, the distinct issue: "Immediate dissolution, or blood."

And this issue embraces more than the fate of these United States. It presents to the whole family of man, the question, whether a constitutional republic, or a democracy— a government of the people, by the same people—can, or cannot, maintain its territorial integrity, against its own domestic foes. It presents the question, whether discontented individuals, too few in numbers to control administration, according to organic law, in any case, can always, upon the pretences made in this case, or on any other pretences, or arbitrarily, without any pretence, break up their Government, and thus practically put an end to free government upon the earth. It forces us to ask: "Is there, in all republics, this inherent, and fatal weakness?" "Must a government, of necessity, be too strong for the liberties of its own people, or too weak to maintain its own existence?"

So viewing the issue, no choice was left but to call out the war power of the Government; and so to resist force, employed for its destruction, by force, for its preservation. . . .

[A]t first, a call was made for seventy-five thousand militia; and rapidly following this, a proclamation was issued for closing the ports of the insurrectionary districts by proceedings in the nature of Blockade. So far all was believed to be strictly legal. At this point the insurrectionists announced their purpose to enter upon the practice of privateering. Other calls were made for volunteers, to serve three years, unless sooner discharged; and also for large additions to the regular Army and Navy. These measures, whether strictly legal or not, were ventured upon, under what appeared to be a popular demand, and a public necessity; trusting, then as now, that Congress would readily ratify them. It is believed that nothing has been done beyond the constitutional competency of Congress.

Soon after the first call for militia, it was considered a duty to authorize the Commanding General, in proper cases, according to his discretion, to suspend the privilege of the writ of habeas corpus; or, in other words, to arrest, and detain, without resort to the ordinary processes and forms of law, such individuals as he might deem dangerous to the public safety. This authority has purposely been exercised but very sparingly. Nevertheless, the legality and propriety of what has been done under it, are questioned; and the attention of the country has been called to the proposition that one who is sworn to "take care that the laws be faithfully executed," should not himself violate them. Of course some consideration was given to the questions of power, and propriety, before this matter was acted upon. The whole of the laws which were required to be faithfully executed, were being resisted, and failing of execution, in nearly one-third of the States. Must they be allowed to finally fail of execution, even had it been perfectly clear, that by the use of the means necessary to their execution, some single law, made in such extreme tenderness of the citizen's liberty, that practically, it relieves more of the guilty, than of the innocent, should, to a very limited extent, be violated? To state the question more directly, are all the laws, but one, to go unexecuted, and the government itself go to pieces, lest that one be violated? Even in such a case, would not the official oath be broken, if the government should be overthrown, when it was believed that disregarding the single law, would tend to preserve it? But it was not believed that this question was presented. It was not believed that any law was violated. The provision of the Constitution that "The privilege of the writ of habeas corpus, shall not be suspended unless when, in cases of rebellion or invasion, the public safety may require it," is equivalent to a provision— is a provision—that such privilege may be suspended when, in cases of rebellion, or invasion, the public safety does require it. It was decided that we have a case of rebellion, and that the public safety does require the qualified suspension of the privilege of the writ which was authorized to be made. Now it is insisted that Congress, and not the Executive, is vested with this power. But the Constitution itself, is silent as to which, or who, is to exercise the power; and as the provision was plainly made for a dangerous emergency, it cannot be believed the framers of the instrument intended, that in every case, the danger should run its course, until Congress could be called together; the very assembling of which might be prevented, as was intended in this case, by the rebellion. . . .

It is now recommended that you give the legal means for making this contest a short, and a decisive one; that you place at the control of the government, for the work, at least four hundred thousand men, and four hundred millions of dollars. That number of men is about one tenth of those of proper ages within the regions where, apparently, all are willing to engage; and the sum is less than a twentythird part of the money value owned by the men who seem ready to devote the whole. A debt of six hundred millions of dollars now, is a less sum per head, than was the debt of our revolution, when we came out of that struggle; and the money value in the country now, bears even a greater proportion to what it was then, than does the population. Surely each man has as strong a motive now, to preserve our liberties, as each had then, to establish them.

A right result, at this time, will be worth more to the world, than ten times the men, and ten times the money. The evidence reaching us from the country, leaves no doubt, that the material for the work is abundant; and that it needs only the hand of legislation to give it legal sanction, and the hand of the Executive to give it practical shape and efficiency. One of the greatest perplexities of the government, is to avoid receiving troops faster than it can provide for them. In a word, the people will save their government, if the government itself, will do its part, only indifferently well. . . .

It was with the deepest regret that the Executive found the duty of employing the war-power, in defence of the government, forced upon him. He could but perform this duty, or surrender the existence of the government. No compromise, by public servants, could, in this case, be a cure; not that compromises are not often proper, but that no popular government can long survive a marked precedent, that those who carry an election, can only save the government from immediate destruction, by giving up the main point, upon which the people gave the election. The people themselves, and not their servants, can safely reverse their own deliberate decisions. As a private citizen, the Executive could not have consented that these institutions shall perish; much less could he, in betrayal of so vast, and so sacred a trust, as these free people had confided to him. He felt that he had no moral right to shrink; nor even to count the chances of his own life, in what might follow. In full view of his great responsibility, he has, so far, done what he has deemed his duty. You will now, according to your own judgment, perform yours. He sincerely hopes that your views, and your action, may so accord with his, as to assure all faithful citizens, who have been disturbed in their rights, of a certain, and speedy restoration to them, under the Constitution, and the laws. And having thus chosen our course, without guile, and with pure purpose, let us renew our trust in God, and go forward without fear, and with manly hearts.

❧ 16 ❧

Abraham Lincoln's Letter to Albert G. Hodges

(1864)

O N NEW YEAR'S DAY 1863, Abraham Lincoln, acting on his own authority as he had during his first months in office, issued the Emancipation Proclamation, which freed "all persons held as slaves within any State or designated part of a State, the people whereof shall then be in rebellion against the United States." Some time later, Kentuckian Albert G. Hodges, the editor of the *Frankfort Commonwealth,* asked the president why he had felt compelled to abandon his long-standing pledge not to interfere with slavery where it already existed. Lincoln replied by letter on April 4, 1864, intending that Hodges make the letter public.

In responding to Hodges, Lincoln argued that it made no sense to observe constitutional niceties while the ultimate purpose of the Constitution—to govern and sustain the Union—was under siege. "Was it possible to lose the nation and yet preserve the Constitution?" he asked, rhetorically. "By general law, life and limb must be protected, yet often a limb must be amputated to save a life; but a life is never wisely given to save a limb." Defending his actions during his first few months in office and afterward, Lincoln added: "I felt that measures otherwise unconstitutional might become lawful by becoming indispensable to the preservation of the Constitution through the preservation of the nation."

Although Lincoln did not mention John Locke, his letter to Hodges was reminiscent of the seventeenth-century English philosopher's discussion of prerogative in his *The Second Treatise of Government.* In the absence of and sometimes in defiance of law, Locke had argued, an executive must obey "this fundamental law of nature and government, viz., that, as much as may be, all the members of society are to be preserved." Prerogative is "the people's permitting their rulers to do several things of their own free choice, where the law was silent, and sometimes, too, against the direct letter of the law, for the public good, and their acquiescing in it when so done." The check on executive power in such an instance is the elected legislature's subsequent decision to accept or reject the propriety of the executive's actions.

Certainly Lincoln could claim that, for the most part, his exercises of prerogative power were vindicated. To be sure, some denounced him as a dictator. But in August 1861, after several weeks of debate, Congress declared most of the president's early actions to be "hereby approved and in all respects legalized and made valid, to the same effect as if they had been issued and done under the previous express authority and direction of the Congress of the United States." In 1862 and 1863 Congress retroactively validated most of Lincoln's other actions.

Not just Congress but the voters endorsed the president's unusual wartime leadership. Lincoln won 55 percent of the popular vote and carried all but three Union states in his bid for reelection in November 1864.

※ ※ ※

My dear Sir:

You ask me to put in writing the substance of what I verbally said the other day in your presence, to Governor [Thomas E.] Bramlette and [former] Senator [Archibald] Dixon, [both of Kentucky]. It was about as follows:

"I am naturally antislavery. If slavery is not wrong, nothing is wrong. I cannot remember when I did not so think and feel, and yet I have never understood that the presidency conferred upon me an unrestricted right to act officially upon this judgment and feeling. It was in the oath I took that I would, to the best of my ability, preserve, protect, and defend the Constitution of the United States. I could not take the office without taking the oath. Nor was it my view that I might take an oath to get power, and break the oath in using the power. I understood, too, that in ordinary civil administration this oath even forbade me to practically indulge my primary abstract judgment on the moral question of slavery. I had publicly declared this many times, and in many ways. And I aver that, to this day, I have done no official act in mere deference to my abstract judgment and feeling on slavery. I did understand, however, that my oath to preserve the Constitution to the best of my ability imposed upon me the duty of preserving, by every indispensable means, that government— that nation, of which that Constitution was the organic law. Was it possible to lose the nation and yet preserve the Constitution? By general law, life and limb must be protected, yet often a limb must be amputated to save a life; but a life is never wisely given to save a limb. I felt that measures otherwise unconstitutional might become lawful by becoming indispensable to the preservation of the Constitution through the preservation of the nation. Right or wrong, I assumed this ground, and now avow it. I could not feel that, to the best of my ability, I had even tried to preserve the Constitution if, to save slavery or any minor matter, I should permit the wreck of government, country, and Constitution all together. When, early in the war, General [John C.] Frémont attempted military emancipation, I forbade it, because I did not then think it an indispensable necessity. When, a little later, General [Simon] Cameron, then Secretary of War, suggested the arming of the blacks, I objected because I did not yet think it an indispensable necessity. When, still later, General [David] Hunter attempted military emancipation, I again forbade it, because I did not yet think the indispensable necessity had come. When in March and May and July, 1862, I made earnest and successive appeals to the border States to favor compensated emancipation, I believed the indispensable necessity to military emancipation and arming the blacks would come unless averted by that measure. They declined the proposition, and I was, in my best judgment, driven to the alternative of either surrendering the Union, and with it the Constitution, or of laying strong hand upon the colored element. I chose the latter. In choosing it, I hoped for greater gain than loss; but of this, I was not entirely confident. More than a year of trial now shows no loss by it in our foreign relations, none in our home popular sentiment, none in our white military force—no loss by it anyhow or anywhere. On the contrary it shows a gain of quite a hundred and thirty thousand soldiers, seamen, and laborers. These are palpable facts, about which, as facts, there can be no caviling. We have the men; and we could not have had them without the measure.

"And now let any Union man who complains of the measure test himself by writing down in one line that he is for subduing the rebellion by force of arms; and in the next, that he is for taking these hundred and thirty thousand men from the Union side and placing them where they would be but for the measure he condemns. If he cannot face his case so stated, it is only because he cannot face the truth."

I add a word which was not in the verbal conversation. In telling this tale I attempt no compliment to my own sagacity. I claim not to have controlled events, but confess plainly that events have controlled me. Now, at the end of three years' struggle, the nation's condition is not what either party, or any man, devised or expected. God alone can claim it. Whither it is tending seems plain. If God now wills the removal of a great wrong, and wills also that we of the North, as well as you of the South, shall pay fairly for our complicity in that wrong, impartial history will find therein new cause to attest and revere the justice and goodness of God. *Yours truly,*

A. Lincoln

❧ 17 ❧
The Gettysburg Address
(1863)

ON JULY 4, 1863, northern armies won two victories that almost ensured the Union eventually would prevail in the Civil War. In the West, the Confederate fortification at Vicksburg, Mississippi, fell to the forces of Gen. Ulysses S. Grant, bringing the strategically vital Mississippi River under complete northern control. In Gettysburg, Pennsylvania, Union forces beat back a Confederate incursion into the North led by Gen. Robert E. Lee.

Four months after these victories, President Abraham Lincoln rode a train from Washington to Gettysburg to attend the November 19 dedication of the cemetery in which six thousand casualties of the Battle of Gettysburg were to be buried. Lincoln was not the main speaker at the dedication. That honor fell to former senator and renowned orator Edward Everett, who delivered a lengthy and moving address to the assembled crowd of around fifteen thousand people. Instead, Lincoln spoke briefly after Everett was finished, his high, clear voice audible to most. On his hat the president wore a mourning band for his recently deceased young son, Willie.

Lincoln's theme was the "nation." The word appears three times in the first two sentences of the address and is invoked again in the peroration. Brief as the Gettysburg Address is, it thematically traces Lincoln's vision of the American experience from past to present to future. The treatment of the past is especially interesting. Lincoln dates the founding of the nation not to the Constitution in 1787, but rather "four score and seven years ago" to 1776, the year the Declaration of Independence proclaimed that "all men are created equal." To Lincoln, equality was the "proposition" to which the new nation was thereby "dedicated."

The brilliance of the Gettysburg Address is that, in the space of only three minutes and 272 words, it solemnly and honestly acknowledged the awful pain suffered by "these honored dead" while defining the war in which they fought as part of the enduring struggle to attain "government of the people, by the people, for the people." Following in the great tradition of Pericles's funeral oration for the Athenian soldiers slain in the Peloponnesian War, and employing the grand cadences of the King James Version of the Bible, Lincoln vowed that because "this nation, under God, shall have a new birth of freedom," the fallen soldiers will not have "died in vain." So profound was the address, one modern scholar has written, that those who heard it "walked off, from those curving graves on the hillside, under a changed sky, into a different America."

⁂ ⁂ ⁂

Four score and seven years ago our fathers brought forth on this continent, a new nation, conceived in Liberty, and dedicated to the proposition that all men are created equal.

Now we are engaged in a great civil war, testing whether that nation or any nation so conceived and so dedicated, can long endure. We are met on a great battle-field of that war. We have come to dedicate a portion of that field, as a final resting place for those who here gave their lives that that nation might live. It is altogether fitting and proper that we should do this.

But, in a larger sense, we can not dedicate—we can not consecrate—we can not hallow—this ground. The brave men, living and dead, who struggled here, have consecrated it, far above our poor power to add or detract. The world will little note, nor long remember what we say here, but it can never forget what they did here. It is for us the living, rather, to be dedicated here to the unfinished work which they who fought here have thus far so nobly advanced. It is rather for us to be here dedicated to the great task remaining before us—that from these honored dead we take increased devotion to that cause for which they gave the last full measure of devotion—that we here highly resolve that these dead shall not have died in vain—that this nation, under God, shall have a new birth of freedom—and that government of the people, by the people, for the people, shall not perish from the earth.

⁊ 18 ⁊

Abraham Lincoln's Second Inaugural Address
(1865)

IN 1864 ABRAHAM LINCOLN became the first president to be elected to a second term since Andrew Jackson accomplished the feat in 1832. Lincoln's opponent was Gen. George B. McClellan, the former commander of the Union armies whom the president had fired for lack of aggressiveness on the battlefield. In nominating

McClellan, the Democratic Party approved a platform that called for a peace convention to restore the Union with slavery intact, criticized Lincoln for violating civil liberties, and accused him of usurping constitutional powers. Victory for the president was by no means certain. In August, after months of discouraging war news, Lincoln had the cabinet sign a pledge to cooperate in the transfer of power to the new administration if, as "seems exceedingly probable . . . this Administration will not be re-elected."

News of fresh military triumphs from Gen. William Tecumseh Sherman in Georgia and Gen. Philip Sheridan in the Shenandoah Valley of Virginia undercut Democratic opposition to the war. On election day, Lincoln carried every Union state but Delaware, Kentucky, and New Jersey to defeat McClellan 212–21 in the Electoral College.

Lincoln delivered his second inaugural address, which could not have lasted more than eight minutes, on March 4, 1865. After four years of war, victory was at hand. The tens of thousands of Republican partisans who gathered outside the Capitol expected their president to utter rousing words of triumph for the Union and condemnation for the Confederacy.

What they heard instead was dramatically different. As Frederick Douglass pointed out, Lincoln's address was more like a sermon than a political speech. The president began by reminding his audience that at the time of his first inauguration four years earlier, "All dreaded [war], all sought to avert it," and "neither party expected for the war the magnitude or the duration which it has already attained." He added that both sides "read the same Bible and pray to the same God," and all "knew that [slavery] was somehow the cause of the war." Instead of accentuating the differences between the virtuous North and the villainous South, Lincoln used words that expressed their similarity: *both, neither, all.*

In September 1862 Lincoln had assessed the widespread northern and southern claims to be acting in accordance with God's will by privately writing, "Both *may* be, and one *must* be wrong." Now, thirty months later, he said, "The prayers of both could not be answered. That of neither has been answered fully." "The Almighty has His own purposes," Lincoln declared, quoting Jesus' fiery words in the Gospel of Matthew: "'Woe unto the world because of offenses.' . . . If we shall suppose that American slavery is one of those offenses which, in the providence of God, must needs come, but which, having continued through His appointed time, He now wills to remove, and that He gives to both North and South this terrible war as the woe due to those by whom the offense came, shall we discern therein any departure from those divine attributes which the believers in a living God always ascribe to Him?"

And then Lincoln spoke, to his increasingly uncomfortable audience, one of the most terrifying passages a president has ever uttered: "[I]f God wills that [this war] continue until all the wealth piled by the bondsman's two hundred and fifty years of unrequited toil shall be sunk, and until every drop of blood drawn with the lash shall be paid by another drawn with the sword . . . so still it must be said 'the judgments of the Lord, are true and righteous altogether.'"

All are guilty, Lincoln told the assembled crowd of pro-Union, northern Republicans who had won the election and were winning the war. North and South alike, their hands stained with the blood of complicity in centuries of slavery, stand where they deserve to stand: before the judgment seat of God. But, Lincoln concluded, despair is no more appropriate a response to this situation than triumph. Judgment belongs to God, but it is for the American people to act as agents of God's grace and mercy. Show "malice toward none," he urged, and "charity for all." In order to "bind up the nation's wounds, . . . care for him who shall have borne the battle and for his widow and his orphan," and "do all which may achieve and cherish a just and a lasting peace among ourselves and with all nations."

The war effectively ended five weeks after Lincoln's inauguration when Confederate general Robert E. Lee surrendered to Gen. Ulysses S. Grant at Appomattox Court House in Virginia on April 9, 1865. Five days later on April 14, Lincoln was shot while attending a play at Ford's Theatre, by Confederate sympathizer John Wilkes Booth, who had been in the crowd that heard the president's second inaugural address. Lincoln died early the next morning.

🎋 🎋 🎋

Fellow-Countrymen:

At this second appearing to take the oath of the Presidential office there is less occasion for an extended address than there was at the first. Then a statement somewhat in detail of a course to be pursued seemed fitting and proper. Now, at the expiration of four years, during which public declarations have been constantly called forth on every point and phase of the great contest which still absorbs the attention and engrosses the energies of the nation, little that is new could be presented. The progress of our arms, upon which all else chiefly depends, is as well known to the public as to myself, and it is, I trust, reasonably satisfactory and encouraging to all. With high hope for the future, no prediction in regard to it is ventured.

On the occasion corresponding to this four years ago all thoughts were anxiously directed to an impending civil war. All dreaded it, all sought to avert it. While the inaugural address was being delivered from this place, devoted altogether to saving the Union without war, insurgent agents were in the city seeking to destroy it without war—seeking to dissolve the Union and divide effects by negotiation. Both parties deprecated war, but one of them would make war rather than let the nation survive, and the other would accept war rather than let it perish, and the war came.

One-eighth of the whole population were colored slaves, not distributed generally over the Union, but localized in the southern part of it. These slaves constituted a peculiar and powerful interest. All knew that this interest was somehow the cause of the war. To strengthen, perpetuate, and extend this interest was the object for which the insurgents would rend the Union even by war, while the Government claimed no right to do more than to restrict the territorial enlargement of it. Neither party expected for the war the magnitude or the duration which it has already attained. Neither anticipated that the cause of the conflict might cease with or even before the conflict itself should cease. Each looked for an easier triumph, and a result less fundamental and astounding. Both read the same Bible and pray to the same God, and each invokes His aid against the other. It may seem strange that any men should dare to ask a just God's assistance in wringing their bread from the sweat of other men's faces, but let us judge not, that we be not judged. The prayers of both could not be answered. That of neither has been answered fully. The Almighty has His own purposes. "Woe unto the world because of offenses; for it must needs be that offenses come, but woe to that man by whom the offense cometh." If we shall suppose that American slavery is one of those offenses which, in the providence of God, must needs come, but which, having continued through His appointed time, He now wills to remove, and that He gives to both North and South this terrible war as the woe due to those by whom the offense came, shall we discern therein any departure from those divine attributes which the believers in a living God always ascribe to Him? Fondly do we hope, fervently do we pray, that this mighty scourge of war may speedily pass away. Yet, if God wills that it continue until all the wealth piled by the bondsman's two hundred and fifty years of unrequited toil shall be sunk, and until every drop of blood drawn with the lash shall be paid by another drawn with the sword, as was said three thousand years ago, so still it must be said "the judgments of the Lord are true and righteous altogether."

With malice toward none, with charity for all, with firmness in the right as God gives us to see the right, let us strive on to finish the work we are in, to bind up the nation's wounds, to care for him who shall have borne the battle and for his widow and his orphan, to do all which may achieve and cherish a just and lasting peace among ourselves and with all nations.

❧ 19 ❧

*Ex parte Milligan**

(1866)

CAN THE PRESIDENT legitimately claim emergency powers in wartime beyond those that are enumerated in the Constitution, as Abraham Lincoln did during the Civil War? The typical response of the Supreme Court to this question has been variable: *yes* in the heat of war, but *no* on later reflection. (For two important exceptions see Documents 33, p. 163, and 54, p. 261.) This pattern of oscillation on matters of presidential war-making was established by the Court during the Civil War and its aftermath.

Midway through the war, the justices were asked to rule on the legality of the naval blockade that President Abraham Lincoln unilaterally imposed on southern

*Go to *http://laws.findlaw.com/us/71/2.html.*

ports after the Confederates seized Fort Sumter in April 1861. The foreign owners of four vessels captured by the Union navy sued for redress because their ships and cargo—the "prizes" of capture—had been sold at public auction. They argued that the blockade was illegal because Congress had not declared war on the Confederacy.

The Court rejected this appeal in an 1863 decision known as the *Prize Cases.* Writing for the majority, Justice Robert C. Grier explained that when American territory is taken by hostile forces, the absence of a congressional declaration of war does not mean that no war exists. In these circumstances, Grier continued, "the President was bound to meet [the insurrection] in the shape it presented itself, without waiting for Congress to baptise it with a name; and no name given to it by him or them could change that fact." Grier went on to say that in crises such as the one Lincoln faced, the Court must defer to the president's judgment.

In 1866, a year after the Civil War ended and Lincoln died, the Court took a more critical view of another of the president's wartime actions. On October 5, 1864, an outspoken southern sympathizer named Lambdin P. Milligan had been arrested in Indiana by order of Gen. Alvin P. Hovey, the Union commander at Indianapolis, on charges of conspiracy to help Confederate prisoners escape and rejoin their army. Lincoln had imposed martial law on portions of some northern states, including Indiana, whose loyalty to the Union he doubted. Milligan was tried by a military commission, even though Indiana was far from the fighting and the state's regular civil courts were open and operating. The commission found Milligan guilty and sentenced him to be hanged.

In *Ex parte Milligan* the Supreme Court ruled in favor of Milligan's claim that the commission had no constitutional authority to try him. Ordering the prisoner released, the Court condemned the government's assertion that in time of war it had the power to impose military trials on civilians even where the regular courts were functioning.

Justice David Davis, a close friend and longtime political ally of the late president, wrote the majority opinion in the case. He began by taking note of the changed circumstances brought about by the cessation of hostilities: "*Now* that the public safety is assured, this question, as well as others, can be discussed and decided without passion or the admixture of any element not required to form a legal judgment." Writing from the vantage point of restored domestic tranquility, Davis ruled: "No doctrine involving more pernicious consequences was ever invented by the wit of man than that any of the [Constitution's] provisions can be suspended during any of the great exigencies of war."

※ ※ ※

MR. JUSTICE DAVIS delivered the opinion of the court. . . .

The importance of the main question . . . cannot be overstated; for it involves the very framework of the government and the fundamental principles of American liberty.

During the late wicked Rebellion, the temper of the times did not allow that calmness in deliberation and discussion so necessary to a correct conclusion of a purely judicial question. *Then,* considerations of safety were mingled with the exercise of power; and feelings and interests prevailed which are happily terminated. *Now* that the public safety is assured, this question, as well as all others, can be discussed and decided without passion or the admixture of any element not required to form a legal judgment. We approach the investigation of this case, fully sensible of the magnitude of the inquiry and the necessity of full and cautious deliberation. . . .

The controlling question in the case is this: Upon the *facts* stated in Milligan's petition, and the exhibits filed, had the military commission mentioned in it *jurisdiction,* legally, to try and sentence him? Milligan, not a resident of one of the rebellious states, or a prisoner of war, but a citizen of Indiana for twenty years past, and never in the military or naval service, is, while at his home, arrested by the military power of the United States, imprisoned, and, on certain criminal charges preferred against him, tried, convicted, and sentenced to be hanged by a military commission, organized under the direction of the military commander of the military district of Indiana. Had this tribunal the *legal* power and authority to try and punish this man?

No graver question was ever considered by this court, nor one which more nearly concerns the rights of the whole people; for it is the birthright of every American citizen when charged with crime, to be tried and punished according to law. The power of punishment is, alone through the means which the laws have provided for that purpose, and if they are ineffectual, there is an immunity from punishment, no matter how great an offender the individual may be, or how much his crimes may have shocked the sense of justice of the country, or endangered its safety. By the protection of the law human rights are secured; withdraw that protection, and they are at the mercy of wicked rulers, or the clamor of an excited people. . . .

The Constitution of the United States is a law for rulers and people, equally in war and in peace, and covers with the shield of its protection all classes of men, at all times, and under all circumstances. No doctrine, involving more pernicious consequences, was ever invented by the wit of man than that any of its provisions can be suspended during any of the great exigencies of government. Such a doctrine leads directly to anarchy or despotism, but the theory of necessity on which it is based is false; for the government, within the Constitution, has all the powers granted to it, which are necessary to preserve its existence; as has been happily proved by the result of the great effort to throw off its just authority.

Have any of the rights guaranteed by the Constitution been violated in the case of Milligan? and if so, what are they?

Every trial involves the exercise of judicial power; and from what source did the military commission that tried him derive their authority? Certainly no part of the judicial power of the country was conferred on them; because the Constitution expressly vests it "in one supreme court and such inferior courts as the Congress may from time to time ordain and establish," and it is not pretended that the commission was a court ordained and established by Congress. They cannot justify on the mandate of the President; because he is controlled by law, and has his appropriate sphere of duty, which is to execute, not to make, the laws; and there is "no unwritten criminal code to which resort can be had as a source of jurisdiction."

But it is said that the jurisdiction is complete under the "laws and usages of war."

It can serve no useful purpose to inquire what those laws and usages are, whence they originated, where found, and on whom they operate; they can never be applied to citizens in states which have upheld the authority of the government, and where the courts are open and their process unobstructed. This court has judicial knowledge that in Indiana the Federal authority was always unopposed, and its courts always open to hear criminal accusations and redress grievances; and no usage of war could sanction a military trial there for any offence whatever of a citizen in civil life, in nowise connected with the military service. Congress could grant no such power; and to the honor of our national legislature be it said, it has never been provoked by the state of the country even to attempt its exercise. One of the plainest constitutional provisions was, therefore, infringed when Milligan was tried by a court not ordained and established by Congress, and not composed of judges appointed during good behavior.

Why was he not delivered to the Circuit Court of Indiana to be proceeded against according to law? No reason of necessity could be urged against it; because Congress had declared penalties against the offences charged, provided for their punishment, and directed that court to hear and determine them. And soon after this military tribunal was ended, the Circuit Court met, peacefully transacted its business, and adjourned. It needed no bayonets to protect it, and required no military aid to execute its judgments. It was held in a state, eminently distinguished for patriotism, by judges commissioned during the Rebellion, who were provided with juries, upright, intelligent, and selected by a marshal appointed by the President. The government had no right to conclude that Milligan, if guilty, would not receive in that court merited punishment; for its records disclose that it was constantly engaged in the trial of similar offences, and was never interrupted in its administration of criminal justice. . . .

Another guarantee of freedom was broken when Milligan was denied a trial by jury. The great minds of the country have differed on the correct interpretation to be given to various provisions of the Federal Constitution; and judicial decision has been often invoked to settle their true meaning; but until recently no one ever doubted that the right of trial by jury was fortified in the organic law against the power of attack. It is *now* assailed; but if ideas can be expressed in words, and language has any meaning, *this right*—one of the most valuable in a free country—is preserved to every one accused of crime who is not attached to the army, or navy, or militia in actual service. . . .

It is claimed that martial law covers with its broad mantle the proceedings of this military commission. The proposition is this: that in a time of war the commander of an armed force (if in his opinion the exigencies of the country demand it, and of which he is to judge), has the power, within the lines of his military district, to suspend all civil rights and their remedies, and subject citizens as well as soldiers to the rule of *his will;* and in the exercise of his lawful authority cannot be restrained, except by his superior officer or the President of the United States.

If this position is sound to the extent claimed, then when war exists, foreign or domestic, and the country is subdivided into military departments for mere convenience, the commander of one of them can, if he chooses, within his limits, on the plea of necessity, with the approval of the Executive, substitute military force for and to the exclusion of the laws, and punish all persons, as he thinks right and proper, without fixed or certain rules.

The statement of this proposition shows its importance; for, if true, republican government is a failure, and there is an end of liberty regulated by law. Martial law, established on such a basis, destroys every guarantee of the Constitution, and effectually renders the "military independent of and superior to the civil power"—the attempt to do which by the King of Great Britain was deemed by our fathers such an offence, that they assigned it to the world as one of the causes which impelled them to declare their independence. Civil liberty and this kind of martial law cannot endure together; the antagonism is irreconcilable; and, in the conflict, one or the other must perish.

This nation, as experience has proved, cannot always remain at peace, and has no right to expect that it will always have wise and humane rulers, sincerely attached to the principles of the Constitution. Wicked men, ambitious of power, with hatred of liberty and contempt of law, may fill the place once occupied by Washington and Lincoln; and if this right is conceded, and the calamities of war again befall us, the dangers to human liberty are frightful to contemplate. If our fathers had failed to provide for just such a contingency, they would have been false to the trust reposed in them. They knew—the history of the world told them—the nation they were founding, be its existence short or long, would be involved in war; how often or how long continued, human foresight could not tell; and that unlimited power, wherever lodged at such a time, was especially hazardous to freemen. For this, and other equally weighty reasons, they secured the inheritance they had fought to maintain, by incorporating in a written constitution the safeguards which *time* had proved were essential to its preservation. Not one of these safeguards can the President, or Congress, or the Judiciary disturb, except the one concerning the writ of *habeas corpus*.

It is essential to the safety of every government that, in a great crisis, like the one we have just passed through, there should be a power somewhere of suspending the writ of *habeas corpus*. In every war, there are men of previously good character, wicked enough to counsel their fellow-citizens to resist the measures deemed necessary by a good government to sustain its just authority and overthrow its enemies; and their influence may lead to dangerous combinations. In the emergency of the times, an immediate public investigation according to law may not be possible; and yet, the peril to the country may be too imminent to suffer such persons to go at large. Unquestionably, there is then an exigency which demands that the government, if it should see fit in the exercise of a proper discretion to make arrests, should not be required to produce the persons arrested in answer to a writ of *habeas corpus*. The Constitution goes no further. It does not say after a writ of *habeas corpus* is denied a citizen, that he shall be tried otherwise than by the course of the common law; if it had intended this result, it was easy by the use of direct words to have accomplished it. The illustrious men who framed that instrument were guarding the foundations of civil liberty against the abuses of unlimited power; they were full of wisdom, and the lessons of history informed them that a trial by an established court, assisted by an impartial jury, was the only sure way of protecting the citizen against oppression and wrong. Knowing this, they limited the suspension to one great right, and left the rest to remain forever inviolable. But, it is insisted that the safety of the country in time of war demands that this broad claim for martial law shall be sustained. If this were true, it could be well said that a country, preserved at the sacrifice of all the cardinal principles of liberty, is not worth the cost of preservation. Happily, it is not so. . . .

❧ 20 ❧

Articles of Impeachment against Andrew Johnson*

(1868)

T HE CONSTITUTION stipulates that the president "shall be removed from office on Impeachment for, and Conviction of, Treason, Bribery, or other high Crimes and Misdemeanors." The House of Representatives is charged to impeach the president, by majority vote. The Senate, with the chief justice of the United States presiding, then tries the president and decides whether to convict and remove or to acquit. A two-thirds majority "of the Members present" is required for conviction.

In all of American history, just two presidents have undergone the entire impeachment process: Andrew Johnson and Bill Clinton. (See Document 50, p. 239.) A Jacksonian Democrat from Tennessee, Johnson was the only southern senator who chose to remain in Congress after his state seceded from the Union in 1861. In 1864, at the request of President Abraham Lincoln, the National Union Party convention (the Republicans decided to change their name in an effort to attract unionist Democrats) nominated Johnson for vice president. Johnson succeeded to the presidency when Lincoln died of an assassin's bullet on April 15, 1865.

As president, Johnson was embroiled in a series of bitter controversies concerning Reconstruction of the South with the Radical Republicans, the wing of the party that took control of Congress in the 1866 elections. Secretary of War Edwin M. Stanton, a Lincoln appointee, sided more with Congress on these issues than with Johnson, who wanted to fire him. Congress protected Stanton by passing the Tenure of Office Act and by overriding Johnson's veto of the bill on March 2, 1867. The new law broke with the precedent established by the First Congress in 1789 by barring the president from removing any Senate-confirmed appointee from office until the Senate approved the nomination of a successor. (See Document 6, p. 43.)

After Congress went into recess in 1867, Johnson took advantage of a loophole in the new law that allowed him to act temporarily when Congress was not in session. He suspended Stanton as secretary of war and replaced him with Gen. Ulysses S. Grant.

---

*Go to *www.law.umkc.edu/faculty/projects/ftrials/impeach/articles.html.*

Reconvening in 1868, however, the Senate disapproved Johnson's action, and Grant turned the office back to Stanton. Johnson thought he had Grant's promise to ignore the Senate vote and thereby force a confrontation with Congress and, ultimately, a decision by the Supreme Court about the constitutionality of the Tenure of Office Act. But Grant decided not to jeopardize his presidential ambitions by siding with the president and alienating congressional Republicans.

In February 1868, acting in explicit defiance of the act, Johnson fired Stanton and appointed Gen. Lorenzo Thomas to replace him. After Thomas tried, unsuccessfully, to persuade Stanton to vacate the building, the House voted on February 21 to open an impeachment inquiry against the president.

The House took little time to act. The ardently radical Committee on Reconstruction quickly prepared an eleven-article impeachment resolution, which the House approved by a 126–47 vote on March 2 and 3, 1868, after only two days of debate. The first eight articles dealt with various aspects of Johnson's violation of the Tenure of Office Act. Article IX accused him of violating another recently enacted law when he bypassed the nation's highest ranking military officer, the general of the army, to give an order to a general in the field. (Johnson considered this law unconstitutional too.) Articles X and XI charged that Johnson's inflammatory speeches in the 1866 congressional election campaign had sought to bring Congress into "disgrace, ridicule, hatred, contempt, and reproach."

Seven members of the House were appointed to present the case for removal in the Senate trial. Johnson's lawyers argued that the president was entitled to violate any law he regarded as unconstitutional in order to bring the issue before the Supreme Court. The lawyers also argued, more narrowly, that the Tenure of Office Act did not bar Johnson from firing Stanton because Stanton had been appointed by a different president. They dismissed Article IX and, especially, Articles X and XI as frivolous (even rude criticism of Congress did not rise to the level of a high crime and misdemeanor).

Thirty-six votes were needed for conviction in the fifty-four-member Senate. By most reckonings, twelve senators (nine of them Democrats) were Johnson supporters and thirty were Johnson opponents. That left the decision in the hands of twelve undecided Republicans, some of whom dreaded the prospect that under the law prevailing at the time, Senate president pro tempore and Reconstruction hard-liner Benjamin Wade of Ohio would succeed to the presidency if Johnson were removed. In votes taken on May 16 and May 26, 1868, seven of the twelve voted not to convict the president. As a result, the margin in favor of conviction was 35–19, one vote shy of the required two-thirds.

Johnson completed his term as president on March 4, 1869. He returned to Tennessee where, after two unsuccessful attempts to win office, he was elected by the state legislature to the U.S. Senate in 1874. On July 31, 1875, five months after his election, Johnson died.

IN THE HOUSE OF REPRESENTATIVES, UNITED STATES,

March 2, 1868

ARTICLES EXHIBITED BY THE HOUSE OF REPRESENTATIVES OF THE UNITED STATES, IN THE NAME OF THEMSELVES AND ALL THE PEOPLE OF THE UNITED STATES, AGAINST ANDREW JOHNSON, PRESIDENT OF THE UNITED STATES, IN MAINTENANCE AND SUPPORT OF THEIR IMPEACHMENT AGAINST HIM FOR HIGH CRIMES AND MISDEMEANORS IN OFFICE.

Article I

That said Andrew Johnson, President of the United States, on the 21st day of February, A.D. 1868, at Washington, in the District of Columbia, unmindful of the high duties of his office, of his oath of office, and of the requirement of the Constitution that he should take care that the laws be faithfully executed, did unlawfully and in violation of the Constitution and laws of the United States issue an order in writing for the removal of Edwin M. Stanton from the office of Secretary for the Department of War, said Edwin M. Stanton having been theretofore duly appointed and commissioned, by and with the advice and consent of the Senate of the United States, as such Secretary; and said Andrew Johnson, President of the United States, on the 12th day of August, A.D. 1867, and during the recess of said Senate, having suspended by his order Edwin M. Stanton from said office, and within twenty days after the first day of the next meeting of said Senate—that is to say, on the 12th day of December, in the year last aforesaid—having reported to said Senate such suspension, with the evidence and reasons for his action in the case and the name of the person designated to perform the duties of such office temporarily until the next meeting of the Senate; and said Senate thereafterwards, on the 13th day of January, A.D. 1868, having duly considered the evidence and reasons reported by said Andrew Johnson for said suspension, and having refused to concur in said suspension, whereby and by force of the provisions of an act entitled "An act regulating the tenure of certain civil offices," passed March 2, 1867, said Edwin M. Stanton did forthwith resume the functions of his office, whereof the said Andrew Johnson had then and there due notice; and said Edwin M. Stanton, by reason of the premises, on said 21st day of February, being lawfully entitled to hold said office of Secretary for the Department of War; which said order for the removal of said Edwin M. Stanton is in substance as follows; that is to say:

EXECUTIVE MANSION,
Washington, D.C., February 21, 1868.

HON. EDWIN M. STANTON,
Washington, D.C.

SIR: By virtue of the power and authority vested in me as President by the Constitution and laws of the United States, you are hereby removed from office as Secretary for the Department of War, and your functions as such will terminate upon the receipt of this communication.

You will transfer to Brevet Major-General Lorenzo Thomas, Adjutant-General of the Army, who has this day been authorized and empowered to act as secretary of War ad interim, all records, books, papers, and other public property now in your custody and charge.

Respectfully yours,
ANDREW JOHNSON

To the Hon. E.M. Stanton, Secretary of War

Which order was unlawfully issued with intent then and there to violate the act entitled "An act regulating the tenure of certain civil offices," passed March 2, 1867, and with the further intent, contrary to the provisions of said act, in violation thereof, and contrary to the provisions of the Constitution of the United States, and without the advice and consent of the Senate of the United States, the said Senate then and there being in session, to remove said Edwin M. Stanton from the office of Secretary for the Department of War, the said Edwin M. Stanton being then and there Secretary for the Department of War, and being then and there in the due and unlawful execution and discharge of the duties of said office; whereby said Andrew Johnson, President of the United States, did then and there commit and was guilty of a high misdemeanor in office. . . .

Article IX

That said Andrew Johnson, President of the United States, on the 22d day of February, A.D. 1868, at Washington, in the District of Columbia, in disregard of the Constitution and the laws of the United States duly enacted, as Commander in Chief of the Army of the United States, did bring before himself then and there William H. Emory, a major-general by brevet in the Army of the United States, actually in command of the Department of Washington and the military forces thereof, and did then and there, as such Commander in Chief, declare to and instruct said Emory that part of a law of the United States, passed March 2, 1867, entitled "An act making appropriations for the support of the Army for the year ending June 30, 1868, and for other purposes," especially the second section thereof, which provides, among other things, that "all orders and instructions relating to military operations issued by the President or Secretary of War shall be issued through the General of the Army, and in case of his inability through the next in rank," was unconstitutional and in contravention of the commission of said Emory, and which said provision of law had been theretofore duly and legally promulgated by general order for the government and direction of the Army of the United States, as the said Andrew Johnson then and there well knew, with intent thereby to induce said Emory, in his official capacity as commander of the Department of Washington, to violate the provisions of said act and to take and receive, act upon, and obey such orders as he, the said Andrew Johnson, might make and give, and which should not be issued through the General of the Army of the United States, according to the provisions of said act, and with the further intent thereby to enable him, and said Andrew Johnson, to prevent the execution of the act entitled "An act regulating the tenure of certain civil offices," passed March 2, 1867, and to unlawfully prevent Edwin M. Stanton, then being Secretary for the Department of War, from holding said office and discharging the duties thereof; whereby said Andrew Johnson, President of the United States, did then and there commit and was guilty of a high misdemeanor in office.

And the House of Representatives, by protestation, saving to themselves the liberty of exhibiting at any time hereafter any further articles or other accusation or impeachment against the said Andrew Johnson, President of the United States, and also of replying to his answers which he shall make unto the articles herein preferred against him, and of offering proof to the same, and every part thereof, and to all and every other article, accusation, or impeachment which shall be exhibited by them, as the case shall require, do demand that the said Andrew Johnson may be put to answer the high crimes and misdemeanors in office here-in charged against him, and that such proceedings, examinations, trials, and judgments may be thereupon had and given as may be agreeable to law and justice.

SCHUYLER COLFAX,
Speaker of the House of Representatives

EDWARD MCPHERSON,
Clerk of the House of Representatives

Attest:
The following additional articles of impeachment were agreed to viz:

IN THE HOUSE OF REPRESENTATIVES, UNITED STATES

March 3, 1868

Article X

That said Andrew Johnson, President of the United States, unmindful of the high duties of his office and the dignity and proprieties thereof, and of the harmony and courtesies which ought to exist and be maintained between the executive and legislative branches of the Government of the United States, designing and intending to set aside the rightful authority and powers of Congress, did attempt to bring into disgrace, ridicule, hatred, contempt, and reproach the Congress of the United States and the several branches thereof, to impair and destroy the regard and respect of all the good people of the United States for the Congress and legislative power thereof (which all officers of the Government ought inviolably to preserve and maintain) and to excite the odium and resentment of all the good people of the United States against Congress and the laws by it duly and constitutionally enacted; and, in pursuance of his said design and intent, openly and publicly, and before divers assemblages of the citizens of the United States, convened in divers parts thereof to meet and receive said Andrew Johnson as the Chief Magistrate of the United States, did, on the 18th day of August, A.D. 1866, and on divers other days and times, as well before as afterwards, make and deliver with a loud voice certain intemperate, inflammatory, and scandalous harangues, and did therein utter loud threats and bitter menaces, as well against Congress as the laws of the United States, duly enacted thereby, amid the cries, jeers, and laughter of the multitudes then assembled and in hearing, which are set forth in the several specifications hereinafter written, in substance and effect, that is to say:

Specification first.—In this, that at Washington, in the District of Columbia in the Executive Mansion, to a committee of citizens who called upon the President of the United States, speaking of and concerning the Congress of the United States, said Andrew Johnson, President of the United States, heretofore, to wit, on the 18th day of August, in the year of our Lord 1866, did, in a loud voice, declare in substance and effect, among other things, that is to say:

"So far as the executive department of the Government is concerned, the effort has been made to restore the Union, to heal the breach, to pour oil into the wounds which were consequent upon the struggle, and (to speak in common phrase) to prepare, as the learned and wise physician would, a plaster healing in character and coextensive with the wound. We thought, and we think, that we had partially succeeded; but as the work progresses, as reconstruction seemed to be taking place and the country was becoming reunited, we found a disturbing and marring element opposing us. In alluding to that element, I shall go no further than your convention and the distinguished gentleman who had delivered to me the report of its proceedings. I shall make no reference to it that I do not believe the time and the occasion justify.

"We have witnessed in one department of the Government every endeavor to prevent the restoration of peace, harmony, and union. We have seen hanging upon the verge of the Government, as it were, a body called, or which assumes to be, the Congress of the United States, while in fact it is a Congress of only a part of the States. We have seen this Congress pretend to be for the Union when its every step and act tended to perpetrate disunion and make a disruption of the States inevitable. We have seen Congress gradually encroach step by step upon constitutional rights and violate, day after day and month after month, fundamental principles of the Government. We have seen a Congress that seemed to forget that there was a limit to the sphere and scope of legislation. We have seen a Congress in a minority assume to exercise power which, allowed to be consummated, would result in despotism or monarchy itself."

Specification second.—In this, that at Cleveland, in the State of Ohio, heretofore, to wit, on the 3d day of September, in the year of our Lord 1866, before a public assemblage of citizens and others, said Andrew Johnson, President of the United States, speaking of and concerning the Congress of the United States did, in a loud voice, declare in substance and effect among other things, that is to say:

"I will tell you what I did do. I called upon your Congress that is trying to break up the Government."

"In conclusion, beside that, Congress had taken much pains to poison their constituents against him. But what had a Congress done? Have they done anything to restore the Union of these States? No; on the contrary, they had done everything to prevent it; and because he stood now where he did when the rebellion commenced he had been denounced as a traitor. Who had run greater risks or made greater sacrifices than himself? But Congress, factious and domineering, had undertaken to poison the minds of the American people."

Specification third.—In this, that at St. Louis, in the State of Missouri, heretofore, to wit, on the 8th day of September, in the year of our Lord 1866, before a public assemblage of citizens and others, said Andrew Johnson, President of the United States, speaking of and concerning the Congress of the United States, did, in a loud voice, declare, in substance and effect, among other things, that is to say:

"Go on. Perhaps if you had a word or two on the subject of New Orleans, you might understand more about it than you do. And if you will go back—if you will go back and ascertain the cause of the riot at New Orleans, perhaps you will not be so prompt in calling out 'New Orleans.' If you will take up the riot at New Orleans and trace it back to its source or its immediate cause, you will find out who was responsible for the blood that was shed there. If you will take up the riot at New Orleans and trace it back to the Radical Congress, you will find that the riot at New Orleans was substantially planned. If you will take up the proceedings in their caucuses, you will understand that they there knew that a convention was to be called which was extinct by its power having expired; that it was said that the intention was that a new government was to be organized, and on the organization of that government the intention was to enfranchise one portion of the population, called the colored population, who had just been emancipated, and at the same time disenfranchise white men. When you design to talk about New Orleans you ought to understand what you are talking about. When you read the speeches that were made, and take up the facts on the Friday and Saturday before that convention sat, you will find that speeches were made incendiary in their character, exciting that portion of the population, the black population, to arm themselves and pre-pare for the shedding of blood. You will also find that that convention did assemble in violation of law, and the intention of that convention was to supersede the reor-ganized authorities in the State government of Louisiana, which had been recog-nized by the Government of the United States; and every man engaged in that rebellion in that convention, with the intention of superseding and upturning the civil government which had been recognized by the Government of the United States, I say that he was a traitor to the Constitution of the United States, and hence you find that another rebellion was commenced having its origin in the Radical Congress.

"So much for the New Orleans riot. And there was the cause and the origin of the blood that was shed; and every drop of blood that was shed is upon their skirts, and they are responsible for it. I could test this thing a little closer, but will not do it here tonight. But when you talk about the causes and consequences that resulted from pro-ceedings of that kind, perhaps as I have been introduced here and you have provoked questions of this kind, though it does not provoke me, I will tell you a few wholesome things that have been done by this Radical Congress in connection with New Orleans and the extension of the elective franchise.

"I know that I have been traduced and abused. I know it has come in advance of me here, as elsewhere, that I have attempted to exercise an arbitrary power in resisting laws that were intended to be forced upon the Government; that I had abandoned the party that elected me, and that I was a traitor because I exercised the veto power in attempting and did arrest for a time a bill that was called a 'Freedman's Bureau' bill; yes, that I was a traitor. And I have been traduced, I have been slandered, I have been maligned, I have been called Judas Iscariot, and all that. Now, my countrymen here tonight, it is very easy to indulge in epithets; it is easy to call a man a Judas and cry out traitor; but when he is called upon to give arguments and facts it is very easy to indulge in epithets; it is easy to call a man a Judas and he was one of the twelve apostles. Oh yes, the twelve apostles had a Christ. The twelve apostles had a Christ, and he never could have had a Judas unless he had had twelve apostles. If I have played the Judas, who has been my Christ that I have played the Judas with? Was it Thad. Stevens? Was it Wendell Philips? Was it Charles Sumner? These are the men that stop and compare themselves with the Saviour; and everybody that differs with them in opinion, and to try and stay and arrest the diabolical and nefarious policy, is to be denounced as a Judas.

"Well, let me say to you, if you will stand by me in this action; if you will stand by me in trying to give the people a fair chance, soldiers and citizens, to participate in these offices, God being willing, I will kick them out, I will kick them out just as fast as I can.

"Let me say to you, in concluding that what I have said I intended to say. I was not provoked into this, and I care not for their menaces, the taunts, and the jeers, I care not for threats, I do not intend to be bullied by my enemies nor overawed by my friends. But, God willing, with your help I will veto their measures whenever any of them come to me."

Which said utterances, declarations, threats, and harangues, highly censurable in any, are peculiarly indecent and unbecoming in the Chief Magistrate of the United States, by means whereof said Andrew Johnson has brought the high office of the President of the United States into contempt, ridicule, and disgrace, to the great scandal of all good citizens, whereby said Andrew Johnson, President of the United States, did commit, and was then and there guilty of, a high misdemeanor in office.

Article XI

That said Andrew Johnson, President of the United States, unmindful of the high duties of his office and of his oath of office, and in disregard of the Constitution and laws of the United States, did heretofore, to wit, on the 18th day of August, A.D. 1866, at the city of Washington, in the District of Columbia, by public speech, declare and affirm in substance that the Thirty-ninth Congress of the United States was not a Congress of the United States authorized by the Constitution to exercise legislative power under the same, but, on the contrary, was a Congress of only part of the States; thereby denying and intending to deny that the legislation of said Congress was valid or obligatory upon him, the said Andrew Johnson, except in so far as he saw fit to approve the same, and also thereby denying and intending to deny the power of the said Thirty-ninth Congress to propose amendments to the Constitution of the United States; and in pursuance of said declaration the said Andrew Johnson, President of the United States, afterwards, to wit, on the 21st day February, A.D. 1868, at the city of Washington, in the District of Columbia, did unlawfully, and in disregard of the requirement of the Constitution that he should take care that the laws be faithfully executed, attempt to prevent the execution of an act entitled "An act regulating the tenure of certain civil offices," passed March 2, 1867, by unlawfully devising and contriving, and attempting to devise and contrive, means by which he should prevent Edwin M. Stanton from forthwith resuming the functions of the office of Secretary for the Department of War, notwithstanding the refusal of the Senate to concur in the suspension theretofore made by said Andrew Johnson of said Edwin M. Stanton from said office of Secretary for the Department of War, and also by further unlawfully devising and contriving, and attempting to devise and contrive, means then and there to prevent the execution of an act entitled "An act making appropriations for the support of the Army for the fiscal year ending June 30, 1868 and for other purposes," approved March 2, 1867, and also to prevent the execution of an act entitled "An act to provide for the more efficient government of the rebel States," passed March 2, 1867, whereby the said Andrew Johnson, President of the United States, did then, to wit, on the 21st day of February, A.D. 1868, at the city of Washington, commit and was guilty of a high misdemeanor in office.

SCHUYLER COLFAX,
Speaker of the House of Representatives

EDWARD MCPHERSON,
Clerk of the House of Representatives

&c 21 &c

The Pendleton Act

(1883)

EFFORTS TO REFORM the federal civil service by replacing the "spoils system," under which government employees were hired and fired by the victorious political party after each election, with a merit system, in which personnel decisions would be made nonpolitically and according to qualifications, were a prominent feature of American politics after the Civil War. These efforts culminated in the passage in 1883 of "An Act to Regulate and Improve the Civil Service of the United States." The law is better known as the Pendleton Act, after its chief sponsor, Sen. George H. Pendleton of Ohio.

President Andrew Jackson established the spoils system. The term was coined in 1832 by Sen. William Marcy of New York, who remarked that political leaders "see nothing wrong in the rule, that to the victor belong the spoils of the enemy." As Jackson made clear in his first annual message to Congress (see Document 13, p. 75), he believed that the skills required for government employment, previously the preserve of a mainly upper-class elite, could be learned by almost anyone and that the president, with the advice of his fellow partisans in Congress, should distribute government jobs widely among those who had supported the party in the election. Later generations of victorious politicians practiced what Jackson preached. Indeed, none wielded spoils more ardently than President Abraham Lincoln during the Civil War.

After the war, abuses of the spoils system—government jobs that were sold to the highest bidder, filled by incompetents, or used to extort bribes—were widely publicized in the press and by political reformers. During the 1870s the administration of President Ulysses S. Grant was especially notorious for its corruption. Rapidly proliferating state and national civil service reform organizations traced much of the administration's peculation to "spoilsmen" appointed to office by Grant.

The death knell for the spoils system was sounded in 1881 when President James A. Garfield was assassinated by Charles J. Guiteau, an obscure Republican partisan who was outraged that he had not received a prominent government job as reward for his labors on behalf of Garfield and the rest of the GOP ticket in the 1880 election. In the atmosphere of revulsion against spoils that followed the assassination, Congress passed the Pendleton Act in 1883.

The Pendleton Act created a bipartisan, three-member Civil Service Commission to help the president oversee the federal personnel system and stated several purposes to guide the commission in its work. Partisan activity, nepotism, and personal connections as reasons for hiring, promoting, and firing government employees were to be replaced by competitive examinations and performance-based promotion and retention policies. Employees were offered protection from having to contribute money or time to political campaigns.

In the short term, only 10.5 percent of the federal workforce—mainly clerical and technical employees—was included in the new "classified civil service." But the act empowered the president to extend its coverage to additional categories of workers. Over time virtually the entire civil service became merit based by virtue of presidential decisions. Ironically, extensions of civil service coverage usually occurred for the most partisan of reasons. A departing president, seeking to protect his patronage appointees from being replaced by his successor, would "blanket them in" by placing their jobs under the protection of the classified civil service.

Be it enacted . . . That the President is authorized to appoint, by and with the advice and consent of the Senate, three persons, not more than two of whom shall be adherents of the same party, as Civil Service Commissioners, and said three commissioners shall constitute the United States Civil Service Commission. Said commissioners shall hold no other official place under the United States.

Sec. 2. That it shall be the duty of said commissioners:

First. To aid the President, as he may request, in preparing suitable rules for carrying this act into effect, and when said rules shall have been promulgated it shall be the duty of all officers of the United States in the departments and offices to which any such rules may relate to aid, in all proper ways, in carrying said rules, and any modifications thereof, into effect.

Second. And, among other things, said rules shall provide and declare, as nearly as the conditions of good administration will warrant, as follows:

First, for open, competitive examinations for testing the fitness of applicants for the public service now classified or to be classified hereunder. Such examinations shall be practical in their character, and so far as may be shall relate to those matters which will fairly test the relative capacity and fitness of the persons examined to discharge the duties of the service into which they seek to be appointed.

Second, that all the offices, places, and employments so arranged or to be arranged in classes shall be filled by selections according to grade from among those graded highest as the results of such competitive examinations.

Third, appointments to the public service aforesaid in the departments at Washington shall be apportioned among the several States and Territories and the District of Columbia upon the basis of population as ascertained at the last preceding census. . . .

Fourth, that there shall be a period of probation before any absolute appointment or employment aforesaid.

Fifth, that no person in the public service is for that reason under any obligations to contribute to any political fund, or to render any political service, and that he will not be removed or otherwise prejudiced for refusing to do so.

Sixth, that no person in said service has any right to use his official authority or influence to coerce the political action of any person or body.

Seventh, there shall be non-competitive examinations in all proper cases before the commission, when competent persons do not compete, after notice has been given of the existence of the vacancy, under such rules as may be prescribed by the commissioners as to the manner of giving notice. . . .

Third. Said commission shall, subject to the rules that may be made by the President, make regulations for, and have control of, such examinations. . . .

Sec. 3. . . . The commission shall, at Washington, and in one or more places in each State and Territory where examinations are to take place, designate and select a suitable number of persons, not less than three, in the official service of the United States, residing in said State or Territory, after consulting the head of the department or office in which such persons serve, to be members of boards of examiners. . . . Such boards of examiners shall be so located as to make it reasonably convenient and inexpensive for applicants to attend before them and where there are persons to be examined in any State or Territory, examinations shall be held therein at least twice in each year. . . .

Sec. 6. That within sixty days after the passage of this act it shall be the duty of the Secretary of the Treasury . . . to arrange in classes the several clerks and persons employed by the collector, naval officer, surveyor, and appraisers, or either of them, or being in the public service, at their respective offices in each customs district where the whole number of said clerks and persons shall be all together as many as fifty. And thereafter, from time to time, on the direction of the President, said Secretary shall make the like classification or arrangement of clerks and persons so employed, in connection with any said office or offices, in any other customs district. And, upon like request, and for the purposes of this act, said Secretary shall arrange in one or more of said classes, or of existing classes, any other clerks, agents, or persons employed under his department in any said district not now classified; and every such arrangement and classification upon being made shall be reported to the President.

Second. Within said sixty days it shall be the duty of the Postmaster-General . . . to separately arrange in classes the several clerks and persons employed, or in the public service, at each post-office, or under any postmaster of the United States, where the whole number of said clerks and persons shall together amount to as many as fifty. And thereafter, from time to time, on the direction of the President, it shall be the duty of the Postmaster-General to arrange in like classes the clerks and persons so employed in the postal service in connection with any other post-office; and every such arrangement and classification upon being made shall be reported to the President.

Third. That from time to time said Secretary, the Postmaster-General, and each of the heads of departments . . . , and each head of an office, shall, on the direction of the President, and for facilitating the execution of this act, respectively revise any then existing classification or arrangement of those in their respective departments and offices, and shall, for the purposes of the examination herein provided for, include in one or more of such classes, so far as practicable, subordinate places, clerks, and officers in the public service pertaining to their respective departments not before classified for examination.

Sec. 7. That after the expiration of six months from the passage of this act no officer or clerk shall be appointed, and no person shall be employed to enter or be promoted in either of the said classes now existing, or that may be arranged hereunder pursuant to said rules, until he has passed an examination, or is shown to be specially exempted from such examination in conformity herewith. But nothing herein contained shall be construed to take from those honorably discharged from the military or naval service . . . nor to take from the President any authority not inconsistent with this act; . . . nor shall any officer not in the executive branch of the government, or any person merely employed as a laborer or workman, be required to be classified hereunder; nor, unless by direction of the Senate, shall any person who has been nominated for confirmation by the Senate be required to be classified or to pass an examination.

Sec. 8. That no person habitually using intoxicating beverages to excess shall be appointed to, or retained in, any office, appointment, or employment to which the provisions of this act are applicable.

Sec. 9. That whenever there are already two or more members of a family in the public service in the grades covered by this act, no other member of such family shall be eligible to appointment to grades.

Sec. 10. That no recommendation of any person who shall apply for office or place under the provisions of this act which may be given by any Senator or member of the House of Representatives, except as to the character or residence of the applicant, shall be received or considered by any person concerned in making any examination or appointment under this act.

Sec. 11. That no Senator, or Representative, or Territorial Delegate of the Congress, or Senator, Representative, or Delegate elect, or any officer or employee of either of said houses, and no executive, judicial, military, or naval officer of the United States, and no clerk or employee of any department, branch or bureau of the executive, judicial, or military or naval service of the United States, shall, directly or indirectly, solicit or receive, or be in any manner concerned in soliciting or receiving, any assessment, subscription, or contribution for any political purpose whatever, from any officer, clerk, or employee of the United States, or any department, branch, or bureau thereof, or from any person receiving any salary or compensation from moneys derived from the Treasury of the United States. . . .

Lord James Bryce, Why Great Men Are Not Chosen President

(1888)

T HE INSTRUCTION given to three generations of college students from 1974 to 2014 by Washington University psychologist Henry L. Roediger III was clear: in the next five minutes, write down the names of as many presidents as you can, in chronological order. The result: most students could name George Washington, John Adams, Thomas Jefferson, and James Madison, as well as several of the presidents since Franklin D. Roosevelt. But when it came to the century–plus between the early and modern eras, they were able to list Abraham Lincoln and scarcely anyone else.

In 1888, midway through this long period that has vanished from historical memory, the celebrated British historian, diplomat, legal scholar, and politician Lord James Bryce published *The American Commonwealth.* The most recent presidents at the time were Andrew Johnson, Ulysses S. Grant, Rutherford B. Hayes, and Grover Cleveland, with Benjamin Harrison on the cusp of election later that year. This roster of generally uncelebrated executives inspired Bryce to include a chapter in his book called "Why Great Men Are Not Chosen President."

Bryce wrote at a time when industry was expanding rapidly in the United States, attracting "much of the best ability, both for thought and for action," into "the business of developing the material resources of the country." He contrasted the American situation to that of Europe, where business opportunities were "comparatively narrow" and the political arena rich in "burning questions."

The late nineteenth century also was a period of strong political parties whose appeal was grounded less in their contrasting political philosophies than in the contest for the spoils that attended electoral success. Despite the recent enactment of the Pendleton Act, government jobs and contracts, not new public policies, were the major prizes of victory in battles for the presidency. Under these circumstances, Bryce argued, "when the choice lies between a brilliant man and a safe man, the safe man is preferred" by the party leaders who controlled the nomination of presidential candidates. "It will be a misfortune to the party," he added, "as well as to the country, if the candidate elected should prove a bad president. But it is a greater misfortune to the party that it should be beaten in the impending election, for the evil of losing national patronage will have come four years sooner."

Bryce wrote in an era when Congress was the dominant branch of government. Legislative supremacy afforded presidents "fewer opportunities for personal distinction," thereby making the office that much less attractive to the nation's most talented individuals. Nor, in an era of "congressional government" (the title of a book published in 1885 by political scientist and future president Woodrow Wilson), did the office require greatness. "After all, too," Bryce added, "a president need not be a man of brilliant intellectual gifts. His main duties are to be prompt and firm in securing the due execution of the laws and maintaining the public peace, careful and upright in the choice of the executive officials of the country."

Wilson and Theodore Roosevelt were among those who read and admired *The American Commonwealth,* which is generally regarded as the best book about the United States by a foreign observer since Alexis de Tocqueville's *Democracy in America.* In less than two decades, these two presidents would inaugurate a new and very different era of presidential leadership.

🐜 🐜 🐜

Europeans often ask, and Americans do not always explain, how it happens that this great office, the greatest in the world, unless we except the papacy, to which anyone can rise by his own merits, is not more frequently filled by great and striking men. In America, which is beyond all other countries the country of a "career open to talents," a country, moreover, in which political life is unusually keen and political ambition widely diffused, it might be expected that the highest place would always be won by a man of brilliant gifts. But from the time when the heroes of the Revolution died out with Jefferson and Adams and Madison, no person except General Grant, had, down till the end of last century, reached the chair whose name would have been remembered had he not been president, and no president except Abraham Lincoln had displayed rare or striking qualities in the chair. Who now knows or cares to know anything about the personality of James K. Polk or Franklin Pierce? The only thing remarkable about them is that being so commonplace they should have climbed so high.

Several reasons may be suggested for the fact, which Americans are themselves the first to admit.

One is that the proportion of first-rate ability drawn into politics is smaller in America than in most European countries. . . . [I]n France, where the half-revolutionary conditions that lasted for some time after 1870, made public life exciting and accessible; in Germany, where an admirably organized civil service cultivates and develops statecraft with unusual success; in England, where many persons of wealth and leisure seek to enter the political arena, while burning questions touch the interests of all classes and make men eager observers of the combatants, the total quantity of talent devoted to parliamentary or administrative work has been larger, relatively to the population, than in America, where much of the best ability, both for thought and for action, for planning and for executing, rushes into a field which is comparatively narrow in Europe, the business of developing the material resources of the country.

Another is that the methods and habits of Congress, and indeed of political life generally, seem to give fewer opportunities for personal distinction, fewer modes in which a man may commend himself to his countrymen by eminent capacity in thought, in speech, or in administration, than is the case in the free countries of Europe. . . .

A third reason is that eminent men make more enemies, and give those enemies more assailable points, than obscure men do. They are therefore in so far less desirable candidates. It is true that the eminent man has also made more friends, that his name is more widely known, and may be greeted with louder cheers. Other things being equal, the famous man is preferable. But other things never are equal. The famous man has probably attacked some leaders in his own party, has supplanted others, has expressed his dislike to the crotchet of some active section, has perhaps committed errors which are capable of being magnified into offences. No man stands long before the public and bears a part in great affairs without giving openings to censorious criticism. Fiercer far than the light which beats upon a throne is the light which beats upon a presidential candidate, searching out all the recesses of his past life. Hence, when the choice lies between a brilliant man and a safe man, the safe man is preferred. Party feeling, strong enough to carry in on its back a man without conspicuous positive merits, is not always strong enough to procure forgiveness for a man with positive faults.

A European finds that this phenomenon needs in its turn to be explained, for in the free countries of Europe brilliancy, be it eloquence in speech, or some striking achievement in war or administration, or the power through whatever means of somehow impressing the popular imagination, is what makes a leader triumphant. Why should it be otherwise in America? Because in America party loyalty and party organization have been hitherto so perfect that anyone put forward by the party will get the full party vote if his character is good and his "record," as they call it, unstained. The safe candidate may not draw in quite so many votes from the moderate men of the other side as the brilliant one would, but he will not lose nearly so many from his own ranks. Even those who admit his mediocrity will vote straight when the moment for voting comes. Besides, the ordinary American voter does not object to mediocrity. He has a lower conception of the qualities requisite to make a statesman than those who direct public opinion in Europe have. He likes his candidate to be sensible, vigorous, and, above all, what he calls "magnetic," and does not value, because he sees no need for, originality or profundity, a fine culture or a wide knowledge. Candidates are selected to be run for nomination by knots of persons who, however expert as party tacticians, are usually commonplace men; and the choice between those selected for nomination is made by a very large body, an assembly of nearly a thousand delegates from the local party organizations over the country, who are certainly no better than ordinary citizens. . . .

It must also be remembered that the merits of a president are one thing and those of a candidate another thing. An eminent American is reported to have said to friends who wished to put him forward, "Gentlemen, let there be no mistake. I should make a good president, but a very bad candidate." Now to a party it is more important that its nominee should be a good candidate than that he should turn out a good president. . . . It will be a misfortune to the party, as well as to the country, if the candidate elected should prove a bad president. But it is a greater misfortune to the party that it should be beaten in the impending election, for the evil of losing national patronage will have come four years sooner. "B" (so reason the leaders), "who is one of our possible candidates, may be an abler man than A, who is the other. But we have a better chance of winning with A than with B, while X, the candidate of our opponents, is anyhow no better than A. We must therefore run A." This reasoning is all the more forcible because the previous career of the possible candidates has generally made it easier to say who will succeed as a candidate than who will succeed as a president; and because the wire-pullers with whom the choice rests are better judges of the former question than of the latter.

After all, too, a president need not be a man of brilliant intellectual gifts. His main duties are to be prompt and firm in securing the due execution of the laws and maintaining the public peace, careful and upright in the choice of the executive officials of the country. Eloquence, whose value is apt to be overrated in all free countries, imagination, profundity of thought or extent of knowledge, are all in so far a gain to him that they make him "a bigger man," and help him to gain a greater influence over the nation, an influence which, if he be a true patriot, he may use for its good. But they are not necessary for the due discharge in ordinary times of the duties of his post. Four-fifths of his work is the same in kind as that which devolves on the chairman of a commercial company or the manager of a railway, the work of choosing good subordinates, seeing that they attend to their business, and taking a sound practical view of such administrative questions as require his decision. Firmness, common sense, and most of all, honesty, an honesty above all suspicion of personal interest, are the qualities which the country chiefly needs in its chief magistrate. . . .

We may now answer the question from which we started. Great men have not often been chosen presidents, first because great men are rare in politics; secondly, because the method of choice does not bring them to the top; thirdly, because they are not, in quiet times, absolutely needed.

✦ 23 ✦

Theodore Roosevelt's and William Howard Taft's Theories of Presidential Power

(1913, 1916)

THEODORE ROOSEVELT, who was elected vice president in 1900, succeeded to the presidency when President William McKinley was assassinated on September 14, 1901. Roosevelt won a full term as president in the 1904 election. He invigorated the office with an energy and initiative not seen since the Lincoln administration but declined to seek reelection in 1908, retiring in favor of his close friend and secretary of war, William Howard Taft. Roosevelt came to regard Taft's leadership as overly cautious and conservative and challenged him for the 1912 Republican presidential nomination. After Taft was renominated, Roosevelt stayed in the race as the candidate of the Progressive, or "Bull Moose," Party. They split the Republican vote in November, and Democrat Woodrow Wilson became president.

Soon after their administrations were over, former presidents Roosevelt and Taft produced a classic exchange on the proper nature of presidential power. Roosevelt articulated his "stewardship" theory of the presidency in *The Autobiography of Theodore Roosevelt,* which was published in 1913. Taft expounded his "literalist" theory in a 1916 book called *Our Chief Magistrate and His Powers.* The exchange is significant not only because of the light it sheds on the conflict that developed between the two former friends and political allies, especially about conservation policy, but also because it offers a striking comparison of the way most presidents regarded the presidency in the nineteenth century (Taft's view) and in the twentieth and twenty-first centuries (Roosevelt's view).

Like Pacificus and Helvidius—that is, Alexander Hamilton and James Madison—more than a century before, Roosevelt and Taft took the Constitution as their point of departure. (See Document 7, p. 47.) But they differed radically on how to interpret that document. Roosevelt believed that the president could do anything that the Constitution or laws did not forbid, and Taft believed that the president could not do anything that the Constitution or laws did not permit.

Roosevelt claimed that while in office, "I acted for the public welfare, I acted for the common well-being of all our people, whenever and in whatever manner was necessary, unless prevented by direct constitutional or legislative prohibition." He regarded the president as "a steward of the people bound actively and affirmatively to do all he could for the people, and not to content himself with the negative merit of keeping his talents undamaged in a napkin."

Taft, on the other hand, believed that "the President can exercise no power which cannot be fairly and reasonably traced to some specific grant of power or justly implied and included within such express grant as proper and necessary to its exercise." He added: "There is no undefined residuum of power which he can exercise because it seems to him to be in the public interest."

Each president's philosophy of executive power helps to explain his actions in office. Taft seldom spoke out publicly in defense of his policies. He neglected the press and, although willing to recommend legislation, stood by as Congress worked its will. In contrast, when Congress resisted Roosevelt's legislative agenda, he broke precedent by embarking on a speech-making tour of the country, "appealing over the heads of the Senate and House leaders to the people, who were the masters of both of us." He used the press to personalize both his administration and his agenda. Roosevelt was "TR," the first president to be known by his initials, and his program was the "Square Deal," which foreshadowed labels such as "New Deal," "New Frontier," and "Great Society." In foreign policy, Roosevelt was active and, on occasion, defiant toward Congress.

※ ※ ※

Theodore Roosevelt

The most important factor in getting the right spirit in my Administration, next to insistence upon courage, honesty, and a genuine democracy of desire to serve the plain people, was my insistence upon the theory that the executive power was limited only by specific restrictions and prohibitions appearing in the Constitution or imposed by Congress under its constitutional powers.

My view was that every executive officer, and above all every executive officer in high position, was a steward of the people bound actively and affirmatively to do all he could for the people, and not to content himself with the negative merit of keeping his talents undamaged in a napkin. I declined to adopt the view that what was imperatively necessary for the nation could not be done by the President unless he could find some specific authorization to do it. My belief was that it was not only his right but his duty to do anything that the needs of the nation demanded unless such action was forbidden by the Constitution or by the laws. Under this interpretation of executive power I did and caused to be done many things not previously done by the President and the heads of the departments. I did not usurp power, but I did greatly broaden the use of executive power. In other words, I acted for the public welfare, I acted for the common well-being of all our people, whenever and in whatever manner was necessary, unless prevented by direct constitutional or legislative prohibition. . . .

The course I followed, of regarding the Executive as subject only to the people, and, under the Constitution, bound to serve the people affirmatively in cases where the Constitution does not explicitly forbid him to render the service, was substantially the course followed by both Andrew Jackson and Abraham Lincoln. Other honorable and well-meaning Presidents, such as James Buchanan, took the opposite and, as it seems to me, narrowly legalistic view that the President is the servant of Congress rather than of the people, and can do nothing, no matter how necessary it be to act, unless the Constitution explicitly commands the action. Most able lawyers who are past middle age take this view, and so do large numbers of well-meaning, respectable citizens. My successor in office [William Howard Taft] took this, the Buchanan, view of the President's powers and duties.

For example, under my administration we found that one of the favorite methods adopted by the men desirous of stealing the public domain was to carry the decision of the secretary of the interior into court. By vigorously opposing such action, and only by so doing, we were able to carry out the policy of properly protecting the public domain. My successor not only took the opposite view, but recommended to Congress the passage of a bill which would have given the courts direct appellate power over the secretary of the interior in these land matters. . . . Fortunately, Congress declined to pass the bill. Its passage would have been a veritable calamity.

I acted on the theory that the President could at any time in his discretion withdraw from entry any of the public lands of the United States and reserve the same for forestry, for water-power sites, for irrigation, and other public purposes. Without such action it would have been impossible to stop the activity of the land-thieves. No one ventured to test its legality by lawsuit. My successor, however, himself questioned it, and referred the matter to Congress. Again Congress showed its wisdom by passing a law which gave the President the power which he had long exercised, and of which my successor had shorn himself.

Perhaps the sharp difference between what may be called the Lincoln-Jackson and the Buchanan-Taft schools, in their views of the power and duties of the President, may be best illustrated by comparing the attitude of my successor toward his Secretary of the Interior, Mr. [Richard A.] Ballinger, when the latter was accused of gross misconduct in office, with my attitude toward my chiefs of department and other subordinate officers. More than once while I was President my officials were attacked by Congress, generally because these officials did their duty well and fearlessly. In every such case I stood by the official and refused to recognize the right of Congress to interfere with me excepting by impeachment or in other constitutional manner. On the other hand, wherever I found the officer unfit for his position, I promptly removed him, even although the most influential men in Congress fought for his retention. The Jackson-Lincoln view is that a President who is fit to do good work should be able to form his own judgment as to his own subordinates, and, above all, of the subordinates standing highest and in closest and most intimate touch with him. My secretaries and their subordinates were responsible to me, and I accepted the responsibility for all their deeds. As long as they were satisfactory to me I stood by them against every critic or assailant, within or without Congress; and as for getting Congress to make up my mind for me about them, the thought would have been inconceivable to me. My successor took the opposite, or Buchanan, view when he permitted and requested Congress to pass judgment on the charges made against Mr. Ballinger as an executive officer. These charges were made to the President; the President had the facts before him and could get at them at any time, and he alone had power to act if the charges were true. However, he permitted and requested Congress to investigate Mr. Ballinger. The party minority of the committee that investigated him, and one member of the majority, declared that the charges were well-founded and that Mr. Ballinger should be removed. The other members of the majority declared the charges ill-founded. The President abode by the view of the majority. Of course believers in the Jackson-Lincoln theory of the presidency would not be content with this town meeting majority and minority method of determining by another branch of the government what it seems the especial duty of the President himself to determine for himself in dealing with his own subordinate in his own department. . . .

William Howard Taft

While it is important to mark out the exclusive field of jurisdiction of each branch of the government, Legislative, Executive and Judicial, it should be said that in the proper working of the government there must be cooperation of all branches, and without a willingness of each branch to perform its function, there will follow a hopeless obstruction to the progress of the whole government. Neither branch can compel the other to affirmative action, and each branch can greatly hinder the other in the attainment of the object of its activities and the exercise of its discretion.

The true view of the Executive functions is, as I conceive it, that the President can exercise no power which cannot be fairly and reasonably traced to some specific grant of power or justly implied and included within such express grant as proper and necessary to its exercise. Such specific grant must be either in the Federal Constitution or in an act of Congress passed in pursuance thereof. There is no undefined residuum of power which he can exercise because it seems to him to be in the public interest, and there is nothing in . . . [Supreme Court] precedents, warranting such an inference. The grants of Executive power are necessarily in general terms in order not to embarrass the Executive within the field of action plainly marked for him, but his jurisdiction must be justified and vindicated by affirmative constitutional or statutory provision, or it does not exist. There have not been wanting, however, eminent men in high public office holding a different view and who have insisted upon the necessity for an undefined residuum of Executive power in the public interest. They have not been confined to the present generation. We may learn this from the complaint of a Virginia statesman, Abel P. Upshur, a strict constructionist of the old school, who succeeded Daniel Webster as Secretary of State under President [John] Tyler. He was aroused by [Justice Joseph] Story's commentaries on the Constitution to write a monograph answering and criticizing them, and in the course of this he comments as follows on the Executive power under the Constitution:

The most defective part of the Constitution beyond all question, is that which related to the Executive Department. It is impossible to read that instrument, without being struck with the loose and unguarded terms in which the powers and duties of the President are pointed out. So far as the legislature is concerned, the limitations of the Constitution, are, perhaps, as precise and strict as they could safely have been made; but in regard to the Executive, the Convention appears to have studiously selected such loose and general expressions, as would enable the President, by implication and construction either to neglect his duties or to enlarge his powers. *We have heard it gravely asserted in Congress that whatever power is neither legislative nor judiciary, is of course executive, and, as such, belongs to the President under the Constitution.* How far a majority of that body would have sustained a doctrine so monstrous, and so utterly at war with the whole genius of our government, it is impossible to say, but this, at least, we know, that it met with no rebuke from those who supported the particular act of Executive power, in defense of which it was urged. Be this as it may, it is a reproach to the Constitution that the Executive trust is so ill-defined, as to leave any plausible pretense even to the insane zeal of party devotion, for attributing to the President of the United States the power of a despot; powers which are wholly unknown in any limited monarchy in the world.

The view that he takes as a result of the loose language defining the Executive powers seems exaggerated. But one must agree with him in his condemnation of the view of the Executive power which he says was advanced in Congress. In recent years there has been put forward a similar view by executive officials and to some extent acted on. Men who are not such strict constructionists of the Constitution as Mr. Upshur may well feel real concern if such views are to receive the general acquiescence. Mr. [James R.] Garfield, when Secretary of the Interior, under Mr. Roosevelt, in his final report to Congress in reference to the power of the Executive over the public domain, said:

Full power under the Constitution was vested in the Executive Branch of the Government and the extent to which that power may be exercised is governed wholly by the discretion of the Executive unless any specific act has been prohibited either by the Constitution or by legislation.

In pursuance of this principle, Mr. Garfield, under an act for the reclamation of arid land by irrigation, which authorized him to make contracts for irrigation works and incur liability equal to the amount on deposit in the Reclamation Fund, made contracts with associations of settlers by which it was agreed that if these settlers would advance money and work, they might receive certificates from the government engineers of the labor and money furnished by them, and that such certificates might be received in the future in the discharge of their legal obligations to the government for water rent and other things under the statute. It became necessary for the succeeding [Taft] administration to pass on the validity of these government certificates. They were held by Attorney-General [George] Wickersham to be illegal, on the ground that no authority existed for their issuance. . . .

My judgment is that the view of Mr. Garfield and Mr. Roosevelt, ascribing an undefined residuum of power to the President is an unsafe doctrine and that it might lead under emergencies to results of an arbitrary character, doing irremediable injustice to private right. The mainspring of such a view is that the Executive is charged with responsibility for the welfare of all the people in a general way, that he is to play the part of a Universal Providence and set all things right, and that anything that in his judgment will help the people he ought to do, unless he is expressly forbidden not to do it. The wide field of action that this would give to the Executive one can hardly limit.

❧ 24 ❧

Woodrow Wilson's Fourteen Points*

(1918)

WOODROW WILSON WAS the only political science professor to ever to be able to implement his theories as president. Wilson, who earned his doctorate at Johns Hopkins University and later became a teacher and president of Princeton University, had argued since his student days that the relationship between the president and Congress should be marked by cooperation rather than conflict. Elected president in 1912 after serving less than two years as governor of New Jersey, Wilson led a newly invigorated Democratic Party. During his first term, Wilson persuaded Congress to enact much of his "New Freedom" agenda, designed to marshal the power of the federal government in order to reduce the power of the large corporations that in recent years had come to dominate the nation's economy.

Wilson also fully ushered in the "rhetorical presidency." He believed the president should lead Congress by leading public opinion. With few exceptions, Wilson's nineteenth-century predecessors had eschewed rhetorical leadership, reflecting the prevailing consensus that such an approach would be unseemly. Most dramatically, in 1913 Wilson addressed Congress in person to rouse support for his tariff bill,

*Go to *http://avalon.law.yale.edu/20th_century/wilson14.asp.*

something no president since John Adams had done. Wilson chose to speak directly to Congress, he told the gathered legislators, to demonstrate "that the President of the United States is a person, not a mere department of the Government hailing Congress from some isolated island of jealous power, sending messages, not speaking naturally and with his own voice—that he is a human being trying to co-operate with other human beings in a common service."

Wilson was reelected in 1916, but despite his campaign's boast that "He kept us out of war," his second term was dominated by the war in Europe, which had been raging since 1914. When the war began, Wilson had announced that the United States would remain neutral. But Germany was convinced that American trade was sustaining its adversaries—France and, especially, Great Britain. In January 1917 Germany declared that it would attack without warning any ship that tried to sail through a wide zone in the Atlantic Ocean. On April 2, after a series of unsuccessful protests to the German government, Wilson asked Congress to declare war on Germany. Four days later it did.

Almost from the moment the United States entered the World War, Wilson wanted to issue a clear statement of American objectives. He was dissuaded from doing so by the argument that any such statement would foster disagreement with the other Allied governments. During the fall of 1917, however, Vladimir Lenin, the leader of the recent Bolshevik revolution in Russia, tried to claim the moral high ground by charging that both sides in the war were fighting for selfish nationalist reasons. Wilson decided to publish a statement of American war objectives that expressed his idealistic purposes.

Wilson delivered the "Fourteen Points" address to Congress on January 8, 1918, with each point describing a war aim. The address was successful in several ways. It defused the Russian charge. It infused the war-weary people of the Allied nations with a sense of moral purpose. Several of Wilson's points—including those guaranteeing freedom of the seas (Point II) and free international trade (Point III)—offered assurances to Germany that made it easier for its government to surrender. Eventually, as part of the armistice that ended the war on November 11, 1918, the Allied governments reluctantly accepted the Fourteen Points as the framework for peace negotiations.

Much of the idealism of Wilson's Fourteen Points was lost in the writing of the Treaty of Versailles. The Allies insisted on steep financial reparations from Germany and divided German colonies among themselves. But parts of Wilson's proposal, including the creation of a League of Nations (Point XIV) that could "afford mutual guarantees of political independence and territorial integrity to great and small states alike," were adopted.

Even greater damage to Wilson's war goals was inflicted at home. War weariness made many Americans reluctant to assume the ongoing postwar involvement in world affairs that membership in the League of Nations would require. Wilson's unprecedented appeal to voters on patriotic grounds to give him a Democratic

Congress in the 1918 midterm elections backfired, and the Republicans won control of both the House of Representatives and Senate. Led by its new Foreign Relations Committee chair, Sen. Henry Cabot Lodge of Massachusetts, the Senate rejected the Treaty of Versailles—including the League of Nations—on November 19, 1919.

❧ ❧ ❧

It will be our wish and purpose that the processes of peace, when they are begun, shall be absolutely open and that they shall involve and permit henceforth no secret understandings of any kind. The day of conquest and aggrandizement is gone by; so is also the day of secret covenants entered into in the interest of particular governments and likely at some unlooked-for moment to upset the peace of the world. It is this happy fact, now clear to the view of every public man whose thoughts do not still linger in an age that is dead and gone, which makes it possible for every nation whose purposes are consistent with justice and the peace of the world to avow now or at any other time the objects it has in view.

We entered this war because violations of right had occurred which touched us to the quick and made the life of our own people impossible unless they were corrected and the world secure once for all against their recurrence. What we demand in this war, therefore, is nothing peculiar to ourselves. It is that the world be made fit and safe to live in; and particularly that it be made safe for every peace-loving nation which, like our own, wishes to live its own life, determine its own institutions, be assured of justice and fair dealing by the other peoples of the world as against force and selfish aggression. All the peoples of the world are in effect partners in this interest, and for our own part we see very clearly that unless justice be done to others it will not be done to us. The programme of the world's peace, therefore, is our programme; and that programme, the only possible programme, as we see it, is this:

I. Open covenants of peace, openly arrived at, after which there shall be no private international understandings of any kind but diplomacy shall proceed always frankly and in the public view.

II. Absolute freedom of navigation upon the seas, outside territorial waters, alike in peace and in war, except as the seas may be closed in whole or in part by international action for the enforcement of international covenants.

III. The removal, so far as possible, of all economic barriers and the establishment of an equality of trade conditions among all the nations consenting to the peace and associating themselves for its maintenance.

IV. Adequate guarantees given and taken that national armaments will be reduced to the lowest point consistent with domestic safety.

V. A free, open-minded, and absolutely impartial adjustment of all colonial claims, based upon a strict observance of the principle that in determining all such questions of sovereignty the interests of the populations concerned must have equal weight with the equitable claims of the government whose title is to be determined.

VI. The evacuation of all Russian territory and such a settlement of all questions affecting Russia as will secure the best and freest cooperation of the other nations of the world in obtaining for her an unhampered and unembarrassed opportunity for the independent determination of her own political development and national policy and assure her of a sincere welcome into the society of free nations under institutions of her own choosing; and, more than a welcome, assistance also of every kind that she may need and may herself desire. The treatment accorded Russia by her sister nations in the months to come will be the acid test of their good will, of their comprehension of her needs as distinguished from their own interests, and of their intelligent and unselfish sympathy.

VII. Belgium, the whole world will agree, must be evacuated and restored, without any attempt to limit the sovereignty which she enjoys in common with all other free nations. No other single act will serve as this will serve to restore confidence among the nations in the laws which they have themselves set and determined for the government of their relations with one another. Without this healing act the whole structure and validity of international law is forever impaired.

VIII. All French territory should be freed and the invaded portions restored, and the wrong done to France by Prussia in 1871 in the matter of Alsace-Lorraine, which has unsettled the peace of the world for nearly fifty years, should be righted, in order that peace may once more be made secure in the interest of all.

IX. A readjustment of the frontiers of Italy should be effected along clearly recognizable lines of nationality.

X. The peoples of Austria-Hungary, whose place among the nations we wish to see safeguarded and assured, should be accorded the freest opportunity to autonomous development.

XI. Rumania, Serbia, and Montenegro should be evacuated; occupied territories restored; Serbia accorded free and secure access to the sea; and the relations of the several Balkan states to one another determined by friendly counsel along historically established lines of allegiance and nationality; and international guarantees of the political and economic independence and territorial integrity of the several Balkan states should be entered into.

XII. The Turkish portion of the present Ottoman Empire should be assured a secure sovereignty, but the other nationalities which are now under Turkish rule should be assured an undoubted security of life and an absolutely unmolested opportunity of autonomous development, and the Dardanelles should be permanently opened as a free passage to the ships and commerce of all nations under international guarantees.

XIII. An independent Polish state should be erected which should include the territories inhabited by indisputably Polish populations, which should be assured a free and secure access to the sea, and whose political and economic independence and territorial integrity should be guaranteed by international covenant.

XIV. A general association of nations must be formed under specific covenants for the purpose of affording mutual guarantees of political independence and territorial integrity to great and small states alike.

In regard to these essential rectifications of wrong and assertions of right we feel ourselves to be intimate partners of all the governments and peoples associated together against the Imperialists. We cannot be separated in interest or divided in purpose. We stand together until the end.

For such arrangements and covenants we are willing to fight and to continue to fight until they are achieved; but only because we wish the right to prevail and desire a just and stable peace such as can be secured only by removing the chief provocations to war, which this programme does remove. We have no jealousy of German greatness, and there is nothing in this programme that impairs it. We grudge her no achievement or distinction of learning or of pacific enterprise such as have made her record very bright and very enviable. We do not wish to injure her or to block in any way her legitimate influence or power. We do not wish to fight her either with arms or with hostile arrangements of trade if she is willing to associate herself with us and the other peace-loving nations of the world in covenants of justice and law and fair dealing. We wish her only to accept a place of equality among the peoples of the world,—the new world in which we now live,—instead of a place of mastery.

❧ 25 ❧

*Myers v. United States**

(1926)

ARTICLE II, SECTION 2, of the Constitution authorizes the president to appoint officials to the executive branch with the "Advice and Consent of the Senate." The Constitution is silent, however, about the role of the president and Senate in removing appointees from office.

As shown in Document 6, p. 43, in 1789 the first Congress to meet under the Constitution accepted Rep. James Madison's argument that unless the president alone could remove uncooperative officials from the executive branch, he could not be held accountable for performing the constitutional duty to "take Care that the Laws be faithfully executed." In passing the laws that created the state department

---

*Go to *http://laws.findlaw.com/us/272/52.html.*

and other departments, Congress acknowledged the president's exclusive power of removal. But in 1867 Congress expressed its disagreement with President Andrew Johnson over post–Civil War reconstruction of the South by passing the Tenure of Office Act. The new act required the president to obtain the consent of the Senate before removing any Senate-confirmed executive appointee. Although Congress backed away from the act after Johnson left office, in 1876 it passed a law to give local postmasters a four-year term, with Senate approval required if the president wanted to fire a postmaster before the term expired. Postmasterships were a form of patronage that members of Congress valued highly and wished to protect both from presidential interference and, when the Pendleton Act became law in 1883, from coverage in the new merit-based civil service. (See Document 21, p. 108.)

In 1920 President Woodrow Wilson, as part of a larger effort to make the executive branch more responsive to his policies, fired Portland, Oregon, postmaster Frank Myers without seeking the Senate's consent. When Myers sued to recover his lost salary, the Justice Department did something it had never done: it asked the Supreme Court to declare a federal law, in this case the 1876 act governing postmasters, to be unconstitutional. In the face of Myers's claim that Congress had created the office of postmaster and could legitimately impose conditions on how postmasters were removed, the Justice Department argued (as Madison had in 1789) that by assigning the president the executive power, the Constitution implicitly granted the removal power as well.

In a 6–3 vote, the Supreme Court affirmed the president's exclusive power of removal and declared the 1876 act unconstitutional. It also voided the 1867 Tenure of Office Act, even though Congress had repealed that act nearly forty years earlier, in 1887. The decision was written by Chief Justice William Howard Taft, who had been president himself. In a sweeping assertion of presidential power that resembled Theodore Roosevelt's "stewardship" theory of the presidency more than Taft's own "literalist" theory (see Document 23, p. 116), Taft declared in his opinion for the Court, "The power of removal is incident to the power of appointment, not to the power of advising and consenting to appointment, and when the grant of executive power is enforced by the express mandate to take care that the laws be faithfully executed, it emphasizes the necessity for including within the executive power as conferred the exclusive power of removal." In dissent, Justice Louis Brandeis argued that to prevent Congress from setting conditions for the term and removal of "inferior [subordinate] executive offices involves an unnecessary and indefensible limitation on the constitutional power of Congress to fix the tenure of the inferior statutory offices." Justice Oliver Wendell Holmes, in a separate dissenting opinion, took an even stronger view of Congress's powers.

Taft's interpretation of the president's removal power, which a clear majority of the Court endorsed, was so broad that it left many wondering whether the Constitution allowed Congress to limit the power at all. Beginning in 1887, Congress had created a number of independent regulatory commissions, such as the Interstate

Commerce Commission and the Federal Trade Commission, which were headed by bipartisan boards whose members served fixed terms rather than at the pleasure of the president. The constitutionality of these commissions would be tested nine years later, in *Humphrey's Executor v. United States* (see Document 27, p. 137).

※ ※ ※

MR. CHIEF JUSTICE TAFT delivered the opinion of the Court.

This case presents the question whether under the Constitution the President has the exclusive power of removing executive officers of the United States whom he has appointed by and with the advice and consent of the Senate.

Myers, appellant's intestate, was on July 21, 1917, appointed by the President, by and with the advice and consent of the Senate, to be a postmaster of the first class at Portland, Or., for a term of four years. On January 20, 1920, Myers' resignation was demanded. He refused the demand. On February 2, 1920, he was removed from office by order of the Postmaster General, acting by direction of the President. February 10th, Myers sent a petition to the President and another to the Senate committee on post offices, asking to be heard, if any charges were filed. He protested to the department against his removal, and continued to do so until the end of his term. He pursued no other occupation and drew compensation for no other service during the interval. On April 21, 1921, he brought this suit in the Court of Claims for his salary from the date of his removal, which, as claimed by supplemental petition filed after July 21, 1921, the end of his term, amounted to $8,838.71. In August, 1920, the President made a recess appointment of one Jones, who took office September 19, 1920. . . .

By the sixth section of the Act of Congress of July 12, 1876, 19 Stat. 80, 81, c. 179, under which Myers was appointed with the advice and consent of the Senate as a first-class postmaster, it is provided that:

'Postmasters of the first, second, and third classes shall be appointed and may be removed by the President by and with the advice and consent of the Senate, and shall hold their offices for four years unless sooner removed or suspended according to law.'

The Senate did not consent to the President's removal of Myers during his term.

If this statute in its requirement that his term should be four years unless sooner removed by the President by and with the consent of the Senate is valid, the appellant, Myers' administratrix, is entitled to recover his unpaid salary for his full term and the judgment of the Court of Claims must be reversed. The government maintains that the requirement is invalid, for the reason that under article 2 of the Constitution the President's power of removal of executive officers appointed by him with the advice and consent of the Senate is full and complete without consent of the Senate. . . .

The question where the power of removal of executive officers appointed by the President by and with the advice and consent of the Senate was vested, was presented early in the first session of the First Congress. There is no express provision respecting removals in the Constitution, except as section 4 of article 2 . . . provides for removal from office by impeachment. The subject was not discussed in the Constitutional Convention. . . .

The vesting of the executive power in the President was essentially a grant of the power to execute the laws. But the President alone and unaided could not execute the laws. He must execute them by the assistance of subordinates. This view has since been repeatedly affirmed by this court. . . . As he is charged specifically to take care that they be faithfully executed, the reasonable implication, even in the absence of express words, was that as part of his executive power he should select those who were to act for him under his direction in the execution of the laws. The further implication must be, in the absence of any express limitation respecting removals, that as his selection of administrative officers is essential to the execution of the laws by him, so must be his power of removing those for whom he cannot continue to be responsible. . . . It was urged that the natural meaning of the term 'executive power' granted the President included the appointment and removal of executive subordinates. If such appointments and removals were not an exercise of the executive power, what were they? They certainly were not the exercise of legislative or judicial power in government as usually understood. . . .

[T]he power of removal, though equally essential to the executive power is different in its nature from that of appointment. . . . A veto by the Senate—a part of the legislative branch of the government—upon removals is a much greater limitation upon the executive branch, and a much more serious blending of the legislative with the executive, than a rejection of a proposed appointment. It is not to be implied. The rejection of a nominee of the President for a particular office does not greatly embarrass him in the conscientious discharge of his high duties in the selection of those who are to aid him, because the President usually has an ample field from which to select for office, according to his preference, competent and capable men. The Senate has full power to reject newly proposed appointees whenever the President shall remove the incumbents. Such a check enables the Senate to prevent the filling of offices with bad or incompetent men, or with those against whom there is tenable objection.

The power to prevent the removal of an officer who has served under the President is different from the authority to consent to or reject his appointment. When a nomination is made, it may be presumed that the Senate is, or may become, as well advised as to the fitness of the nominee as the President, but in the nature of things the defects in ability or intelligence or loyalty in the administration of the laws of one who has served as an officer under the President are facts as to which the President, or his trusted subordinates, must be better informed than the Senate, and the power to remove him may therefore be regarded as confined for very sound and practical reasons, to the governmental authority which has administrative control. The power of removal is incident to the power of appointment, not to the power of advising and consenting to appointment, and when the grant of the executive power is enforced by the express mandate to take care that the laws be faithfully executed, it emphasizes the necessity for including within the executive power as conferred the exclusive power of removal. . . .

A reference of the whole power of removal to general legislation by Congress is quite out of keeping with the plan of government devised by the framers of the Constitution. It could never have been intended to leave to Congress unlimited discretion to vary fundamentally the operation of the great independent executive branch of government and thus most seriously to weaken it. It would be a delegation by the convention to Congress of the function of defining the primary boundaries of another of the three great divisions of government. The inclusion of removals of executive officers in the executive power vested in the President by article 2 according to its usual definition, and the implication of his power of removal of such officers from the provision of section 2 expressly recognizing in him the power of their appointment, are a much more natural and appropriate source of the removing power.

It is reasonable to suppose also that had it been intended to give to Congress power to regulate or control removals in the manner suggested, it would have been included among the specifically enumerated legislative powers in article 1, or in the specified limitations on the executive power in article 2. The difference between the grant of legislative power under article 1 to Congress which is limited to powers therein enumerated, and the more general grant of the executive power to the President under article 2 is significant. The fact that the executive power is given in general terms strengthened by specific terms where emphasis is appropriate, and limited by direct expressions where limitation is needed, and that no express limit is placed on the power of removal by the executive is a convincing indication that none was intended. . . .

We come now to consider an argument, advanced and strongly pressed on behalf of the complainant, that this case concerns only the removal of a postmaster, that a postmaster is an inferior officer, and that such an office was not included within the legislative decision of 1789, which related only to superior officers to be appointed by the President by and with the advice and consent of the Senate. . . .

The power to remove inferior executive officers, like that to remove superior executive officers, is an incident of the power to appoint them, and is in its nature an executive power. The authority of Congress given by the excepting clause to vest the appointment of such inferior officers in the heads of departments carries with it authority incidentally to invest the heads of departments with power to remove. It has been the practice of Congress to do so and this court has recognized that power. . . . But the court never has held, nor reasonably could hold, although it is argued to the contrary on behalf of the appellant, that the excepting clause enables Congress to draw to itself, or to either branch of it, the power to remove or the right to participate in the exercise of that power. To do this would be to go beyond the words and implications of that clause, and to infringe the constitutional principle of the separation of governmental powers. . . .

What, then, are the elements that enter into our decision of this case? We have, first, a construction of the Constitution made by a Congress which was to provide by legislation for the organization of the government in accord with the Constitution which had just then been adopted, and in which there were, as Representatives and Senators, a considerable number of those who had been members of the convention that framed the Constitution and presented it for ratification. It was the Congress that launched the government. It was the Congress that rounded out the Constitution itself by the proposing of the first 10 amendments, which had in effect been promised to the people as a consideration for the ratification. It was the Congress in which Mr. Madison, one of the first in the framing of the Constitution, led also in the organization of the government under it. It was a Congress whose constitutional decisions have always been regarded, as they should be regarded, as of the greatest weight in the interpretation of that fundamental instrument. This construction was followed by the legislative department and the executive department continuously for 78 years [until passage of the Tenure of Office Act of 1867]. . . .

We are now asked to set aside this construction thus buttressed and adopt an adverse view, because the Congress of the United States did so during a heated political difference of opinion between the then President and the majority leaders of Congress over the reconstruction measures adopted as a means of restoring to their proper status the states which attempted to withdraw from the Union at the time of the Civil War. The extremes to which the majority in both Houses carried legislative measures in that matter are now recognized by all who calmly review the history of that episode in our government leading to articles of impeachment against President Johnson and his acquittal. Without animadverting on the character of the measures taken, we are certainly justified in saying that they should not be given the weight affecting proper constitutional construction to be accorded to that reached by the First Congress of the United States during a political calm and acquiesced in by the whole government for three-quarters of a century, especially when the new construction contended for has never been acquiesced in by either the executive or the judicial departments. While this court has studiously avoided deciding the issue until it was presented in such a way that it could not be avoided, in the references it has made to the history of the question, and in the presumptions it has indulged in favor of a statutory construction not inconsistent with the legislative decision of 1789, it has indicated a trend of view that we should not and cannot ignore. When on the merits we find our conclusion strongly favoring the view which prevailed in the First Congress, we have no hesitation in holding that conclusion to be correct; and it therefore follows that the Tenure of Office Act of 1867, in so far as it attempted to prevent the President from removing executive officers who had been appointed by him by and with the advice and consent of the Senate, was invalid, and that subsequent legislation of the same effect was equally so.

For the reasons given, we must therefore hold that the provision of the law of 1876 by which the unrestricted power of removal of first-class postmasters is denied to the President is in violation of the Constitution and invalid. This leads to an affirmance of the judgment of the Court of Claims. . . .

Judgment affirmed.

MR. JUSTICE BRANDEIS, DISSENTING.

. . . May the President, having acted under the statute in so far as it creates the office and authorizes the appointment, ignore, while the Senate is in session, the provision which prescribes the condition under which a removal may take place?

It is this narrow question, and this only, which we are required to decide. We need not consider what power the President, being Commander-in-Chief, has over officers in the Army and the Navy. We need not determine whether the President, acting alone, may remove high political officers. We need not even determine whether, acting alone, he may remove inferior civil officers when the Senate is not in session. It was in session when the President purported to remove Myers, and for a long time thereafter. . . .

The argument is that appointment and removal of officials are executive prerogatives; that the grant to the President of 'the executive power' confers upon him, as inherent in the office, the power to exercise these two functions without restriction by Congress, except in so far as the power to restrict his exercise of then is expressly conferred upon Congress by the Constitution; that in respect to appointment certain restrictions of the executive power are so provided for; but that in respect to removal there is no express grant to Congress of any power to limit the President's prerogative. The simple answer to the argument is this: The ability to remove a subordinate executive officer, being an essential of effective government, will, in the absence of express constitutional provision to the contrary, be deemed to have been vested in some person or body. . . . But it is not a power inherent in a chief executive. The President's power of removal from statutory civil inferior offices, like the power of appointment to them, comes immediately from Congress. It is true that the exercise of the power of removal is said to be an executive act, and that when the Senate grants or withholds consent to a removal by the President, it participates in an executive act. But the Constitution has confessedly granted to Congress the legislative power to create offices, and to prescribe the tenure thereof; and it has not in terms denied to Congress the power to control removals. To prescribe the tenure involves prescribing the conditions under which incumbency shall cease. For the possibility of removal is a condition or qualification of the tenure. When Congress provides that the incumbent shall hold the office for four years unless sooner removed with the consent of the Senate, it prescribes the term of the tenure. . . .

The separation of the powers of government did not make each branch completely autonomous. It left each in some measure, dependent upon the others, as it left to each power to exercise, in some respects, functions in their nature executive, legislative and judicial. Obviously the President cannot secure full execution of the laws, if Congress denies to him adequate means of doing so. Full execution may be defeated because Congress declines to create offices indispensable for that purpose; or because Congress, having created the office, declines to make the indispensable appropriation; or because Congress, having both created the office and made the appropriation, prevents, by restrictions which it imposes, the appointment of officials who in quality and character are indispensable to the efficient execution of the law. If, in any such way, adequate means are denied to the President, the fault will lie with Congress. The President performs his full constitutional duty, if, with the means and instruments provided by Congress and within the limitations prescribed by it, he uses his best endeavors to secure the faithful execution of the laws enacted. . . .

The doctrine of the separation of powers was adopted by the convention of 1787 not to promote efficiency but to preclude the exercise of arbitrary power. The purpose was not to avoid friction, but, by means of the inevitable friction incident to the distribution of the governmental powers among three departments, to save the people from autocracy. . . .

MR. JUSTICE HOLMES, DISSENTING.

. . . We have to deal with an office that owes its existence to Congress and that Congress may abolish to-morrow. Its duration and the pay attached to it while it lasts depend on Congress alone. Congress alone confers on the President the power to appoint to it and at any time may transfer the power to other hands. With such power over its own creation, I have no more trouble in believing that Congress has power to prescribe a term of life for it free from any interference than I have in accepting the undoubted power of Congress to decree its end. I have equally little trouble in accepting its power to prolong the tenure of an incumbent until Congress or the Senate shall have assented to his removal. The duty of the President to see that the laws be executed is a duty that does not go beyond the laws or require him to achieve more than Congress sees fit to leave within his power.

❧ 26 ❧

Franklin D. Roosevelt's First Inaugural Address

(1933)

FRANKLIN D. ROOSEVELT was the last president to be inaugurated on March 4. The Twentieth Amendment (1933) advanced the start of the president's term to January 20, but not in time to affect Roosevelt's first inauguration. During the long winter between Roosevelt's landslide election against President Herbert C. Hoover in November 1932 and his inauguration the following March, the Great Depression that had sunk the nation into economic inactivity worsened. Factories for producing goods and land for growing crops were abundant, but they had fallen into disuse. On February 14 Roosevelt was the target of an assassination attempt in Miami by an unemployed bricklayer.

Roosevelt saw one of his main challenges as restoring the people's confidence in government and raising their morale. It was a challenge to which he was well suited, despite his privileged upbringing on a family estate in Hyde Park, New York. Although Roosevelt's bout with polio in the early 1920s left him disabled for the rest of his life, it also gave the self-confident and infectiously optimistic president a newfound empathy for those who suffer. In the best-remembered line of his 1933 inaugural address, one of the first to be broadcast nationally by radio, Roosevelt proclaimed that "the only thing we have to fear is fear itself—nameless, unreasoning, unjustified terror which paralyzes needed efforts to convert retreat into advance."

Roosevelt also used the address to make clear his contempt for the probusiness policies of the Harding, Coolidge, and Hoover administrations. "The money changers have fled from their high seats in the temple of our civilization," he said.

"We may now restore that temple to the ancient truths. The measure of that restoration lies in the extent to which we apply social values more noble than mere monetary profit."

Roosevelt pledged to "act, and act quickly" to combat the Great Depression, using and perhaps extending the full powers of the presidency to do so. "It is to be hoped," Roosevelt said, "that the normal balance of executive and legislative authority may be wholly adequate to meet the unprecedented task before us. . . . But in the event that . . . the national emergency is still critical . . . I shall ask the Congress for the one remaining instrument to meet the crisis—broad executive power to wage a war against the emergency as great as the power that would be given me if we were in fact invaded by a foreign foe."

Roosevelt's cousin, former president Theodore Roosevelt, was the first to describe the presidency as a "bully pulpit" for moral leadership. Franklin Roosevelt made full use of that pulpit in 1933 and afterward. Responding to his inaugural address, around 500,000 people wrote to express their thanks and support in an unprecedented outpouring of mail to the White House. A little more than a week after his inauguration, on March 13, Roosevelt delivered the first of twenty-seven informal radio addresses, called "fireside chats," which marked a revolutionary change in presidential communications. (See Document 29, p. 146.)

In his acceptance speech at the 1932 Democratic Convention, Roosevelt had pledged "a new deal for the American people." The vague words became the catchphrase for his presidency. More than anything else, "New Deal" came to mean presidentially sponsored government programs to support both the general goal of economic prosperity and the particular needs of people who were suffering economic distress.

𝒜 𝒜 𝒜

President Hoover, Mr. Chief Justice, my friends:

This is a day of national consecration, and I am certain that my fellow Americans expect that on my induction into the Presidency I will address them with a candor and a decision which the present situation of our nation impels.

This is pre-eminently the time to speak the truth, the whole truth, frankly and boldly. Nor need we shrink from honestly facing conditions in our country today. This great nation will endure as it has endured, will revive and will prosper.

So first of all let me assert my firm belief that the only thing we have to fear is fear itself—nameless, unreasoning, unjustified terror which paralyzes needed efforts to convert retreat into advance.

In every dark hour of our national life a leadership of frankness and vigor has met with that understanding and support of the people themselves which is essential to victory. I am convinced that you will again give that support to leadership in these critical days.

In such a spirit on my part and on yours we face our common difficulties. They concern, thank God, only material things. Values have shrunken to fantastic levels; taxes have risen; our ability to pay has fallen; government of all kinds is faced by serious curtailment of income; the means of exchange are frozen in the currents of trade; the withered leaves of industrial enterprise lie on every side; farmers find no markets for their produce; the savings of many years in thousands of families are gone.

More important, a host of unemployed citizens face the grim problem of existence, and an equally great number toil with little return. Only a foolish optimist can deny the dark realities of the moment.

Yet our distress comes from no failure of substance. We are stricken by no plague of locusts. Compared with the perils which our forefathers conquered because they believed and were not afraid, we have still much to be thankful for. Nature still offers her bounty and human efforts have multiplied it. Plenty is at our doorstep, but a generous use of it languishes in the very sight of the supply.

Primarily, this is because the rulers of the exchange of mankind's goods have failed through their own stubbornness and their own incompetence, have admitted their failure and abdicated. Practices of the unscrupulous money changers stand indicted in the court of public opinion, rejected by the hearts and minds of men. True, they have tried, but their efforts have been cast in the pattern of an outworn tradition. Faced by failure of credit, they have proposed only the lending of more money.

Stripped of the lure of profit by which to induce our people to follow their false leadership, they have resorted to exhortations, pleading tearfully for restored confidence. They know only the rules of a generation of self-seekers.

They have no vision, and when there is no vision the people perish.

The money changers have fled from their high seats in the temple of our civilization. We may now restore that temple to the ancient truths.

The measure of the restoration lies in the extent to which we apply social values more noble than mere monetary profit.

Happiness lies not in the mere possession of money; it lies in the joy of achievement, in the thrill of creative effort.

The joy and moral stimulation of work no longer must be forgotten in the mad chase of evanescent profits. These dark days will be worth all they cost us if they teach us that our true destiny is not to be ministered unto but to minister to ourselves and to our fellow-men.

Recognition of the falsity of material wealth as the standard of success goes hand in hand with the abandonment of the false belief that public office and high political position are to be valued only by the standards of pride of place and personal profit; and there must be an end to a conduct in banking and in business which too often has given to a sacred trust the likeness of callous and selfish wrongdoing.

Small wonder that confidence languishes, for it thrives only on honesty, on honor, on the sacredness of obligations, on faithful protection, on unselfish performance. Without them it cannot live.

Restoration calls, however, not for changes in ethics alone. This nation asks for action, and action now.

Our greatest primary task is to put people to work. This is no unsolvable problem if we face it wisely and courageously.

It can be accomplished in part by direct recruiting by the government itself, treating the task as we would treat the emergency of a war, but at the same time, through this employment accomplishing greatly needed projects to stimulate and reorganize the use of our natural resources.

Hand in hand with this, we must frankly recognize the overbalance of population in our industrial centers and, by engaging on a national scale in the redistribution, endeavor to provide a better use of the land for those best fitted for the land.

The task can be helped by definite efforts to raise the values of agricultural products and with this the power to purchase the output of our cities.

It can be helped by preventing realistically the tragedy of the growing loss, through foreclosure, of our small homes and our farms.

It can be helped by insistence that the Federal, State and local governments act forthwith on the demand that their cost be drastically reduced.

It can be helped by the unifying of relief activities which today are often scattered, uneconomical and unequal. It can be helped by national planning for and supervision of all forms of transportation and of communications and other utilities which have a definitely public character.

There are many ways in which it can be helped, but it can never be helped merely by talking about it. We must act, and act quickly.

Finally, in our progress toward a resumption of work we require two safeguards against a return of the evils of the old order; there must be a strict supervision of all banking and credits and investments, there must be an end to speculation with other people's money, and there must be provision for an adequate but sound currency.

These are the lines of attack. I shall presently urge upon a new Congress in special session detailed measures for their fulfillment, and I shall seek the immediate assistance of the several States.

Through this program of action we address ourselves to putting our own national house in order and making income balance outgo.

Our international trade relations, though vastly important, are, in point of time and necessity, secondary to the establishment of a sound national economy.

I favor as a practical policy the putting of first things first. I shall spare no effort to restore world trade by international economic readjustment, but the emergency at home cannot wait on that accomplishment.

The basic thought that guides these specific means of national recovery is not narrowly nationalistic.

It is the insistence, as a first consideration, upon the interdependence of the various elements in, and parts of, the United States—a recognition of the old and permanently important manifestation of the American spirit of the pioneer.

It is the way to recovery. It is the immediate way. It is the strongest assurance that the recovery will endure.

In the field of world policy I would dedicate this nation to the policy of the good neighbor—the neighbor who resolutely respects himself and, because he does so, respects the rights of others—the neighbor who respects his obligations and respects the sanctity of his agreements in and with a world of neighbors.

If I read the temper of our people correctly, we now realize as we have never before, our interdependence on each other; that we cannot merely take, but we must give as well; that if we are to go forward we must move as a trained and loyal army willing to sacrifice for the good of a common discipline, because, without such discipline, no progress is made, no leadership becomes effective.

We are, I know, ready and willing to submit our lives and property to such discipline because it makes possible a leadership which aims at a larger good.

This I propose to offer, pledging that the larger purposes will bind upon us all as a sacred obligation with a unity of duty hitherto evoked only in time of armed strife.

With this pledge taken, I assume unhesitatingly the leadership of this great army of our people, dedicated to a disciplined attack upon our common problems.

Action in this image and to this end is feasible under the form of government which we have inherited from our ancestors.

Our Constitution is so simple and practical that it is possible always to meet extraordinary needs by changes in emphasis and arrangement without loss of essential form.

That is why our constitutional system has proved itself the most superbly enduring political mechanism the modern world has produced. It has met every stress of vast expansion of territory, of foreign wars, of bitter internal strife, of world relations.

It is to be hoped that the normal balance of executive and legislative authority may be wholly adequate to meet the unprecedented task before us. But it may be that an unprecedented demand and need for undelayed action may call for temporary departure from that normal balance of public procedure.

I am prepared under my constitutional duty to recommend the measures that a stricken nation in the midst of a stricken world may require.

These measures, or such other measures as the Congress may build out of its experience and wisdom, I shall seek, within my constitutional authority, to bring to speedy adoption.

But in the event that the Congress shall fail to take one of these two courses, and in the event that the national emergency is still critical, I shall not evade the clear course of duty that will then confront me.

I shall ask the Congress for the one remaining instrument to meet the crisis— broad executive power to wage a war against the emergency as great as the power that would be given me if we were in fact invaded by a foreign foe.

For the trust reposed in me I will return the courage and the devotion that befit the time. I can do no less.

We face the arduous days that lie before us in the warm courage of national unity; with the clear consciousness of seeking old and precious moral values; with the clean satisfaction that comes from the stern performance of duty by old and young alike.

We aim at the assurance of a rounded and permanent national life.

We do not distrust the future of essential democracy. The people of the United States have not failed. In their need they have registered a mandate that they want direct, vigorous action.

They have asked for discipline and direction under leadership. They have made me the present instrument of their wishes. In the spirit of the gift I take it.

In this dedication of a nation we humbly ask the blessing of God. May He protect each and every one of us! May He guide me in the days to come!

❧ 27 ❧
*Humphrey's Executor v. United States**
(1935)

FOR NEARLY A CENTURY AND A HALF, controversy about the president's removal power vexed the political system. The Constitution, so clear in stating that presidential appointments to the executive branch must obtain "the Advice and Consent of the Senate," was silent about the Senate's role, if any, in removing appointees from office. In 1789 the First Congress had acknowledged the president's exclusive power of removal. (See Document 6, p. 43.) But in 1867 Congress passed the Tenure of Office Act, which required the president to obtain the Senate's consent before replacing any Senate-confirmed appointee.

After Andrew Johnson, at whom the tenure act was aimed, left office, Congress softened the removal requirement but did not eliminate it. In 1926 the Supreme Court weighed in, strengthening the president's power by declaring in *Myers v. United States* that a law requiring the Senate's consent before the president could fire a postmaster was unconstitutional. (See Document 25, p. 125.) A former president, Chief Justice William Howard Taft, wrote the opinion of the Court. "The power of removal is incident to the [president's] power of appointment," Taft ruled, "not to the [Senate's] power of advising and consenting."

Taft's opinion was so sweeping in its defense of the president's removal power as to suggest that no government officials except legislators, judges, and the vice president were immune from presidential dismissal for any reason. By implication, members of an independent regulatory agency such as the Interstate Commerce Commission (ICC) and the Federal Trade Commission (FTC) served at the pleasure of the president, even though Congress had assigned these members terms of fixed duration that, by law, could be abridged only for "inefficiency, neglect of duty, or malfeasance in office."

In 1933 President Franklin D. Roosevelt wrote a series of letters to William E. Humphrey, an outspoken administration critic who had been appointed to a seven-year term on the FTC by President Herbert C. Hoover in 1931. Roosevelt's

*Go to *http://laws.findlaw.com/us/295/602.html.*

first letter asked Humphrey to resign as commissioner so that "the aims and purposes of the Administration with respect to the work of the Commission can be carried out most effectively with personnel of my own choosing." (The FTC had jurisdiction over several New Deal programs.) When Humphrey refused, Roosevelt notified him on October 7 that he was fired.

Humphrey died in early 1934, never having accepted the legality of his removal. The executor of his estate sued the government for the salary Humphrey was not paid after being forced from office. The executor argued that Roosevelt had fired Humphrey for legally impermissible political reasons.

The case reached the Supreme Court, which sided with Humphrey's executor by a unanimous 9–0 vote. Writing for the Court, Justice George Sutherland argued that the *Myers* ruling did not apply to a situation like Humphrey's. Because Frank Myers, a postmaster, had been employed by a federal agency that clearly was "an arm or an eye of the Executive," the president's constitutional responsibility as chief executive included the power to remove him, unfettered by Congress. But the FTC, like other independent regulatory agencies, was "an administrative body created by Congress to carry into effect legislative policies," and Congress had the constitutional right to legislate its own guidelines for removing Humphrey or any other employee.

The Supreme Court's decision in *Humphrey's Executor* was announced on May 27, 1935. It was one of a historically unprecedented series of decisions in 1935 and 1936 that overturned presidential actions and administration-supported laws. Yet *Humphrey's Executor* reportedly infuriated Roosevelt more than any other case—he took it as a personal insult by the justices—and, in the opinion of some of his aides, provoked the president to try to "pack" the Court. (See Document 29, p. 146.)

⁂ ⁂ ⁂

MR. JUSTICE SUTHERLAND delivered the opinion of the Court. . . .

First. The question first to be considered is whether, by the provisions of §1 of the Federal Trade Commission Act already quoted, the President's power is limited to removal for the specific causes enumerated therein. . . .

The commission is to be non-partisan; and it must, from the very nature of its duties, act with entire impartiality. It is charged with the enforcement of no policy except the policy of the law. Its duties are neither political nor executive, but predominantly quasi-judicial and quasi-legislative. Like the Interstate Commerce Commission, its members are called upon to exercise the trained judgment of a body of experts "appointed by law and informed by experience." *Illinois Central R.R. Co. v. Interstate Commerce Comm'n,* 206 U.S. 441, 454; *Standard Oil Co. v. United States,* 283 U.S. 235, 238–239.

The legislative reports in both houses of Congress clearly reflect the view that a fixed term was necessary to the effective and fair administration of the law. . . .

The debates in both houses demonstrate that the prevailing view was that the commission was not to be "subject to anybody in the government but . . . only to the people of the United States"; free from "political domination or control" or the "probability or possibility of such a thing"; to be "separate and apart from any existing department of the government—not subject to the orders of the President."

More to the same effect appears in the debates, which were long and thorough and contain nothing to the contrary. While the general rule precludes the use of these debates to explain the meaning of the words of the statute, they may be considered as reflecting light upon its general purposes and the evils which it sought to remedy. *Federal Trade Comm'n v. Raladam Co.*, 283 U.S. 643, 650.

Thus, the language of the act, the legislative reports, and the general purposes of the legislation as reflected by the debates, all combine to demonstrate the Congressional intent to create a body of experts who shall gain experience by length of service—a body which shall be independent of executive authority, *except in its selection,* and free to exercise its judgment without the leave or hindrance of any other official or any department of the government. To the accomplishment of these purposes, it is clear that Congress was of opinion that length and certainty of tenure would vitally contribute. And to hold that, nevertheless, the members of the commission continue in office at the mere will of the President, might be to thwart, in large measure, the very ends which Congress sought to realize by definitely fixing the term of office.

We conclude that the intent of the act is to limit the executive power of removal to the causes enumerated, the existence of none of which is claimed here; and we pass to the second question.

Second. To support its contention that the removal provision of § 1, as we have just construed it, is an unconstitutional interference with the executive power of the President, the government's chief reliance is *Myers v. United States,* 272 U.S. 52. That case has been so recently decided, and the prevailing and dissenting opinions so fully review the general subject of the power of executive removal, that further discussion would add little of value to the wealth of material there collected. These opinions examine at length the historical, legislative and judicial data bearing upon the question, beginning with what is called "the decision of 1789" in the first Congress and coming down almost to the day when the opinions were delivered. They occupy 243 pages of the volume in which they are printed. Nevertheless, the narrow point actually decided was only that the President had power to remove a postmaster of the first class, without the advice and consent of the Senate as required by act of Congress. In the course of the opinion of the court, expressions occur which tend to sustain the government's contention, but these are beyond the point involved and, therefore, do not come within the rule of *stare decisis.* In so far as they are out of harmony with the views here set forth, these expressions are disapproved. . . .

The office of a postmaster is so essentially unlike the office now involved that the decision in the *Myers* case cannot be accepted as controlling our decision here. A postmaster is an executive officer restricted to the performance of executive functions. He is charged with no duty at all related to either the legislative or judicial power. The actual decision in the *Myers* case finds support in the theory that such an officer is merely one of the units in the executive department and, hence, inherently subject to the exclusive and illimitable power of removal by the Chief Executive, whose subordinate and aid he is. Putting aside *dicta,* which may be followed if sufficiently persuasive but which are not controlling, the necessary reach of the decision goes far enough to include all purely executive officers. It goes no farther;—much less does it include an officer who occupies no place in the executive department and who exercises no part of the executive power vested by the Constitution in the President.

The Federal Trade Commission is an administrative body created by Congress to carry into effect legislative policies embodied in the statute in accordance with the legislative standard therein prescribed, and to perform other specified duties as a legislative or as a judicial aid. Such a body cannot in any proper sense be characterized as an arm or an eye of the executive. Its duties are performed without executive leave and, in the contemplation of the statute, must be free from executive control. In administering the provisions of the statute in respect of "unfair methods of competition"—that is to say in filling in and administering the details embodied by that general standard—the commission acts in part quasi-legislatively and in part quasi-judicially. In making investigations and reports thereon for the information of Congress under § 6, in aid of the legislative power, it acts as a legislative agency. Under § 7, which authorizes the commission to act as a master in chancery under rules prescribed by the court, it acts as an agency of the judiciary. To the extent that it exercises any executive function—as distinguished from executive power in the constitutional sense—it does so in the discharge and effectuation of its quasi-legislative or quasi-judicial powers, or as an agency of the legislative or judicial departments of the government.[1]

If Congress is without authority to prescribe causes for removal of members of the trade commission and limit executive power of removal accordingly, that power at once becomes practically all-inclusive in respect of civil officers with the exception of the judiciary provided for by the Constitution. The Solicitor General, at the bar, apparently recognizing this to be true, with commendable candor, agreed that his view in respect of the removability of members of the Federal Trade Commission necessitated a like view in respect of the Interstate Commerce Commission and the Court of Claims. We are thus confronted with the serious question whether not only the members of these quasi-legislative and quasi-judicial bodies, but the judges of the legislative Court of Claims, exercising judicial power (*Williams v. United States,* 289 U.S. 553, 565–567), continue in office only at the pleasure of the President.

We think it plain under the Constitution that illimitable power of removal is not possessed by the President in respect of officers of the character of those just named. The authority of Congress, in creating quasi-legislative or quasi-judicial agencies, to require them to act in discharge of their duties independently of executive control cannot well be doubted; and that authority includes, as an appropriate incident, power to fix the period during which they shall continue in office, and to forbid their removal except for cause in the meantime. For it is quite evident that one who holds his office only during the pleasure of another, cannot be depended upon to maintain an attitude of independence against the latter's will.

The fundamental necessity of maintaining each of the three general departments of government entirely free from the control or coercive influence, direct or indirect, of either of the others, has often been stressed and is hardly open to serious question. So much is implied in the very fact of the separation of the powers of these departments by the Constitution; and in the rule which recognizes their essential co-equality. The sound application of a principle that makes one master in his own house precludes him from imposing his control in the house of another who is master there. James Wilson, one of the framers of the Constitution and a former justice of this court, said that the independence of each department required that its proceedings "should be free from the remotest influence, direct or indirect, of either of the other two powers." Andrews, *The Works of James Wilson* (1896), vol. 1, p. 367. And Mr. Justice Story in the first volume of his work on the Constitution, 4th ed., § 530, citing No. 48 of the *Federalist,* said that neither of the departments in reference to each other "ought to possess, directly or indirectly, an overruling influence in the administration of their respective powers." And see *O'Donoghue v. United States, supra,* at pp. 530–531.

The power of removal here claimed for the President falls within this principle, since its coercive influence threatens the independence of a commission, which is not only wholly disconnected from the executive department, but which, as already fully appears, was created by Congress as a means of carrying into operation legislative and judicial powers, and as an agency of the legislative and judicial departments. . . .

The result of what we now have said is this: Whether the power of the President to remove an officer shall prevail over the authority of Congress to condition the power by fixing a definite term and precluding a removal except for cause, will depend upon the character of the office; the *Myers* decision, affirming the power of the President alone to make the removal is confined to purely executive officers; and as to officers of the kind here under consideration, we hold that no removal can be made during the prescribed term for which the officer is appointed, except for one or more of the causes named in the applicable statute.

To the extent that, between the decision in the *Myers* case, which sustains the unrestrictable power of the President to remove purely executive officers, and our present decision that such power does not extend to an office such as that here involved, there shall remain a field of doubt, we leave such cases as may fall within it for future consideration and determination as they may arise. . . .

NOTE

1. The provision of § 6 (d) of the act which authorizes the President to direct an investigation and report by the commission in relation to alleged violations of the anti-trust acts, is so obviously collateral to the main design of the act as not to detract from the force of this general statement as to the character of that body.

28

United States v. Curtiss-Wright Export Corp.*

(1936)

U NITED STATES V. CURTISS-WRIGHT EXPORT CORP. is arguably the Supreme
Court's most important decision concerning the president's constitutional
powers in foreign affairs. The expansive view of presidential authority that the
decision endorsed is all the more remarkable because in 1935 and 1936 the Court
was unusually hostile to the New Deal domestic policies of President Franklin D.
Roosevelt. Indeed, the author of the Court's opinion in the case, Justice George
Sutherland, was one of the New Deal's most ardent judicial foes. Yet, in *United
States v. Curtiss-Wright,* Sutherland and his fellow justices promulgated a constitutional theory that echoed Alexander Hamilton's Pacificus letters by describing
"the President as the sole organ of the federal government in the field of international relations," even though the Constitution did not explicitly confer such a
role. (See Document 7, p. 47.)

The *Curtiss-Wright* case was triggered by the government's effort to limit the
so-called Chaco War between Bolivia and Paraguay, which had taken 100,000
lives and jeopardized the peace of much of South America. On May 28, 1934,
Congress passed a joint resolution granting the president power to prohibit, at his
discretion, the sale of any or all American-made arms to the two nations. Later
that day, Roosevelt issued an order banning all such sales.

Curtiss-Wright Export Corporation was indicted in 1936 for conspiring to sell
military equipment to Bolivia in violation of the president's order. The corporation and its officers responded by challenging in federal court the constitutionality of the law under which Roosevelt acted. They claimed that Congress had made
an unconstitutional delegation of power to the president.

In favoring the president's position in the case, the Court could simply have
decided that Congress's delegation of power was constitutional. But in several
recent rulings that overturned Roosevelt's New Deal domestic programs, Sutherland and his conservative colleagues had accused Congress of delegating power to
the president indiscriminately and improperly. The Court needed a new constitutional theory to justify the actions of the president and Congress in the *Curtiss-
Wright* case.

Sutherland found his theory in the concept of sovereignty. The United States
had been formed as a nation, he noted, by thirteen previously separate states.
These states had domestic powers at the time they united and, in writing the

*Go to *http://laws.findlaw.com/us/299/304.html.*

Constitution, they had described which of these powers would be granted to the national government. But, Sutherland argued, because the states never had power to deal in international relations, the national government formed by the Constitution did not have to rely for its foreign affairs powers on any explicit constitutional authorization. Instead, as the plan of government for a nation, the Constitution implicitly granted the national government all the traditional sovereign powers that any nation wields, except as specifically limited by the document itself.

The sovereign powers of the United States in international affairs, Sutherland continued, obviously reside in the president. "[H]e, not Congress, has the better opportunity of knowing the conditions which prevail in foreign countries, and especially is this true in time of war. He has his confidential sources of information. He has his agents in the form of diplomatic, consular, and other officials," Sutherland wrote. Indeed, the Court's opinion suggested that Roosevelt may not even have needed Congress's permission to ban the sale of arms to Bolivia and Paraguay.

⁂ ⁂ ⁂

MR. JUSTICE SUTHERLAND delivered the opinion of the Court. . . .

Whether, if the Joint Resolution had related solely to internal affairs it would be open to the challenge that it constituted an unlawful delegation of legislative power to the Executive, we find it unnecessary to determine. The whole aim of the resolution is to affect a situation entirely external to the United States, and falling within the category of foreign affairs. The determination which we are called to make, therefore, is whether the Joint Resolution, as applied to that situation, is vulnerable to attack under the rule that forbids a delegation of the law-making power. In other words, assuming (but not deciding) that the challenged delegation, if it were confined to internal affairs, would be invalid, may it nevertheless be sustained on the ground that its exclusive aim is to afford a remedy for a hurtful condition within foreign territory?

It will contribute to the elucidation of the question if we first consider the differences between the powers of the federal government in respect of foreign or external affairs and those in respect of domestic or internal affairs. That there are differences between them, and that these differences are fundamental, may not be doubted.

The two classes of powers are different, both in respect of their origin and their nature. The broad statement that the federal government can exercise no powers except those specifically enumerated in the Constitution, and such implied powers as are necessary and proper to carry into effect the enumerated powers, is categorically true only in respect of our internal affairs. In that field, the primary purpose of the Constitution was to carve from the general mass of legislative powers *then possessed by the states* such portions as it was thought desirable to vest in the federal government, leaving those not included in the enumeration still in the states. *Carter v. Carter Coal Co.,* 298

U.S. 238, 294. That this doctrine applies only to powers which the states had, is self evident. And since the states severally never possessed international powers, such powers could not have been carved from the mass of state powers but obviously were transmitted to the United States from some other source. During the colonial period, those powers were possessed exclusively by and were entirely under the control of the Crown. By the Declaration of Independence, "the Representatives of the United States of America" declared the United [not the several] Colonies to be free and independent states, and as such to have "full Power to levy War, conclude Peace, contract Alliances, establish Commerce and to do all other Acts and Things which Independent States may of right do."

As a result of the separation from Great Britain by the colonies acting as a unit, the powers of external sovereignty passed from the Crown not to the colonies severally, but to the colonies in their collective and corporate capacity as the United States of America. Even before the declaration, the colonies were a unit in foreign affairs, acting through a common agency—namely the Continental Congress, composed of delegates from the thirteen colonies. That agency exercised the powers of war and peace, raised an army, created a navy, and finally adopted the Declaration of Independence. Rulers come and go; governments end and forms of government change; but sovereignty survives. A political society cannot endure without a supreme will somewhere. Sovereignty is never held in suspense. When, therefore, the external sovereignty of Great Britain in respect of the colonies ceased, it immediately passed to the Union. *See Penhallow v. Doane,* 3 Dall. 54, 80–81. That fact was given practical application almost at once. The treaty of peace, made on September 23, 1783, was concluded between his Brittanic Majesty and the "United States of America." 8 Stat.—European Treaties—80. . . .

It results that the investment of the federal government with the powers of external sovereignty did not depend upon the affirmative grants of the Constitution. The powers to declare and wage war, to conclude peace, to make treaties, to maintain diplomatic relations with other sovereignties, if they had never been mentioned in the Constitution, would have vested in the federal government as necessary concomitants of nationality. . . .

Not only, as we have shown, is the federal power over external affairs in origin and essential character different from that over internal affairs, but participation in the exercise of the power is significantly limited. In this vast external realm, with its important, complicated, delicate and manifold problems, the President alone has the power to speak or listen as a representative of the nation. He *makes* treaties with the advice and consent of the Senate; but he alone negotiates. Into the field of negotiation the Senate cannot intrude; and Congress itself is powerless to invade it. As [John] Marshall said in his great argument of March 7, 1800, in the House of Representatives, "The President is the sole organ of the nation in its external relations, and its sole representative with foreign nations." Annals, 6th Cong., col. 613. . . .

It is important to bear in mind that we are here dealing not alone with an authority vested in the President by an exertion of legislative power, but with such an authority plus the very delicate, plenary and exclusive power of the President as the sole organ of the federal government in the field of international relations—a power which does not require as a basis for its exercise an act of Congress, but which, of course, like every other governmental power, must be exercised in subordination to the applicable provisions of the Constitution. It is quite apparent that if, in the maintenance of our international relations, embarrassment—perhaps serious embarrassment—is to be avoided and success for our aims achieved, congressional legislation which is to be made effective through negotiation and inquiry within the international field must often accord to the President a degree of discretion and freedom from statutory restriction which would not be admissible were domestic affairs alone involved. Moreover, he, not Congress, has the better opportunity of knowing the conditions which prevail in foreign countries, and especially is this true in time of war. He has his confidential sources of information. He has his agents in the form of diplomatic, consular and other officials. Secrecy in respect of information gathered by them may be highly necessary, and the premature disclosure of it productive by harmful results. Indeed, so clearly is this true that the first President refused to accede to a request to lay before the House of Representatives the instructions, correspondence and documents relating to the negotiation of the Jay Treaty—a refusal the wisdom of which was recognized by the House itself and has never since been doubted. . . .

The marked difference between foreign affairs and domestic affairs in this respect is recognized by both houses of Congress in the very form of their requisitions for information from the executive departments. In the case of every department except the Department of State, the resolution *directs* the official to furnish the information. In the case of the State Department, dealing with foreign affairs, the President is *requested* to furnish the information "if not incompatible with the public interest." A statement that to furnish the information is not compatible with the public interest rarely, if ever, is questioned.

When the President is to be authorized by legislation to act in respect of a matter intended to affect a situation in foreign territory, the legislator properly bears in mind the important consideration that the form of the President's action—or, indeed, whether he shall act at all—may well depend, among other things, upon the nature of the confidential information which he has or may thereafter receive, or upon the effect which his action may have upon our foreign relations. This consideration, in connection with what we have already said on the subject, discloses the unwisdom of requiring Congress in this field of governmental power to lay down narrowly definite standards by which the President is to be governed. . . .

We deem it unnecessary to consider, *seriatim,* the several clauses which are said to evidence the unconstitutionality of the Joint Resolution as involving an unlawful delegation of legislative power. It is enough to summarize by saying that, both upon principle and in accordance with precedent, we conclude there is sufficient warrant for the broad discretion vested in the President to determine whether the enforcement of the statute will have a beneficial effect upon the reestablishment of peace in the affected countries; whether he shall make proclamation to bring the resolution into operation; whether and when the resolution shall cease to operate and to make proclamation accordingly; and to prescribe limitations and exceptions to which the enforcement of the resolution shall be subject. . . .

29

Franklin D. Roosevelt's
"Court-Packing" Address
(1937)

O N February 5, 1937, President Franklin D. Roosevelt, reacting to a long string of Supreme Court decisions that were hostile to the New Deal, asked Congress to add as many as six new positions to the Court, one for every sitting justice aged seventy or older who refused to retire.

Roosevelt's frustration with the Supreme Court was long-simmering. When he became president in 1933, the Court was dominated by conservatives. In 1935 and 1936 it overturned an unprecedented number of important federal laws that Roosevelt and Congress had enacted to combat the Great Depression, including the National Industrial Recovery Act, the Agricultural Adjustment Act, and the Railway Pension Act. Other significant New Deal laws, such as the Social Security Act and the National Labor Relations Act, seemed doomed to a similar fate as soon as they came before the justices.

Privately, Roosevelt raged against the Court. Publicly, he was relatively quiet, fearing an adverse political reaction to any assault he might launch on the long-respected judicial branch. In 1936 Roosevelt ran a cautious campaign for reelection and was returned to office by the largest electoral vote majority in history, 523–8. Scarcely two weeks after his inauguration on January 20, 1937, however, the president revealed to a startled cabinet, Congress, and nation his proposal to expand the number of Supreme Court justices from nine to fifteen, which would enable him to appoint six New Deal sympathizers to the Court immediately.

In a severe political miscalculation, Roosevelt initially defended the Court-packing plan as an effort to relieve the workload of the justices, six of whom (including most of the conservatives) were in their seventies. This rationale was both inaccurate—Chief Justice Charles Evans Hughes was able to demonstrate easily to Congress that the Court was efficiently handling its caseload—and transparently insincere. Critics attacked the president for disguising his real intention, which was to impose a liberal majority on the Court.

On March 9 Roosevelt gave one of his celebrated "fireside chats" to a national radio audience. In it, he changed tactics and spoke frankly of his concern that "the Court has been acting not as a judicial body, but as a policy-making body." He conceded his intention of "'packing the Court' . . . [i]f by that phrase [is meant] . . . that I would appoint Justices who will not undertake to override the judgment of the Congress on legislative policy."

Politically, Roosevelt's speech was too little, too late. The Court-packing plan was dead. But in a series of decisions beginning later in March, Justice Owen Roberts, previously an ally of the Court's four most resolute conservatives, began voting to uphold New Deal laws. Several other justices retired within a few years, and Roosevelt appointed nine new justices before leaving office. Although his later claim that he had lost the Court-packing battle but won the war was too facile (the battle was a major defeat in its own right, and it marked the birth of the conservative coalition of Republicans and southern Democrats that dominated Congress for decades), Roosevelt never had another problem with the Supreme Court.

🐎 🐎 🐎

. . . Tonight, sitting at my desk in the White House, I make my first radio report to the people in my second term of office.

I am reminded of that evening in March, four years ago, when I made my first radio report to you. We were then in the midst of the great banking crisis.

Soon after, with the authority of the Congress, we asked the Nation to turn over all of its privately held gold, dollar for dollar, to the Government of the United States.

Today's recovery proves how right that policy was.

But when, almost two years later, it came before the Supreme Court its constitutionality was upheld only by a five-to-four vote. The change of one vote would have thrown all the affairs of this great Nation back into hopeless chaos. In effect, four Justices ruled that the right under a private contract to exact a pound of flesh was more sacred than the main objectives of the Constitution to establish an enduring Nation.

In 1933 you and I knew that we must never let our economic system get completely out of joint again—that we could not afford to take the risk of another great depression.

We also became convinced that the only way to avoid a repetition of those dark days was to have a government with power to prevent and to cure the abuses and the inequalities which had thrown that system out of joint.

We then began a program of remedying those abuses and inequalities—to give balance and stability to our economic system—to make it bombproof against the causes of 1929.

Today we are only part-way through that program—and recovery is speeding up to a point where the dangers of 1929 are again becoming possible, not this week or month perhaps, but within a year or two.

National laws are needed to complete that program. Individual or local or state effort alone cannot protect us in 1937 any better than ten years ago. . . .

The American people have learned from the depression. For in the last three national elections an overwhelming majority of them voted a mandate that the Congress and the President begin the task of providing that protection—not after long years of debate, but now.

The Courts, however, have cast doubts on the ability of the elected Congress to protect us against catastrophe by meeting squarely our modern social and economic conditions. . . .

Last Thursday I described the American form of Government as a three horse team provided by the Constitution to the American people so that their field might be plowed. The three horses are, of course, the three branches of government—the Congress, the Executive and the Courts. Two of the horses are pulling in unison today; the third is not. Those who have intimated that the President of the United States is trying to drive that team, overlook the simple fact that the President, as Chief Executive, is himself one of the three horses.

It is the American people themselves who are in the driver's seat.

It is the American people themselves who want the furrow plowed.

It is the American people themselves who expect the third horse to pull in unison with the other two.

I hope that you have re-read the Constitution of the United States in these past few weeks. Like the Bible, it ought to be read again and again.

It is an easy document to understand when you remember that it was called into being because the Articles of Confederation under which the original thirteen States tried to operate after the Revolution showed the need of a National Government with power enough to handle national problems. In its Preamble, the Constitution states that it was intended to form a more perfect Union and promote the general welfare; and the powers given to the Congress to carry out those purposes can be best described by saying that they were all the powers needed to meet each and every problem which then had a national character and which could not be met by merely local action.

But the framers went further. Having in mind that in succeeding generations many other problems then undreamed of would become national problems, they gave to the Congress the ample broad powers "to levy taxes . . . and provide for the common defense and general welfare of the United States."

That, my friends, is what I honestly believe to have been the clear and underlying purpose of the patriots who wrote a Federal Constitution to create a National Government with national power, intended as they said, "to form a more perfect union . . . for ourselves and our posterity."

For nearly twenty years there was no conflict between the Congress and the Court. Then Congress passed a statute which, in 1803, the Court said violated an express provision of the Constitution. The Court claimed the power to declare it unconstitutional and did so declare it. But a little later the Court itself admitted that it was an extraordinary power to exercise and through Mr. Justice [Bushrod] Washington laid down this limitation upon it: "It is but a decent respect due to the wisdom, the integrity and the patriotism of the legislative body, by which any law is passed, to presume in favor of its validity until its violation of the Constitution is proved beyond all reasonable doubt."

But since the rise of the modern movement for social and economic progress through legislation, the Court has more and more often and more and more boldly asserted a power to veto laws passed by the Congress and State Legislatures in complete disregard of this original limitation.

In the last four years the sound rule of giving statutes the benefit of all reasonable doubt has been cast aside. The Court has been acting not as a judicial body, but as a policy-making body. . . .—a super-legislature, as one of the justices has called it—reading into the Constitution words and implications which are not there, and which were never intended to be there. . . .

I want—as all Americans want—an independent judiciary as proposed by the framers of the Constitution. That means a Supreme Court that will enforce the Constitution as written—that will refuse to amend the Constitution by the arbitrary exercise of judicial power—amendment by judicial say-so. It does not mean a judiciary so independent that it can deny the existence of facts universally recognized.

How then could we proceed to perform the mandate given us? It was said in last year's Democratic platform, "If these problems cannot be effectively solved within the Constitution, we shall seek such clarifying amendment as will assure the power to enact those laws, adequately to regulate commerce, protect public health and safety, and safeguard economic security." In other words, we said we would seek an amendment only if every other possible means by legislation were to fail.

When I commenced to review the situation with the problem squarely before me, I came by a process of elimination to the conclusion that, short of amendments, the only method which was clearly constitutional, and would at the same time carry out other much needed reforms, was to infuse new blood into all our Courts. We must have men worthy and equipped to carry out impartial justice. But, at the same time, we must have Judges who will bring to the Courts a present-day sense of the Constitution—Judges who will retain in the Courts the judicial functions of a court, and reject the legislative powers which the courts have today assumed.

In forty-five out of the forty-eight States of the Union, Judges are chosen not for life but for a period of years. In many States Judges must retire at the age of seventy. Congress has provided financial security by offering life pensions at full pay for Federal Judges on all Courts who are willing to retire at seventy. In the case of Supreme Court Justices, that pension is $20,000 a year. But all Federal Judges, once appointed, can, if they choose, hold office for life, no matter how old they may get to be.

What is my proposal? It is simply this: whenever a Judge or Justice of any Federal Court has reached the age of seventy and does not avail himself of the opportunity to retire on a pension, a new member shall be appointed by the President then in office, with the approval, as required by the Constitution, of the Senate of the United States.

The plan has two chief purposes. By bringing into the judicial system a steady and continuing stream of new and younger blood, I hope, first, to make the administration of all Federal justice speedier and, therefore, less costly; secondly, to bring to the decision of social and economic problems younger men who have had personal experience and contact with modern facts and circumstances under which average men have to live and work. This plan will save our national Constitution from hardening of the judicial arteries.

The number of Judges to be appointed would depend wholly on the decision of present Judges now over seventy, or those who would subsequently reach the age of seventy.

If, for instance, any one of the six Justices of the Supreme Court now over the age of seventy should retire as provided under the plan, no additional place would be created. Consequently, although there never can be more than fifteen, there may be only fourteen, or thirteen, or twelve. And there may be only nine. . . .

Those opposing this plan have sought to arouse prejudice and fear by crying that I am seeking to "pack" the Supreme Court and that a baneful precedent will be established.

What do they mean by the words "packing the Court"?

Let me answer this question with a bluntness that will end all *honest* misunderstanding of my purposes.

If by that phrase "packing the Court" it is charged that I wish to place on the bench spineless puppets who would disregard the law and would decide specific cases as I wished them to be decided, I make this answer: that no President fit for his office would appoint, and no Senate of honorable men fit for their office would confirm, that kind of appointees to the Supreme Court.

But if by that phrase the charge is made that I would appoint and the Senate would confirm Justices worthy to sit beside present members of the Court who understand those modern conditions, that I will appoint Justices who will not undertake to override the judgment of the Congress on legislative policy, that I will appoint Justices who will act as Justices and not as legislators—if the appointment of such Justices can be called "packing the Courts," then I say that I and with me the vast majority of the American people favor doing just that thing—now.

Is it a dangerous precedent for the Congress to change the number of the Justices? The Congress has always had, and will have, that power. The number of Justices has been changed several times before, in the Administrations of John Adams and Thomas Jefferson—both signers of the Declaration of Independence—Andrew Jackson, Abraham Lincoln and Ulysses S. Grant. . . .

It is the clear intention of our public policy to provide for a constant flow of new and younger blood into the Judiciary. Normally every President appoints a large number of District and Circuit Judges and a few members of the Supreme Court. Until my first term practically every President of the United States had appointed at least one member of the Supreme Court. President [William Howard] Taft appointed five members and named a Chief Justice; President [Woodrow] Wilson, three; President [Warren G.] Harding, four, including a Chief Justice.

Such a succession of appointments should have provided a Court well-balanced as to age. But chance and the disinclination of individuals to leave the Supreme bench have now given us a Court in which five Justices will be over seventy-five years of age before next June and one over seventy. Thus a sound public policy has been defeated. . . .

I have thus explained to you the reasons that lie behind our efforts to secure results by legislation within the Constitution. I hope that thereby the difficult process of constitutional amendment may be rendered unnecessary . . .

And remember one thing more. Even if an amendment were passed, and even if in the years to come it were to be ratified, its meaning would depend upon the kind of Justices who would be sitting on the Supreme Court bench. An amendment, like the rest of the Constitution, is what the Justices say it is rather than what its framers or you might hope it is. . . .

I am in favor of action through legislation:

First, because I believe that it can be passed at this session of the Congress.

Second, because it will provide a reinvigorated, liberal-minded Judiciary necessary to furnish quicker and cheaper justice from bottom to top.

Third, because it will provide a series of Federal Courts willing to enforce the Constitution as written, and unwilling to assert legislative powers by writing into it their own political and economic policies.

During the past half century the balance of power between the three great branches of the Federal Government, has been tipped out of balance by the Courts in direct contradiction of the high purposes of the framers of the Constitution. It is my purpose to restore that balance. You who know me will accept my solemn assurance that in a world in which democracy is under attack, I seek to make American democracy succeed. You and I will do our part.

ᢓᚲ 30 ᢓᚲ

Report of the Brownlow Committee

(1937)

T HE FIRST INAUGURATION of Franklin D. Roosevelt as president, on March 4, 1933, was followed by an explosion of legislative activity aimed at combating the Great Depression. During Roosevelt's fabled "first hundred days," Congress passed more than a dozen pieces of major administration-sponsored legislation. After the 1934 midterm elections, in which the president's party broke historical precedent by gaining seats in the House of Representatives and the Senate, Congress passed additional legislation. Cumulatively, these laws created a large and active role for the federal government in the nation's economy.

Because Roosevelt doubted the loyalty and competence of most of the existing departments and agencies, which had been created in less active times and were staffed mainly by Republican appointees, he persuaded Congress to authorize new agencies to carry out many of his programs. By adding so many components to the executive branch, however, Roosevelt created an administrative monster. He was frustrated by his inability to get the information he needed from the bureaucracy or to communicate his desires for action to it effectively.

On March 20, 1936, Roosevelt appointed the Committee on Administrative Management, better known as the Brownlow Committee after its chairman, Louis D. Brownlow. The other two members were political scientists Charles E. Merriam and Luther Gulick. The committee's charge was to design and recommend an overhaul of the executive branch that would make it more efficient and responsive to the president. On January 8, 1937, Brownlow and his colleagues issued their report, which Roosevelt accepted wholeheartedly.

Arguing that "the president needs help," the Brownlow Committee recommended that the president be authorized to hire six personal assistants "possessed of high competence, great physical vigor, and a passion for anonymity." Their task would be to help the president "in obtaining quickly and without delay all pertinent information possessed by any of the executive departments so as to guide him in making responsible decisions; and after decisions have been made, to assist him in seeing to it that every administrative department and agency affected is promptly informed."

In addition to these personal staff positions, the Brownlow Committee recommended the creation of the Executive Office of the President (EOP) to serve the long-term interests of the presidency as an institution. The main components of the EOP would be the Bureau of the Budget, then housed in the Treasury Department, and the Civil Service Commission, an independent agency.

After receiving the Brownlow Committee's report, Roosevelt immediately asked Congress for authorization to implement its recommendations. Angry over the president's effort to "pack" the Supreme Court (see Document 7, p. 47). Congress did not approve the president's request until April 1939. Even then, the Civil Service Commission was left independent. On September 8, 1939, Roosevelt issued Executive Order 8248, and the Brownlow Committee's major proposals took effect.

༄ ༄ ༄

. . . Our Presidency unites at least three important functions. From one point of view the President is a political leader—leader of a party, leader of the Congress, leader of a people. From another point of view he is head of the Nation in the ceremonial sense of the term, the symbol of our American national solidarity. From still another point of view the President is the Chief Executive and administrator within the Federal system and service. In many types of government these duties are divided or only in part combined, but in the United States they have always been united in one and the same person whose duty it is to perform all of these tasks.

Your Committee on Administrative Management has been asked to investigate and report particularly upon the last function; namely, that of administrative management—the organization for the performance of the duties imposed upon the President in exercising the executive power vested in him by the Constitution of the United States. . . .

Since the Civil War, as the tasks and responsibilities of our Government have grown with the growth of the Nation in sweep and power, some notable attempts have been made to keep our administrative system abreast of the new times. The assassination of President [James] Garfield by a disappointed office seeker aroused the Nation against the spoils system and led to the enactment of the civil-service law of 1883. We have struggled to make the principle of this law effective for half a century. The confusion in fiscal management led to the establishment of the Bureau of the Budget and the budgetary system in 1921. We still strive to realize the goal set for the Nation at that time. And, indeed, many other important forward steps have been taken.

Now we face again the problem of governmental readjustment, in part as the result of the activities of the Nation during the desperate years of the industrial depression, in part because of the very growth of the Nation, and in part because of the vexing social problems of our times. There is room for vast increase in our national productivity and there is much bitter wrong to set right in neglected ways of human life. There is need for improvement of our governmental machinery to meet new conditions and to make us ready for the problems just ahead. . . .

Fortunately the foundations of effective management in public affairs, no less than in private, are well known. They have emerged universally wherever men have worked together for some common purpose, whether through the state, the church, the private association, or the commercial enterprise. They have been written into constitutions, charters, and articles of incorporation, and exist as habits of work in the daily life of all organized peoples. Stated in simple terms these canons of efficiency require the establishment of a responsible and effective chief executive as the center of energy, direction, and administrative management; the systematic organization of all activities in the hands of qualified personnel under the direction of the chief executive; and to aid him in this, the establishment of appropriate managerial and staff agencies. There must also be provision for planning, a complete fiscal system, and means for holding the Executive accountable for his program. . . .

While in general principle our organization of the Presidency challenges the admiration of the world, yet in equipment for administrative management our Executive Office is not fully abreast of the trend of our American times, either in business or in government. Where, for example, can there be found an executive in any way comparable upon whom so much petty work is thrown? Or who is forced to see so many persons on unrelated matters and to make so many decisions on the basis of what may be, because of the very press of work, incomplete information? How is it humanly possible to know fully the affairs and problems of over 100 separate major agencies, to say nothing of being responsible for their general direction and coordination?

These facts have been known for many years and are so well appreciated that it is not necessary for us to prove again that the President's administrative equipment is far less developed than his responsibilities, and that a major task before the American Government is to remedy this dangerous situation. What we need is not a new principle, but a modernizing of our managerial equipment. . . .

In this broad program of administrative reorganization the White House itself is involved. The President needs help. His immediate staff assistance is entirely inadequate. He should be given a small number of executive assistants who would be his direct aides in dealing with the managerial agencies and administrative departments of the Government. These assistants, probably not exceeding six in number, would be in addition to his present secretaries, who deal with the public, with the Congress, and with the press and the radio. These aides would have no power to make decisions or issue instructions in their own right. They would not be interposed between the President and the heads of his departments. They would not be assistant presidents in any sense. Their function would be, when any matter was presented to the President for action affecting any part of the administrative work of the Government, to assist him in obtaining quickly and without delay all pertinent information possessed by any of the executive departments so as to guide him in making his responsible decisions; and then when decisions have been made, to assist him in seeing to it that every administrative department and agency affected is promptly informed. Their effectiveness in assisting the President will, we think, be directly proportional to their ability to discharge their functions with restraint. They would remain in the background, issue orders, make no decisions, emit no public statements. Men for these positions should be carefully chosen by the President from within and without the Government. They should be men in whom the President has personal confidence and whose character and attitude is such that they would not attempt to exercise power on their own account. They should be possessed of high competence, great physical vigor, and a passion for anonymity. They should be installed in the White House itself, directly accessible to the President. In the selection of these aides the President should be free to call on departments from time to time for the assignment of persons who, after a tour of duty as his aides, might be restored to their old positions.

This recommendation arises from the growing complexity and magnitude of the work of the President's office. Special assistance is needed to insure that all matters coming to the attention of the President have been examined from the over-all managerial point of view, as well as from all standpoints that would bear on policy and operation. It also would facilitate the flow upward to the President of information upon which he is to base his decisions and the flow downward from the President of the decisions once taken for execution by the department or departments affected. Thus such a staff would not only aid the President but would also be of great assistance to the several executive departments and to the managerial agencies in simplifying executive contacts, clearance, and guidance.

The President should also have at his command a contingent fund to enable him to bring in from time to time particular persons possessed of particular competency for a particular purpose and whose services he might usefully employ for short periods of time.

The President in his regular office staff should be given a greater number of positions so that he will not be compelled, as he has been compelled in the past, to use for his own necessary work persons carried on the payrolls of other departments.

If the President be thus equipped he will have but the ordinary assistance that any executive of a large establishment is afforded as a matter of course.

In addition to this assistance in his own office the President must be given direct control over and be charged with immediate responsibility for the great managerial functions of the Government which affect all of the administrative departments. . . . These functions are personnel management, fiscal and organizational management, and planning management. Within these three groups may be comprehended all of the essential elements of business management.

The development of administrative management in the Federal Government requires the improvement of the administration of these managerial activities, not only by the central agencies in charge, but also by the departments and bureaus. The central agencies need to be strengthened and developed as managerial arms of the Chief Executive, better equipped to perform their central responsibilities and to provide the necessary leadership in bringing about improved practices throughout the Government.

The three managerial agencies, the Civil Service Administration, the Bureau of the Budget, and the National Resources Board should be a part and parcel of the Executive Office. Thus the President would have reporting to him directly the three managerial institutions whose work and activities would affect all of the administrative departments.

The budgets for the managerial agencies should be submitted to the Congress by the President as a part of the budget for the Executive Office. This would distinguish these agencies from the operating administrative departments of the Government, which should report to the President through the heads of departments who collectively compose his Cabinet. Such an arrangement would materially aid the President in his work of supervising the administrative agencies and would enable the Congress and the people to hold him to strict accountability for their conduct. . . .

[In addition to these recommendations concerning

1. the White House staff and

2. the three managerial agencies,]

3. The merit system should be extended upward, outward, and downward to cover all non–policy-determining posts, and the civil service system should be reorganized and opportunities established for a career system attractive to the talent of the Nation.

4. The whole Executive Branch of Government should be overhauled and the present 100 agencies reorganized under a few large departments in which every executive activity would find its place.

5. The fiscal system should be extensively revised in the light of the best governmental and private practice, particularly with reference to financial records, audit, and accountability of the Executive to the Congress. . . .

Franklin D. Roosevelt's Executive Order
on Japanese American Internment

(1942)

F RANKLIN D. ROOSEVELT was elected to an unprecedented third presidential
term in 1940. His strongest claim to reelection was the recent outbreak of
World War II in Europe and Asia, and the public's sense that only an experienced
president could successfully navigate the world's treacherous shoals on behalf of
the United States. On December 7, 1941, less than a year after FDR's third inauguration, Japan launched a surprise air attack that destroyed nearly all of America's
Pacific fleet, anchored at the Pearl Harbor naval station in Hawaii. The following
day Roosevelt asked Congress to declare war on Japan, and it did so quickly and
almost unanimously. (Only one member of the House of Representatives, and no
senators, dissented.) Three days later, on December 11, Japan's European allies,
Germany and Italy, declared war on the United States. Roosevelt immediately
became a wartime president. "Dr. New Deal," he said, had helped to cure the
depression but now must give way to "Dr. Win-the-War."

Americans were baffled by the success of the Japanese attack, which was followed
by an additional series of naval defeats in the Pacific. Residents of the West Coast
feared for their safety. In this atmosphere of confusion and near panic, a search for
scapegoats began. Offering no evidence, a commission appointed by the president
and chaired by Supreme Court Justice Owen Roberts concluded on January 24,
1942, that unnamed Americans of Japanese descent had provided the government
of Japan with the information it needed to destroy Pearl Harbor. By the end of the
month the entire California congressional delegation, the state's Democratic governor, and Republican State Attorney General Earl Warren were demanding that all
of the more than 100,000 Japanese Americans living on the West Coast be rounded
up and taken to internment camps for the duration of the war.

Assistant Secretary of War John J. McCloy, who was charged with deciding what
to do on behalf of the Roosevelt administration, said, "If it is a question of the safety
of the country or the Constitution of the United States, why the Constitution is just
a scrap of paper to me." On February 8, in the face of objections from Federal Bureau
of Investigation Director J. Edgar Hoover, Attorney General Francis Biddle, and
Deputy Army Chief of Staff Mark Clark, Roosevelt invoked "the authority invested
in me as President of the United States, and Commander in Chief of the Army and
Navy" and issued Executive Order 9066. The order authorized "the Secretary of
War, and the Military Commanders whom he may from time to time designate" to
declare that certain parts of the country were "military areas . . . from which any or

all persons may be excluded." In removing these persons from their homes, the secretary also was authorized to provide "such transportation, food, shelter, and other accommodations as may be necessary." Although the words "Japanese Americans," "West Coast," and "internment camps" did not appear in the order, its clear purpose was to force Japanese Americans living on the West Coast into internment camps, and this was its effect.

One internee, Fred Korematsu, resisted removal, was arrested, and in 1944 appealed his conviction to the Supreme Court. As had been its custom during previous wars, the Court sided with the president in the case of *Korematsu v. United States,* citing wartime necessity.

❧ ❧ ❧

Executive Order Authorizing the Secretary of War to Prescribe Military Areas

Whereas the successful prosecution of the war requires every possible protection against espionage and against sabotage to national-defense material, national-defense premises, and national-defense utilities as defined in Section 4, Act of April 20, 1918, 40 Stat. 533, as amended by the Act of November 30, 1940, 54 Stat. 1220, and the Act of August 21, 1941, 55 Stat. 655 (U.S.C., Title 50, Sec. 104);

Now, therefore, by virtue of the authority vested in me as President of the United States, and Commander in Chief of the Army and Navy, I hereby authorize and direct the Secretary of War, and the Military Commanders whom he may from time to time designate, whenever he or any designated Commander deems such action necessary or desirable, to prescribe military areas in such places and of such extent as he or the appropriate Military Commander may determine, from which any or all persons may be excluded, and with respect to which, the right of any person to enter, remain in, or leave shall be subject to whatever restrictions the Secretary of War or the appropriate Military Commander may impose in his discretion. The Secretary of War is hereby authorized to provide for residents of any such area who are excluded therefrom, such transportation, food, shelter, and other accommodations as may be necessary, in the judgment of the Secretary of War or the said Military Commander, and until other arrangements are made, to accomplish the purpose of this order. The designation of military areas in any region or locality shall supersede designations of prohibited and restricted areas by the Attorney General under the Proclamations of December 7 and 8, 1941, and shall supersede the responsibility and authority of the Attorney General under the said Proclamations in respect of such prohibited and restricted areas.

I hereby further authorize and direct the Secretary of War and the said Military Commanders to take such other steps as he or the appropriate Military Commander may deem advisable to enforce compliance with the restrictions applicable to each Military area hereinabove authorized to be designated, including the use of Federal troops and other Federal Agencies, with authority to accept assistance of state and local agencies.

I hereby further authorize and direct all Executive Departments, independent establishments and other Federal Agencies, to assist the Secretary of War or the said Military Commanders in carrying out this Executive Order, including the furnishing of medical aid, hospitalization, food, clothing, transportation, use of land, shelter, and other supplies, equipment, utilities, facilities, and services.

This order shall not be construed as modifying or limiting in any way the authority heretofore granted under Executive Order No. 8972, dated December 12, 1941, nor shall it be construed as limiting or modifying the duty and responsibility of the Federal Bureau of Investigation, with respect to the investigation of alleged acts of sabotage or the duty and responsibility of the Attorney General and the Department of Justice under the Proclamations of December 7 and 8, 1941, prescribing regulations for the conduct and control of alien enemies, except as such duty and responsibility is superseded by the designation of military areas hereunder.

Franklin D. Roosevelt
The White House,
February 19, 1942.

≈§ 32 §≈

The Truman Doctrine

(1947)

S CARCELY WAS WORLD WAR II won in 1945 than severe tensions emerged between the United States and Great Britain and their chief wartime ally, the Soviet Union. Complicating matters further was the unexpected death of President Franklin D. Roosevelt on April 12, 1945, and Vice President Harry S. Truman's immediate succession to the presidency.

In the course of defeating Germany's eastern army, Soviet troops and tanks occupied nearly all of Eastern Europe even as American and British forces were advancing from the west. Despite the Soviet government's assurances to the contrary, it gradually became clear that it had no intention of withdrawing from Poland, Czechoslovakia, Bulgaria, Hungary, Romania, eastern Germany, and the other countries it occupied. In addition, the Soviets were working hard to aid Communist Party candidates for office in France, Italy, and other western European democracies that had been liberated by the United States and Great Britain and were holding free elections. No one could be certain how extensive the ambitions of the Soviet Union and its leader, Josef Stalin, were.

Although Truman, a former senator from Missouri, was an inexperienced president when he took office, he surrounded himself with experienced foreign policy statesmen, including three successive secretaries of state: James F. Byrnes, George C. Marshall, and Dean Acheson. Advised by them and others, especially Soviet expert George F. Kennan, Truman adopted a policy of containment, whose purpose was to keep the burgeoning Soviet empire from further extending its borders.

Containment received a severe test in 1947, when a nearly bankrupt Great Britain made clear that it lacked the resources to protect Greece and Turkey against Soviet-assisted communist aggression. Truman resolved to seek financial assistance for the two nations' beleaguered governments from Congress, which had come under Republican control in the 1946 midterm election and was strongly opposed to the president's domestic agenda. Briefed on the Greece and Turkey situation at a White House meeting, Senate Foreign Relations Committee chair Arthur Vandenberg pledged his support for financial assistance, and then told Truman, "Mr. President, the only way you are ever going to get this is to make a speech and scare the hell out of the country."

Truman addressed Congress and a national radio audience on March 12, 1947. He asked legislators to "to provide authority for assistance to Greece and Turkey in the amount of $400,000,000 for the period ending June 30, 1948." More generally, he enunciated a guiding philosophy—soon dubbed the Truman Doctrine—for the United States in the postwar world. "It must be the policy of the United States," the president declared, "to support free peoples who are resisting attempted subjugation by armed minorities or by outside pressures."

Truman was far from renowned as an orator. But his March 12 speech had a dramatic effect on public opinion. Before the speech only ones about one-fifth of Americans thought foreign problems were the most important ones facing the country. Afterward more than half did. In this altered climate of opinion, Congress voted by a two-thirds majority to approve the president's request for aid.

🦐 🦐 🦐

Mr. President, Mr. Speaker, Members of the Congress of the United States:

The gravity of the situation which confronts the world today necessitates my appearance before a joint session of the Congress. The foreign policy and the national security of this country are involved.

One aspect of the present situation, which I wish to present to you at this time for your consideration and decision, concerns Greece and Turkey.

The United States has received from the Greek Government an urgent appeal for financial and economic assistance. Preliminary reports from the American Economic Mission now in Greece and reports from the American Ambassador in Greece corroborate the statement of the Greek Government that assistance is imperative if Greece is to survive as a free nation.

I do not believe that the American people and the Congress wish to turn a deaf ear to the appeal of the Greek Government.

Greece is not a rich country. Lack of sufficient natural resources has always forced the Greek people to work hard to make both ends meet. Since 1940, this industrious and peace loving country has suffered invasion, four years of cruel enemy occupation, and bitter internal strife.

When forces of liberation entered Greece they found that the retreating Germans had destroyed virtually all the railways, roads, port facilities, communications, and merchant marine. More than a thousand villages had been burned. Eighty-five per cent of the children were tubercular. Livestock, poultry, and draft animals had almost disappeared. Inflation had wiped out practically all savings.

As a result of these tragic conditions, a militant minority, exploiting human want and misery, was able to create political chaos which, until now, has made economic recovery impossible.

Greece is today without funds to finance the importation of those goods which are essential to bare subsistence. Under these circumstances the people of Greece cannot make progress in solving their problems of reconstruction. Greece is in desperate need of financial and economic assistance to enable it to resume purchases of food, clothing, fuel and seeds. These are indispensable for the subsistence of its people and are obtainable only from abroad. Greece must have help to import the goods necessary to restore internal order and security, so essential for economic and political recovery.

The Greek Government has also asked for the assistance of experienced American administrators, economists and technicians to insure that the financial and other aid given to Greece shall be used effectively in creating a stable and self-sustaining economy and in improving its public administration.

The very existence of the Greek state is today threatened by the terrorist activities of several thousand armed men, led by Communists, who defy the government's authority at a number of points, particularly along the northern boundaries. A Commission appointed by the United Nations Security Council is at present investigating disturbed conditions in northern Greece and alleged border violations along the frontier between Greece on the one hand and Albania, Bulgaria, and Yugoslavia on the other.

Meanwhile, the Greek Government is unable to cope with the situation. The Greek army is small and poorly equipped. It needs supplies and equipment if it is to restore the authority of the government throughout Greek territory. Greece must have assistance if it is to become a self-supporting and self-respecting democracy.

The United States must supply that assistance. We have already extended to Greece certain types of relief and economic aid but these are inadequate.

There is no other country to which democratic Greece can turn.

No other nation is willing and able to provide the necessary support for a democratic Greek government.

The British Government, which has been helping Greece, can give no further financial or economic aid after March 31. Great Britain finds itself under the necessity of reducing or liquidating its commitments in several parts of the world, including Greece.

We have considered how the United Nations might assist in this crisis. But the situation is an urgent one requiring immediate action and the United Nations and its related organizations are not in a position to extend help of the kind that is required.

It is important to note that the Greek Government has asked for our aid in utilizing effectively the financial and other assistance we may give to Greece, and in improving its public administration. It is of the utmost importance that we supervise the use of any funds made available to Greece; in such a manner that each dollar spent will count toward making Greece self-supporting, and will help to build an economy in which a healthy democracy can flourish.

No government is perfect. One of the chief virtues of a democracy, however, is that its defects are always visible and under democratic processes can be pointed out and corrected. The Government of Greece is not perfect. Nevertheless it represents eighty-five per cent of the members of the Greek Parliament who were chosen in an election last year. Foreign observers, including 692 Americans, considered this election to be a fair expression of the views of the Greek people.

The Greek Government has been operating in an atmosphere of chaos and extremism. It has made mistakes. The extension of aid by this country does not mean that the United States condones everything that the Greek Government has done or will do. We have condemned in the past, and we condemn now, extremist measures of the right or the left. We have in the past advised tolerance, and we advise tolerance now.

Greece's neighbor, Turkey, also deserves our attention.

The future of Turkey as an independent and economically sound state is clearly no less important to the freedom-loving peoples of the world than the future of Greece. The circumstances in which Turkey finds itself today are considerably different from those of Greece. Turkey has been spared the disasters that have beset Greece. And during the war, the United States and Great Britain furnished Turkey with material aid.

Nevertheless, Turkey now needs our support.

Since the war Turkey has sought financial assistance from Great Britain and the United States for the purpose of effecting that modernization necessary for the maintenance of its national integrity.

That integrity is essential to the preservation of order in the Middle East.

The British government has informed us that, owing to its own difficulties can no longer extend financial or economic aid to Turkey.

As in the case of Greece, if Turkey is to have the assistance it needs, the United States must supply it. We are the only country able to provide that help.

I am fully aware of the broad implications involved if the United States extends assistance to Greece and Turkey, and I shall discuss these implications with you at this time.

One of the primary objectives of the foreign policy of the United States is the creation of conditions in which we and other nations will be able to work out a way of life free from coercion. This was a fundamental issue in the war with Germany and Japan. Our victory was won over countries which sought to impose their will, and their way of life, upon other nations.

To ensure the peaceful development of nations, free from coercion, the United States has taken a leading part in establishing the United Nations, The United Nations is designed to make possible lasting freedom and independence for all its members. We shall not realize our objectives, however, unless we are willing to help free peoples to maintain their free institutions and their national integrity against aggressive movements that seek to impose upon them totalitarian regimes. This is no more than a frank recognition that totalitarian regimes imposed on free peoples, by direct or indirect aggression, undermine the foundations of international peace and hence the security of the United States.

The peoples of a number of countries of the world have recently had totalitarian regimes forced upon them against their will. The Government of the United States has made frequent protests against coercion and intimidation, in violation of the Yalta agreement, in Poland, Rumania, and Bulgaria. I must also state that in a number of other countries there have been similar developments.

At the present moment in world history nearly every nation must choose between alternative ways of life. The choice is too often not a free one.

One way of life is based upon the will of the majority, and is distinguished by free institutions, representative government, free elections, guarantees of individual liberty, freedom of speech and religion, and freedom from political oppression.

The second way of life is based upon the will of a minority forcibly imposed upon the majority. It relies upon terror and oppression, a controlled press and radio, fixed elections, and the suppression of personal freedoms.

I believe that it must be the policy of the United States to support free peoples who are resisting attempted subjugation by armed minorities or by outside pressures.

I believe that we must assist free peoples to work out their own destinies in their own way.

I believe that our help should be primarily through economic and financial aid which is essential to economic stability and orderly political processes.

The world is not static, and the status quo is not sacred. But we cannot allow changes in the status quo in violation of the Charter of the United Nations by such methods as coercion, or by such subterfuges as political infiltration. In helping free and independent nations to maintain their freedom, the United States will be giving effect to the principles of the Charter of the United Nations.

It is necessary only to glance at a map to realize that the survival and integrity of the Greek nation are of grave importance in a much wider situation. If Greece should fall under the control of an armed minority, the effect upon its neighbor, Turkey, would be immediate and serious. Confusion and disorder might well spread throughout the entire Middle East.

Moreover, the disappearance of Greece as an independent state would have a profound effect upon those countries in Europe whose peoples are struggling against great difficulties to maintain their freedoms and their independence while they repair the damages of war.

It would be an unspeakable tragedy if these countries, which have struggled so long against overwhelming odds, should lose that victory for which they sacrificed so much. Collapse of free institutions and loss of independence would be disastrous not only for them but for the world. Discouragement and possibly failure would quickly be the lot of neighboring peoples striving to maintain their freedom and independence.

Should we fail to aid Greece and Turkey in this fateful hour, the effect will be far reaching to the West as well as to the East.

We must take immediate and resolute action.

I therefore ask the Congress to provide authority for assistance to Greece and Turkey in the amount of $400,000,000 for the period ending June 30, 1948. In requesting these funds, I have taken into consideration the maximum amount of relief assistance which would be furnished to Greece out of the $350,000,000 which I recently requested that the Congress authorize for the prevention of starvation and suffering in countries devastated by the war.

In addition to funds, I ask the Congress to authorize the detail of American civilian and military personnel to Greece and Turkey, at the request of those countries, to assist in the tasks of reconstruction, and for the purpose of supervising the use of such financial and material assistance as may be furnished. I recommend that authority also be provided for the instruction and training of selected Greek and Turkish personnel.

Finally, I ask that the Congress provide authority which will permit the speediest and most effective use, in terms of needed commodities, supplies, and equipment, of such funds as may be authorized.

If further funds, or further authority, should be needed for purposes indicated in this message, I shall not hesitate to bring the situation before the Congress. On this subject the Executive and Legislative branches of the Government must work together.

This is a serious course upon which we embark.

I would not recommend it except that the alternative is much more serious. The United States contributed $341,000,000,000 toward winning World War II. This is an investment in world freedom and world peace.

The assistance that I am recommending for Greece and Turkey amounts to little more than 1 tenth of 1 per cent of this investment. It is only common sense that we should safeguard this investment and make sure that it was not in vain.

The seeds of totalitarian regimes are nurtured by misery and want. They spread and grow in the evil soil of poverty and strife. They reach their full growth when the hope of a people for a better life has died. We must keep that hope alive.

The free peoples of the world look to us for support in maintaining their freedoms.

If we falter in our leadership, we may endanger the peace of the world—and we shall surely endanger the welfare of our own nation.

Great responsibilities have been placed upon us by the swift movement of events.

I am confident that the Congress will face these responsibilities squarely.

⋙ 33 ⋙
*Youngstown Sheet & Tube Co. v. Sawyer**
(1952)

IN JUNE 1950 troops from communist North Korea invaded South Korea, an American ally. At the behest of the United States, the Security Council of the recently formed United Nations (UN) passed a resolution condemning the invasion and asking UN member nations to "render every assistance" to South Korea. President Harry S. Truman, relying on the resolution and on his constitutional

*Go to *http://laws.findlaw.com/us/343/579.html.*

authority as commander in chief, committed American men and materiel to South Korea's defense without asking Congress to declare war.

The fighting did not go as well as Truman had hoped, and the longer the war lasted, the more unpopular it and the president became. On April 8, 1952, when a labor dispute in the steel industry made the situation even more uncertain, Truman ordered Secretary of Commerce Charles Sawyer "to take possession of and operate the plants and facilities of certain steel companies," including the Youngstown Sheet & Tube Company in Youngstown, Ohio. Truman acted partly out of fear that an impending strike for higher wages by the United Steelworkers union would jeopardize his government's ability to maintain both its military effort in Korea and its commitment to supply arms to Western Europe. He was not alone in this belief. Secretary of Defense Robert Lovett and Secretary of State Dean Acheson agreed with the president.

Truman had authority under the Labor-Management Relations Act of 1947 (better known as the Taft-Hartley Act) to impose a court-ordered, eighty-day "cooling-off" period on both labor and management whenever the nation's health or safety was imperiled. But because Truman had opposed the act and pledged to seek its repeal, he grounded his authority to seize the mills in his constitutional status "as President of the United States and Commander in Chief of the Armed Forces." Truman was aware that previous presidents, including Abraham Lincoln and Franklin D. Roosevelt, had seized private property without prior congressional authorization. He also knew that only once—and never while American troops were still fighting—had the Supreme Court declared a wartime presidential action unconstitutional. (See Document 19, p. 95.)

Truman conceded in an April 9, 1952, report that Congress had the power to countermand his steel seizure order, confident that it would not do so. In this assessment he was correct. Although certain that the steel companies would sue to have the Supreme Court declare the order unconstitutional, Truman expected the Court's support as well, not just because of the long history of judicial deference to the president in foreign and military matters, but also because he had appointed three of the nine justices and believed that at least three others would take an expansive view of presidential prerogative. In this assessment he was wrong.

On June 2, 1952, ruling in the case of *Youngstown Sheet & Tube Co. v. Sawyer* (also known as the Steel Seizure Case), the Supreme Court declared Truman's order to Secretary Sawyer unconstitutional by a 6–3 vote. Because seven of the nine justices, including all six in the majority, wrote separate opinions and only three endorsed Justice Hugo L. Black's opinion of the Court in its entirety, the full implications of this ruling for presidential power were unclear. But one finding on which a majority of justices agreed was that Congress had foreclosed the president from seizing industries during national emergencies when it rejected a proposed amendment to the Taft-Hartley Act that would have conferred such authority.

Although Truman lost the case, his claim that the president has an inherent, unstated constitutional power to act in times of national emergency was accepted, to one degree or another, by a majority of the justices. Black rejected this argument, but Robert H. Jackson's concurring opinion turned out to be of more enduring influence. Jackson argued that presidential power is variable: strong when supported by Congress, moderate when Congress is silent, and "at its lowest ebb" when exercised in opposition to Congress.

※ ※ ※

MR. JUSTICE BLACK delivered the opinion of the Court.

We are asked to decide whether the President was acting within his constitutional power when he issued an order directing the Secretary of Commerce [Charles Sawyer] to take possession of and operate most of the Nation's steel mills. The mill owners argue that the President's order amounts to lawmaking, a legislative function which the Constitution has expressly confided to the Congress and not to the President. The Government's position is that the order was made on findings of the President that his action was necessary to avert a national catastrophe which would inevitably result from a stoppage of steel production, and that in meeting this grave emergency the President was acting within the aggregate of his constitutional powers as the Nation's Chief Executive and the Commander in Chief of the Armed Forces of the United States. . . .

The President's power, if any, to issue the order must stem either from an act of Congress or from the Constitution itself. There is no statute that expressly authorizes the President to take possession of property as he did here. Nor is there any act of Congress to which our attention has been directed from which such a power can fairly be implied. Indeed, we do not understand the Government to rely on statutory authorization for this seizure. There are two statutes which do authorize the President to take both personal and real property under certain conditions. However, the Government admits that these conditions were not met and that the President's order was not rooted in either of the statutes. The Government refers to the seizure provisions of one of these statutes (§ 201 (b) of the Defense Production Act) as "much too cumbersome, involved, and time-consuming for the crisis which was at hand."

Moreover, the use of the seizure technique to solve labor disputes in order to prevent work stoppages was not only unauthorized by any congressional enactment; prior to this controversy, Congress had refused to adopt that method of settling labor disputes. When the Taft-Hartley Act was under consideration in 1947, Congress rejected an amendment which would have authorized such governmental seizures in cases of emergency. . . .

It is clear that if the President had authority to issue the order he did, it must be found in some provision of the Constitution. And it is not claimed that express constitutional language grants this power to the President. The contention is that presidential power should be implied from the aggregate of his powers under the Constitution. Particular reliance is placed on provisions in Article II which says that "The executive Power shall be vested in a President . . ."; that "he shall take

Care that the Laws be faithfully executed"; and that he "shall be Commander in Chief of the Army and Navy of the United States."

The order cannot properly be sustained as an exercise of the President's military power as Commander in Chief of the Armed Forces. The Government attempts to do so by citing a number of cases upholding broad powers in military commanders engaged in day-to-day fighting in a theater of war. Such cases need not concern us here. Even though "theater of war" be an expanding concept, we cannot with faithfulness to our constitutional system hold that the Commander in Chief of the Armed Forces has the ultimate power as such to take possession of private property in order to keep labor disputes from stopping production. This is a job for the Nation's lawmakers, not for its military authorities.

Nor can the seizure order be sustained because of the several constitutional provisions that grant executive power to the President. In the framework of our Constitution, the President's power to see that the laws are faithfully executed refutes the idea that he is to be a lawmaker. The Constitution limits his functions in the lawmaking process to the recommending of laws he thinks wise and the vetoing of laws he thinks bad. And the Constitution is neither silent nor equivocal about who shall make laws which the President is to execute. The first section of the first article says that "All legislative Powers herein granted shall be vested in a Congress of the United States. . . ." After granting many powers to the Congress, Article I goes on to provide that Congress may "make all Laws which shall be necessary and proper for carrying into Execution the foregoing Powers, and all other Powers vested by this Constitution in the Government of the United States, or in any Department or Officer thereof."

The President's order does not direct that a congressional policy be executed in a manner prescribed by Congress—it directs that a presidential policy be executed in a manner prescribed by the President. . . .

It is said that other Presidents without congressional authority have taken possession of private business enterprises in order to settle labor disputes. But even if this be true, Congress has not thereby lost its exclusive constitutional authority to make laws necessary and proper to carry out the powers vested by the Constitution "in the Government of the United States, or any Department or Officer thereof."

The Founders of this Nation entrusted the lawmaking power to the Congress alone in both good and bad times. It would do no good to recall the historical events, the fears of power and the hopes for freedom that lay behind their choice. Such a review would but confirm our holding that this seizure order cannot stand.

The judgment of the District Court is Affirmed.

MR. JUSTICE JACKSON, concurring in the judgment and opinion of the Court. . . .

A judge, like an executive adviser, may be surprised at the poverty of really useful and unambiguous authority applicable to concrete problems of executive power as they actually present themselves. Just what our forefathers did envision, or would have envisioned had they foreseen modern conditions, must be divined from materials almost as enigmatic as the dreams Joseph was called upon to interpret for Pharaoh. A century and a half of partisan debate and scholarly speculation yields no net result but only supplies more or less apt quotations from respected sources on each side of any question. They largely cancel each other. And court decisions are indecisive because of the judicial practice of dealing with the largest questions in the most narrow way.

The actual art of governing under our Constitution does not and cannot conform to judicial definitions of the power of any of its branches based on isolated clauses or even single Articles torn from context. While the Constitution diffuses power the better to secure liberty, it also contemplates that practice will integrate the dispersed powers into a workable government. It enjoins upon its branches separateness but interdependence, autonomy but reciprocity. Presidential powers are not fixed but fluctuate, depending upon their disjunction or conjunction with those of Congress. We may well begin by a somewhat over-simplified grouping of practical situations in which a President may doubt, or others may challenge, his powers, and by distinguishing roughly the legal consequences of this factor of relativity.

1. When the President acts pursuant to an express or implied authorization of Congress, his authority is at its maximum, for it includes all that he possesses in his own right plus all that Congress can delegate. In these circumstances, and in these only, may he be said (for what it may be worth) to personify federal sovereignty. If his act is held unconstitutional under these circumstances, it usually means that the Federal Government as an undivided whole lacks power. A seizure executed by the President pursuant to an Act of Congress would be supported by the strongest of presumptions and the widest latitude of judicial interpretation, and the burden of persuasion would rest heavily upon any who might attack it.

2. When the President acts in absence of either a congressional grant or denial of authority, he can only rely upon his own independent powers, but there is a zone of twilight in which he and Congress may have concurrent authority, or in which its distribution is uncertain. Therefore, congressional inertia, indifference or quiescence may sometimes, at least as a practical matter, enable, if not invite, measures on independent presidential responsibility. In this area, any actual test of power is likely to depend on the imperatives of events and contemporary imponderables rather than on abstract theories of law.

3. When the President takes measures incompatible with the expressed or implied will of Congress, his power is at its lowest ebb, for then he can rely only upon his own constitutional powers minus any constitutional powers of Congress over the matter. Courts can sustain exclusive presidential control in such a case only by disabling the Congress from acting upon the subject. Presidential claim to a power at once so conclusive and preclusive must be scrutinized with caution, for what is at stake is the equilibrium established by our constitutional system.

Into which of these classifications does this executive seizure of the steel industry fit? It is eliminated from the first by admission, for it is conceded that no congressional authorization exists for this seizure. That takes away also the support of the many precedents and declarations which were made in relation, and must be confined, to this category.

Can it then be defended under flexible tests available to the second category? It seems clearly eliminated from that class because Congress has not left seizure of private property an open field but has covered it by three statutory policies inconsistent with this seizure. In cases where the purpose is to supply needs of the Government itself, two courses are provided: one, seizure of a plant which fails to comply with obligatory orders placed by the Government; another, condemnation of facilities, including temporary use under the power of eminent domain. The third is applicable where it is the general economy of the country that is to be protected rather than exclusive governmental interests. None of these were invoked. In choosing a different and inconsistent way of his own, the President cannot claim that it is necessitated or invited by failure of Congress to legislate upon the occasions, grounds and methods for seizure of industrial properties.

This leaves the current seizure to be justified only by the severe tests under the third grouping, where it can be supported only by any reminder of executive power after subtraction of such powers as Congress may have over the subject. In short, we can sustain the President only by holding that seizure of such strike-bound industries is within his domain and beyond control by Congress. Thus, this Court's first review of such seizures occurs under circumstances which leave presidential power most vulnerable to attack and in the least favorable of possible constitutional postures. . . .

The Solicitor General seeks the power of seizure in three clauses of the Executive Article, the first reading, "The executive Power shall be vested in a President of the United States of America." Lest I be thought to exaggerate, I quote the interpretation which his brief puts upon it: "In our view, this clause constitutes a grant of all the executive powers of which the Government is capable." If that be true, it is difficult to see why the forefathers bothered to add several specific items, including some trifling ones. . . .

The clause on which the Government next relies is that "The President shall be Commander in Chief of the Army and Navy of the United States. . . ." These cryptic words have given rise to some of the most persistent controversies in our constitutional history. Of course, they imply something more than an empty title. But just what authority goes with the name has plagued presidential advisers who would not waive or narrow it by nonassertion yet cannot say where it begins or ends. It undoubtedly puts the Nation's armed forces under presidential command. Hence, this loose appellation is sometimes advanced as support for any presidential action, internal or external, involving use of force, the idea being that it vests power to do anything, anywhere, that can be done with an army or navy.

That seems to be the logic of an argument tendered at our bar—that the President having, on his own responsibility, sent American troops abroad derives from that act "affirmative power" to seize the means of producing a supply of steel for them. To quote, "Perhaps the most forceful illustration of the scope of Presidential power in this connection is the fact that American troops in Korea, whose safety and effectiveness are so directly involved here, were sent to the field by an exercise of the President's constitutional powers." Thus, it is said, he has invested himself with "war powers."

I cannot foresee all that it might entail if the Court should indorse this argument. Nothing in our Constitution is plainer than that declaration of a war is entrusted only to Congress. . . .

There are indications that the Constitution did not contemplate that the title Commander in Chief *of the Army and Navy* will constitute him also Commander in Chief of the country, its industries and its inhabitants. He has no monopoly of "war powers," whatever they are. While Congress cannot deprive the President of the command of the army and navy, only Congress can provide him an army or navy to command. It is also empowered to make rules for the "Government and Regulation of land and naval Forces," by which it may to some unknown extent impinge upon even command functions. . . .

We should not use this occasion to circumscribe, much less to contract, the lawful role of the President as Commander in Chief. I should indulge the widest latitude of interpretation to sustain his exclusive function to command the instruments of national force, at least when turned against the outside world for the security of our society. But, when it is turned inward, not because of rebellion but because of a lawful economic struggle between industry and labor, it should have no such indulgence. His command power is not such an absolute as might be implied from that office in militaristic system but is subject to limitations consistent with a constitutional Republic whose law and policy-making branch is a representative Congress. The purpose of lodging dual titles in one man was to insure that the civilian would control the military, not to enable the military to subordinate the presidential office. No penance would ever expiate the sin against free government of holding that a President can escape control of executive powers by law through assuming his military role. What the power of command may include I do not try to envision, but I think it is not a military prerogative, without support of law, to seize persons or property because they are important or even essential for the military and naval establishment.

The third clause in which the Solicitor General finds seizure powers is that "he shall take Care that the Laws be faithfully executed. . . ." That authority must be matched against words of the Fifth Amendment that "No person shall be . . . deprived of life, liberty or property, without due process of law. . . ." One gives a governmental authority that reaches so far as there is law, the other gives a private right that authority shall go no farther. These signify about all there is of the principle that ours is a government of laws, not of men, and that we submit ourselves to rulers only if under rules.

The Solicitor General lastly grounds support of the seizure upon nebulous, inherent powers never expressly granted but said to have accrued to the office from the customs and claims of preceding administrations. The plea is for a resulting power to deal with a crisis or an emergency according to the necessities of the case, the unarticulated assumption being that necessity knows no law. . . .

In the practical working of our Government we already have evolved a technique within the framework of the Constitution by which normal executive powers may be considerably expanded to meet an emergency. Congress may and has granted extraordinary authorities which lie dormant in normal times but may be called into play by the Executive in war or upon proclamation of a national emergency. In 1939, upon congressional request, the Attorney General listed ninety-nine such separate statutory grants by Congress of emergency or wartime executive powers. They were invoked from time to time as need appeared. Under this procedure we retain Government by law—special, temporary law, perhaps, but law nonetheless. The public may know the extent and limitations of the powers that can be asserted, and persons affected may be informed from the statute of their rights and duties.

In view of the ease, expedition and safety with which Congress can grant and has granted large emergency powers, certainly ample to embrace this crisis, I am quite unimpressed with the argument that we should affirm possession of them without statute. Such power either has no beginning or it has no end. If it exists, it need submit to no legal restraint. I am not alarmed that it would plunge us straightway into dictatorship, but it is at least a step in that wrong direction.

As to whether there is imperative necessity for such powers, it is relevant to note the gap that exists between the President's paper powers and his real powers. The Constitution does not disclose the measure of the actual controls wielded by the modern presidential office. That instrument must be understood as an Eighteenth-Century sketch of a government hoped for, not as a blueprint of the Government that is. Vast accretions of federal power, eroded from that reserved by the States, have magnified the scope of presidential activity. Subtle shifts take place in the centers of real power that do not show on the face of the Constitution.

Executive power has the advantage of concentration in a single head in whose choice the whole Nation has a part, making him the focus of public hopes and expectations. In drama, magnitude and finality his decisions so far overshadow any others that almost alone he fills the public eye and ear. No other personality in public life can begin to compete with him in access to the public mind through modern methods of communications. By his prestige as head of state and his influence upon public opinion he exerts a leverage upon those who are supposed to check and balance his power which often cancels their effectiveness.

Moreover, [the] rise of the party system has made a significant extra constitutional supplement to real executive power. No appraisal of his necessities is realistic which overlooks that he heads a political system as well as a legal system. Party loyalties and interests, sometimes more binding than law, extend his effective control into branches of government other than his own and he often may win, as a political leader, what he cannot command under the Constitution. Indeed, Woodrow Wilson, commenting on the President as leader both of his party and of the Nation, observed, "If he rightly interpret the national thought and boldly insist upon it, he is irresistible. . . . His office is anything he has the sagacity and force to make it." I cannot be brought to believe that this country will suffer if the Court refuses further to aggrandize the presidential office, already so potent and so relatively immune from judicial review, at the expense of Congress.

But I have no illusion that any decision by this Court can keep power in the hands of Congress if it is not wise and timely in meeting its problems. A crisis that challenges the President equally, or perhaps primarily, challenges Congress. If not good law, there was worldly wisdom in the maxim attributed to Napoleon that "The tools belong to the man who can use them." We may say that power to legislate for emergencies belongs in the hands of Congress, but only Congress itself can prevent power from slipping through its fingers.

The essence of our free Government is "leave to live by no man's leave, underneath the law"—to be governed by those impersonal forces which we call law. Our Government is fashioned to fulfill this concept so far as humanly possible. The Executive, except for recommendation and veto, has no legislative power. The executive action we have here originates in the individual will of the President and represents an exercise of authority without law. No one, perhaps not even the President, knows the limits of the power he may seek to exert in this instance and the parties affected cannot learn the limit of their rights. We do not know today what powers over labor or property would be claimed to flow from Government possession if we should legalize it, what rights to compensation would be claimed or recognized, or on what contingency it would end. With all its defects, delays and inconveniences, men have discovered no technique for long preserving free government except that the Executive be under the law, and that the law be made by parliamentary deliberations.

Such institutions may be destined to pass away. But it is the duty of the Court to be last, not first, to give them up.

❦ 34 ❦
Dwight D. Eisenhower's Little Rock Executive Order
(1957)

T HE CONSTITUTION VESTS the "executive Power" in the "President of the United States of America" and charges the president to "take Care that the Laws be faithfully executed." Taken in combination, these constitutional clauses have given rise to a presidential power that is not mentioned in the Constitution: the power to issue executive orders. Nearly fourteen thousand executive orders have been issued by presidents from George Washington to Barack Obama, all but around a thousand of them in the twentieth and twenty-first centuries. The legal authority for each of these orders has been grounded in statutes enacted by Congress or in the president's constitutional authority. In most cases, the orders have either established executive agencies, changed executive decision-making procedures, modified bureaucratic rules and practices, or given force and substance to statutes.

The train of events that led to President Dwight D. Eisenhower's issuance of Executive Order 10730 began with the Supreme Court's declaration in *Brown v. Board of Education* (1954) that legally segregated public schools violate the Constitution. The southern states, taking heart from Eisenhower's refusal to publicly endorse the wisdom of the Court's decision, responded by strenuously resisting school integration. When the school board of Little Rock, Arkansas, decided to inaugurate a six-year plan of integration by admitting a small number of African American students to all-white Central High School in September 1957, Gov. Orval Faubus intervened. On September 2 Faubus, defying an order by the federal district court for the Eastern District of Arkansas, deployed his state's national guard to prevent the nine black students designated by the school board from enrolling at Central. Mobs of angry, sometimes violent whites surrounded the school.

Eisenhower may have had doubts about mandatory school integration, but he had none about defiance of the law. He also was concerned about the Soviet Union's use of the crisis to portray the United States as racist to the newly independent countries of Africa and Asia. After an unsuccessful September 14 meeting with Faubus at the president's summer home in Newport, Rhode Island, Eisenhower issued a proclamation on September 23 "to command all persons engaged in obstruction of justice to cease and desist therefrom, and to disperse forthwith." The next day, after Faubus and the mob ignored the proclamation, Eisenhower issued an executive order directing Secretary of Defense Charles Wilson to federalize the Arkansas national guard and to deploy approximately one thousand armed paratroopers from the army's 101st Airborne Division to Little Rock. That night, Eisenhower addressed the nation on television, having returned to Washington from Newport in order to buttress the "firmness" of his remarks by "speaking from the House of Lincoln, of Jackson and of Wilson."

Eisenhower grounded his power to issue Executive Order 10730 in "the authority vested in me by the Constitution and statutes of the United States," including several Civil War–era laws concerning "unlawful obstruction," "rebellion," and "interference with state and Federal law." He explained that he had issued the proclamation the previous day because one of the laws required that he do so before actually deploying the armed forces in a domestic situation.

Once the paratroopers arrived, the mob dispersed and Central High was integrated, at least on a token basis. But Faubus, who was seeking reelection in 1958 (he won overwhelmingly), remained defiant and even closed the schools in Little Rock for the rest of the academic year. School desegregation only became widespread in the South in the early 1970s.

Eisenhower was not the first president to issue an executive order on behalf of civil rights. During World War II Franklin D. Roosevelt ordered an easing of racial segregation in defense plants, and in 1948 Harry S. Truman integrated the armed forces with an executive order. Nor would Eisenhower be the last. Lyndon B. Johnson, for example, used an executive order to direct businesses contracting with the federal government to create affirmative action hiring programs.

⁂ ⁂ ⁂

Executive Order 10730

The White House
U.S. Naval Base
Newport, R.I.

PROVIDING ASSISTANCE FOR THE REMOVAL OF AN
OBSTRUCTION OF JUSTICE WITHIN THE STATE OF ARKANSAS

Whereas, on Sept. 23, 1957, I issued proclamation No. 3204 reading in part as follows:

"Whereas, certain persons in the State of Arkansas, individually and in unlawful assemblages, combinations, and conspiracies, have wilfully obstructed the enforcement of orders of the United States District Court for the Eastern District of Arkansas with respect to matters relating to enrollment and attendance at public schools, particularly at Central High School, located in Little Rock School District, Little Rock, Ark., and

"Whereas, such wilful obstruction of justice hinders the execution of the laws of that state and of the United States, and makes it impracticable to enforce such laws by the ordinary course of judicial proceedings, and

"Whereas, such obstruction of justice constitutes a denial of the equal protection of the laws secured by the Constitution of the United States and impedes the course of justice under those laws;

"Now, therefore, I, Dwight D. Eisenhower, President of the United States, under and by the virtue of the authority vested in me by the Constitution and statutes of the United States, including Chapter 15 of Title 10, of the United States Code, particularly Sections 332, 333 and 334 thereof, do command all persons engaged in such obstruction of justice to cease and desist therefrom, and to disperse forthwith" and

Whereas, the command contained in that proclamation has not been obeyed and wilful obstruction of enforcement of said court order still exists and threatens to continue;

Now, therefore, by virtue of the authority vested in me by the Constitution and statutes of the United States, including Chapter 15 and Title 10, particularly Sections 332, 333 and 334 thereof, and Section 301 of Title Three, of the United States Code; it is hereby ordered as follows:

"Section 1. I hereby authorize and direct the Secretary of Defense to order into the active military service of the United States, as he may deem appropriate to carry out the purposes of this order, any or all of the units of the National Guard of the United States and of the Air National Guard of the United States within the State of Arkansas to serve in the active military service of the United States for an indefinite period and until relieved by appropriate order.

"Section 2. The Secretary of Defense is authorized and directed to take all appropriate steps to enforce any order of the United States District Court for the Eastern District of Arkansas for the removal of an obstruction of justice in the State of Arkansas with respect to matters relating to enrollment and attendance at public schools in the Little Rock School District, Little Rock, Arkansas. In carrying out the provisions of this section, the

Secretary of Defense is authorized to use the units and members thereof, ordered into active military service of the United States pursuant to section 1 of this order.

"Section 3. In furtherance of the enforcement of the aforementioned order of the United States District Court for the Eastern District of Arkansas, the Secretary of Defense is authorized to use such forces of the armed forces of the United States as he may deem necessary.

"Section 4. The Secretary of Defense is authorized to delegate to the Secretary of the Army or the Secretary of the Air Force, or both, any of the authority conferred upon him by this order."

❧ 35 ❧

John F. Kennedy's Inaugural Address

(1961)

ON JANUARY 20, 1961, as on most presidential inauguration days, the nation was governed by one president until noon and by another afterward. The contrast between outgoing president Dwight D. Eisenhower and his incoming successor, John F. Kennedy, was dramatic and visible. The youngest man ever to be elected president (Kennedy was forty-three) was replacing the oldest man yet to leave the office (Eisenhower was seventy). A Democrat was replacing a Republican. A celebrated World War II combat hero was replacing the celebrated World War II supreme commander. A professional politician who had served three terms in the House of Representatives and was in his second term as senator from Massachusetts was replacing a career military leader whose first and only elective office was the presidency. Most important, perhaps, Kennedy's election replaced a defender of caution, prudence, and restraint with an advocate of change and energetic leadership.

The new president's inaugural address, delivered outdoors from the East Front of the Capitol on a bright but bitterly cold day, accentuated most of these contrasts. Kennedy emphasized his youth by noting that "the torch has been passed to a new generation of Americans—born in this century." He reached out to the Soviet Union: "Let us never negotiate out of fear. But let us never fear to negotiate." But he also pledged that "we shall pay any price, bear any burden, meet any hardship, support any friend, oppose any foe to assure the survival and the success of liberty." Finally, in the best-remembered sentence of his presidency, Kennedy summoned the idealism of the American people: "ask not what your country can do for you—ask what you can do for your country."

Kennedy's foreign policy was prefigured by his inaugural address. He negotiated an important nuclear test ban treaty with the Soviet Union. But he also resisted communist aggression in a number of global settings, including Berlin, Cuba, and Vietnam. Scholars continue to debate whether Kennedy, who sent

16,500 American soldiers to help defend South Vietnam, would have escalated the war further if he had lived to serve a second term.

Tragically, Kennedy did not survive even his first term. During the fall of 1963, the president made several trips around the country to build support for his 1964 reelection bid. On November 22, while riding through Dallas, Texas, in an open car, Kennedy was shot in the head and neck. Shortly afterward, he died at a nearby hospital without having regained consciousness. The police quickly apprehended his assassin, ex-Marine and communist sympathizer Lee Harvey Oswald. But Oswald's own murder while in police custody by Dallas nightclub owner Jack Ruby fostered speculation that the Kennedy assassination may have been the product of a conspiracy. A special presidential commission headed by Chief Justice Earl Warren concluded in 1964 that Oswald acted alone.

The combination of Kennedy's youth and glamour and his sudden, violent death has given the late president a special place in the consciousness of the American people. Polls often find that the public regards Kennedy as one of the greatest presidents in history, a verdict not shared by even admiring historians.

※ ※ ※

We observe today not a victory of party but a celebration of freedom—symbolizing an end as well as a beginning—signifying renewal as well as change. For I have sworn before you and Almighty God the same solemn oath our forebears prescribed nearly a century and three quarters ago.

The world is very different now. For man holds in his mortal hands the power to abolish all forms of human poverty and all forms of human life. And yet the same revolutionary beliefs for which our forebears fought are still at issue around the globe—the belief that the rights of man come not from the generosity of the state but from the hand of God.

We dare not forget today that we are the heirs of that first revolution. Let the word go forth from this time and place, to friend and foe alike, that the torch has been passed to a new generation of Americans—born in this century, tempered by war, disciplined by a hard and bitter peace, proud of our ancient heritage—and unwilling to witness or permit the slow undoing of those human rights to which this nation has always been committed, and to which we are committed today at home and around the world.

Let every nation know, whether it wishes us well or ill, that we shall pay any price, bear any burden, meet any hardship, support any friend, oppose any foe to assure the survival and the success of liberty.

This much we pledge—and more.

To those old allies whose cultural and spiritual origins we share, we pledge the loyalty of faithful friends. United, there is little we cannot do in a host of cooperative ventures. Divided, there is little we can do—for we dare not meet a powerful challenge at odds and split asunder.

To those new states whom we welcome to the ranks of the free, we pledge our word that one form of colonial control shall not have passed away merely to be replaced by a far more iron tyranny. We shall not always expect to find them supporting our view. But we shall always hope to find them strongly supporting their own freedom—and to remember that, in the past, those who foolishly sought power by riding the back of the tiger ended up inside.

To those peoples in the huts and villages of half the globe struggling to break the bonds of mass misery, we pledge our best efforts to help them help themselves, for whatever period is required—not because the communists may be doing it, not because we seek their votes, but because it is right. If a free society cannot help the many who are poor, it cannot save the few who are rich.

To our sister republics south of our border, we offer a special pledge—to convert our good words into good deeds—in a new alliance for progress—to assist free men and free governments in casting off the chains of poverty. But this peaceful revolution of hope cannot become the prey of hostile powers. Let all our neighbors know that we shall join with them to oppose aggression or subversion anywhere in the Americas. And let every other power know that this Hemisphere intends to remain the master of its own house.

To that world assembly of sovereign states, the United Nations, our last best hope in an age where the instruments of war have far outpaced the instruments of peace, we renew our pledge of support—to prevent it from becoming merely a forum for invective—to strengthen its shield of the new and the weak—and to enlarge the area in which its writ may run.

Finally, to those nations who would make themselves our adversary, we offer not a pledge but a request: that both sides begin anew the quest for peace, before the dark powers of destruction unleashed by science engulf all humanity in planned or accidental self-destruction.

We dare not tempt them with weakness. For only when our arms are sufficient beyond doubt can we be certain beyond doubt that they will never be employed.

But neither can two great and powerful groups of nations take comfort from our present course—both sides overburdened by the cost of modern weapons, both rightly alarmed by the steady spread of the deadly atom, yet both racing to alter that uncertain balance of terror that stays the hand of mankind's final war.

So let us begin anew—remembering on both sides that civility is not a sign of weakness, and sincerity is always subject to proof. Let us never negotiate out of fear. But let us never fear to negotiate.

Let both sides explore what problems unite us instead of belaboring those problems which divide us.

Let both sides, for the first time, formulate serious and precise proposals for the inspection and control of arms—and bring the absolute power to destroy other nations under the absolute control of all nations.

Let both sides seek to invoke the wonders of science instead of its terrors. Together let us explore the stars, conquer the deserts, eradicate disease, tap the ocean depths and encourage the arts and commerce.

Let both sides unite to heed in all corners of the earth the command of Isaiah—to "undo the heavy burdens . . . (and) let the oppressed go free."

And if a beach-head of cooperation may push back the jungle of suspicion, let both sides join in creating a new endeavor, not a new balance of power, but a new world of law, where the strong are just and the weak secure and the peace preserved.

All this will not be finished in the first one hundred days. Nor will it be finished in the first one thousand days, nor in the life of this Administration, nor even perhaps in our lifetime on this planet. But let us begin.

In your hands, my fellow citizens, more than mine, will rest the final success or failure of our course. Since this country was founded, each generation of Americans has been summoned to give testimony to its national loyalty. The graves of young Americans who answered the call to service surround the globe.

Now the trumpet summons us again—not as a call to bear arms, though arms we need—not as a call to battle, though embattled we are—but a call to bear the burden of a long twilight struggle, year in and year out, "rejoicing in hope, patient in tribulation"—a struggle against the common enemies of man: tyranny, poverty, disease and war itself.

Can we forge against these enemies a grand and global alliance, North and South, East and West, that can assure a more fruitful life for all mankind? Will you join in that historic effort?

In the long history of the world, only a few generations have been granted the role of defending freedom in its hours of maximum danger. I do not shrink from this responsibility—I welcome it. I do not believe that any of us would exchange places with any other people or any other generation. The energy, the faith, the devotion which we bring to this endeavor will light our country and all who serve it—and the glow from that fire can truly light the world.

And so, my fellow Americans: ask not what your country can do for you—ask what you can do for your country.

My fellow citizens of the world: ask not what America will do for you, but what together we can do for the freedom of man.

Finally, whether you are citizens of America or citizens of the world, ask of us here the same high standards of strength and sacrifice which we ask of you. With a good conscience our only sure reward, with history the final judge of our deeds, let us go forth to lead the land we love, asking His blessing and His help, but knowing that here on earth God's work must truly be our own.

✦ 36 ✦

The Cuban Missile Crisis
John F. Kennedy's Letter to Soviet Premier Nikita Khrushchev

(1962)

SOON AFTER TAKING OFFICE IN 1961, President John F. Kennedy endorsed a plan developed by the Central Intelligence Agency (CIA) during the Eisenhower administration to arm, train, and transport approximately fourteen hundred Cuban exiles to Cuba to overthrow the communist government of Fidel Castro. The April 17, 1961, operation, known as the Bay of Pigs invasion after the location where the exile forces landed, was a complete failure. All but two hundred of the invading Cubans were captured, and the United States was embarrassed before the world. Soon afterward, speaking at a press conference, Kennedy accepted full blame for the failure.

Both Castro and his patron, Soviet leader Nikita Khrushchev, were convinced that the United States would launch a subsequent full-scale invasion of Cuba. For this reason and one other—the Soviet Union's desire to add to the twenty nuclear missiles it already had aimed directly at the United States—Khrushchev secretly placed sixty-six intermediate-range missiles in Cuba.

On October 15, 1962, Kennedy received photographic evidence of the Soviet nuclear presence in Cuba. He secretly formed an "executive committee" (ExComm) of high administration officials to prepare the American response. ExComm included Secretary of State Dean Rusk, Secretary of Defense Robert S. McNamara, Attorney General Robert F. Kennedy, Vice President Lyndon B. Johnson, CIA Director John McCone, Joint Chiefs of Staff Chair Maxwell Taylor, National Security Adviser McGeorge Bundy, and various subcabinet officials. Publicly, the president carried on business as usual, even appearing at a rally for Democratic congressional candidates in Chicago.

ExComm's initial judgment was that the United States should launch an air strike against the missile sites. Taking a more cautious and less overtly aggressive approach, Kennedy decided instead to impose a naval blockade around Cuba to prevent Soviet ships from delivering supplies. Through diplomatic channels and in a televised address to the nation on October 22 (the first public report of what was happening), Kennedy then demanded that the Soviet missiles be withdrawn. Nuclear war between the United States and the Soviet Union seemed more likely than at any time in the history of the Cold War.

Soviet reaction to the blockade and to the president's demand was hard to ascertain. Khrushchev sent a conciliatory message on October 26, but a harsh one followed on October 27. Kennedy decided to ignore the second message and reply to the first. Kennedy's October 27 letter to Khrushchev laid out part of the basis for the agreement that ended the crisis: the Soviets would remove their missiles in return for the president's public pledge not to invade Cuba. Khrushchev responded favorably the following day. In 1989, at a conference of former Soviet and American officials who had participated in the Cuban missile crisis, it was confirmed that Kennedy also secretly promised to remove American nuclear missiles from near the Soviet border in Turkey.

🎎 🎎 🎎

Dear Mr. Chairman:

I have read your letter of October 26th with great care and welcomed the statement of your desire to seek a prompt solution to the problem. The first thing that needs to be done, however, is for work to cease on offensive missile bases in Cuba and for all weapons systems in Cuba capable of offensive use to be rendered inoperable, under effective United Nations arrangements.

Assuming this is done promptly, I have given my representatives in New York instructions that will permit them to work out this weekend—in cooperation with the Acting Secretary General [of the United Nations] and your representative—an arrangement for a permanent solution to the Cuban problem along the lines suggested in your letter of October 26th. As I read your letter, the key elements of your proposals—which seem generally acceptable as I understand them—are as follows:

1) You would agree to remove these weapons systems from Cuba under appropriate United Nations observation and supervision; and undertake, with suitable safeguards, to halt the further introduction of such weapons systems into Cuba.

2) We, on our part, would agree—upon the establishment of adequate arrangements through the United Nations to ensure the carrying out and continuation of these commitments—(a) to remove promptly the quarantine measures now in effect and (b) to give assurances against an invasion of Cuba. I am confident that other nations of the Western Hemisphere would be prepared to do likewise.

If you will give your representative similar instructions, there is no reason why we should not be able to complete these arrangements and announce them to the world within a couple of days. The effect of such a settlement on easing world tensions would enable us to work toward a more general arrangement regarding "other armaments," as proposed in your second letter which you made public. I would like to say again that the United States is very much interested in reducing tensions and halting the arms race; and if your letter signifies that you are prepared to discuss a detente affecting NATO and the Warsaw Pact, we are quite prepared to consider with our allies any useful proposals.

But the first ingredient, let me emphasize, is the cessation of work on missile sites in Cuba and measures to render such weapons inoperable, under effective international guarantees. The continuation of this threat, or a prolonging of this discussion concerning Cuba by linking these problems to the broader questions of European and world security, would surely lead to an intensification of the Cuban crisis and a grave risk to the peace of the world. For this reason I hope we can quickly agree along the lines outlined in this letter and in your letter of October 26th.

❧ 37 ❧
Lyndon B. Johnson's "Great Society" Speech*
(1964)

V ICE PRESIDENT LYNDON B. JOHNSON succeeded to the presidency when President John F. Kennedy was assassinated in Dallas, Texas, on November 22, 1963. Arriving that evening in Washington, Johnson pledged to a national television audience that the watchword of his administration would be: "Let us

*Go to *http://www.h-net.org/~hst306/documents/great.html.*

continue." Capitalizing on the grieving public's disposition to support virtually anything the slain president had proposed, Johnson persuaded Congress to enact most of the unfinished business of Kennedy's "New Frontier" agenda in 1964, including the most sweeping civil rights act in history and a large reduction in federal income taxes.

Johnson, who had served as Senate majority leader during the 1950s and unsuccessfully challenged Kennedy for the 1960 Democratic presidential nomination, also wanted to make his own mark on history. Within a few months, he offered "Great Society" as the catchphrase for his administration. In a May 22, 1964, commencement address at the University of Michigan, Johnson developed a broad outline of the Great Society theme.

According to Johnson, the United States already had become "the rich society and the powerful society" and now was challenged to reach "upward." The effort to build a Great Society would have two main goals. The first was "an end to poverty and racial injustice." The other was "to advance the quality of our American civilization." As Johnson described it, "the Great Society is a place where every child can find knowledge to enrich his mind and to enlarge his talents. It is a place where leisure is a welcome chance to build and reflect, not a feared cause of boredom and restlessness. It is a place where the city of man serves not only the needs of the body and the demands of commerce, but the desire for beauty and the hunger for community."

Johnson ran for president in 1964 against Republican senator Barry Goldwater of Arizona, an ardent conservative whom critics labeled a dangerous extremist. In addition to winning a personal landslide victory, Johnson brought in on his coat-tails a Congress that was two-thirds Democratic. In 1965 and 1966, the Eighty-ninth Congress passed a long list of Great Society initiatives: the Voting Rights Act, the Older Americans Act, the Freedom of Information Act, and legislation to establish or advance Medicare and Medicaid, the National Endowment of the Arts and Humanities, the Department of Transportation, the Department of Housing and Urban Development, highway beautification, and urban mass transit.

Yet these accomplishments, although substantial, did not fulfill Johnson's vision of the Great Society. Problems developed in the implementation of many of the programs, and poverty proved to be more intractable than he had imagined. In addition, the war in Vietnam, which he escalated, diverted attention and funding from the president's domestic agenda.

※ ※ ※

. . . The purpose of protecting the life of our Nation and preserving the liberty of our citizens is to pursue the happiness of our people. Our success in that pursuit is the test of our success as a nation. For a century we labored to settle and to subdue a continent. For half a century, we called upon unbounded invention and untiring industry to create an order of plenty for all of our people. The challenge of the next half century is whether we have the wisdom to use that wealth to enrich and elevate our national life, and to advance the quality of our American civilization.

Your imagination, your initiative and your indignation will determine whether we build a society where progress is the servant of our needs, or a society where old values and new visions are buried under unbridled growth.

For in your time we have the opportunity to move not only toward the rich society and the powerful society, but upward to the Great Society. The Great Society rests on abundance and liberty for all. It demands an end to poverty and racial injustice, to which we are totally committed in our time. But that is just the beginning.

The Great Society is a place where every child can find knowledge to enrich his mind and to enlarge his talents. It is a place where leisure is a welcome chance to build and reflect, not a feared cause of boredom and restlessness. It is a place where the city of man serves not only the needs of the body and the demands of commerce, but the desire for beauty and the hunger for community.

It is a place where man can renew contact with nature. It is a place which honors creation for its own sake and for what it adds to the understanding of the race. It is a place where men are more concerned with the quality of their goals than the quantity of their goods. But most of all, the great society is not a safe harbor, a resting place, a final objective, a finished work. It is a challenge constantly renewed, beckoning us toward a destiny where the meaning of our lives matches the marvelous products of our labor.

So I want to talk to you today about three places where we begin to build the Great Society—in our cities, in our countryside, and in our classrooms. . . .

Aristotle said, "Men come together in cities in order to live, but they remain together in order to live the good life."

It is harder and harder to live the good life in American cities today. The catalogue of ills is long: There is the decay of the centers and the despoiling of the suburbs. There is not enough housing for our people or transportation for our traffic. Open land is vanishing and old landmarks are violated. Worst of all, expansion is eroding the precious and time-honored values of community with neighbors and communion with nature. The loss of these values breeds loneliness and boredom and indifference. Our society will never be great until our cities are great. Today the frontier of imagination and innovation is inside those cities, and not beyond their borders. . . .

A second place where we begin to build the Great Society is in our countryside. We have always prided ourselves on being not only America the strong and America the free, but America the beautiful. Today that beauty is in danger. The water we drink, the food we eat, the very air that we breathe, are threatened with pollution. Our parks are overcrowded, our seashores overburdened. Green fields and dense forests are disappearing.

A few years ago we were greatly concerned about the Ugly American. Today we must act to prevent an Ugly America.

For once the battle is lost, once our natural splendor is destroyed, it can never be recaptured. And once man can no longer walk with beauty or wonder at nature, his spirit will wither and his sustenance be wasted.

A third place to build the Great Society is in the classrooms of America. There your children's lives will be shaped. Our society will not be great until every young mind is set free to scan the farthest reaches of thought and imagination. We are still far from that goal. . . . In many places, classrooms are overcrowded and curricula are outdated. Most of our qualified teachers are underpaid, and many of our paid teachers are unqualified.

So we must give every child a place to sit and a teacher to learn from. Poverty must not be a bar to learning, and learning must offer an escape from poverty.

But more classrooms and more teachers are not enough. We must seek an educational system which grows in excellence as it grows in size. This means better training for our teachers. It means preparing youth to enjoy their hours of leisure as well as their hours of labor. It means exploring new techniques of teaching, to find new ways to stimulate the love of learning and the capacity for creation.

These are three of the central issues of the Great Society. While our government has many programs directed at those issues, I do not pretend that we have the full answer to those problems. But I do promise this: We are going to assemble the best thought and the broadest knowledge from all over the world to find those answers for America. . . .

There are those timid souls who say this battle cannot be won, that we are condemned to a soulless wealth. I do not agree. We have the power to shape the civilization that we want. But we need your will, your labor, your hearts, if we are to build that kind of society.

Those who came to this land sought to build more than just a new country. They sought a free world.

So I have come here today to your campus to say that you can make their vision our reality. Let us from this moment begin our work so that in the future men will look back and say: It was then, after a long and weary way, that man turned the exploits of his genius to the full enrichment of his life.

Thank you. Goodbye.

---

৯৪ 38 ৯৪

Lyndon B. Johnson's Gulf of Tonkin Message*

(1964)

T WO THEMES DOMINATED the five-and-one-half-year presidency of Lyndon B. Johnson: the Great Society (see Document 37, p. 179) and the war in Vietnam. Much to Johnson's distress, the latter gradually overshadowed the former.

After winning its battle for independence from France in 1954, Vietnam was divided by treaty into two countries: communist North Vietnam, which was headed by the hero of the revolution, Ho Chi Minh, and anticommunist South

---

*For the text of the Gulf of Tonkin Resolution passed by Congress, go to *http://avalon.law.yale
.edu/20th_century/tonkin-g.asp#joint*.

Vietnam. Unsatisfied with the persistence of this arrangement, which was meant to be temporary, North Vietnam and Vietcong guerrillas in the South fought the South Vietnamese government in an effort to reunify the country under communist rule. President Dwight D. Eisenhower sent weapons and economic aid to South Vietnam. His successor, John F. Kennedy, added 16,500 U.S. military advisers to the South Vietnamese war effort.

In early 1964 aides to Johnson privately drafted a congressional resolution that would give the president a virtual blank check to conduct the Vietnam War as he saw fit. Johnson feared that such a proposal would generate too much controversy. But on August 2 and 4, 1964, reports reached Washington that two American naval destroyers, the *Maddox* and the *C. Turner Joy,* had been attacked by North Vietnamese patrol boats in the Gulf of Tonkin. The attack was described as unprovoked. In truth, at the time of the attack the *Maddox* was gathering sensitive intelligence information and the South Vietnamese navy was assaulting North Vietnam. But these facts became public only when the Senate Foreign Relations Committee uncovered them in 1968.

On August 5, 1964, Johnson sent what became known as the "Gulf of Tonkin message" to Congress, urging it to pass a resolution of support for his leadership. The resolution stated, "Congress approves and supports the determination of the President, as Commander-in-Chief, to take all necessary measures to repel any armed attack against the forces of the United States and to prevent further aggression." It also declared that the United States was "prepared, as the President determines, to take all necessary steps, including the use of armed force, to assist any member or protocol state of the Southeast Asia Collective Defense Treaty requesting assistance in defense of its freedom," including South Vietnam. Two days later, the House of Representatives passed the Gulf of Tonkin Resolution unanimously and the Senate approved it by a vote of 88–2.

In later years, as the American military commitment in Vietnam became much larger and more controversial, Johnson claimed that the Gulf of Tonkin Resolution provided ample authority for his administration's policies, which eventually included maintaining an active combat force of more than 500,000 American soldiers in Vietnam. Publicly, Undersecretary of State Nicholas Katzenbach told Congress in 1967 that the resolution, in conjunction with American treaty obligations, was the "functional equivalent" of a declaration of war. Privately, Johnson compared the resolution to "grandma's nightshirt—it covered everything."

Despite the American military effort, the Vietcong and North Vietnamese continued their assault on the government of South Vietnam. The war became increasingly unpopular in the United States, first on college campuses, then across the country. In a largely symbolic act, Congress repealed the Gulf of Tonkin Resolution on December 31, 1970. By then, Johnson had withdrawn from politics and Richard Nixon, a Republican, had been elected president in 1968.

In 1973, after four years in office, the Nixon administration concluded an agreement with North Vietnam that ended direct U.S. participation in the fighting in exchange for the return of American prisoners of war. Nixon secretly promised South Vietnamese president Nguyen Van Thieu that the United States would not allow his government to be overthrown by the communists. But Nixon resigned as president in 1974 (see Document 43, p. 205), and when South Vietnam was unable to defend itself against a North Vietnamese offensive in 1975, Congress refused to allow President Gerald R. Ford to assist South Vietnam militarily in any way.

⁂ ⁂ ⁂

To the Congress of the United States:

Last night I announced to the American people that the North Vietnamese regime had conducted further deliberate attacks against U.S. naval vessels operating in international waters, and that I had therefore directed air action against gun boats and supporting facilities used in these hostile operations. This air action has now been carried out with substantial damage to the boats and facilities. Two U.S. aircraft were lost in the action.

After consultation with the leaders of both parties in the Congress, I further announced a decision to ask the Congress for a Resolution expressing the unity and determination of the United States in supporting freedom and in protecting peace in Southeast Asia.

These latest actions of the North Vietnamese regime have given a new and grave turn to the already serious situation in Southeast Asia. Our commitments in that area are well known to the Congress. They were first made in 1954 by President Eisenhower. They were further defined in the Southeast Asia Collective Defense Treaty approved by the Senate in February 1955.

This Treaty with its accompanying protocol obligates the United States and other members to act in accordance with their Constitutional processes to meet Communist aggression against any of the parties or protocol states.

Our policy in Southeast Asia has been consistent and unchanged since 1954. I summarized it on June 2 in four simple propositions:

1. *America keeps her word.* Here as elsewhere, we must and shall honor our commitments.

2. *The issue is the future of Southeast Asia as a whole.* A threat to any nation in that region is a threat to all, and a threat to us.

3. *Our purpose is peace.* We have no military, political or territorial ambitions in the area.

4. *This is not just a jungle war, but a struggle for freedom on every front of human activity.* Our military and economic assistance to South Vietnam and Laos in particular has the purpose of helping these countries to repel aggression and strengthen their independence.

The threat to the free nations of Southeast Asia has long been clear. The North Vietnamese regime has constantly sought to take over South Vietnam and Laos. This Communist regime has violated the Geneva Accords for Vietnam. It has systematically conducted a campaign of subversion, which includes the direction, training, and supply of personnel and arms for the conduct of guerrilla warfare in South Vietnamese territory. In Laos, the North Vietnamese regime has maintained military forces, used Laotian territory for infiltration into South Vietnam, and most recently carried out combat operations—all in direct violation of the Geneva Agreements of 1962.

In recent months, the actions of the North Vietnamese regime have become steadily more threatening. In May, following new acts of Communist aggression in Laos, the United States undertook reconnaissance flights over Laotian territory, at the request of the Government of Laos. These flights had the essential mission of determining the situation in territory where Communist forces were preventing inspection by the International Control Commission. When the Communists attacked these aircraft, I responded by furnishing escort fighters with instructions to fire when fired upon. Thus, these latest North Vietnamese attacks on our naval vessels are not the first direct attack on armed forces of the United States.

As President of the United States I have concluded that I should now ask the Congress, on its part, to join in affirming the national determination that all such attacks will be met, and that the U.S. will continue in its basic policy of assisting the free nations of the area to defend their freedom.

As I have repeatedly made clear, the United States intends no rashness, and seeks no wider war. We must make it clear to all that the United States is united in its determination to bring about the end of Communist subversion and aggression in the area. We seek the full and effective restoration of the international agreements signed in Geneva in 1954, with respect to South Vietnam, and again in Geneva in 1962, with respect to Laos.

I recommend a Resolution expressing the support of the Congress for all necessary action to protect our armed forces and to assist nations covered by the SEATO [Southeast Asia Treaty Organization] Treaty. At the same time, I assure the Congress that we shall continue readily to explore any avenues of political solution that will effectively guarantee the removal of Communist subversion and the preservation of the independence of the nations of the area.

The Resolution could well be based upon similar resolutions enacted by the Congress in the past—to meet the threat to Formosa in 1955, to meet the threat to the Middle East in 1957, and to meet the threat in Cuba in 1962. It could state in the simplest terms the resolve and support of the Congress for action to deal appropriately with attacks against our armed forces and to defend freedom and preserve peace in southeast Asia in accordance with the obligations of the United States under the Southeast Asia Treaty. I urge the Congress to enact such a Resolution promptly and thus to give convincing evidence to the aggressive Communist nations, and to the world as a whole, that our policy in Southeast Asia will be carried forward—and that the peace and security of the area will be preserved.

The events of this week would in any event have made the passage of a Congressional Resolution essential. But there is an additional reason for doing so at a time when we are entering on three months of political campaigning. Hostile nations must understand that in such a period the United States will continue to protect its national interests, and that in these matters there is no division among us.

❧ 39 ❧
Lyndon B. Johnson's "Equality
of Result" Speech
(1965)

L YNDON B. JOHNSON emphasized civil rights and racial justice more than any
American president in history. As Senate majority leader during the 1950s,
he helped to enact the Civil Rights Act of 1957 and the Civil Rights Act of 1960,
both of them modest measures but the first to pass Congress since Reconstruction. Nevertheless, as a Texan with a deep southern accent, Johnson faced suspicion from liberals and civil rights groups when he assumed the presidency after
John F. Kennedy was assassinated on November 22, 1963. Would he champion
Kennedy's recently introduced and much more powerful civil rights bill or would
he let it languish?

Johnson not only championed the Civil Rights Act of 1964, he also used his
superior legislative skills to persuade Congress to pass a stronger bill than anyone
expected, especially in the areas of employment discrimination and access to public accommodations. On March 7, 1965, responding to public outrage at the violence that greeted civil rights marchers in Selma, Alabama, he introduced voting
rights legislation. Eight days after the march, Johnson borrowed the slogan of the
civil rights movement and told Congress and a national television audience that
in passing such a bill, "we shall overcome." Congress passed the Voting Rights
Act in August.

Even as the battle to secure voting rights was being fought, Johnson turned to
a different race-related subject in a June 6, 1965, commencement address at historically black Howard University. After saluting the progress toward freedom
that had been secured by the civil rights movement and the three branches of the
federal government, Johnson said, "freedom is not enough. . . . You do not take a
person who, for years, has been hobbled by chains and liberate him, bring him up
to the starting line of a race and then say, 'you are free to compete with all the others,' and still justly believe that you have been completely fair." Pointing to the
many ways that African Americans still lagged whites in economic prosperity, he
declared that "the next and the more profound stage of the battle for civil rights"
would be to achieve "not just equality as a right and a theory but equality as a fact
and equality as a result."

Johnson's speech laid the groundwork for subsequent federal efforts to mandate
"affirmative action" on behalf of racial minorities seeking economic and educational opportunity. Much more than the freedom agenda represented by the Civil

Rights Act of 1964 and the Voting Rights Act of 1965, these efforts would prove politically and constitutionally controversial for decades when whites saw them coming at their expense.

🐎 🐎 🐎

Dr. [James M.] Nabrit, [president of Howard University], my fellow Americans:

I am delighted at the chance to speak at this important and this historic institution. Howard has long been an outstanding center for the education of Negro Americans. Its students are of every race and color and they come from many countries of the world. It is truly a working example of democratic excellence.

Our earth is the home of revolution. In every corner of every continent men charged with hope contend with ancient ways in the pursuit of justice. They reach for the newest of weapons to realize the oldest of dreams, that each may walk in freedom and pride, stretching his talents, enjoying the fruits of the earth.

Our enemies may occasionally seize the day of change, but it is the banner of our revolution they take. And our own future is linked to this process of swift and turbulent change in many lands in the world. But nothing in any country touches us more profoundly, and nothing is more freighted with meaning for our own destiny than the revolution of the Negro American.

In far too many ways American Negroes have been another nation: deprived of freedom, crippled by hatred, the doors of opportunity closed to hope.

In our time change has come to this Nation, too. The American Negro, acting with impressive restraint, has peacefully protested and marched, entered the courtrooms and the seats of government, demanding a justice that has long been denied. The voice of the Negro was the call to action. But it is a tribute to America that, once aroused, the courts and the Congress, the President and most of the people, have been the allies of progress.

Thus we have seen the high court of the country declare that discrimination based on race was repugnant to the Constitution, and therefore void. We have seen in 1957, and 1960, and again in 1964, the first civil rights legislation in this Nation in almost an entire century.

As majority leader of the United States Senate, I helped to guide two of these bills through the Senate. And, as your President, I was proud to sign the third. And now very soon we will have the fourth—a new law guaranteeing every American the right to vote.

No act of my entire administration will give me greater satisfaction than the day when my signature makes this bill, too, the law of this land.

The voting rights bill will be the latest, and among the most important, in a long series of victories. But this victory—as Winston Churchill said of another triumph for freedom— "is not the end. It is not even the beginning of the end. But it is, perhaps, the end of the beginning."

That beginning is freedom; and the barriers to that freedom are tumbling down. Freedom is the right to share, share fully and equally, in American society—to vote, to hold a job, to enter a public place, to go to school. It is the right to be treated in every part of our national life as a person equal in dignity and promise to all others.

But freedom is not enough. You do not wipe away the scars of centuries by saying: Now you are free to go where you want, and do as you desire, and choose the leaders you please.

You do not take a person who, for years, has been hobbled by chains and liberate him, bring him up to the starting line of a race and then say, "you are free to compete with all the others," and still justly believe that you have been completely fair.

Thus it is not enough just to open the gates of opportunity. All our citizens must have the ability to walk through those gates.

This is the next and the more profound stage of the battle for civil rights. We seek not just freedom but opportunity. We seek not just legal equity but human ability, not just equality as a right and a theory but equality as a fact and equality as a result.

For the task is to give 20 million Negroes the same chance as every other American to learn and grow, to work and share in society, to develop their abilities—physical, mental and spiritual, and to pursue their individual happiness.

To this end equal opportunity is essential, but not enough, not enough. Men and women of all races are born with the same range of abilities. But ability is not just the product of birth. Ability is stretched or stunted by the family that you live with, and the neighborhood you live in—by the school you go to and the poverty or the richness of your surroundings. It is the product of a hundred unseen forces playing upon the little infant, the child, and finally the man.

This graduating class at Howard University is witness to the indomitable determination of the Negro American to win his way in American life.

The number of Negroes in schools of higher learning has almost doubled in 15 years. The number of nonwhite professional workers has more than doubled in 10 years. The median income of Negro college women tonight exceeds that of white college women. And there are also the enormous accomplishments of distinguished individual Negroes—many of them graduates of this institution, and one of them the first lady ambassador in the history of the United States.

These are proud and impressive achievements. But they tell only the story of a growing middle class minority, steadily narrowing the gap between them and their white counterparts.

But for the great majority of Negro Americans—the poor, the unemployed, the uprooted, and the dispossessed—there is a much grimmer story. They still, as we meet here tonight, are another nation. Despite the court orders and the laws, despite the legislative victories and the speeches, for them the walls are rising and the gulf is widening.

Here are some of the facts of this American failure.

Thirty-five years ago the rate of unemployment for Negroes and whites was about the same. Tonight the Negro rate is twice as high.

In 1948 the 8 percent unemployment rate for Negro teenage boys was actually less than that of whites. By last year that rate had grown to 23 percent, as against 13 percent for whites unemployed.

Between 1949 and 1959, the income of Negro men relative to white men declined in every section of this country. From 1952 to 1963 the median income of Negro families compared to white actually dropped from 57 percent to 53 percent.

In the years 1955 through 1957, 22 percent of experienced Negro workers were out of work at some time during the year. In 1961 through 1963 that proportion had soared to 29 percent.

Since 1947 the number of white families living in poverty has decreased 27 percent while the number of poorer nonwhite families decreased only 3 percent.

The infant mortality of nonwhites in 1940 was 70 percent greater than whites. Twenty-two years later it was 90 percent greater.

Moreover, the isolation of Negro from white communities is increasing, rather than decreasing as Negroes crowd into the central cities and become a city within a city.

Of course Negro Americans as well as white Americans have shared in our rising national abundance. But the harsh fact of the matter is that in the battle for true equality too many—far too many—are losing ground every day.

We are not completely sure why this is. We know the causes are complex and subtle. But we do know the two broad basic reasons. And we do know that we have to act.

First, Negroes are trapped—as many whites are trapped—in inherited, gateless poverty. They lack training and skills. They are shut in, in slums, without decent medical care. Private and public poverty combine to cripple their capacities.

We are trying to attack these evils through our poverty program, through our education program, through our medical care and our other health programs, and a dozen more of the Great Society programs that are aimed at the root causes of this poverty.

We will increase, and we will accelerate, and we will broaden this attack in years to come until this most enduring of foes finally yields to our unyielding will.

But there is a second cause—much more difficult to explain, more deeply grounded, more desperate in its force. It is the devastating heritage of long years of slavery; and a century of oppression, hatred, and injustice.

For Negro poverty is not white poverty. Many of its causes and many of its cures are the same. But there are differences-deep, corrosive, obstinate differences—radiating painful roots into the community, and into the family, and the nature of the individual.

These differences are not racial differences. They are solely and simply the consequence of ancient brutality, past injustice, and present prejudice. They are anguishing to observe. For the Negro they are a constant reminder of oppression. For the white they are a constant reminder of guilt. But they must be faced and they must be dealt with and they must be overcome, if we are ever to reach the time when the only difference between Negroes and whites is the color of their skin.

Nor can we find a complete answer in the experience of other American minorities. They made a valiant and a largely successful effort to emerge from poverty and prejudice.

The Negro, like these others, will have to rely mostly upon his own efforts. But he just can not do it alone. For they did not have the heritage of centuries to overcome, and they did not have a cultural tradition which had been twisted and battered by endless years of hatred and hopelessness, nor were they excluded—these others— because of race or color—a feeling whose dark intensity is matched by no other prejudice in our society.

Nor can these differences be understood as isolated infirmities. They are a seamless web. They cause each other. They result from each other. They reinforce each other.

Much of the Negro community is buried under a blanket of history and circumstance. It is not a lasting solution to lift just one corner of that blanket. We must stand on all sides and we must raise the entire cover if we are to liberate our fellow citizens.

One of the differences is the increased concentration of Negroes in our cities. More than 73 percent of all Negroes live in urban areas compared with less than 70 percent of the whites. Most of these Negroes live in slums. Most of these Negroes live together—a separated people.

Men are shaped by their world. When it is a world of decay, ringed by an invisible wall, when escape is arduous and uncertain, and the saving pressures of a more hopeful society are unknown, it can cripple the youth and it can desolate the men.

There is also the burden that a dark skin can add to the search for a productive place in our society. Unemployment strikes most swiftly and broadly at the Negro, and this burden erodes hope. Blighted hope breeds despair. Despair brings indifferences to the learning which offers a way out. And despair, coupled with indifferences, is often the source of destructive rebellion against the fabric of society.

There is also the lacerating hurt of early collision with white hatred or prejudice, distaste or condescension. Other groups have felt similar intolerance. But success and achievement could wipe it away. They do not change the color of a man's skin. I have seen this uncomprehending pain in the eyes of the little, young Mexican-American schoolchildren that I taught many years ago. But it can be overcome. But, for many, the wounds are always open.

Perhaps most important—its influence radiating to every part of life—is the breakdown of the Negro family structure. For this, most of all, white America must accept responsibility. It flows from centuries of oppression and persecution of the Negro man. It flows from the long years of degradation and discrimination, which have attacked his dignity and assaulted his ability to produce for his family.

This, too, is not pleasant to look upon. But it must be faced by those whose serious intent is to improve the life of all Americans.

Only a minority—less than half—of all Negro children reach the age of 18 having lived all their lives with both of their parents. At this moment, tonight, little less than two-thirds are at home with both of their parents. Probably a majority of all Negro children receive federally-aided public assistance sometime during their childhood.

The family is the cornerstone of our society. More than any other force it shapes the attitude, the hopes, the ambitions, and the values of the child. And when the family collapses it is the children that are usually damaged. When it happens on a massive scale the community itself is crippled.

So, unless we work to strengthen the family, to create conditions under which most parents will stay together—all the rest: schools, and playgrounds, and public assistance, and private concern, will never be enough to cut completely the circle of despair and deprivation.

There is no single easy answer to all of these problems.

Jobs are part of the answer. They bring the income which permits a man to provide for his family.

Decent homes in decent surroundings and a chance to learn—an equal chance to learn—are part of the answer.

Welfare and social programs better designed to hold families together are part of the answer.

Care for the sick is part of the answer.

An understanding heart by all Americans is another big part of the answer.

And to all of these fronts—and a dozen more—I will dedicate the expanding efforts of the Johnson administration.

But there are other answers that are still to be found. Nor do we fully understand even all of the problems. Therefore, I want to announce tonight that this fall I intend to call a White House conference of scholars, and experts, and outstanding Negro leaders—men of both races—and officials of Government at every level.

This White House conference's theme and title will be "To Fulfill These Rights."

Its object will be to help the American Negro fulfill the rights which, after the long time of injustice, he is finally about to secure.

To move beyond opportunity to achievement.

To shatter forever not only the barriers of law and public practice, but the walls which bound the condition of many by the color of his skin.

To dissolve, as best we can, the antique enmities of the heart which diminish the holder, divide the great democracy, and do wrong—great wrong—to the children of God.

And I pledge you tonight that this will be a chief goal of my administration, and of my program next year, and in the years to come. And I hope, and I pray, and I believe, it will be a part of the program of all America.

For what is justice?

It is to fulfill the fair expectations of man.

Thus, American justice is a very special thing. For, from the first, this has been a land of towering expectations. It was to be a nation where each man could be ruled by the common consent of all—enshrined in law, given life by institutions, guided by men themselves subject to its rule. And all—all of every station and origin—would be touched equally in obligation and in liberty.

Beyond the law lay the land. It was a rich land, glowing with more abundant promise than man had ever seen. Here, unlike any place yet known, all were to share the harvest.

And beyond this was the dignity of man. Each could become whatever his qualities of mind and spirit would permit—to strive, to seek, and, if he could, to find his happiness.

This is American justice. We have pursued it faithfully to the edge of our imperfections, and we have failed to find it for the American Negro.

So, it is the glorious opportunity of this generation to end the one huge wrong of the American Nation and, in so doing, to find America for ourselves, with the same immense thrill of discovery which gripped those who first began to realize that here, at last, was a home for freedom.

All it will take is for all of us to understand what this country is and what this country must become.

The Scripture promises: "I shall light a candle of understanding in thine heart, which shall not be put out."

Together, and with millions more, we can light that candle of understanding in the heart of all America.

And, once lit, it will never again go out.

⊰ 40 ⊱

Richard Nixon's China Trip Announcement

(1971)

RICHARD NIXON'S ELECTION as president in 1968 marked the greatest political comeback in American history. After losing the 1960 election to John F. Kennedy, Nixon was defeated two years later in a bid to become governor of California. The day after that defeat, Nixon angrily announced his retirement from politics. "You won't have Nixon to kick around anymore," he told a stunned audience of reporters, "because, gentlemen, this is my last press conference." Nevertheless, in 1968 Nixon won the Republican presidential nomination with a series of primary victories that convinced party leaders he could still appeal to voters. On election day he eked out a victory over Vice President Hubert H. Humphrey, the Democratic nominee. Nixon's winning margin was almost as narrow as his losing margin to Kennedy eight years earlier.

Nixon's political career had been constructed on a foundation of anticommunism. In his first election to the House of Representatives in 1946, Nixon accused incumbent Democrat Jerry Voorhis of being a socialist. Nixon gained national fame when he became the chair of a subcommittee of the House Un-American Activities Committee in 1948 and uncovered evidence that Alger Hiss, a former high-ranking official of the State Department, was a communist spy. Running for the Senate in 1950, Nixon called his opponent, Helen Gahagan Douglas, the "pink lady" (not a "red" communist exactly, but not a patriot either). Renowned for his claims that Democratic leaders were soft on communism, Nixon was chosen in 1952 to run for vice president on the Republican ticket headed by Dwight D. Eisenhower.

Nixon's rise to political prominence on the basis of anticommunism both shaped and reflected the tenor of the times. In the late 1940s the United States and the Soviet Union had ended their World War II alliance and entered into a cold war. The long-standing friendship between the United States and China also came to an end when, in 1949, a communist revolution led by Mao Zedong overthrew the government of Chiang Kai-shek. Even after Chiang and his supporters fled to the offshore island of Formosa (renamed Taiwan), the United States continued to recognize his regime as the legitimate government of China. Diplomatic relations between the United States and the Maoist government of mainland China were virtually nonexistent, and the rhetoric of the two nations was mutually hostile.

Politically, few Democrats or liberal Republicans during the 1950s and 1960s dared broach the subject of better relations with China, for fear of bringing down the wrath of conservatives such as Nixon. It was all the more surprising, then, that on July 15, 1971, President Nixon appeared on national television to announce in a three-and-one-half-minute statement that he would be traveling to China sometime in early 1972 at the invitation of the communist government. The purpose of the visit, Nixon said, would be "to seek the normalization of relations" between the United States and China. The president also revealed that the trip had been arranged at his direction through a series of secret visits to China by his national security adviser, Henry Kissinger, during the preceding two years. Nixon made the China trip, which was politically and diplomatically successful, in February 1972.

Many analysts believe that only a staunch anticommunist like Nixon could have ended American hostility to such a bitter enemy without provoking widespread political opposition. Part of his motive seems to have been to take advantage of the developing tensions between China and the Soviet Union by forging a relationship between the United States and China. Playing each communist nation against the other, Nixon also was welcomed to the Soviet Union by Leonid Brezhnev in May 1972. The two leaders concluded their meeting by signing a strategic arms limitation treaty.

Nixon's trips to China and the Soviet Union were the first by an American president. "Summit" meetings (Winston Churchill coined the term in 1953) between the president and the leader of one or more other nations were rare until World War II but have become common since then.

🐎 🐎 🐎

Good evening.

I have requested this television time tonight to announce a major development in our efforts to build a lasting peace in the world.

As I have pointed out on a number of occasions over the past three years, there can be no stable and enduring peace without the participation of the Peoples [sic] Republic of China and its 750 million people. That is why I have undertaken initiatives in several areas to open the door for more normal relations between our two countries.

In pursuance of that goal, I sent Dr. Kissinger, my Assistant for National Security Affairs, to Peking during his recent world tour for the purpose of having talks with

Premier Chou En-lai. The announcement I shall now read is being issued simultaneously in Peking and in the United States.

"Premier Chou En-lai and Dr. Henry Kissinger, President Nixon's Assistant for National Security Affairs, held talks in Peking from July 9 to 11, 1971. Knowing of President Nixon's expressed desire to visit the Peoples Republic of China, Premier Chou En-lai, on behalf of the Government of the Peoples Republic of China, has extended an invitation to President Nixon to visit China at an appropriate date before May 1972. President Nixon has accepted the invitation with pleasure."

The meeting between the leaders of China and the United States is to seek the normalization of relations between the two countries and also to exchange views on questions of concern to the two sides. In anticipation of the inevitable speculation which will follow this announcement, I want to put our policy in the clearest possible context.

Our action in seeking a new relationship with the Peoples Republic of China will not be at the expense of our old friends. It is not directed against any other nation. We seek friendly relations with all nations. Any nation can be our friend without being any other nation's enemy.

I have taken this action because of my profound conviction that all nations will gain from a reduction of tensions and a better relationship between the United States and the Peoples Republic of China.

It is in that spirit that I will undertake what I deeply hope will become a journey for peace, peace not just for our generation, but for future generations on this earth we share together.

Thank you and good night.

❧ 41 ❧

The McGovern–Fraser Commission Report

(1971)

ONE MAJOR COMPLAINT of Vice President Hubert H. Humphrey's defeated opponents at the 1968 Democratic National Convention was that they had not been given a fair chance to compete in the delegate selection process. Only about one-third of the convention's delegates were chosen in primaries; the remaining two-thirds were appointed by state party leaders, many of them before the election year even began. The one-third strongly supported antiwar candidates Sen. Eugene McCarthy of Minnesota and, until he was assassinated on June 4, Sen. Robert F. Kennedy of New York. The two-thirds translated their superior numbers into control of the convention and the nomination of their favorite candidate, Humphrey.

Although the 1968 convention made few changes in its own structure, it voted to require that all Democratic voters receive "full, meaningful and timely opportunity to participate in the selection of delegates" to the 1972 convention.

To implement the convention's decision, in February 1969 the Democratic National Committee created the Commission on Party Structure and Delegate Selection, chaired by Sen. George McGovern of South Dakota and, later, by Rep. Donald Fraser of Minnesota. The McGovern–Fraser Commission, as it came to be known, issued its report, *Mandate for Change,* in September 1971. The report included eighteen detailed guidelines that the state parties were obliged to follow in choosing delegates to the 1972 convention.

Although the McGovern–Fraser Commission received little attention at the time, it transformed the presidential nominating process. The commission banned a number of traditional practices, including the "unit rule" that allowed each state party to award all of its votes to the candidate who had a majority of the delegation. The commission also required that racial minorities, women, and young voters be represented at the national convention in proportion to their share of the population in each state. Most important, the commission demanded that all convention delegates be chosen in an open, participatory process, either a presidential primary or a caucus in which any Democrat could vote.

To the surprise and dismay of the McGovern–Fraser Commission, most states decided to go the simpler, primary route. By the end of the decade, the number of presidential primaries had doubled from seventeen to thirty-five. Because the new primaries required changes in state laws, state Republican parties usually followed the Democrats' lead.

The McGovern–Fraser reforms affected not just the process but also the politics of presidential nominations. In 1960 John F. Kennedy, a Democrat, and eight years later, Richard Nixon, a Republican, had entered primaries, but only as a strategy to persuade the party leaders who controlled nominations that they were electable. In 1968, after Lyndon B. Johnson withdrew from the presidential race in March, Humphrey received the Democratic nomination without entering a single primary. But since 1972 party leaders have had no choice but to accept the verdict of the primaries. No one has been nominated for president by either of the two major parties without defeating their rivals at the ballot box.

<hr />

On November 19 and 20, 1969, the Commission, meeting in open session in Washington, D.C., adopted the following Guidelines for delegate selection. . . .

A–1 Discrimination on the basis of race, color, creed, or national origin

The 1964 Democratic National Convention adopted a resolution which conditioned the seating of delegations at future conventions on the assurance that discrimination in any State Party affairs on the grounds of race, color, creed or national origin did not occur. The 1968 Convention adopted the 1964 Convention resolution for inclusion in the Call to the 1972 Convention. In 1966, the Special Equal Rights

Committee, which had been created in 1964, adopted six anti-discrimination standards—designated as the "six basic elements"—for the State Parties to meet. These standards were adopted by the Democratic National Committee in January 1968 as its official policy statement.

These actions demonstrate the intention of the Democratic Party to ensure a full opportunity for all minority group members to participate in the delegate selection process. To supplement the requirements of the 1964 and 1968 Conventions, the Commission requires that:

1. State Parties add the six basic elements of the Special Equal Rights Committee to their Party rules and take appropriate steps to secure their implementation;

2. State Parties overcome the effects of past discrimination by affirmative steps to encourage minority group participation, including representation of minority groups on the national convention delegation in reasonable relationship to the group's presence in the population of the State.

A–2 Discrimination on the basis of age or sex

The Commission believes that discrimination on the grounds of age or sex is inconsistent with full and meaningful opportunity to participate in the delegate selection process. Therefore, the Commission requires State Parties to eliminate all vestiges of discrimination on these grounds. Furthermore, the Commission requires State Parties to overcome the effects of past discrimination by affirmative steps to encourage representation on the national convention delegation of young people— defined as people of not more than thirty nor less than eighteen years of age—and women in reasonable relationship to their presence in the population of the State. Moreover, the Commission requires State Parties to amend their Party rules to allow and encourage any Democrat of eighteen years or more to participate in all party affairs.

When State law controls, the Commission requires State Parties to make all feasible efforts to repeal, amend, or otherwise modify such laws to accomplish the stated purpose. . . .

A–5 Existence of party rules

In order for rank-and-file Democrats to have a full and meaningful opportunity to participate in the delegate selection process, they must have access to the substantive and procedural rules which govern the process. In some States the process is not regulated by law or rule, but by resolution of the State Committee and by tradition. In other States, the rules exist, but generally are inaccessible. In still others, rules and laws regulate only the formal aspects of the selection process (e.g., date and place of the State convention) and leave to Party resolution or tradition the more substantive matters (e.g., intrastate apportionment of votes; rotation of alternates; nomination of delegates).

The Commission believes that any of these arrangements is inconsistent with the spirit of the Call in that they permit excessive discretion on the part of Party officials, which may be used to deny or limit full and meaningful opportunity to participate.

Therefore, the Commission requires State Parties to adopt and make available readily accessible statewide Party rules and statutes which prescribe the State's delegate selection process with sufficient details and clarity. . . .

Furthermore, the Commission requires State Parties to adopt rules which will facilitate maximum participation among interested Democrats in the processes by which National Convention delegates are selected. Among other things, these rules should provide for dates, times, and public places which would be most likely to encourage interested Democrats to attend all meetings involved in the delegate selection process.

The Commission requires State Parties to adopt explicit written Party rules which provide for uniform times and dates of all meetings involved in the delegate selection process. These meetings and events include caucuses, conventions, committee meetings, primaries, filing deadlines, and Party enrollment periods. Rules regarding time and date should be uniform in two senses. First, each stage of the delegate selection process should occur at a uniform time and date throughout the State. Second, the time and date should be uniform from year to year. . . .

B–2 Clarity of purpose

An opportunity for full participation in the delegate selection process is not meaningful unless each Party member can clearly express his preference for candidates for delegates to the National Convention, or for those who will select such delegates. In many States, a Party member who wishes to affect the selection of the delegation must do so by voting for delegates or Party officials who will engage in many activities unrelated to the delegate selection process.

Whenever other Party business is mixed, without differentiation, with the delegate selection process, the Commission requires State Parties to make it clear to voters how they are participating in a process that will nominate their Party's candidate for President. Furthermore, in States which employ a convention or committee system, the Commission requires State Parties to clearly designate the delegate selection procedures as distinct from other Party business. . . .

B–5 Unit rule

In 1968, many States used the unit rule at various stages in the processes by which delegates were selected to the National Convention. The 1968 Convention defined unit rule, did not enforce the unit rule on any delegate in 1968, and added language to the 1972 Call requiring that "the unit rule not be used in any stage of the delegate selection process." In light of the Convention action, the Commission requires State Parties to add to their explicit written rules provisions which forbid the use of the unit rule or the practice of instructing delegates to vote against their stated preferences at any stage of the delegate selection process.

B–6 Adequate representation of minority views on presidential candidates at each stage in the delegate selection process

The Commission believes that a full and meaningful opportunity to participate in the delegate selection process is precluded unless the presidential preference of each

Democrat is fairly represented at all levels of the process. Therefore, the Commission urges each State Party to adopt procedures which will provide fair representation of minority views on presidential candidates and recommends that the 1972 Convention adopt a rule requiring State Parties to provide for the representation of minority views to the highest level of the nominating process.

The Commission believes that there are at least two different methods by which a State Party can provide for such representation. First, in at-large elections it can divide delegate votes among presidential candidates in proportion to their demonstrated strength. Second, it can choose delegates from fairly apportioned districts no larger than congressional districts. . . .

C–2 Automatic (ex-officio) delegates . . .

In some States, certain public or Party officeholders are delegates to county, State and National Conventions by virtue of their official position. The Commission believes that State laws, Party rules and Party resolutions which so provide are inconsistent with the Call to the 1972 Convention for three reasons:

1. The Call requires all delegates to be chosen by primary, convention or committee procedures. Achieving delegate status by virtue of public or Party office is not one of the methods sanctioned by the 1968 Convention.

2. The Call requires all delegates to be chosen by a process which begins within the calendar year of the Convention. Ex-officio delegates usually were elected (or appointed) to their positions before the calendar year of the Convention.

3. The Call requires all delegates to be chosen by a process in which all Democrats have a full and meaningful opportunity to participate. Delegate selection by a process in which certain places on the delegation are not open to competition among Democrats is inconsistent with a full and meaningful opportunity to participate.

Accordingly, the Commission requires State Parties to repeal Party rules or resolutions which provide for ex-officio delegates. When State law controls, the Commission requires State Parties to make all feasible efforts to repeal, amend or otherwise modify such laws to accomplish the stated purpose. . . .

C–4 Premature delegate selection (timeliness)

The 1968 Convention adopted language adding to the Call to the 1972 Convention the requirement that the delegate selection process must begin within the calendar year of the Convention. In many States, Governors, State Chairmen, State, district and county committees who are chosen before the calendar year of the Convention, select—or choose agents to select—the delegates. These practices are inconsistent with the Call.

The Commission believes that the 1968 Convention intended to prohibit any untimely procedures which have any direct bearing on the process by which National Convention delegates are selected. The process by which delegates are nominated is such a procedure. Therefore, the Commission requires State Parties to prohibit any practices by which officials elected or appointed before the calendar year choose nominating committees or propose or endorse a slate of delegates—even when the possibility for a challenge to such slate or committee is provided.

When State law controls, the Commission requires State Parties to make all feasible efforts to repeal, amend, or modify such laws to accomplish the stated purposes. . . .

Conclusion

The Guidelines that we have adopted are designed to open the door to all Democrats who seek a voice in their Party's most important decision: the choice of its presidential nominee. We are concerned with the opportunity to participate, rather than the actual level of participation, although the number of Democrats who vote in their caucuses, meetings and primaries is an important index of the opportunities available to them.

As members of the Commission, we are less concerned with the product of the meetings than the process, although we believe that the product will be improved in the give and take of open, fairly conducted meetings.

We believe that popular participation is more than a proud heritage of our party, more even than a first principle. We believe that popular control of the Democratic Party is necessary for its survival.

We do not believe this is an idle threat. When we view our past history and present policies alongside that of the Republican Party, we are struck by one unavoidable fact: our Party is the only major vehicle for peaceful, progressive change in the United States.

If we are not an open party; if we do not represent the demands of change, then the danger is not that people will go to the Republican Party; it is that there will no longer be a way for people committed to orderly change to fulfill their needs and desires within our traditional political system. It is that they will turn to third and fourth party politics or the anti-politics of the street.

We believe that our Guidelines offer an alternative for these people. We believe that the Democratic Party can meet the demands for participation with their adoption. We trust that all Democrats will give the Guidelines their careful consideration.

We are encouraged by the response of state Parties to date. In 40 states and territories the Democratic Party has appointed reform commissions (or subcommittees of the state committee) to investigate ways of modernizing party procedures. Of these, 17 have already issued reports and recommendations. In a number of states, party rules and state laws have already been revised, newly written or amended to insure the opportunity for participation in Party matters by all Democrats. . . .

All of these efforts lead us to the conclusion that the Democratic Party is bent on meaningful change. A great European statesman once said, "All things are possible, even the fact that an action in accord with honor and honesty ultimately appears to be a prudent political investment." We share this sentiment. We are confident that party reform, dictated by our Party's heritage and principles, will insure a strong, winning and united Party.

❧ 42 ❧
The War Powers Resolution
(1973)

T HE AMERICAN FAILURE in the Vietnam War tested the nation's belief during
the post–World War II era that the executive branch, with its superior
sources of information, its unity of command, and its ability to act with dispatch,
should be responsible for determining when and how the United States will go to
war. In 1973 Congress passed the War Powers Resolution and, after President
Richard Nixon vetoed the measure, overrode his veto on November 7 by a margin
of 284–135 in the House of Representatives and 75–18 in the Senate.

The War Powers Resolution requires the president to consult with Congress
"in every possible instance" before committing American armed forces to hostile
or dangerous situations. After making such a commitment, the president is
charged to report his actions in writing to congressional leaders. Within sixty or,
by special presidential request, ninety days, American forces must be withdrawn
unless Congress votes to authorize their continued involvement. Even within that
period, Congress can vote to withdraw the forces.

Despite the act's overwhelming support in Congress, its opponents proved prescient in their criticisms. Conservatives echoed Nixon, who vetoed the act as being
"both unconstitutional and dangerous to the best interests of our Nation." A few liberals, led by Democratic senator Thomas F. Eagleton of Missouri, noted that the act
effectively sanctions virtually any presidential use of force for ninety days. Although
Congress has the legal power to force a withdrawal, charged Frank Church, a Democratic senator from Idaho, "I cannot imagine a situation where a President would take
us into a foreign war of major proportions under circumstances that would not cause
both the public and Congress to rally around the flag, at least for sixty days."

Since 1973 presidents have questioned the constitutionality of the War Powers
Resolution. Military operations were undertaken by Presidents Gerald R. Ford (the
Vietnam evacuation and *Mayaguez* rescue), Jimmy Carter (the attempted Iranian
hostage rescue), Ronald Reagan (the Lebanon mission, Grenada invasion, bombing
of Libya, and naval escort of oil tankers in the Persian Gulf), George H. W. Bush
(the Panama invasion and Persian Gulf War), Bill Clinton (the bombing of Iraq
and ordering of troops to Somalia, Haiti, and Bosnia), George W. Bush (the wars in
Afghanistan and Iraq), and Barack Obama (aerial attacks against despotic regimes
and terrorists throughout much of the Middle East). In few instances has the president complied with the letter, much less the spirit, of the resolution. Prior consultation with Congress has typically been perfunctory or nonexistent. Written
reports often have not been filed.

Congress has seldom voted to start the sixty-day clock, and never when it mattered. In 1983 Congress decreed that the clock started ticking when Reagan invaded Grenada. (He did not consult with Congress before launching the invasion.) But the troops returned home victorious in a few days, making the time requirement irrelevant.

To be sure, because of the War Powers Resolution, a president would find it more difficult to involve the United States in a drawn-out, Vietnam-style war without congressional support or acquiescence, which is why the elder Bush and, later, the younger sought congressional resolutions authorizing the use of force against Iraq in 1990 and 2002, respectively. They, along with Obama, who sought a similar resolution to authorize the use of force against the self-described Islamic State in 2015, claimed that although they desired such a resolution, they did not need one in order to act. But the main lesson of more than four decades of experience under the War Powers Resolution is that law cannot substitute for political will if Congress intends to curb the president's role in making war.

🐾 🐾 🐾

SECTION 1. This joint resolution may be cited as the "War Powers Resolution."

SECTION 2. (a) It is the purpose of this joint resolution to fulfill the intent of the framers of the Constitution of the United States and insure that the collective judgment of both the Congress and the president will apply to the introduction of United States armed forces into hostilities, or into situations where imminent involvement in hostilities is clearly indicated by the circumstances, and to the continued use of such forces in hostilities or in such situations.

(b) Under article 1, section 8, of the Constitution, it is specifically provided that the Congress shall have the power to make all laws necessary and proper for carrying into execution, not only its own powers but also all other powers vested by the Constitution in the government of the United States, or in any department or officer thereof.

(c) The constitutional powers of the president as commander-in-chief to introduce United States armed forces into hostilities, or into situations where imminent involvement in hostilities is clearly indicated by the circumstances, are exercised only pursuant to (1) a declaration of war, (2) specific statutory authorization, or (3) a national emergency created by attack upon the United States, its territories or possessions, or its armed forces.

SECTION 3. The president in every possible instance shall consult with Congress before introducing United States armed forces into hostilities or into situations where imminent involvement in hostilities is clearly indicated by the circumstances, and after every such introduction shall consult regularly with the Congress until United States armed forces are no longer engaged in hostilities or have been removed from such situations.

SECTION 4. (a) In the absence of a declaration of war, in any case in which United States armed forces are introduced—

(1) into hostilities or into situations where imminent involvement in hostilities is clearly indicated by the circumstances;

(2) into the territory, airspace, or waters of a foreign nation, while equipped for combat, except for deployments which relate solely to supply, replacement, repair, or training of such forces; or

(3) in numbers which substantially enlarge United States armed forces equipped for combat already located in a foreign nation;

the President shall submit within 48 hours to the Speaker of the House of Representatives and to the president pro tempore of the Senate a report, in writing, setting forth—

(A) the circumstances necessitating the introduction of United States armed forces;

(B) the constitutional and legislative authority under which such introduction took place; and

(C) the estimated scope and duration of the hostilities or involvement.

(b) The president shall provide such other information as the Congress may request in the fulfillment of its constitutional responsibilities with respect to committing the nation to war and to the use of United States armed forces abroad.

(c) Whenever United States armed forces are introduced into hostilities or into any situation described in subsection (a) of this section, the president shall, so long as such armed forces continue to be engaged in such hostilities or situation, report to the Congress periodically on the status of such hostilities or situation as well as on the scope and duration of such hostilities or situation, but in no event shall he report to the Congress less often than once every six months.

SECTION 5. (a) Each report submitted pursuant to section 4(a) (1) shall be transmitted to the Speaker of the House of Representatives and to the president pro tempore of the Senate on the same calendar day. Each report so transmitted shall be referred to the Committee on Foreign Affairs of the House of Representatives and to the Committee on Foreign Relations of the Senate for appropriate action. If, when the report is transmitted, the Congress has adjourned sine die or has adjourned for any period in excess of three calendar days, the Speaker of the House of Representatives and the president pro tempore of the Senate, if they deem it advisable (or if petitioned by at least 30 percent of the membership of their respective houses) shall jointly request the president to convene Congress in order that it may consider the report and take appropriate action pursuant to this section.

(b) Within sixty calendar days after a report is submitted or is required to be submitted pursuant to section 4(a) (1), whichever is earlier, the president shall terminate any use of United States armed forces with respect to which such report was submitted (or required to be submitted), unless the Congress (1) has declared war or has enacted a specific authorization for such use of United States armed forces, (2) has extended by law such sixty-day period, or (3) is physically unable to meet as a result of an armed attack upon the United States. Such sixty-day period shall be extended for not more than an additional thirty days if the president determines and certifies to the Congress in writing that unavoidable military necessity respecting the safety of the United States armed forces requires the continued use of such armed forces in the course of bringing about a prompt removal of such forces.

(c) Notwithstanding subsection (b), at any time that United States armed forces are engaged in hostilities outside the territory of the United States, its possessions and territories without a declaration of war or specific statutory authorization, such forces shall be removed by the president if the Congress so directs by concurrent resolution.

SECTION 6. (a) Any joint resolution or bill introduced pursuant to section 5(b) at least thirty calendar days before the expiration of the sixty-day period specified in such section shall be referred to the Committee on Foreign Affairs of the House of Representatives or the Committee on Foreign Relations of the Senate, as the case may be, and such committee shall report one such joint resolution or bill, together with its recommendations, not later than twenty-four calendar days before the expiration of the sixty-day period specified in such section, unless such house shall otherwise determine by the yeas and nays.

(b) Any joint resolution or bill so reported shall become the pending business of the house in question (in the case of the Senate the time for debate shall be equally divided between the proponents and the opponents), and shall be voted on within three calendar days thereafter, unless such house shall otherwise determine by yeas and nays.

(c) Such a joint resolution or bill passed by one house shall be referred to the committee of the other house named in subsection (a) and shall be reported out not later than fourteen calendar days before the expiration of the sixty-day period specified in section 5(b). The joint resolution or bill so reported shall become the pending business of the house in question and shall be voted on within three calendar days after it has been reported, unless such house shall otherwise determine by yeas and nays.

(d) In the case of any disagreement between the two houses of Congress with respect to a joint resolution or bill passed by both houses, conferees shall be promptly appointed and the committee of conference shall make and file a report with respect to such resolution or bill not later than four calendar days before the expiration of the sixty-day period specified in section 5(b). In the event the conferees are unable to agree within forty-eight hours, they shall report back to their respective houses in disagreement. Notwithstanding any rule in either house concerning the printing of conference reports in the Record or concerning any delay in the consideration of such reports, such report shall be acted on by both houses not later than the expiration of such sixty-day period.

SECTION 7. (a) Any concurrent resolution introduced pursuant to section 5(c) shall be referred to the Committee on Foreign Affairs of the House of Representatives or the Committee on Foreign Relations of the Senate, as the case may be, and one such concurrent resolution shall be reported out by such committee together with its recommendations within fifteen calendar days, unless such house shall otherwise determine by the yeas and nays.

(b) Any concurrent resolution so reported shall become the pending business of the house in question (in the case of the Senate the time for debate shall be equally divided between the proponents and the opponents) and shall be voted on within three calendar days thereafter, unless such house shall otherwise determine by yeas and nays.

(c) Such a concurrent resolution passed by one house shall be referred to the committee of the other house named in subsection (a) and shall be reported out by such committee together with its recommendations within fifteen calendar days and shall thereupon become the pending business of such house and shall be voted upon within three calendar days, unless such house shall otherwise determine by yeas and nays.

(d) In the case of any disagreement between the two houses of Congress with respect to a concurrent resolution passed by both houses, conferees shall be promptly appointed and the committee of conference shall make and file a report with respect to such concurrent resolution within six calendar days after the legislation is referred to the committee of conference. Notwithstanding any rule in either house concerning the printing of conference reports in the Record or concerning any delay in the consideration of such reports, such report shall be acted on by both houses not later than six calendar days after the conference report is filed. In the event the conferees are unable to agree within forty-eight hours, they shall report back to their respective houses in disagreement.

SECTION 8. (a) Authority to introduce United States armed forces into hostilities or into situations wherein involvement in hostilities is clearly indicated by the circumstances shall not be inferred—

(1) from any provision of law (whether or not in effect before the date of the enactment of this joint resolution), including any provision contained in any appropriation act, unless such provision specifically authorizes the introduction of United States armed forces into hostilities or into such situations and states that it is intended to constitute specific statutory authorization within the meaning of this joint resolution; or

(2) from any treaty heretofore or henceafter ratified unless such treaty is implemented by legislation specifically authorizing the introduction of United States armed forces into hostilities or into such situations and stating that it is intended to constitute specific statutory authorization within the meaning of this joint resolution.

(b) Nothing in this joint resolution shall be construed to require any further specific statutory authorization to permit members of United States armed forces to participate jointly with members of the armed forces of one or more foreign countries in the headquarters operations of high-level military commands which were established prior to the date of enactment of this joint resolution and pursuant to the United Nations Charter or any treaty ratified by the United States prior to such date.

(c) For purposes of this joint resolution, the term "introduction of United States armed forces" includes the assignment of members of such armed forces to command, coordinate, participate in the movement of, or accompany the regular or irregular military forces of any foreign country or government when such military forces are engaged, or there exists an imminent threat that such forces will become engaged, in hostilities.

(d) Nothing in this joint resolution—

(1) is intended to alter the constitutional authority of the Congress or of the president, or the provisions of existing treaties; or

(2) shall be construed as granting any authority to the president with respect to the introduction of United States armed forces into hostilities or into situations wherein involvement in hostilities is clearly indicated by the circumstances which authority he would not have had in the absence of this joint resolution.

SECTION 9. If any provision of this joint resolution or the application thereof to any person or circumstance is held invalid, the remainder of the joint resolution and the application of such provision to any other person or circumstance shall not be affected thereby.

SECTION 10. This joint resolution shall take effect on the date of its enactment.
     Passed over presidential veto Nov. 7, 1973.

❧ 43 ❧

Proposed Articles of Impeachment against Richard Nixon

(1974)

O N JULY 17, 1972, five burglars secretly employed by the Committee to Re-elect the President (better known by its acronym, CREEP) were caught breaking into the offices of the Democratic National Committee in the Watergate Hotel and office complex in Washington, D.C. The chain of command that had authorized the break-in, as well as a host of other illegal and unethical campaign activities, reached high into the administration of President Richard Nixon. In an effort to avoid embarrassing revelations, Nixon and some of his closest aides in the White House responded to news of the burglary by trying to obstruct official investigations into what happened. A combination of actions brought to light evidence of Nixon's involvement in the Watergate cover-up, including: diligent investigations by reporters Bob Woodward and Carl Bernstein of the *Washington Post* in 1972 and 1973; hearings by a special Senate committee chaired by Democratic senator Sam Ervin of North Carolina during the summer of 1973; testimony before the Ervin committee by White House counsel John Dean and other participants in the Watergate affair regarding their own, each other's, and (in Dean's case) the president's culpability; and the release of secret White House tape recordings.

In February 1974 the House Judiciary Committee began to consider impeaching the president for "high Crimes and Misdemeanors" in the second of only three serious presidential impeachment inquiries in American history. (See Documents 20, p. 100, and 50, p. 239.) Between July 27 and 29, the committee decided to recommend three articles of impeachment to the full House of Representatives.

Article I, which the committee approved by a bipartisan 27–11 vote, charged that Nixon had violated his oath to "preserve, protect, and defend the Constitution" as well as his constitutional responsibility to "take Care that the Laws be faithfully executed" with actions that obstructed the administration of justice in the Watergate case. These actions included: withholding evidence, condoning perjury, approving the payment of "hush money" to the five who were caught breaking into the Watergate, interfering with lawful investigations, and making false and misleading statements.

Article II, approved 28–10, contended that the president had misused and abused both his executive authority and the resources of various executive agencies, including the Federal Bureau of Investigation (FBI), the Central Intelligence Agency (CIA), the Internal Revenue Service, and the Justice Department's Criminal Division and Office of Watergate Special Prosecution Force. This article involved the Watergate cover-up and other misdeeds, such as a covert break-in, sponsored by White House operatives, into the office of Dr. Lewis Fielding, who was psychiatrist to former Defense Department employee Daniel Ellsberg. In particular, White House tapes revealed that Nixon had ordered the CIA to tell the FBI not to investigate the Watergate break-in too carefully for the false reason that national security would be jeopardized.

Article III, approved 21–17, charged Nixon with contempt of Congress for not cooperating with the House Judiciary Committee's impeachment investigation.

Because the committee's working standard for an impeachable offense was that it be an indictable crime "to the manifest injury of the people of the United States," it voted down two other proposed articles of impeachment. The first, which faulted the president for secretly bombing Cambodia, was judged not to be criminal. The second, Nixon's evasion of income taxes, was found to be a personal rather than a political crime.

※ ※ ※

Resolution

Impeaching Richard M. Nixon, President of the United States, of high crimes and misdemeanors.

Resolved, That Richard M. Nixon, President of the United States, is impeached for high crimes and misdemeanors, and that the following articles of impeachment be exhibited to the Senate:

Articles of impeachment exhibited by the House of Representatives of the United States of America in the name of itself and of all of the people of the United States of America, against Richard M. Nixon, President of the United States of America, in maintenance and support of its impeachment against him for high crimes and misdemeanors.

Article I

In his conduct of the office of President of the United States, Richard M. Nixon, in violation of his constitutional oath faithfully to execute the office of President of the United States and, to the best of his ability, preserve, protect, and defend the Constitution of the United States, and in violation of his constitutional duty to take care that the laws be faithfully executed, has prevented, obstructed, and impeded the administration of justice, in that:

On June 17, 1972, and prior thereto, agents of the Committee for the Re-election of the President committed unlawful entry of the headquarters of the Democratic National Committee in Washington, District of Columbia, for the purpose of securing political intelligence. Subsequent thereto, Richard M. Nixon, using the powers of his high office, engaged personally and through his subordinates and agents, in a course of conduct or plan designed to delay, impede, and obstruct the investigation of such unlawful entry; to cover up, conceal and protect those responsible; and to conceal the existence and scope of other unlawful covert activities.

The means used to implement this course of conduct or plan included one or more of the following:

(1) making or causing to be made false or misleading statements to lawfully authorized investigative officers and employees of the United States;

(2) withholding relevant and material evidence or information from lawfully authorized investigative officers and employees of the United States;

(3) approving, condoning, acquiescing in, and counseling witnesses with respect to the giving of false or misleading statements to lawfully authorized investigative officers and employees of the United States and false or misleading testimony in duly instituted judicial and congressional proceedings;

(4) interfering or endeavoring to interfere with the conduct of investigations by the Department of Justice of the United States, the Federal Bureau of Investigation, the Office of Watergate Special Prosecution Force, and Congressional Committees;

(5) approving, condoning, and acquiescing in, the surreptitious payment of substantial sums of money for the purpose of obtaining the silence or influencing the testimony of witnesses, potential witnesses or individuals who participated in such unlawful entry and other illegal activities;

(6) endeavoring to misuse the Central Intelligence Agency, an agency of the United States;

(7) disseminating information received from officers of the Department of Justice of the United States to subjects of investigations conducted by lawfully authorized investigative officers and employees of the United States, for the purpose of aiding and assisting such subjects in their attempts to avoid criminal liability;

(8) making false or misleading public statements for the purpose of deceiving the people of the United States into believing that a thorough and complete investigation had been conducted with respect to allegations of misconduct on the part of personnel of the executive branch of the United States and personnel of the Committee to Re-elect the President, and that there was no involvement of such personnel in such misconduct; or

(9) endeavoring to cause prospective defendants, and individuals duly tried and convicted, to expect favored treatment and consideration in return for their silence or false testimony, or rewarding individuals for their silence or false testimony.

In all of this, Richard M. Nixon has acted in a manner contrary to his trust as President and subversive of constitutional government, to the great prejudice of the cause of law and justice and to the manifest injury of the people of the United States.

Wherefore Richard M. Nixon, by such conduct, warrants impeachment and trial, and removal from office.

Article II

Using the powers of the office of President of the United States, Richard M. Nixon, in violation of his constitutional oath faithfully to execute the office of President of the United States and, to the best of his ability, preserve, protect, and defend the Constitution of the United States, and in disregard of his constitutional duty to take care that the laws be faithfully executed, has repeatedly engaged in conduct violating the constitutional rights of citizens, impairing the due and proper administration of justice and the conduct of lawful inquiries, or contravening the laws governing agencies of the executive branch and the purposes of these agencies.

This conduct has included one or more of the following:

(1) He has, acting personally and through his subordinates and agents, endeavored to obtain from the Internal Revenue Service, in violation of the constitutional rights of citizens, confidential information contained in income tax returns for purposes not authorized by law, and to cause, in violation of the constitutional rights of citizens, income tax audits or other income tax investigations to be initiated or conducted in a discriminatory manner.

(2) He misused the Federal Bureau of Investigation, the Secret Service, and other executive personnel, in violation or disregard of the constitutional rights of citizens, by directing or authorizing such agencies or personnel to conduct or continue electronic surveillance or other investigations for purposes unrelated to national security, the enforcement of laws, or any other lawful function of his office; he did direct, authorize, or permit the use of information obtained thereby for purposes unrelated to national security, the enforcement of laws, or any other lawful function of his office; and he did direct the concealment of certain records made by the Federal Bureau of Investigation of electronic surveillance.

(3) He has, acting personally and through his subordinates and agents, in violation or disregard of the constitutional rights of citizens, authorized and permitted to be maintained a secret investigative unit within the office of the President, financed in part with money derived from campaign contributions, which unlawfully utilized the resources of the Central Intelligence Agency, engaged in covert and unlawful activities, and attempted to prejudice the constitutional right of an accused to a fair trial.

(4) He has failed to take care that the laws were faithfully executed by failing to act when he knew or had reason to know that his close subordinates endeavored to impede and frustrate lawful inquiries by duly constituted executive, judicial, and legislative entities concerning the unlawful entry into the headquarters of the Democratic National Committee, and the cover-up thereof, and concerning other unlawful activities, including those relating to the confirmation of Richard Kleindienst as Attorney General of the United States, the electronic surveillance of private citizens, the break-in into the offices of Dr. Lewis Fielding, and the campaign financing practices of the Committee to Re-elect the President.

(5) In disregard of the rule of law, he knowingly misused the executive power by interfering with agencies of the executive branch, including the Federal Bureau of Investigation, the Criminal Division, and the Office of Watergate Special Prosecution Force, of the Department of Justice, and the Central Intelligence Agency, in violation of his duty to take care that the laws be faithfully executed.

In all of this, Richard M. Nixon has acted in a manner contrary to his trust as President and subversive of constitutional government, to the great prejudice of the cause of law and justice and to the manifest injury of the people of the United States.

Wherefore Richard M. Nixon, by such conduct, warrants impeachment and trial, and removal from office.

Article III

In his conduct of the office of President of the United States, Richard M. Nixon, contrary to his oath faithfully to execute the office of President of the United States and, to the best of his ability, preserve, protect, and defend the Constitution of the United States, and in violation of his constitutional duty to take care that the laws be faithfully executed, has failed without lawful cause or excuse to produce papers and things as directed by duly authorized subpoenas issued by the Committee on the Judiciary of the House of Representatives on April 11, 1974, May 15, 1974, May 30, 1974, and June 24, 1974, and willfully disobeyed such subpoenas. The subpoenaed papers and things were deemed necessary by the Committee in order to resolve by direct evidence fundamental, factual questions relating to Presidential direction, knowledge, or approval of actions demonstrated by other evidence to be substantial grounds for impeachment of the President. In refusing to produce these papers and things, Richard M. Nixon, substituting his judgment as to what materials were necessary for the inquiry, interposed the powers of the Presidency against the lawful subpoenas of the House of Representatives, thereby assuming to himself functions and judgments necessary to the exercise of the sole power of impeachment vested by the Constitution in the House of Representatives.

In all of this, Richard M. Nixon has acted in a manner contrary to his trust as President and subversive of constitutional government, to the great prejudice of the cause of law and justice, and to the manifest injury of the people of the United States.

Wherefore Richard M. Nixon, by such conduct, warrants impeachment and trial, and removal from office.

❧ 44 ❧
United States v. Nixon*
(1974)

I N JUNE 1973 the special Senate Watergate committee, chaired by Democratic senator Sam Ervin of North Carolina, learned in testimony from former White House aide Alexander P. Butterfield that President Richard Nixon had installed a secret, voice-activated audio-taping system in the Oval Office and in some other presidential offices. The revelation seemed to indicate that conclusive evidence existed that could prove the truth or falsehood of the president's and other administration officials' versions of the Watergate affair. As such, it marked a turning point in the investigation. It also touched off a lengthy political and legal battle for control of the tapes.

Several investigating bodies, including the Senate committee, the House Judiciary Committee, and the Watergate special prosecutor, subpoenaed a number of tapes in late 1973 and early 1974. At various times, bending to overwhelming political pressure, Nixon released transcripts of selected taped conversations. But he continued to claim that the president's right to executive privilege justified his decision not to comply with the subpoenas. Eventually, the request of Special Watergate Prosecutor Leon Jaworski, who stated that he needed sixty-four tapes as evidence in the criminal trial of several former Nixon aides, came before the Supreme Court for review.

On July 24, 1974, the Court ruled, 8–0, that Nixon must turn over the tapes to John J. Sirica, the judge in the criminal trial. (Justice William Rehnquist, as a former Nixon administration official, disqualified himself from the case.) Chief Justice Warren E. Burger, writing for all of his colleagues, granted the existence of a limited executive privilege under the Constitution, a doctrine the Court had never before declared. Burger wrote that under the separation of powers, the "President and those who assist him must be free to explore alternatives in the process of shaping policies and making decisions and to do so in a way many would be unwilling to express except privately." But, Burger continued, executive privilege does not outweigh the explicit constitutional right that defendants have to a fair trial and due process. Therefore, "absent a claim of need to protect military, diplomatic or sensitive national security secrets," executive privilege must give way to a proper subpoena. The Court ordered Nixon to turn over the tapes to Jaworski.

*Go to *http://laws.findlaw.com/us/418/683.html.*
For oral arguments, go to *http://www.oyez.org/cases/1970-1979/1974/1974_73_1766.*

Nixon had considered defying the Supreme Court decision if the justices' vote was close. (Four of them were Nixon appointees.) But in the face of a unanimous ruling, he agreed to turn over the tapes to Sirica. One tape in particular turned out to be a "smoking gun" that persuaded even Nixon's Republican supporters in Congress that he was guilty of "high Crimes and Misdemeanors." In three separate conversations between Nixon and his chief of staff, H. R. Haldeman, on June 23, 1972, Nixon approved a plan proposed by Haldeman to have top officials at the Central Intelligence Agency tell L. Patrick Gray, the acting director of the Federal Bureau of Investigation, not to conduct a serious investigation of the June 17 Watergate burglary on bogus national security grounds. Facing certain impeachment and removal after the tapes were released, Nixon announced in a televised address to the nation on August 8, 1974, that he would resign the presidency effective noon the following day.

※ ※ ※

MR. CHIEF JUSTICE BURGER delivered the opinion of the Court. . . .

[W]e turn to the claim that the subpoena should be quashed because it demands "confidential conversations between a President and his close advisors that it would be inconsistent with the public interest to produce." The first contention is a broad claim that the separation of powers doctrine precludes judicial review of a President's claim of privilege. The second contention is that if he does not prevail on the claim of absolute privilege, the court should hold as a matter of constitutional law that privilege prevails over the subpoena *duces tecum*.

In the performance of assigned constitutional duties each branch of the Government must initially interpret the Constitution, and the interpretation of its powers by any branch is due great respect from the others. The President's counsel, as we have noted, reads the Constitution as providing the absolute privilege of confidentiality for all presidential communications. Many decisions of this court, however, have unequivocally reaffirmed the holding of *Marbury v. Madison* (1803), that "it is emphatically the province and duty of the judicial department to say what the law is." . . .

No holding of the Court has defined the scope of judicial power specifically relating to the enforcement of a subpoena for confidential presidential communications for use in a criminal prosecution, but other exercises of powers by the Executive Branch and the Legislative Branch have been found invalid as in conflict with the Constitution. *Powell v. McCormack* (1969), *Youngstown Sheet and Tube v. Sawyer* (1952). . . . Since this Court has consistently exercised the power to construe and delineate claims arising under express powers, it must follow that the court has authority to interpret claims with respect to powers alleged to derive from enumerated powers. . . .

In support of his claim of absolute privilege, the President's counsel urges two grounds, one of which is common to all governments and one of which is peculiar to our system of separation of powers. The first ground is the valid need for protection of communications between high government officials and those who advise and assist them in the performance of their manifold duties; the importance of this confidentiality is too plain to require further discussion. Human experience teaches that those who expect public dissemination of their remarks may well temper candor with a concern for appearances and for their own interests to the detriment of the decisionmaking process. Whatever the nature of the privilege of confidentiality of presidential communications in the exercise of Art. II powers the privilege can be said to derive from the supremacy of each branch within its own assigned area of constitutional duties. Certain powers and privileges flow from the nature of enumerated powers; the protection of the confidentiality of presidential communications has similar constitutional underpinnings.

The second ground asserted by the President's counsel in support of the claim of absolute privilege rests on the doctrine of separation of powers. Here it is argued that the independence of the Executive Branch within its own sphere, *Humphrey's Executor v. United States* (1935), *Kilbourn v. Thompson* (1881), insulates a president from a judicial subpoena in an ongoing criminal prosecution, and thereby protects confidential presidential communications.

However, neither the doctrine of separation of powers, nor the need for confidentiality of high level communications, without more, can sustain an absolute, unqualified presidential privilege of immunity from judicial process under all circumstances. The President's need for complete candor and objectivity from advisers calls for great deference from the courts. However, when the privilege depends solely on the broad undifferentiated claim of public interest in the confidentiality of such conversations, a confrontation with other values arises. Absent a claim of need to protect military, diplomatic or sensitive national security secrets, we find it difficult to accept the argument that even the very important interest in confidentiality of presidential communications is significantly diminished by production of such material for *in camera* inspection with all the protection that a district court will be obliged to provide.

The impediment that an absolute, unqualified privilege would place in the way of the primary constitutional duty of the Judicial Branch to do justice in criminal prosecutions would plainly conflict with the function of the courts under Art. III. In designing the structure of our Government and dividing and allocating the sovereign power among three coequal branches, the Framers of the Constitution sought to provide a comprehensive system, but the separate powers were not intended to operate with absolute independence.

"While the Constitution diffuses power the better to secure liberty, it also contemplates that practice will integrate the dispersed powers into a workable government. It enjoins upon its branches separateness but interdependence, autonomy but reciprocity." *Youngstown Sheet & Tube Co. v. Sawyer* (1952) (Jackson, J., concurring).

To read Art. II powers of the President as providing an absolute privilege as against a subpoena essential to enforcement of criminal statutes on no more than a generalized claim of the public interest in confidentiality of nonmilitary and nondiplomatic discussions would upset the constitutional balance of "a workable government" and gravely impair the role of the courts under Art. III.

Since we conclude that the legitimate needs of the judicial process may outweigh presidential privilege, it is necessary to resolve those competing interests in a manner that preserves the essential functions of each branch. The right and indeed the duty to resolve that question does not free the judiciary from according high respect to the representations made on behalf of the President. *United States v. Burr* (1807).

The expectation of a President to the confidentiality of his conversations and correspondence, like the claim of confidentiality of judicial deliberations, for example, has all the values to which we accord deference for the privacy of all citizens and added to those values the necessity for protection of the public interest in candid, objective, and even blunt or harsh opinions in presidential decisionmaking. A President and those who assist him must be free to explore alternatives in the process of shaping policies and making decisions and to do so in a way many would be unwilling to express except privately. These are the considerations justifying a presumptive privilege for presidential communications. The privilege is fundamental to the operation of government and inextricably rooted in the separation of powers under the Constitution. In *Nixon v. Sirica* (1973), the Court of Appeals held that such presidential communications are "presumptively privileged," and this position is accepted by both parties in the present litigation. We agree with Mr. Chief Justice Marshall's observation, therefore, that "in no case of this kind would a court be required to proceed against the President as against an ordinary individual." *United States v. Burr* (CCD Va. 1807).

But this presumptive privilege must be considered in light of our historic commitment to the rule of law. This is nowhere more profoundly manifest than in our view that "the twofold aim [of criminal justice] is that guilt shall not escape or innocence suffer." *Berger v. United States* (1935). We have elected to employ an adversary system of criminal justice in which the parties contest all issues before a court of law. The need to develop all relevant facts in the adversary system is both fundamental and comprehensive. The ends of criminal justice would be defeated if judgments were to be founded on a partial or speculative presentation of the facts. The very integrity of the judicial system and public confidence in the system depend on full disclosure of all the facts, within the framework of the rules of evidence. To ensure that justice is done, it is imperative to the function of courts that compulsory process be available for the production of evidence needed either by the prosecution or by the defense. . . .

In this case the President challenges a subpoena served on him as a third party requiring the production of materials for use in a criminal prosecution on the claim that he has a privilege against disclosure of confidential communications. He does not place his claim of privilege on the ground they are military or diplomatic secrets. As to these areas of Art. II duties the courts have traditionally shown the utmost deference to presidential responsibilities. . . .

No case of the Court, however, has extended this high degree of deference to a President's generalized interest in confidentiality. Nowhere in the Constitution, as we have noted earlier, is there any explicit reference to a privilege of confidentiality, yet to the extent this interest relates to the effective discharge of a President's powers, it is constitutionally based.

The right to the production of all evidence at a criminal trial similarly has constitutional dimensions. The Sixth Amendment explicitly confers upon every defendant in a criminal trial the right "to be confronted with the witnesses against him" and "to have compulsory process for obtaining witnesses in his favor." Moreover, the Fifth Amendment also guarantees that no person shall be deprived of liberty without due process of law. It is the manifest duty of the courts to vindicate those guarantees and to accomplish that it is essential that all relevant and admissible evidence be produced.

In this case we must weigh the importance of the general privilege of confidentiality of presidential communications in performance of his responsibilities against the inroads of such a privilege on the fair administration of criminal justice. The interest in preserving confidentiality is weighty indeed and entitled to great respect. However we cannot conclude that advisers will be moved to temper the candor of their remarks by the infrequent occasions of disclosure because of the possibility that such conversations will be called for in the context of criminal prosecution.

On the other hand, the allowance of the privilege to withhold evidence that is demonstrably relevant in a criminal trial would cut deeply into the guarantee of due process of law and gravely impair the basic function of the courts. A President's acknowledged need for confidentiality in the communications of his office is general in nature, whereas the constitutional need for production of relevant evidence in a criminal proceeding is specific and central to the fair adjudication of a particular criminal case in the administration of justice. Without access to specific facts a criminal prosecution may be totally frustrated. The President's broad interest in confidentiality of communications will not be vitiated by disclosure of a limited number of conversations preliminarily shown to have some bearing on the pending criminal cases.

We conclude that when the ground for asserting privilege as to subpoenaed materials sought for use in a criminal trial is based only on the generalized interest in confidentiality, it cannot prevail over the fundamental demands of due process of law in the fair administration of criminal justice. The generalized assertion of privilege must yield to the demonstrated, specific need for evidence in a pending criminal trial. . . .

⊰ 45 ⊱

Gerald R. Ford's Pardon of Richard Nixon

(1974)

SINCE THE ENACTMENT of the Twenty-fifth Amendment in 1967, the president has been charged to fill any vacancy that arises in the vice presidency by nominating a replacement, subject to confirmation by a majority of both houses of Congress. After Vice President Spiro T. Agnew resigned in the face of federal bribery and tax evasion charges in October 1973, President Richard Nixon nominated House Republican leader Gerald R. Ford of Michigan to the office. Congress confirmed the nomination overwhelmingly, and Ford was sworn in on November 27. Less than a year later, on August 9, 1974, Ford succeeded to the presidency when Nixon resigned.

Resignation left Nixon subject to indictment, trial, and possible conviction for obstructing justice in the Watergate investigation. (See Documents 43, p. 205, and 44, p. 210.) On Sunday morning, September 8, 1974, Ford announced to a national television audience that he was exercising his constitutional power to grant Nixon a "full, free and absolute pardon . . . for all offenses against the United States which he . . . has committed or may have committed" as president. Ford's exercise of the pardon power—the only constitutional power of the presidency that cannot be checked by Congress or the Supreme Court—effectively freed Nixon from prosecution for any federal crime.

In announcing the pardon, Ford noted several reasons for his decision, including the former president's health and mental anguish and the difficulty of securing a fair trial. More than anything else, Ford believed that "someone must write 'The End'" to the Watergate affair, lest "ugly passions . . . again be aroused."

Nixon received the pardon with a statement conceding only "mistakes and misjudgments" in his handling of the Watergate affair. Responding to critics who complained that Ford should have insisted on a stronger apology, administration officials maintained that, legally, the act of accepting the pardon was a confession of guilt by the former president.

Ford paid a severe political price for the Nixon pardon. He was roundly criticized in Congress and the media, and his public approval rating instantly dropped twenty percentage points in the polls. When the House Judiciary Committee conducted hearings to investigate why the pardon was granted, Ford appeared personally to deny that he and Nixon had made any secret arrangement to exchange the promise of a pardon for Nixon's agreement to resign. Ford's appearance marked the first time that a president testified under oath before a congressional committee.

Ford's loss of public support enfeebled his presidency in the face of major foreign and domestic problems. At home, inflation and unemployment rose steadily, producing an unprecedented "stagflation" that standard economic remedies did not address. Abroad, South Vietnam fell to the communists and the Soviet Union took advantage of weakened American resolve by successfully aiding revolutions in various developing countries. Congressional Republicans suffered substantial losses in the 1974 elections. Ford himself was the victim of two serious assassination attempts in September 1975, and he nearly lost the 1976 Republican presidential nomination to Ronald Reagan, the conservative former governor of California. In the course of beating back Reagan's challenge, Ford dropped his appointed vice president, Nelson A. Rockefeller, the liberal former governor of New York, from the ticket in favor of Kansas senator Robert Dole.

Ford waged a hard and generally effective campaign against the Democratic presidential nominee, former Georgia governor Jimmy Carter, in the 1976 election. But he was defeated narrowly, bringing his two-and-one-half-year presidency to an end.

❧ ❧ ❧

Ladies and gentlemen, I have come to a decision which I felt I should tell you, and all of my fellow American citizens, as soon as I was certain in my own mind and in my own conscience that it was the right thing to do.

I have learned already in this office that the difficult decisions always come to this desk. I must admit that many of them do not look at all the same as the hypothetical questions that I have answered freely and perhaps too fast on previous occasions. My customary policy is to try and get all the facts and to consider the opinions of my countrymen and to take counsel with my most valued friends. But these seldom agree, and in the end the decision is mine.

To procrastinate, to agonize and to wait for a more favorable turn of events that may never come, or more compelling external pressures that may as well be wrong as right, is itself a decision of sorts and a weak course for a President to follow.

I have promised to uphold the Constitution, to do what is right as God gives me to see the right, and to do the very best that I can for America. I have asked your help and your prayers not only when I became President, but many times since.

The Constitution is the supreme law of our land and it governs our actions as citizens. Only the laws of God, which govern our consciences, are superior to it. As we are a nation under God, so I am sworn to uphold our laws with the help of God. And I have sought such guidance and searched my own conscience with special diligence to determine the right thing for me to do with respect to my predecessor in this place, Richard Nixon, and his loyal wife and family.

Theirs is an American tragedy in which we all have played a part. It could go on and on and on, or someone must write "The End" to it.

I have concluded that only I can do that. And if I can, I must.

There are no historic or legal precedents to which I can turn in this matter, none that precisely fit the circumstances of a private citizen who has resigned the presidency of the United States. But it is common knowledge that serious allegations and accusations hang like a sword over our former President's head, threatening his health, as he tries to reshape his life, a great part of which was spent in the service of this country and by the mandate of its people.

After years of bitter controversy and divisive national debate, I have been advised and I am compelled to conclude that many months and perhaps more years will have to pass before Richard Nixon could obtain a fair trial by jury in any jurisdiction of the United States under governing decisions of the Supreme Court.

I deeply believe in equal justice for all Americans, whatever their station or former station. The law, whether human or divine, is no respecter of persons but the law is a respecter of reality. The facts as I see them are that a former President of the United States, instead of enjoying equal treatment with any other citizen accused of violating the law, would be cruelly and excessively penalized either in preserving the presumption of his innocence or in obtaining a speedy determination of his guilt in order to repay a legal debt to society.

During this long period of delay and potential litigation, ugly passions would again be aroused, and our people would again be polarized in their opinions, and the credibility of our free institutions of government would again be challenged at home and abroad. In the end, the courts might well hold that Richard Nixon had been denied due process and the verdict of history would even more be inconclusive with respect to those charges arising out of the period of his presidency of which I am presently aware.

But it is not the ultimate fate of Richard Nixon that most concerns me—though surely it deeply troubles every decent and every compassionate person. My concern is the immediate future of this great country. In this I dare not depend upon my personal sympathy as a longtime friend of the former President nor my professional judgment as a lawyer. And I do not.

As President, my primary concern must always be the greatest good of all the people of the United States, whose servant I am.

As a man, my first consideration is to be true to my own convictions and my own conscience.

My conscience tells me clearly and certainly that I cannot prolong the bad dreams that continue to reopen a chapter that is closed. My conscience tells me that only I, as President, have the constitutional power to firmly shut and seal this book. My conscience says it is my duty, not merely to proclaim domestic tranquility, but to use every means that I have to ensure it.

I do believe that the buck stops here, that I cannot rely upon public opinion polls to tell me what is right. I do believe that right makes might, and that if I am wrong 10 angels swearing I was right would make no difference. I do believe with all my heart and mind and spirit that I, not as President, but as a humble servant of God, will receive justice without mercy if I fail to show mercy.

Finally, I feel that Richard Nixon and his loved ones have suffered enough, and will continue to suffer no matter what I do, no matter what we as a great and good nation can do together to make his goal of peace come true.

Now, therefore, I, Gerald R. Ford, President of the United States, pursuant to the pardon power conferred upon me by Article II, Section 2, of the Constitution, have granted and by these presents do grant a full, free, and absolute pardon unto Richard Nixon for all offenses against the United States which he, Richard Nixon, has committed or may have committed or taken part in during the period from January 20, 1969, through August 9, 1974.

In witness whereof, I have hereunto set my hand this 8th day of September in the year of our Lord Nineteen Hundred Seventy Four, and of the independence of the United States of America the 199th.

❧ 46 ❧

Walter F. Mondale's Memo to Jimmy Carter on the Role of the Vice President*

(1976)

NOT EVERY AMERICAN ADMIRES CONGRESS, agrees with the Supreme Court, or supports the president. But, except for the vice presidency, no constitutional office has been the object of ridicule. Even some vice presidents have ruefully joined in the fun. Woodrow Wilson's vice president, Thomas R. Marshall,

*Go to *http://www.mnhs.org/collections/upclose/Mondale-CarterMemo-Transcription.pdf.*

liked to tell about two brothers: "One ran away to sea; the other was elected vice president. And nothing was heard of either of them again." John Nance Garner, who was Franklin D. Roosevelt's first vice president, famously declared: "The vice presidency isn't worth a pitcher of warm piss."

Historically, the vice presidency's main problem lay in its design. The Constitutional Convention assigned the vice president only two duties: to preside over the Senate (a position that is significant only when the vice president breaks a tie vote) and to succeed to the presidency if the president dies, resigns, becomes disabled, or is impeached and removed. These duties stranded the vice president in a constitutional no-man's land, somewhere between the executive and legislative branches.

Since the Carter administration, however, the vice presidency has grown in prestige and influence, even though its constitutional authority is substantially unchanged. Much of the credit for this transformation lies in the agreement forged between Jimmy Carter and Walter F. Mondale in response to a memo that Vice President–elect Mondale wrote to President-elect Carter on December 9, 1976, six weeks before the beginning of their term.

Carter was the first in a series of state governors, including Ronald Reagan, Bill Clinton, and George W. Bush, to be elected president from 1976 to 2004. Like his successors, Carter realized that he needed a vice president with Washington experience to help him meet the challenges of his new job. Mondale had served two terms in the Senate when Carter selected him as his running mate.

A protégé of his fellow Minnesotan, former vice president Hubert H. Humphrey, Mondale knew how frustrating the vice presidency could be. Humphrey especially warned Mondale against getting tied down with specific responsibilities, which tended to be time-consuming but peripheral. Accordingly, Mondale proposed that his main responsibility be as "general adviser" to the president, consulting with Carter on virtually every matter that crossed the president's desk. As vice president, Mondale argued, he was in a "unique position" to perform this role because he was "the only other public official elected nationwide, not affected by specific obligations or institutional interests of either the Congressional or Executive branch, and able to look at the government as a whole."

To make his advice useful, Mondale wrote, he would need access to the full range of information that Carter received, a professional staff, the right to participate in all important meetings and, most important, "access to you" in the form of weekly private sessions and an office in the West Wing of the White House. Mondale promised not to neglect some other recently developed vice-presidential chores, such as "congressional relations," "political action," and "liaison with special groups." But service as president of the Senate, he predicted, "will take a minimum amount of time."

Carter approved Mondale's memo in full, not just on paper but in practice. Subsequent presidents and vice presidents have accepted the Carter–Mondale innovations and institutionalized them. Clinton's vice president, Al Gore, and George W. Bush's, Richard Cheney, were if anything even more influential than Mondale, and Vice President Joseph Biden became a major player in the Obama White House.

🐾 🐾 🐾

December 9, 1976
TO: JIMMY CARTER
FROM: WALTER F. MONDALE
RE: THE ROLE OF THE VICE PRESIDENT IN THE
CARTER ADMINISTRATION

I. Background

Defining an appropriate and meaningful role for the Vice President has been a problem throughout the history of this country. While custom and statute have changed the office gradually over 200 years, generally speaking, the Vice President has performed a role characterized by ambiguity, disappointment, and even antagonism. Arthur Schlesinger, Jr. concludes "history has shown the American Vice Presidency to be a job of spectacular and, I believe, incurable frustration."

Other commentators as well as former Vice Presidents have focused on particular problems of the office. Competition with the President, conflict with the White House staff, lack of meaningful assignments, lack of authority, and inadequate access to vital information are most frequently mentioned.

I have spoken at length with Vice President Rockefeller, former Vice President Humphrey, and their staffs to try to understand more fully the many dimensions of the position. Further, through other conversations and reading what literature is available, I have tried to supplement my understanding. Finally, my staff prepared a Constitutional history of the office and a comparison of the duties and staffing of the Humphrey and Rockefeller Vice Presidencies.

It is my hope in this memorandum that I can outline a set of relationships, functions and assignments that will be workable and productive for the administration. I am committed to do everything possible to make this administration a success. I fully realize that my personal and political success is totally tied to yours and the achievements of your administration.

II. Our Basic Relationship—General Adviser

I believe the most important contribution I can make is to serve as a general adviser to you. I would hope my experience in government and politics would assist me in giving you advice on the major questions facing you.

The position of being the only other public official elected nationwide, not affected by specific obligations or institutional interests of either the Congressional or Executive branch, and able to look at the government as a whole, does put me in a unique position to advise. Further, my political role around the country as well as my established relationships in Washington should allow me to keep in close touch with many different groups and viewpoints.

The biggest single problem of our recent administrations has been the failure of the President to be exposed to independent analysis not conditioned by what it is thought he wants to hear or often what others want him to hear. I hope to offer impartial advice and help assure that you are not shielded from points of view that you should hear. I will not be the only source of such advice. Yet, I think my position enables me to help maintain the free flow of ideas and information which is indispensable to a healthy and productive administration.

In order to fulfill the role of a general adviser satisfactorily, I think the following are necessary:

1. Frequent and comprehensive intelligence briefings from the CIA and other intelligence agencies of similar depth to those you receive. Advance warning of major issues to be discussed at meetings of the NSC and other significant groups is necessary as well as the ability to request additional briefings and responses on areas of special concern.
   Senator Humphrey emphasized the importance of this point to me repeatedly. He was not given adequate briefings and was, therefore, unable to participate effectively on the NSC or in this general arena of foreign and defense policy.

2. *A special relationship with other members of the Executive branch.* I would hope that I could expect the same or nearly the same level of responsiveness from key administration officials in seeking information that you would receive. Providing sound advice to you requires from them complete candor and cooperation in providing information. I do not believe I could evaluate and/or assess key problems without this relationship. I think it would be important to make this point to the Cabinet and other key officials at the very beginning of the administration.

3. *Participation in Meetings of Key Groups.* Participation in Cabinet meetings, discussions with the Congressional leadership, meetings of the National Security Council, Domestic Council and the economic policy group (whatever form it takes) would be extremely valuable in fulfilling the advisory role.

4. *A seasoned, experienced staff representative on the NSC and Domestic Council who I can call on to meet my needs.* I think it is terribly important that I have a staff capability on these two Councils whose priority is to assist me in performing my functions. Humphrey was not given staff support which combined with the lack of briefings made his role on the NSC almost insignificant.

5. *Relationship with White House Staff.* I think it is critical that my office be well informed on the activities of the White House. I believe it would be helpful if representatives of my office could participate in appropriate White House staff meetings. I hope we can maintain the excellent relationship our two staffs developed during the campaign and have maintained during the transition. Also, my staff is available to you or the White House staff for any assignments or tasks for which they may be needed.

6. *Access to you.*[1] I suggest that we plan to meet once per week at a minimum of 30 minutes to an hour. Rockefeller currently has this arrangement with President Ford and recommends it highly. This would be a time for me to report on my activities, offer advice and get assignments from you. We, of course, could cancel the meeting if we did not need the time. In addition to our regular meeting, I would hope I could depend on having access whenever necessary. Of course, I would be available whenever you might want to meet.

III. General Functions

A. Trouble-Shooting. As problems arise, I would like to be available to respond to your direction and help solve them as quickly as possible. Within this general category, two areas emerge.

1. *Investigation.* I believe I could perform a very valuable function in attempting to provide background and analysis for you in special areas of concern. This function could range from gathering information on an issue or area of government about which you are restless or uncomfortable to conducting a full-scale, formal investigation such as Rockefeller did in the case of the CIA. An example of one area well suited for this approach is that of task force on hard crime and official lawlessness suggested in the campaign.

2. *Arbitration.* The sometimes conflicting and sometimes parallel assignments of governmental functions to different departments and agencies produces inefficiency and interdepartmental disputes, as you well know. With your support, I think I could play an important role in resolving such problems. This would probably be done in an assignment-by-assignment basis.[2]

B. Foreign Representation. Nearly everyone, most notably the former Vice Presidents I have spoken with, agrees that the Vice President can play a very significant role through foreign travel. The foreign travel I do can be used to express your interest in selected foreign policy areas, give us an additional presence abroad, and provide you with a first-hand assessment of foreign leaders and situations.

I would tentatively suggest (subject to conversations with the Secretary of State) that in the early weeks of the administration we consider the advantages of short trips to the industrialized nations (Canada, Western Europe and Japan). Such trips would enable me to reassure our allies, discuss the objectives of a possible economic summit, and assess the internal economic prospects of our leading economic partners. I am advised that travel in the early days can be very productive in part because it is too soon for the host countries to expect specific responses to their problems.

It would be made clear, both publicly and privately, that such a trip was *an information gathering mission, not a negotiating mission.* The itinerary would be worked out with your senior Cabinet officials and advisers. It would be conducted with minimum publicity from the standpoint of the United States but with appropriate attention to dramatizing the Vice President's visit as a gesture of your interest in the countries concerned.

IV. Specific Function

The Constitution mandates that I serve as President of the Senate. The duties are ceremonial with the exception of casting tie-breaking votes. I assume this responsibility will take a minimum amount of time.

V. Possible Additional Functions

Based on my analysis of the history of the office, the following are functions which are the most promising or in this situation seem to merit serious exploration.

A. *Congressional Relations.* I think I can be helpful to you in your relations with the Congress in two important respects:

1. I think I can advise you on what to expect from the Congress on significant issues, how to interpret their actions, and what approaches will be most productive. Twelve years in the Senate gives me a substantial background for analysis and interpretation.
2. I can advise and assist your Congressional liaison office. This should be done on an informal basis so that my role is not thought of as a lobbyist. Yet, on major initiatives, I could conduct key conversations and become more operational.

B. *Political Action.* Every Vice President in recent history has played a significant political role for the President. I assume I would do the same. I can be helpful through keeping our administration on the offensive politically and representing us around the country, with the Party, and with special constituencies such as labor. I would assume this would be a continuing role, meshed with the off-year election campaigns and the re-election campaign of 1980.

On an allied point, an immediate assessment of election laws, together with recommendations for Congressional action, is very much needed before the next election. Campaign finance, primary laws, voter registration, and other critical areas are much in need of review. I would be interested in conducting such a review and recommending a legislative package if you would find it valuable.

C. *Liaison with Special Groups.* The Vice President has served in the past as a special liaison to elected officials (particularly Mayors and Governors). Agnew established an office of intergovernmental relations for a time which was disbanded. Humphrey served as a point of contact and advocate for the elected officials.

The key danger in regard to this function is that the Vice President's office is devoted to doing agency work for local and state government which could be handled better through direct contact between the elected official and the agency concerned.

I suggest maintaining the Vice President's office as a key contact point for Mayors and Governors with adequate safeguards against the danger noted above. The proper execution of this possible function will require additional discussion.

D. *Special Role with Domestic Council.* Depending on the functions of the Domestic Council, a leadership role with the Council might be considered. The Council is currently the only group concerned with a long-range policy planning function and with the integration of domestic policy recommendations. These functions would be consistent with the domestic overview required as an adviser to the President and with the possible role as an arbitrator in interdepartmental conflicts. Your determination of the functions of the Council will bear directly on what role would be appropriate for me to play.

E. *Special Role with Economic Policy Board.* The coordination of domestic and international economic policy will be extremely important. A special role with the Economic Policy Board could be considered.

VI. Additional Commitments

A. *Minnesota.* I would like very much to be able to continue to devote some time and attention to my special relationship to the people of Minnesota. Special projects, some liaison work, concern about appointments, and regular contacts in Minnesota and Washington would be included. That time would not be substantial, but this private commitment to be able to continue to serve the people of my state would be very meaningful to me.

B. *A Role for Joan with the National Foundation on the Arts and Humanities.* I would like to assist Joan in structuring a useful and rewarding role with the National Foundation as the primary vehicle for her continued involvement in the arts. She is extremely effective in this area. In the early stages, this might involve my showing a special interest in this agency.

VIII. Conclusion

I am optimistic that we can develop a relationship and a set of functions which will allow me to contribute to the administration in a substantial way. That optimism has been maintained and nourished from our first conversation in Plains through the campaign and further reinforced in the past month of working together. I look forward to a productive working relationship and a close friendship throughout the administration and beyond.

The role outlined above would, in my judgment, clearly fulfill the most important constitutional obligation of the office—that is, being prepared to take over the Presidency should that be required. The relationship and assignments suggested were not focused on that obligation, but I think they do meet the test.

NOTES

1. Historically, there has been substantial variation in access and proximity. It was not until President Kennedy that the Vice President had an office in proximity to the White House (EOB). On one occasion (Agnew) the office of the Vice President was actually in the White House. I prefer to think of access in the terms expressed here and would prefer to maintain the space with adequate staff offices in the Executive Office Building.

2. Humphrey felt he could be very effective in this area. He noted that the President did not have sufficient time to consider many of the problems that arose between departments and agencies.

❧ 47 ❧
Jimmy Carter's "Crisis of Confidence" Speech*
(1979)

FORMER GEORGIA GOVERNOR Jimmy Carter's narrow victory over Gerald R. Ford in the 1976 election marked the first time that a challenger had unseated an incumbent president since Franklin D. Roosevelt defeated Herbert C. Hoover in 1932. Although Carter, a Democrat, stressed domestic issues in his campaign, he initially was unsuccessful in enacting most of his policies into law. By the summer of 1979 Carter had become more surefooted in his dealings with Congress, but the nation was plagued by gasoline shortages, raging inflation, and soaring interest rates. The president's public approval rating sank like a stone.

On July 5, 1979, Carter began an unprecedented effort to revive his presidency. Convinced by his advisers that most people would not watch, he canceled a televised address on energy policy (his fifth) that was scheduled for that evening. The next day, Carter went to Camp David, the presidential retreat in Maryland's Catoctin Mountains, to reflect on the underlying causes of the energy crisis and the nation's other problems. During the week that followed, he met with more than one hundred invited visitors, including political, business, labor, and religious leaders, to discuss politics, public policy, and even philosophy. He also made some unannounced helicopter trips to visit average families in their homes.

On the evening of July 15 Carter returned to Washington and gave a nationally televised speech from the Oval Office that dealt in part with energy (he proposed a ten-year, $142 billion program to obtain national energy independence), but dwelt mainly on the "crisis of confidence" that he believed was enfeebling the American spirit.

Carter's speech began with an extended mea culpa, quoting criticisms of his leadership from some of the people with whom he had spoken during his retreat. He then described his perception of "a fundamental threat to American democracy," namely, a "crisis of the American spirit" marked by loss of faith in the country and confidence in the future. "Restoring that faith and that confidence to America is now the most important task we face," the president concluded.

Although Carter never spoke the word, his address soon became known as the "malaise" speech. Critics charged that the president, who had been elected by praising the American people as "good and honest and decent and competent and compassionate and filled with love," was now blaming them for his own failure to solve soluble problems. The public's reaction was initially more positive, but Carter quickly dissipated whatever political gains he made by firing five cabinet members

*Go to *http://www.pbs.org/wgbh/amex/carter/filmmore/ps_crisis.html.*

224

during the week following the speech. To a nation unused to having its president undertake soul-searching retreats, the firings reinforced doubts about the stability and competence of Carter's leadership. He was defeated for reelection in 1980 by former California governor Ronald Reagan in the largest electoral vote landslide in history against an incumbent president.

※ ※ ※

GOOD EVENING.

This is a special night for me. Exactly three years ago on July 15, 1976, I accepted the nomination of my party to run for President of the United States. I promised you a President who is not isolated from the people, who feels your pain and who shares your dreams and who draws his strength and his wisdom from you.

During the past 3 years I have spoken to you on many occasions about national concerns, the energy crisis, reorganizing the Government, our Nation's economy and issues of war and especially peace. But over those years the subjects of the speeches, the talks and the press conferences have become increasingly narrow, focused more and more on what the isolated world of Washington thinks is important. Gradually you have heard more and more about what the Government thinks or what the Government should be doing and less and less about our Nation's hopes, our dreams and our vision of the future.

Ten days ago I had planned to speak to you again about a very important subject—energy. For the fifth time I would have described the urgency of the problem and laid out a series of legislative recommendations to the Congress. But as I was preparing to speak, I began to ask myself the same question that I now know has been troubling many of you. Why have we not been able to get together as a nation to resolve our serious energy problem?

It's clear that the true problems of our Nation are much deeper—deeper than gasoline lines or energy shortages, deeper even than inflation or recession. And I realize more than ever that as President I need your help. So, I decided to reach out and to listen to the voices of America.

I invited to Camp David people from almost every segment of our society—business and labor, teachers and preachers, Governors, mayors and private citizens. And then I left Camp David to listen to other Americans, men and women like you. It has been an extraordinary 10 days, and I want to share with you what I've heard.

First of all, I got a lot of personal advice. Let me quote a few of the typical comments that I wrote down.

This from a Southern governor: "Mr. President, you are not leading this Nation—you're just managing the Government."

"You don't see the people enough any more."

"Some of your Cabinet members don't seem loyal. There is not enough discipline among your disciples."

"Don't talk to us about politics or the mechanics of government, but about an understanding of our common good."

"Mr. President, we're in trouble. Talk to us about blood and sweat and tears."

"If you lead, Mr. President, we will follow."

Many people talked about themselves and about the condition of our Nation. This from a young woman in Pennsylvania: "I feel so far from government. I feel like ordinary people are excluded from political power."

And this from a young Chicano: "Some of us have suffered from recession all our lives."

"Some people have wasted energy, but others haven't had anything to waste."

And this from a religious leader: "No material shortage can touch the important things like God's love for us or our love for one another."

And I like this one particularly from a black woman who happens to be the mayor of a small Mississippi town: "The big shots are not the only ones who are important. Remember, you can't sell anything on Wall Street unless someone digs it up somewhere else first."

This kind of summarized a lot of other statements: "Mr. President, we are confronted with a moral and a spiritual crisis."

Several of our discussions were on energy and I have a notebook full of comments and advice. I'll read just a few.

"We can't go on consuming 40 percent more energy than we produce. When we import oil we are also importing inflation plus unemployment."

"We've got to use what we have. The Middle East has only 5 percent of the world's energy, but the United States has 24 percent."

And this is one of the most vivid statements: "Our neck is stretched over the fence and OPEC [Organization of Petroleum Exporting Countries] has the knife."

"There will be other cartels and other shortages. American wisdom and courage right now can set a path to follow in the future."

This was a good one: "Be bold, Mr. President. We may make mistakes, but we are ready to experiment."

And this one from a labor leader got to the heart of it: "The real issue is freedom. We must deal with the energy problem on a war footing."

And the last that I'll read: "When we enter the moral equivalent of war, Mr. President, don't issue us BB guns."

These 10 days confirmed my belief in the decency and the strength and the wisdom of the American people, but it also bore out some of my longstanding concerns about our Nation's underlying problems.

I know, of course, being President, that government actions and legislation can be very important. That is why I've worked hard to put my campaign promises into law—and I have to admit, with just mixed success. But after listening to the American people I have been reminded again that all the legislation in the world can't fix what's wrong with America. So, I want to speak to you first tonight about a subject even more serious than energy or inflation. I want to talk to you right now about a fundamental threat to American democracy.

I do not mean our political and civil liberties. They will endure. And I do not refer to the outward strength of America, a nation that is at peace tonight everywhere in the world, with unmatched economic power and military might.

The threat is nearly invisible in ordinary ways. It is a crisis of confidence. It is a crisis that strikes at the very heart and soul and spirit of our national will. We can see this crisis in the growing doubt about the meaning of our own lives and in the loss of a unity of purpose for our Nation.

The erosion of our confidence in the future is threatening to destroy the social and the political fabric of America.

The confidence that we have always had as a people is not simply some romantic dream or a proverb in a dusty book that we read just on the Fourth of July. It is the idea we founded our Nation on and has guided our development as a people. Confidence in the future has supported everything else—public institutions and private enterprise, our own families, and the very Constitution of the United States. Confidence has defined our course and has served as a link between generations. We've always believed in something called progress. We've always had a faith that the days of our children would be better than our own.

Our people are losing that faith, not only in government itself, but in the ability as citizens to serve as the ultimate rulers and shapers of our democracy. As a people we know our past and we are proud of it. Our progress has been part of the living history of America, even the world. We always believed that we were part of a great movement of humanity itself called democracy, involved in the search for freedom and that belief has always strengthened us in our purpose. But just as we are losing our confidence in the future, we are also beginning to close the door on our past.

In a Nation that was proud of hard work, strong families, close knit communities, and our faith in God, too many of us now tend to worship self-indulgence and consumption. Human identity is no longer defined by what one does, but by what one owns. But we've discovered that owning things and consuming things does not satisfy our longing for meaning. We've learned that piling up material goods cannot fill the emptiness of lives which have no confidence or purpose.

The symptoms of this crisis of the American spirit are all around us. For the first time in the history of our country the majority of our people believe that the next 5 years will be worse than the past 5 years. Two-thirds of our people do not even vote. The productivity of American workers is actually dropping and the willingness of Americans to save for the future has fallen below that of all other people in the Western world.

As you know, there is a growing disrespect for government and for churches and for schools, the news media, and other institutions. This is not a message of happiness or reassurance, but it is the truth and it is a warning.

These changes did not happen overnight. They've come upon us gradually over the last generation, years that were filled with shocks and tragedy.

We were sure that ours was a nation of the ballot, not the bullet, until the murders of John Kennedy and Robert Kennedy and Martin Luther King Jr. We were taught that our armies were always invincible and our causes were always just, only to suffer the agony of Vietnam. We respected the Presidency as a place of honor until the shock of Watergate.

We remember when the phrase "sound as a dollar" was an expression of absolute dependability, until 10 years of inflation began to shrink our dollars and our savings. We believed that our Nation's resources were limitless until 1973 when we had to face a growing dependence on foreign oil.

These wounds are still very deep. They have never been healed.

Looking for a way out of this crisis, our people have turned to the Federal Government and found it isolated from the mainstream of our Nation's life. Washington, D.C., has become an island. The gap between our citizens and our government has never been so wide. The people are looking for honest answers, not easy answers; clear leadership, not false claims and evasiveness and politics as usual.

What you see too often in Washington and elsewhere around the country is a system of government that seems incapable of action. You see a Congress twisted and pulled in every direction by hundreds of well-financed and powerful special interests.

You see every extreme position defended to the last vote, almost to the last breath by one unyielding group or another. You often see a balanced and a fair approach that demands sacrifice, a little sacrifice from everyone, abandoned like an orphan without support and without friends.

Often you see paralysis and stagnation and drift. You don't like it, and neither do I. What can we do?

First of all, we must face the truth and then we can change our course. We simply must have faith in each other, faith in our ability to govern ourselves and faith in the future of this Nation.

Restoring that faith and that confidence to America is now the most important task we face. It is a true challenge of this generation of Americans.

One of the visitors to Camp David last week put it this way: "We've got to stop crying and start sweating, stop talking and start walking, stop cursing and start praying. The strength we need will not come from the White House, but from every house in America."

We know the strength of America. We are strong. We can regain our unity. We can regain our confidence. We are the heirs of generations who survived threats much more powerful and awesome than those that challenge us now. Our fathers and mothers were strong men and women who shaped a new society during the Great Depression, who fought world wars and who carved out a new charter of peace for the world.

We ourselves are the same Americans who just 10 years ago put a man on the moon. We are the generation that dedicated our society to the pursuit of human rights and equality. And we are the generation that will win the war on the energy problem and in that process rebuild the unity and confidence of America.

We are at a turning point in our history. There are two paths to choose. One is a path I warned about tonight, the path that leads to fragmentation and self-interest. Down that road lies a mistaken idea of freedom, the right to grasp for ourselves some advantage over others. That path would be one of constant conflict between narrow interests ending in chaos and immobility. It is a certain route to failure.

All the traditions of our past, all the lessons of our heritage, all the promises of our future point to another path, the path of common purpose and the restoration of American values. That path leads to true freedom for our Nation and ourselves. We can take the first steps down that path as we begin to solve our energy problem.

Energy will be the immediate test of our ability to unite this Nation and it can also be the standard around which we rally. On the battlefield of energy we can win for our Nation a new confidence, and we can seize control again of our common destiny.

In little more than two decades we've gone from a position of energy independence to one in which almost half the oil we use comes from foreign countries, at prices that are going through the roof. Our excessive dependence on OPEC has already taken a tremendous toll on our economy and our people. This is the direct cause of the long lines which have made millions of you spend aggravating hours waiting for gasoline. It's a cause of the increased inflation and unemployment that we now face. This intolerable dependence on foreign oil threatens our economic independence and the very security of our Nation.

The energy crisis is real. It is worldwide. It is a clear and present danger to our Nation. These are facts and we simply must face them. . . .

Twelve hours from now I will speak again in Kansas City, to expand and to explain further our energy program. Just as the search for solutions to our energy shortages has now led us to a new awareness of our Nation's deeper problems, so our willingness to work for those new solutions in energy can strengthen us to attack those deeper problems.

I will continue to travel this country, to hear the people of America. You can help me to develop a national agenda for the 1980s. I will listen and I will act. We will act together. These were the promises I made three years ago and I intend to keep them.

Little by little we can and we must rebuild our confidence. We can spend until we empty our treasuries, and we may summon all the wonders of science. But we can succeed only if we tap our greatest resources—America's people, America's values, and America's confidence.

I have seen the strength of America in the inexhaustible resources of our people. In the days to come, let us renew that strength in the struggle for an energy-secure nation.

In closing, let me say this: I will do my best, but I will not do it alone. Let your voice be heard. Whenever you have a chance, say something good about our country. With God's help and for the sake of our Nation, it is time for us to join hands in America. Let us commit ourselves together to a rebirth of the American spirit. Working together with our common faith we cannot fail.

Thank you and good night.

✷ 48 ✷
Ronald Reagan's First Inaugural Address
(1981)

R ONALD REAGAN was a professional movie and television actor and a New Deal Democrat for most of his adult life. In 1966, four years after changing his party registration, Reagan entered elective politics by running successfully for governor of California as a conservative Republican. After leaving the governorship in 1975, Reagan challenged Republican incumbent Gerald R. Ford for their party's 1976 presidential nomination. Although Reagan was defeated, he came very close to winning. His strong conservative credentials and exceptional ability as an on-screen communicator, which had been honed throughout his career in show business, made him a formidable candidate in any election he entered.

In 1980 Reagan swept easily to the Republican nomination. His main rival was former United Nations ambassador George H. W. Bush, whom he tapped at the convention as his vice-presidential running mate. Capitalizing on severe economic conditions and the year-long seizure of fifty-two American hostages by militant revolutionaries in Iran, Reagan defeated President Jimmy Carter by 489 electoral votes to 49.

Reagan's inauguration as president also was unprecedented in some ways. Two weeks shy of his seventieth birthday, Reagan was the oldest person ever to take the oath of office. (William Henry Harrison, at sixty-eight, previously was the oldest.) Reagan was inaugurated on the West Front of the Capitol, not the traditional East Front. Parts of his speech were coordinated with network television cameras that showed viewers the Washington Monument, the Jefferson and Lincoln memorials, and Arlington National Cemetery as he spoke of them.

Reagan's first inaugural address advanced the two main themes of his political career, his 1980 campaign, and, subsequently, his presidency: the failings of big government ("government is not the solution to our problem; government is the problem") and a fervent optimism that national problems could be overcome with conservative policies. "The economic ills we suffer . . . will go away," Reagan proclaimed. "They will go away because we as Americans have the capacity now, as we've had in the past, to do whatever needs to be done to preserve this last and greatest bastion of freedom."

Congress enacted Reagan's program of tax cuts, spending reductions for social welfare, and spending increases for defense in 1981. During his eight years as president, inflation, interest rates, and unemployment fell. After a severe recession in 1982, the economy grew rapidly. But the combination of reduced tax revenues and soaring defense spending caused the national debt to triple from approximately $1 trillion to $3 trillion by the time Reagan left office in 1989.

※ ※ ※

To a few of us here today this is a solemn and most momentous occasion. And, yet, in the history of our Nation it is a commonplace occurrence. The orderly transfer of authority as called for in the Constitution routinely takes place, as it has for almost two centuries, and few of us stop to think how unique we really are. In the eyes of many in the world, this every-4-year ceremony we accept as normal is nothing less than a miracle.

Mr. President [Carter], I want our fellow citizens to know how much you did to carry on this tradition. By your gracious cooperation in the transition process you have shown a watching world that we are a united people pledged to maintaining a political system which guarantees individual liberty to a greater degree than any other, and I thank you and your people for all your help in maintaining the continuity which is the bulwark of our Republic.

The business of our Nation goes forward. These United States are confronted with an economic affliction of great proportions. We suffer from the longest and one of the worst sustained inflations in our national history. It distorts our economic decisions, penalizes thrift and crushes the struggling young and the fixed-income elderly alike. It threatens to shatter the lives of millions of our people.

Idle industries have cast workers into unemployment, human misery, and personal indignity. Those who do work are denied a fair return for their labor by a tax system which penalizes successful achievement and keeps us from maintaining full productivity.

But great as our tax burden is, it has not kept pace with public spending. For decades we have piled deficit upon deficit, mortgaging our future and our children's future for the temporary convenience of the present. To continue this long trend is to guarantee tremendous social, cultural, political, and economic upheavals.

You and I, as individuals, can, by borrowing, live beyond our means, but for only a limited period of time. Why, then, should we think that collectively, as a nation, we're not bound by that same limitation? We must act today in order to preserve tomorrow. And let there be no misunderstanding—we are going to begin to act, beginning today.

The economic ills we suffer have come upon us over several decades. They will not go away in days, weeks, or months, but they will go away. They will go away because we as Americans have the capacity now, as we've had in the past, to do whatever needs to be done to preserve this last and greatest bastion of freedom.

In this present crisis, government is not the solution to our problem; government is the problem. From time to time we've been tempted to believe that society has become too complex to be managed by self-rule, that government by an elite group is superior to government for, by, and of the people. Well, if no one among us is capable of governing himself, then who among us has the capacity to govern someone else? All of us together—in and out of government—must bear the burden. The solutions we seek must be equitable with no one group singled out to pay a higher price.

We hear much of special interest groups. Well, our concern must be for a special interest group that has been too long neglected. It knows no sectional boundaries or ethnic and racial divisions, and it crosses political party lines. It is made up of men and women who raise our food, patrol our streets, man our mines and factories, teach our children, keep our homes, and heal us when we're sick—professionals, industrialists, shopkeepers, clerks, cabbies, and truck drivers. They are, in short, "We the people," this breed called Americans.

Well, this administration's objective will be a healthy, vigorous, growing economy that provides equal opportunities for all Americans with no barriers born of bigotry or discrimination. Putting America back to work means putting all Americans back to work. Ending inflation means freeing all Americans from the terror of runaway living costs. All must share in the productive work of this "new beginning," and all must share in the bounty of a revived economy. With the idealism and fair play which are the core of our system and our strength, we can have a strong and prosperous America at peace with itself and the world.

So, as we begin, let us take inventory. We are a nation that has a government—not the other way around. And this makes us special among the nations of the Earth. Our government has no power except that granted it by the people. It is time to check and reverse the growth of government which shows signs of having grown beyond the consent of the governed.

It is my intention to curb the size and influence of the Federal establishment and to demand recognition of the distinction between the powers granted to the Federal Government and those reserved to the States or to the people. All of us need to be reminded that the Federal Government did not create the States; the States created the Federal Government.

Now so there will be no misunderstanding, it's not my intention to do away with government. It is rather to make it work—work with us, not over us; to stand by our side, not ride on our back. Government can and must provide opportunity, not smother it; foster productivity, not stifle it.

If we look to the answer as to why for so many years we achieved so much, prospered as no other people on Earth, it was because here in this land we unleashed the energy and individual genius of man to a greater extent than has ever been done before. Freedom and the dignity of the individual have been more available and assured here than in any other place on Earth. The price for this freedom at times has been high. But we have never been unwilling to pay that price.

It is no coincidence that our present troubles parallel and are proportionate to the intervention and intrusion in our lives that result from unnecessary and excessive growth of government. It is time for us to realize that we're too great a nation to limit ourselves to small dreams. We're not, as some would have us believe, doomed to an inevitable decline. I do not believe in a fate that will fall on us no matter what we do. I do believe in a fate that will fall on us if we do nothing. So, with all the creative energy at our command, let us begin an era of national renewal. Let us renew our determination, our courage, and our strength. And let us renew our faith and our hope.

We have every right to dream heroic dreams. Those who say we're in a time when there are no heroes, they just don't know where to look. You can see heroes every day going in and out of factory gates. Others, a handful in number, produce food enough to feed all of us and much of the world beyond. You meet heroes across a counter. And they're on both sides of that counter. There are entrepreneurs with faith in themselves and faith in an idea who create new jobs, new wealth and opportunity. They're individuals and families whose taxes support the government and whose voluntary gifts support church, charity, culture, art, and education. Their patriotism is quiet but deep. Their values sustain our national life.

Now, I have used the words "they" and "their" in speaking of these heroes. I could say "you" and "your," because I'm addressing the heroes of whom I speak—you, the citizens of this blessed land. Your dreams, your hopes, your goals are going to be the dreams, the hopes, and the goals of this administration, so help me God.

We shall reflect the compassion that is so much a part of your makeup. How can we love our country and not love our countrymen; and loving them, reach out a hand when they fall, heal them when they're sick, and provide opportunity to make them self-sufficient so they will be equal in fact and not just in theory?

Can we solve the problems confronting us? Well, the answer is an unequivocal and emphatic "yes." To paraphrase Winston Churchill, I do not take the oath I've just taken with the intention of presiding over the dissolution of the world's strongest economy.

In the days ahead I will propose removing the roadblocks that have slowed our economy and reduced productivity. Steps will be taken aimed at restoring the balance between the various levels of government. Progress may be slow, measured in inches and feet, not miles, but we will progress. It is time to reawaken this industrial giant, to get government back within its means, and to lighten our punitive tax burden. And these will be our first priorities, and on these principles, there will be no compromise.

On the eve of our struggle for independence a man who might have been one of the greatest among the Founding Fathers, Dr. Joseph Warren, president of the Massachusetts Congress, said to his fellow Americans, "Our country is in danger, but not to be despaired of. . . . On you depend the fortunes of America. You are to decide the important question on which rests the happiness and liberty of millions yet unborn. Act worthy of yourselves."

Well, I believe we, the Americans of today, are ready to act worthy of ourselves, ready to do what must be done to ensure happiness and liberty for ourselves, our children, and our children's children. And as we renew ourselves here in our own land, we will be seen as having greater strength throughout the world. We will again be the exemplar of freedom and a beacon of hope for those who do not now have freedom.

To those neighbors and allies who share our ideal of freedom, we will strengthen our historic ties and assure them of our support and firm commitment. We will match loyalty with loyalty. We will strive for mutually beneficial relations. We will not use our friendship to impose on their sovereignty, for our own sovereignty is not for sale.

As for the enemies of freedom, those who are potential adversaries, they will be reminded that peace is the highest aspiration of the American people. We will negotiate for it, sacrifice for it; we will not surrender it now or ever.

Our forbearance should never be misunderstood. Our reluctance for conflict should not be misjudged as a failure of will. When action is required to preserve our national security, we will act. We will maintain sufficient strength to prevail if need be, knowing that if we do so we have the best chance of never having to use that strength.

Above all we must realize that no arsenal or no weapon in the arsenals of the world is so formidable as the will and moral courage of free men and women. It is a weapon our adversaries in today's world do not have. It is a weapon that we as Americans do have. Let that be understood by those who practice terrorism and prey upon their neighbors.

I'm told that tens of thousands of prayer meetings are being held on this day, and for that I'm deeply grateful. We are a nation under God, and I believe God intended for us to be free. It would be fitting and good, I think, if each Inaugural Day in future years should be declared a day of prayer.

This is the first time in our history that this ceremony has been held, as you've been told, on this West Front of the Capitol. Standing here, one faces a magnificent vista, opening up on this city's special beauty and history. At the end of this open mall are those shrines to the giants on whose shoulders we stand.

Directly in front of me, the monument to a monumental man, George Washington, father of our country. A man of humility who came to greatness reluctantly. He led America out of revolutionary victory into infant nationhood. Off to one side, the stately memorial to Thomas Jefferson. The Declaration of Independence flames with his eloquence. And then, beyond the Reflecting Pool, the dignified columns of the Lincoln Memorial. Whoever would understand in his heart the meaning of America will find it in the life of Abraham Lincoln.

Beyond these monuments to heroism is the Potomac River, and on the far shore the sloping hills of Arlington National Cemetery, with its row upon row of simple white markers bearing crosses or Stars of David. They add up to only a tiny fraction of the price that has been paid for our freedom.

Each one of those markers is a monument to the kind of hero I spoke of earlier. Their lives ended in places called Belleau Wood, The Argonne, Omaha Beach, Salerno, and halfway around the world on Guadalcanal, Tarawa, Pork Chop Hill, the Chosin Reservoir, and in a hundred rice paddies and jungles of a place called Vietnam. Under one such marker lies a young man, Martin Treptow, who left his job in a small town barbershop in 1917 to go to France with the famed Rainbow Division. There, on the western front, he was killed trying to carry a message between battalions under heavy artillery fire.

We're told that on his body was found a diary. On the flyleaf under the heading, "My Pledge," he had written these words: "America must win this war. Therefore I will work, I will save, I will sacrifice, I will endure, I will fight cheerfully and do my utmost, as if the issue of the whole struggle depended on me alone."

The crisis we are facing today does not require of us the kind of sacrifice that Martin Treptow and so many thousands of others were called upon to make. It does require, however, our best effort, and our willingness to believe in ourselves and to believe in our capacity to perform great deeds, to believe that together and with God's help we can and will resolve the problems which confront us.

And after all, why shouldn't we believe that? We are Americans.

God bless you, and thank you.

❧ 49 ❧
*Clinton v. City of New York**
(1998)

BILL CLINTON'S FIRST THREE YEARS in office were unusually turbulent. His early difficulties had several sources. Clinton was elected in 1992 without much of a mandate, winning only 43 percent of the popular vote in a three-way contest with Republican incumbent George H. W. Bush and independent candidate

*Go to *http://laws.findlaw.com/us/524/417.html.*
For oral arguments, go to *http://www.oyez.org/cases/1990-1999/1997/1997_97_1374.*

H. Ross Perot. As the longtime governor of Arkansas, the new president was inexperienced in the ways of Washington. In addition, Democrats in Congress, who had controlled the House of Representatives for forty years and the Senate for almost as long, were unsympathetic to their new president's goal of moving the party toward the political center.

Clinton's difficulties manifested themselves in a number of ways, including bad press relations, an undisciplined staff, controversial appointments, and a host of political scandals. In 1994 his most ambitious legislative initiative, a sweeping overhaul of the nation's health care system developed by first lady Hillary Rodham Clinton, was defeated in Congress. Even the enactment in 1993 of Clinton's five-year, $500 billion deficit reduction plan was politically costly, at least in the short term. Many voters disliked the spending cuts and tax increases that lay at the heart of his plan. The Republicans took control of both the House and Senate in the 1994 midterm elections, and in early 1995 they seized the policy initiative so firmly that Clinton was forced to assert, "The president is relevant here."

Clinton's political comeback was grounded in his embrace of "triangulation," a strategy he developed in 1995 in conjunction with his backstage political adviser, Dick Morris. Morris persuaded Clinton that it was important not only to stake out a position at the political center, midway between liberal congressional Democrats and conservative congressional Republicans, but also to find new issues that would allow the president to rise above the conventional left–right political spectrum. The three points of the new political triangle would then be occupied by traditional Democrats and Republicans at opposite ends of the baseline, with Clinton hovering at a point above and between them. Clinton embraced Morris's strategy, including a Republican-favored bill to grant the president a line-item veto. In truth, the strategy was consistent with his longstanding effort to forge a "third way" between orthodox liberalism and conservatism.

The precedent established by George Washington that after Congress legislates a president must either "approve all the parts of a bill, or reject it in toto" had been a long-standing irritant to political conservatives, who objected that Congress often lards important bills with extraneous earmarks for "pork-barrel" programs. During the 1980s, as federal budget deficits soared, President Ronald Reagan urged Congress to grant presidents a line-item veto that would enable them to sign some parts of a newly enacted money bill while vetoing others. Republican candidates made the line-item veto a prominent part of their "Contract with America" in the 1994 midterm elections and enacted it into law after they won control of Congress. Clinton, who along with forty-two other state governors had enjoyed the line-item veto as governor of Arkansas, enthusiastically signed the legislation, even though Congress had delayed its effective date until January 1997 in hopes that a new Republican president would take power.

The line-item veto law allowed the president to cancel any new spending projects, narrowly targeted tax breaks, and entitlement programs within five days of signing a money bill. If Congress wanted to restore a canceled provision, it would have to pass a "disapproval" bill. If the president vetoed the disapproval bill, a two-thirds majority of both houses was required to override the veto. Between January 1997 and June 1998 Clinton used the line-item veto to cancel eighty-two provisions in eleven laws, ranging from $15,000 for a new police training center in Arab, Alabama, to $30 million for an air force program to intercept an asteroid in space. Congress overrode thirty-eight of the cancellations, all of them in a single military construction bill. In all, Clinton's use of the line-item veto saved $869 million in spending and tax breaks.

The line-item veto had been controversial from the start, especially among liberal Democrats. Critics charged that it did little to curb wasteful government spending in the states. Instead, state legislatures often forestalled vetoes of favored spending programs by granting governors pet projects of their own. Constitutional scholars defended George Washington's position that Article I, section 7, allows the president to veto only a "Bill," not "part of a Bill."

The critics lost their case in the political arena but won it on constitutional grounds. On June 25, 1998, a six-member majority of the Supreme Court overturned the Line Item Veto Act in response to lawsuits filed by the City of New York, which objected to Clinton's veto of a tax break tied to the Medicaid program, and by the Snake River (Idaho) Potato Growers, who had lost a capital gains tax advantage for farmers' cooperatives. Relying on the presentment clause in Article I, section 7, Justice John Paul Stevens wrote that line-item vetoes are "the functional equivalent of partial repeal of acts of Congress" even though "there is no provision in the Constitution that authorizes the President to enact, to amend, or to repeal statutes." In dissent, Justice Antonin Scalia argued that the Court's interpretation of the presentment clause was too narrow and doctrinaire.

🐾 🐾 🐾

JUSTICE STEVENS delivered the opinion of the Court.

The Line Item Veto Act was enacted in April 1996 and became effective on January 1, 1997. . . . [In June] the President exercised his authority to cancel one provision in the Balanced Budget Act of 1997 and two provisions in the Taxpayer Relief Act of 1997. Appellees, claiming that they had been injured by two of those cancellations, filed these cases in the District Court. That Court again held the statute invalid, and we again expedited our review. We now hold that these appellees have standing to challenge the constitutionality of the Act and, reaching the merits, we agree that the cancellation procedures set forth in the Act violate the Presentment Clause, Art. I, §7, cl. 2, of the Constitution. . . .

The Line Item Veto Act gives the President the power to "cancel in whole" three types of provisions that have been signed into law: "(1) any dollar amount of discretionary budget authority; (2) any item of new direct spending; or (3) any limited tax benefit." It is undisputed that the New York case involves an "item of new direct spending" and that the Snake River case involves a "limited tax benefit" as those terms are defined in the Act. It is also undisputed that each of those provisions had been signed into law pursuant to Article I, §7, of the Constitution before it was canceled.

The Act requires the President to adhere to precise procedures whenever he exercises his cancellation authority. In identifying items for cancellation he must consider the legislative history, the purposes, and other relevant information about the items. He must determine, with respect to each cancellation, that it will "(i) reduce the Federal budget deficit; (ii) not impair any essential Government functions; and (iii) not harm the national interest." Moreover, he must transmit a special message to Congress notifying it of each cancellation within five calendar days (excluding Sundays) after the enactment of the canceled provision. It is undisputed that the President meticulously followed these procedures in these cases.

A cancellation takes effect upon receipt by Congress of the special message from the President. If, however, a "disapproval bill" pertaining to a special message is enacted into law, the cancellations set forth in that message become "null and void." The Act sets forth a detailed expedited procedure for the consideration of a "disapproval bill," but no such bill was passed for either of the cancellations involved in these cases.

A majority vote of both Houses is sufficient to enact a disapproval bill. The Act does not grant the President the authority to cancel a disapproval bill, but he does, of course, retain his constitutional authority to veto such a bill.

The effect of a cancellation is plainly stated in §691e [of the Line Item Veto Act], which defines the principal terms used in the Act. With respect to both an item of new direct spending and a limited tax benefit, the cancellation prevents the item "from having legal force or effect."

Thus, under the plain text of the statute, the two actions of the President that are challenged in these cases prevented one section of the Balanced Budget Act of 1997 and one section of the Taxpayer Relief Act of 1997 "from having legal force or effect." The remaining provisions of those statutes, with the exception of the second canceled item in the latter, continue to have the same force and effect as they had when signed into law.

In both legal and practical effect, the President has amended two Acts of Congress by repealing a portion of each. "[R]epeal of statutes, no less than enactment, must conform with Art. I." *INS v. Chadha* (1983). There is no provision in the Constitution that authorizes the President to enact, to amend, or to repeal statutes. Both Article I and Article II assign responsibilities to the President that directly relate to the lawmaking process, but neither addresses the issue presented by these cases. The President "shall from time to time give to the Congress Information on the State of the Union, and recommend to their Consideration such Measures as he shall judge necessary and expedient. . . ." Art. II, §3. Thus, he may initiate and influence legislative proposals. Moreover, after a bill has passed both Houses of Congress, but "before it become[s] a Law," it must be presented to the President. If he approves it, "he shall sign it, but if

not he shall return it, with his Objections to that House in which it shall have originated, who shall enter the Objections at large on their Journal, and proceed to reconsider it." Art. I, §7, cl. 2.

His "return" of a bill, which is usually described as a "veto," is subject to being
overridden by a two-thirds vote in each House.

There are important differences between the President's "return" of a bill pursuant
to Article I, §7, and the exercise of the President's cancellation authority pursuant to
the Line Item Veto Act. The constitutional return takes place before the bill becomes
law; the statutory cancellation occurs after the bill becomes law. The constitutional
return is of the entire bill; the statutory cancellation is of only a part. Although the
Constitution expressly authorizes the President to play a role in the process of enacting statutes, it is silent on the subject of unilateral Presidential action that either
repeals or amends parts of duly enacted statutes.

There are powerful reasons for construing constitutional silence on this profoundly
important issue as equivalent to an express prohibition. The procedures governing the
enactment of statutes set forth in the text of Article I were the product of the great
debates and compromises that produced the Constitution itself. Familiar historical
materials provide abundant support for the conclusion that the power to enact statutes may only "be exercised in accord with a single, finely wrought and exhaustively
considered, procedure." *INS v. Chadha.* Our first President understood the text of the
Presentment Clause as requiring that he either "approve all the parts of a Bill, or
reject it in toto." . . .

If the Line Item Veto Act were valid, it would authorize the President to create a
different law, one whose text was not voted on by either House of Congress or presented to the President for signature. Something that might be known as "Public
Law 105–33 as modified by the President" may or may not be desirable, but it is
surely not a document that may "become a law" pursuant to the procedures designed
by the Framers of Article I, §7, of the Constitution. . . .

JUSTICE SCALIA, dissenting.

. . . [T]he crux of the matter [is] whether Congress's authorizing the President to
cancel an item of spending gives him a power that our history and traditions show
must reside exclusively in the Legislative Branch. I may note, to begin with, that the
Line Item Veto Act is not the first statute to authorize the President to "cancel"
spending items. In *Bowsher v. Synar* (1986), we addressed the constitutionality of the
Balanced Budget and Emergency Deficit Control Act of 1985, which required the
President, if the federal budget deficit exceeded a certain amount, to issue a "sequestration" order mandating spending reductions specified by the Comptroller General.
The effect of sequestration was that "amounts sequestered . . . shall be permanently
cancelled." We held that the Act was unconstitutional, not because it impermissibly
gave the Executive legislative power, but because it gave the Comptroller General, an
officer of the Legislative Branch over whom Congress retained removal power, "the
ultimate authority to determine the budget cuts to be made," "functions . . . plainly
entailing execution of the law in constitutional terms." The President's discretion
under the Line Item Veto Act is certainly broader than the Comptroller General's

discretion was under the 1985 Act, but it is no broader than the discretion tradition-ally granted the President in his execution of spending laws.

Insofar as the degree of political, "law-making" power conferred upon the Execu-tive is concerned, there is not a dime's worth of difference between Congress's autho-rizing the President to cancel a spending item, and Congress's authorizing money to be spent on a particular item at the President's discretion. And the latter has been done since the Founding of the Nation. From 1789–1791, the First Congress made lump-sum appropriations for the entire Government—"sum[s] not exceeding" speci-fied amounts for broad purposes. From a very early date Congress also made permis-sive individual appropriations, leaving the decision whether to spend the money to the President's unfettered discretion. . . .

The short of the matter is this: Had the Line Item Veto Act authorized the President to "decline to spend" any item of spending contained in the Balanced Budget Act of 1997, there is not the slightest doubt that authorization would have been constitu-tional. What the Line Item Veto Act does instead—authorizing the President to "cancel" an item of spending—is technically different. But the technical difference does not relate to the technicalities of the Presentment Clause, which have been fully complied with; and the doctrine of unconstitutional delegation, which is at issue here, is preeminently not a doctrine of technicalities. The title of the Line Item Veto Act, which was perhaps designed to simplify for public comprehension, or perhaps merely to comply with the terms of a campaign pledge, has succeeded in faking out the Supreme Court. The President's action it authorizes in fact is not a line item veto and thus does not offend Art. I, §7; and insofar as the substance of that action is concerned, it is no different from what Congress has permitted the President to do since the forma-tion of the Union. . . .

❧ 50 ❧
Articles of Impeachment against Bill Clinton*
(1998)

IN DECEMBER 1998, Bill Clinton became the second president ever to be impeached by the House of Representatives. Like his predecessor Andrew Johnson (see Document 20, p. 100), Clinton was acquitted by the Senate and served the remainder of his term. Unlike Johnson, Clinton maintained wide-spread approval from the American people for the job he was doing as president.

The roots of Clinton's impeachment lay in the Ethics in Government Act of 1978, a Watergate-era measure that had been renewed at Clinton's urging in 1993. The act required a panel of federal judges to appoint an independent

---

*Go to *http://www.washingtonpost.com/wp-srv/politics/special/clinton/stories/impeachvote121198.htm.*

counsel whenever the attorney general concluded that a high-level executive official may have committed a crime. In 1994 Attorney General Janet Reno appointed former Reagan administration solicitor general Kenneth Starr to investigate Clinton's possible involvement during the late 1970s in an Arkansas real estate scheme known as Whitewater. In subsequent years, Starr's investigation broadened, eventually centering on the president's testimony in a sexual harassment lawsuit brought against him by Paula Jones, a former Arkansas state employee. The suit was thrown out of federal court, but by then Clinton had testified in a sworn deposition that he never had "sexual relations" or "an affair" with former White House intern Monica Lewinsky, who was one of several women about whom he was asked. Starr regarded this testimony as perjurious. He also suspected the president of obstructing justice by trying to persuade Lewinsky to perjure herself when giving a deposition for the Jones case in return for his help in getting a lucrative job in New York.

Clinton's sexual relationship with Lewinsky became public in January 1998 and dominated the news for more than a year. On August 6 Lewinsky, in exchange for a promise of immunity from prosecution, testified to Starr's Whitewater grand jury that she and the president had a number of sexual encounters in the White House. When the federal courts ruled that Starr had the authority to subpoena Clinton to testify before the grand jury, the president agreed to appear on August 17. Although Clinton admitted in a televised address that evening that his relationship with Lewinsky "was not appropriate. In fact, it was wrong," Starr believed that the president had lied to the grand jury about the full extent of his wrongdoing. Zealously fulfilling one of the independent counsel's responsibilities under the Ethics in Government Act, Starr shared with the House of Representatives his opinion that the president had committed impeachable offenses.

On December 19, 1998, the House adopted two articles of impeachment recommended by its Judiciary Committee and rejected two others. By a vote of 228–206, with only five Republicans and five Democrats crossing party lines, the House approved an article that accused Clinton of providing the grand jury "perjurious, false and misleading testimony" concerning his relationship with Lewinsky. After voting down another of the committee's proposed articles, which involved Clinton's deposition in the Paula Jones lawsuit, the House adopted a second article, charging the president with obstruction of justice for a series of actions to "delay, impede, cover up, and conceal the existence of evidence" related to the Jones case. Five Democrats voted for this article, and twelve Republicans voted against it. The House then rejected the final proposed article, which accused the president of abuse of power and "a pattern of deceit and obstruction," by a vote of 285–148.

The Senate formally convened on January 7, 1999, to deal with the two articles of impeachment approved by the House. Chief Justice William H. Rehnquist presided, as mandated by the Constitution. On February 12 the Senate voted 55–45 against conviction on Article I—twenty-two votes short of the two-thirds majority necessary to remove the president. Ten Republicans joined all forty-five Democrats in voting "not guilty." The Senate divided 50–50 on Article II, with five Republicans joining all the Democrats in voting not to convict.

Partisan politics colored the Clinton impeachment controversy. The Republicans controlled both houses of Congress, which helps to explain why Clinton was impeached. But they lacked a two-thirds majority in the Senate, which along with strong public approval of Clinton's record of peace and prosperity, helps to explain why he was not convicted and removed.

In contrast, bipartisan politics allowed the Ethics in Government Act to expire when it came up for renewal later in 1999. Republicans and Democrats alike felt they had been burned during the act's twenty-six year history by overzealous independent counsels and were happy to see the law die.

꙰ ꙰ ꙰

Resolution, Impeaching William Jefferson Clinton, President of the United States, for high crimes and misdemeanors.

Resolved, that William Jefferson Clinton, President of the United States, is impeached for high crimes and misdemeanors, and that the following articles of impeachment be exhibited to the United States Senate:

Articles of impeachment exhibited by the House of Representatives of the United States of America in the name of itself and of the people of the United States of America, against William Jefferson Clinton, President of the United States of America, in maintenance and support of its impeachment against him for high crimes and misdemeanors.

Article I

In his conduct while President of the United States, William Jefferson Clinton, in violation of his constitutional oath faithfully to execute the office of the President of the United States, and, to the best of his ability, preserve, protect, and defend the Constitution of the United States, and in violation of his constitutional duty to take care that the laws be faithfully executed, has willfully corrupted and manipulated the judicial process of the United States for his personal gain and exoneration, impeding the administration of justice, in that:

On August 17, 1998, William Jefferson Clinton swore to tell the truth, the whole truth, and nothing but the truth before a Federal grand jury of the United States. Contrary to that oath, William Jefferson Clinton willfully provided perjurious, false and misleading testimony to the grand jury concerning one or more of the following: (1) the nature and details of his relationship with a subordinate government employee; (2) prior perjurious, false and misleading testimony he gave in a Federal civil rights action brought against him; (3) prior false and misleading statements he allowed his attorney to make to a Federal judge in that civil rights action; and (4) his corrupt efforts to influence the testimony of witnesses and to impede the discovery of evidence in that civil rights action.

In doing this, William Jefferson Clinton has undermined the integrity of his office, has brought disrepute on the Presidency, has betrayed his trust as President, and has acted in a manner subversive of the rule of law and justice, to the manifest injury of the people of the United States.

Wherefore, William Jefferson Clinton, by such conduct, warrants impeachment and trial, and removal from office and disqualification to hold and enjoy any office of honor, trust or profit under the United States.

Article II

In his conduct while President of the United States, William Jefferson Clinton, in violation of his constitutional oath faithfully to execute the office of President of the United States and, to the best of his ability, preserve, protect, and defend the Constitution of the United States, and in violation of his constitutional duty to take care that the laws be faithfully executed, has prevented, obstructed, and impeded the administration of justice, and has to that end engaged personally, and through his subordinates and agents, in a course of conduct or scheme designed to delay, impede, cover up, and conceal the existence of evidence and testimony related to a Federal civil rights action brought against him in a duly instituted judicial proceeding.

The means used to implement this course of conduct or scheme included one or more of the following acts:

(1) On or about December 17, 1997, William Jefferson Clinton corruptly encouraged a witness in a Federal civil rights action brought against him to execute a sworn affidavit in that proceeding that he knew to be perjurious, false and misleading.

(2) On or about December 17, 1997, William Jefferson Clinton corruptly encouraged a witness in a Federal civil rights action brought against him to give perjurious, false and misleading testimony if and when called to testify personally in that proceeding.

(3) On or about December 28, 1997, William Jefferson Clinton corruptly engaged in, encouraged, or supported a scheme to conceal evidence that had been subpoenaed in a Federal civil rights action brought against him.

(4) Beginning on or about December 7, 1997, and continuing through and including January 14, 1998, William Jefferson Clinton intensified and succeeded in an effort to secure job assistance to a witness in a Federal civil rights action brought against him in order to corruptly prevent the truthful testimony of that witness in that proceeding at a time when the truthful testimony of that witness would have been harmful to him.

(5) On January 17, 1998, at his deposition in a Federal civil rights action brought against him, William Jefferson Clinton corruptly allowed his attorney to make false and misleading statements to a Federal judge characterizing an affidavit, in order to prevent questioning deemed relevant by the judge. Such false and

misleading statements were subsequently acknowledged by his attorney in a communication to that judge.

(6) On or about January 18 and January 20–21, 1998, William Jefferson Clinton related a false and misleading account of events relevant to a Federal civil rights action brought against him to a potential witness in that proceeding, in order to corruptly influence the testimony of that witness.

(7) On or about January 21, 23 and 26, 1998, William Jefferson Clinton made false and misleading statements to potential witnesses in a Federal grand jury proceeding in order to corruptly influence the testimony of those witnesses. The false and misleading statements made by William Jefferson Clinton were repeated by the witnesses to the grand jury, causing the grand jury to receive false and misleading information.

In all of this, William Jefferson Clinton has undermined the integrity of his office, has brought disrepute on the Presidency, has betrayed his trust as President, and has acted in a manner subversive of the rule of law and justice, to the manifest injury of the people of the United States.

Wherefore, William Jefferson Clinton, by such conduct, warrants impeachment and trial, and removal from office and disqualification to hold and enjoy any office of honor, trust or profit under the United States.

❧ 51 ❧

*Bush v. Gore**

(2000)

THE 2000 ELECTION WAS A VIRTUAL TIE, with the deadlock ultimately resolved by the U.S. Supreme Court. In the end, the campaign that pitted Gov. George W. Bush of Texas, the Republican nominee, against Vice President Al Gore, his Democratic opponent, was less decisive than the *Bush v. Gore* legal case.

The "postelection election" of 2000 began in the predawn hours of Wednesday, November 8, when the television networks, which earlier had declared Bush the winner on the basis of his projected victory in Florida, decided that Florida was actually too close to call. Gore dispatched a team of lawyers to Tallahassee to investigate charges by local Democrats that they had been cheated out of their votes. Claiming that voting machines had failed to count all of his ballots and therefore had thwarted the will of the people, Gore called for a hand count in four

*Go to *http://laws.findlaw.com/us/531/98.html.*
For oral arguments, go to *http://www.oyez.org/cases/2000-2009/2000/2000_00_949.*

counties known to be strongly Democratic and controlled by Democratic election commissions. The central claim of Gore's legal challenge, which was supported by the Florida Supreme Court, also dominated by Democrats, was that the state's voting machines were flawed. A hand count would show the true intent of the voters and, in all likelihood, overcome Bush's minuscule lead, which had shrunk from a reported 1,784 votes on election night to 327 votes after a statewide machine recount was conducted a few days later.

Bush's lawyers appealed to the U.S. Supreme Court to stop the hand recount ordered by the state supreme court in the four disputed counties. They argued that the Florida court's decision violated both the Constitution's provision that the state legislature must determine how a state's electors will be chosen and the 1887 Electoral Count Act's requirement, passed in the wake of the disputed 1876 Hayes–Tilden election, that electors must be chosen according to state laws enacted by the legislature before election day. Bush's lawyers also claimed that the recount violated the equal protection clause of the Fourteenth Amendment, because no uniform standards would govern the recounting of votes in the state's different counties.

Even as the lawyers from both sides chased each other from courtroom to courtroom, Bush pressed advantages that he alone enjoyed. Florida secretary of state Katherine Harris, who under state law was charged to certify the results of the election and oversee any recounts that took place, had cochaired the state's Bush campaign. The state legislature, which arguably had the power under the Electoral Count Act to appoint a slate of electors if all other approaches failed, was heavily Republican. The governor of Florida was Bush's brother. As governor, Jeb Bush was charged by the Electoral Count Act to officially notify the National Archives in Washington which slate of electors his state had chosen. Republican presidents had appointed seven of the nine justices of the U.S. Supreme Court, which on December 9 agreed to the Bush legal team's request to resolve the controversy. Bush also benefited from the simple passage of time. Because the Electoral Count Act required that states decide by December 12 which candidate's slate of electors had been chosen, any recounts presumably would have to be completed by then.

Discerning the intent of voters who had imperfectly marked their ballots was the main subject of the Supreme Court decision. A seven-justice majority decreed that the counting process ordered by the Florida Supreme Court, which required a manual recount of every "under-vote" (that is, every ballot for which a machine had failed to register a vote for president), was unconstitutional. By failing to establish a uniform standard that every county in the state would use to judge the voters' intention, the Florida court had violated the Fourteenth Amendment's requirement that states protect the right of individuals to the "equal protection of the laws."

The Court divided more closely and bitterly in the second, decisive part of its ruling. In a 5–4 vote, the Court found that the Florida court had also violated the Constitution by overruling the state legislature, which had indicated its intention to take advantage of an Electoral Count Act provision that insulates a state's electors from challenge as long as they are certified by December 12. Because any recount would frustrate the constitutional prerogative of the state legislature to determine how electors are chosen, the Court decreed, "we reverse the judgment of the Supreme Court of Florida ordering the recount to proceed." The Supreme Court issued its decision on the evening of December 12, leaving Florida no time to recount the votes even if identical procedures for doing so could be implemented in every county.

Gore graciously conceded the election the next day. But his surrender did not take place without considerable protest from others. Gore's supporters were emboldened by Justice John Paul Stevens's dissenting opinion, in which he condemned the Court's majority for emphasizing the state's need to certify its electoral votes by December 12 rather than enforcing Florida's obligation to determine the intention of its voters. "Although we may never know with complete certainty the identity of the winner of this year's Presidential election," Stevens wrote, "the identity of the loser is perfectly clear. It is the Nation's confidence in the judge as an impartial guardian of the rule of law."

❧ ❧ ❧

PER CURIAM.

. . . The individual citizen has no federal constitutional right to vote for electors for the President of the United States unless and until the state legislature chooses a statewide election as the means to implement its power to appoint members of the Electoral College. U.S. Const., Art. II, §1. This is the source for the statement in *McPherson* v. *Blacker,* 146 U.S. 1, 35 (1892), that the State legislature's power to select the manner for appointing electors is plenary; it may, if it so chooses, select the electors itself, which indeed was the manner used by State legislatures in several States for many years after the Framing of our Constitution. *Id.,* at 28–33. History has now favored the voter, and in each of the several States the citizens themselves vote for Presidential electors. When the state legislature vests the right to vote for President in its people, the right to vote as the legislature has prescribed is fundamental; and one source of its fundamental nature lies in the equal weight accorded to each vote and the equal dignity owed to each voter. . . .

The right to vote is protected in more than the initial allocation of the franchise. Equal protection applies as well to the manner of its exercise. Having once granted the right to vote on equal terms, the State may not, by later arbitrary and disparate treatment, value one person's vote over that of another. See, *e.g., Harper* v. *Virginia Bd. of Elections,* 383 U.S. 663, 665 (1966) ("[O]nce the franchise is granted to the electorate, lines may not be drawn which are inconsistent with the Equal Protection Clause of the Fourteenth Amendment"). It must be remembered that "the right of suffrage can be denied by a debasement or dilution of the weight of a citizen's vote just as effectively as by wholly prohibiting the free exercise of the franchise." *Reynolds* v. *Sims,* 377 U.S. 533, 555 (1964).

There is no difference between the two sides of the present controversy on these basic propositions. Respondents say that the very purpose of vindicating the right to vote justifies the recount procedures now at issue. The question before us, however, is whether the recount procedures the Florida Supreme Court has adopted are consistent with its obligation to avoid arbitrary and disparate treatment of the members of its electorate.

Much of the controversy seems to revolve around ballot cards designed to be perforated by a stylus but which, either through error or deliberate omission, have not been perforated with sufficient precision for a machine to count them. In some cases a piece of the card—a chad—is hanging, say by two corners. In other cases there is no separation at all, just an indentation.

The Florida Supreme Court has ordered that the intent of the voter be discerned from such ballots. . . . The recount mechanisms implemented in response to the decisions of the Florida Supreme Court do not satisfy the minimum requirement for non-arbitrary treatment of voters necessary to secure the fundamental right. Florida's basic command for the count of legally cast votes is to consider the "intent of the voter. . . ." This is unobjectionable as an abstract proposition and a starting principle. The problem inheres in the absence of specific standards to ensure its equal application. . . .

A monitor in Miami-Dade County testified at trial that he observed that three members of the county canvassing board applied different standards in defining a legal vote. 3 Tr. 497, 499 (Dec. 3, 2000). And testimony at trial also revealed that at least one county changed its evaluative standards during the counting process. Palm Beach County, for example, began the process with a 1990 guideline which precluded counting completely attached chads, switched to a rule that considered a vote to be legal if any light could be seen through a chad, changed back to the 1990 rule, and then abandoned any pretense of a *per se* rule, only to have a court order that the county consider dimpled chads legal. This is not a process with sufficient guarantees of equal treatment. . . .

The State Supreme Court ratified this uneven treatment. It mandated that the recount totals from two counties, Miami-Dade and Palm Beach, be included in the certified total. The court also appeared to hold *sub silentio* that the recount totals from Broward County, which were not completed until after the original November 14 certification by the Secretary of State, were to be considered part of the new certified vote totals even though the county certification was not contested by Vice President Gore. Yet each of the counties used varying standards to determine what was a legal vote. . . .

The question before the Court is not whether local entities, in the exercise of their expertise, may develop different systems for implementing elections. Instead, we are presented with a situation where a state court with the power to assure uniformity has ordered a statewide recount with minimal procedural safeguards. When a court orders a statewide remedy, there must be at least some assurance that the rudimentary requirements of equal treatment and fundamental fairness are satisfied. . . .

Upon due consideration of the difficulties identified to this point, it is obvious that the recount cannot be conducted in compliance with the requirements of equal protection and due process without substantial additional work. It would require not only the adoption (after opportunity for argument) of adequate statewide standards for determining what is a legal vote, and practicable procedures to implement them, but also orderly judicial review of any disputed matters that might arise. . . .

The Supreme Court of Florida has said that the legislature intended the State's electors to "participat[e] fully in the federal electoral process," as provided in 3 U.S.C. § 5. ___ So. 2d, at ___ (slip op. at 27); see also *Palm Beach Canvassing Bd.* v. *Harris*, 2000 WL 1725434, *13 (Fla. 2000). That statute, in turn, requires that any controversy or contest that is designed to lead to a conclusive selection of electors be completed by December 12. That date is upon us, and there is no recount procedure in place under the State Supreme Court's order that comports with minimal constitutional standards. Because it is evident that any recount seeking to meet the December 12 date will be unconstitutional for the reasons we have discussed, we reverse the judgment of the Supreme Court of Florida ordering a recount to proceed.

Seven Justices of the Court agree that there are constitutional problems with the recount ordered by the Florida Supreme Court that demand a remedy. . . .

None are more conscious of the vital limits on judicial authority than are the members of this Court, and none stand more in admiration of the Constitution's design to leave the selection of the President to the people, through their legislatures, and to the political sphere. When contending parties invoke the process of the courts, however, it becomes our unsought responsibility to resolve the federal and constitutional issues the judicial system has been forced to confront.

The judgment of the Supreme Court of Florida is reversed, and the case is remanded for further proceedings not inconsistent with this opinion.

CHIEF JUSTICE REHNQUIST, with whom JUSTICE SCALIA and JUSTICE THOMAS join, concurring.

We join the *per curiam* opinion. We write separately because we believe there are additional grounds that require us to reverse the Florida Supreme Court's decision. . . .

Article II, §1, cl. 2, provides that "[e]ach State shall appoint, in such Manner as the *Legislature* thereof may direct," electors for President and Vice President. (Emphasis added.)

Acting pursuant to its constitutional grant of authority, the Florida Legislature has created a detailed, if not perfectly crafted, statutory scheme that provides for appointment of Presidential electors by direct election. Fla. Stat. §103.011 (2000). Under the statute, "[v]otes cast for the actual candidates for President and Vice President shall be counted as votes cast for the presidential electors supporting such candidates." *Ibid.* The legislature has designated the Secretary of State as the "chief election officer," with the responsibility to "[o]btain and maintain uniformity in the application, operation, and interpretation of the election laws." §97.012. The state legislature has delegated to county canvassing boards the duties of administering elections. §102.141. Those boards are responsible for providing results to the state Elections Canvassing Commission, comprising the Governor, the Secretary of State, and the Director of the Division of Elections. §102.111. Cf. *Boardman* v. *Esteva*, 323 So. 2d 259, 268, n. 5 (1975) ("The election process . . . is committed to the executive branch of government through duly designated officials all charged with specific duties. . . . [The] judgments [of these officials] are entitled to be regarded by the courts as presumptively correct . . .").

After the election has taken place, the canvassing boards receive returns from precincts, count the votes, and in the event that a candidate was defeated by .5% or less, conduct a mandatory recount. Fla. Stat. §102.141(4) (2000). The county canvassing boards must file certified election returns with the Department of State by 5 p.m. on the seventh day following the election. §102.112(1). The Elections Canvassing Commission must then certify the results of the election. §102.111(1).

The state legislature has also provided mechanisms both for protesting election returns and for contesting certified election results. Section 102.166 governs protests. Any protest must be filed prior to the certification of election results by the county canvassing board. §102.166(4)(b). Once a protest has been filed, "the county canvassing board may authorize a manual recount." §102.166(4)(c). If a sample recount conducted pursuant to §102.166(5) "indicates an error in the vote tabulation which could affect the outcome of the election," the county canvassing board is instructed to: "(a) Correct the error and recount the remaining precincts with the vote tabulation system; (b) Request the Department of State to verify the tabulation software; or (c) Manually recount all ballots," §102.166(5). In the event a canvassing board chooses to conduct a manual recount of all ballots, §102.166(7) prescribes procedures for such a recount.

Contests to the certification of an election, on the other hand, are controlled by §102.168. The grounds for contesting an election include "[r]eceipt of a number of illegal votes or rejection of a number of legal votes sufficient to change or place in doubt the result of the election." §102.168(3)(c). Any contest must be filed in the appropriate Florida circuit court, Fla. Stat. §102.168(1), and the canvassing board or election board is the proper party defendant, §102.168(4). Section 102.168(8) provides that "[t]he circuit judge to whom the contest is presented may fashion such orders as he or she deems necessary to ensure that each allegation in the complaint is investigated, examined, or checked, to prevent or correct any alleged wrong, and to provide any relief appropriate under such circumstances." In Presidential elections, the contest period necessarily terminates on the date [December 12] set by 3 U.S.C. §5 for concluding the State's "final determination" of election controversies. . . .

Surely when the Florida Legislature empowered the courts of the State to grant "appropriate" relief, it must have meant relief that would have become final by the cut-off date of 3 U.S.C. §5. In light of the inevitable legal challenges and ensuing appeals to the Supreme Court of Florida and petitions for certiorari to this Court, the entire recounting process could not possibly be completed by that date. . . .

Given all these factors, . . . the remedy prescribed by the Supreme Court of Florida cannot be deemed an "appropriate" one as of December 8. It significantly departed from the statutory framework in place on November 7, and authorized open-ended further proceedings which could not be completed by December 12, thereby preventing a final determination by that date.

For these reasons, in addition to those given in the *per curiam,* we would reverse.

JUSTICE STEVENS, with whom JUSTICE GINSBURG and JUSTICE BREYER join, dissenting.

The Constitution assigns to the States the primary responsibility for determining the manner of selecting the Presidential electors. See Art. II, §1, cl. 2. When questions arise about the meaning of state laws, including election laws, it is our settled practice to accept the opinions of the highest courts of the States as providing the final answers. On rare occasions, however, either federal statutes or the Federal Constitution may require federal judicial intervention in state elections. This is not such an occasion.

The federal questions that ultimately emerged in this case are not substantial. Article II provides that "[e]ach *State* shall appoint, in such Manner as the Legislature *thereof* may direct, a Number of Electors." *Ibid.* (emphasis added). It does not create state legislatures out of whole cloth, but rather takes them as they come—as creatures born of, and constrained by, their state constitutions. . . . [T]he Florida Legislature's own decision to employ a unitary code for all elections indicates that it intended the Florida Supreme Court to play the same role in Presidential elections that it has historically played in resolving electoral disputes. The Florida Supreme Court's exercise of appellate jurisdiction therefore was wholly consistent with, and indeed contemplated by, the grant of authority in Article II. . . .

What must underlie petitioners' entire federal assault on the Florida election procedures is an unstated lack of confidence in the impartiality and capacity of the state judges who would make the critical decisions if the vote count were to proceed. Otherwise, their position is wholly without merit. The endorsement of that position by the majority of this Court can only lend credence to the most cynical appraisal of the work of judges throughout the land. It is confidence in the men and women who administer the judicial system that is the true backbone of the rule of law. Time will one day heal the wound to that confidence that will be inflicted by today's decision. One thing, however, is certain. Although we may never know with complete certainty the identity of the winner of this year's Presidential election, the identity of the loser is perfectly clear. It is the Nation's confidence in the judge as an impartial guardian of the rule of law.

I respectfully dissent.

George W. Bush's War on Terrorism Address*

(2001)

O N THE MORNING OF SEPTEMBER 11, 2001, nineteen terrorists of the Afghanistan-based al Qaeda network seized control of four airborne passenger jets as they departed from airports in Boston, Washington, and Newark. Two of the planes crashed into the twin towers of the World Trade Center in New York City, causing both buildings to crumble. Another plane crashed into the Pentagon near Washington, D.C. The fourth plane, which almost certainly was targeted to destroy the Capitol or White House, crashed in a remote area of western Pennsylvania after a band of passengers fought the terrorists for control of the cockpit. More than three thousand people were killed in the attacks.

President George W. Bush was reading to children at a Florida elementary school when the attacks occurred. Security concerns delayed his return to Washington until that evening. Even more than it usually does in times of international crisis, the nation rallied to the support of the president. Bush's job approval rating was 51 percent in public opinion polls taken just before the attacks, the lowest of any modern president at the eight-month mark of his administration. Within days his rating rose to 90 percent, the highest ever recorded by a modern president.

In the course of formulating the American response to the attacks, Bush consulted closely with his national security team, including Secretary of State Colin Powell, Secretary of Defense Donald Rumsfeld, and Vice President Richard B. Cheney, as well as with the leaders of allied nations, especially British prime minister Tony Blair. The result was a new approach to fighting terrorism. Previous presidents had treated terrorist incidents on American soil mostly as a law enforcement problem to be dealt with in the courts. Bush instructed the Federal Bureau of Investigation to emphasize prevention rather than prosecution. Previous presidents had fought terrorism abroad mostly through covert operations and occasional bombing raids. Bush marshaled the armed services to prepare air, sea, and ground military operations.

On the evening of September 20, with Prime Minister Blair in the gallery of the House chamber, Bush addressed an expectant audience consisting of Congress and, via television, radio, and the Internet, the American people and many of the leaders and peoples of the world. Vowing to bring al Qaeda and its leader, Osama bin Laden, to justice, Bush demanded the full cooperation of the Islamic fundamentalist

*Go to *http://www.washingtonpost.com/wp-srv/nation/specials/attacked/transcripts/bushaddress_092001.html*

Taliban government of Afghanistan. "Deliver to the United States authorities all the leaders of al Qaeda who hide in your land . . . ," Bush said. He then warned that the Taliban "will hand over the terrorists, or they will share in their fate." In subsequent weeks, when the Taliban government did not act, Bush used American troops, intelligence agents, and financial resources to foment a civil war in Afghanistan that toppled the regime.

Bush made clear that patience would be required to achieve the larger American goal of stamping out terrorism. The war on terrorism "will not end until every terrorist group of global reach has been found, stopped and defeated," Bush vowed. He also warned foreign governments that "any nation that continues to harbor or support terrorism will be regarded by the United States as a hostile regime." To help protect the United States against subsequent attacks, Bush announced the appointment of Pennsylvania governor Tom Ridge to head the new White House Office of Homeland Security. In June 2002 Bush asked Congress to elevate that office to a cabinet department, and it did so later that year. Ridge was quickly confirmed by the Senate as the first secretary of homeland security.

Americans' unity behind the president gradually waned. Some critics focused on the threats to civil liberties that the war on terrorism posed, both for citizens and for suspected foreign terrorists who were captured, detained, and sometimes tortured. Others focused on the failure to capture Osama bin Laden, which they traced to Bush's subsequent focus on waging war against Iraq. The fighting in Afghanistan continued for the duration of the Bush presidency and well into the presidency of his successor, Barack Obama.

🦂 🦂 🦂

Mr. Speaker, Mr. President Pro Tempore, members of Congress, and fellow Americans: In the normal course of events, Presidents come to this chamber to report on the state of the Union. Tonight, no such report is needed. It has already been delivered by the American people. . . .

We have seen the state of our Union in the endurance of rescuers, working past exhaustion. We have seen the unfurling of flags, the lighting of candles, the giving of blood, the saying of prayers—in English, Hebrew, and Arabic. We have seen the decency of a loving and giving people who have made the grief of strangers their own.

My fellow citizens, for the last nine days, the entire world has seen for itself the state of our Union—and it is strong.

Tonight we are a country awakened to danger and called to defend freedom. Our grief has turned to anger, and anger to resolution. Whether we bring our enemies to justice, or bring justice to our enemies, justice will be done.

I thank the Congress for its leadership at such an important time. All of America was touched on the evening of the tragedy to see Republicans and Democrats joined together on the steps of this Capitol, singing "God Bless America." And you did more than sing; you acted, by delivering $40 billion to rebuild our communities and meet the needs of our military. . . .

And on behalf of the American people, I thank the world for its outpouring of support. America will never forget the sounds of our National Anthem playing at Buckingham Palace, on the streets of Paris, and at Berlin's Brandenburg Gate.

We will not forget South Korean children gathering to pray outside our embassy in Seoul, or the prayers of sympathy offered at a mosque in Cairo. We will not forget moments of silence and days of mourning in Australia and Africa and Latin America.

Nor will we forget the citizens of 80 other nations who died with our own: dozens of Pakistanis; more than 130 Israelis; more than 250 citizens of India; men and women from El Salvador, Iran, Mexico and Japan; and hundreds of British citizens. America has no truer friend than Great Britain. Once again, we are joined together in a great cause—so honored the British Prime Minister has crossed an ocean to show his unity of purpose with America. Thank you for coming, friend.

On September the 11th, enemies of freedom committed an act of war against our country. Americans have known wars—but for the past 136 years, they have been wars on foreign soil, except for one Sunday in 1941. Americans have known the casualties of war—but not at the center of a great city on a peaceful morning. Americans have known surprise attacks—but never before on thousands of civilians. All of this was brought upon us in a single day—and night fell on a different world, a world where freedom itself is under attack.

Americans have many questions tonight. Americans are asking: Who attacked our country? The evidence we have gathered all points to a collection of loosely affiliated terrorist organizations known as al Qaeda. They are the same murderers indicted for bombing American embassies in Tanzania and Kenya, and responsible for bombing the USS *Cole*.

Al Qaeda is to terror what the mafia is to crime. But its goal is not making money; its goal is remaking the world—and imposing its radical beliefs on people everywhere.

The terrorists practice a fringe form of Islamic extremism that has been rejected by Muslim scholars and the vast majority of Muslim clerics—a fringe movement that perverts the peaceful teachings of Islam. The terrorists' directive commands them to kill Christians and Jews, to kill all Americans, and make no distinction among military and civilians, including women and children.

This group and its leader—a person named Osama bin Laden—are linked to many other organizations in different countries, including the Egyptian Islamic Jihad and the Islamic Movement of Uzbekistan. There are thousands of these terrorists in more than 60 countries. They are recruited from their own nations and neighborhoods and brought to camps in places like Afghanistan, where they are trained in the tactics of terror. They are sent back to their homes or sent to hide in countries around the world to plot evil and destruction.

The leadership of al Qaeda has great influence in Afghanistan and supports the Taliban regime in controlling most of that country. In Afghanistan, we see al Qaeda's vision for the world.

Afghanistan's people have been brutalized—many are starving and many have fled. Women are not allowed to attend school. You can be jailed for owning a television.

Religion can be practiced only as their leaders dictate. A man can be jailed in Afghanistan if his beard is not long enough.

The United States respects the people of Afghanistan—after all, we are currently its largest source of humanitarian aid—but we condemn the Taliban regime. It is not only repressing its own people, it is threatening people everywhere by sponsoring and sheltering and supplying terrorists. By aiding and abetting murder, the Taliban regime is committing murder.

And tonight, the United States of America makes the following demands on the Taliban: Deliver to United States authorities all the leaders of al Qaeda who hide in your land. Release all foreign nationals, including American citizens, you have unjustly imprisoned. Protect foreign journalists, diplomats and aid workers in your country. Close immediately and permanently every terrorist training camp in Afghanistan, and hand over every terrorist, and every person in their support structure, to appropriate authorities. Give the United States full access to terrorist training camps, so we can make sure they are no longer operating.

These demands are not open to negotiation or discussion. The Taliban must act, and act immediately. They will hand over the terrorists, or they will share in their fate.

I also want to speak tonight directly to Muslims throughout the world. We respect your faith. It's practiced freely by many millions of Americans, and by millions more in countries that America counts as friends. Its teachings are good and peaceful, and those who commit evil in the name of Allah blaspheme the name of Allah. The terrorists are traitors to their own faith, trying, in effect, to hijack Islam itself. The enemy of America is not our many Muslim friends; it is not our many Arab friends. Our enemy is a radical network of terrorists, and every government that supports them.

Our war on terror begins with al Qaeda, but it does not end there. It will not end until every terrorist group of global reach has been found, stopped and defeated.

Americans are asking, why do they hate us? They hate what we see right here in this chamber—a democratically elected government. Their leaders are self-appointed. They hate our freedoms—our freedom of religion, our freedom of speech, our freedom to vote and assemble and disagree with each other.

They want to overthrow existing governments in many Muslim countries, such as Egypt, Saudi Arabia, and Jordan. They want to drive Israel out of the Middle East. They want to drive Christians and Jews out of vast regions of Asia and Africa.

These terrorists kill not merely to end lives, but to disrupt and end a way of life. With every atrocity, they hope that America grows fearful, retreating from the world and forsaking our friends. They stand against us, because we stand in their way.

We are not deceived by their pretenses to piety. We have seen their kind before. They are the heirs of all the murderous ideologies of the 20th century. By sacrificing human life to serve their radical visions—by abandoning every value except the will to power—they follow in the path of fascism, and Nazism, and totalitarianism. And they will follow that path all the way, to where it ends: in history's unmarked grave of discarded lies.

Americans are asking: How will we fight and win this war? We will direct every resource at our command—every means of diplomacy, every tool of intelligence, every instrument of law enforcement, every financial influence, and every necessary weapon of war—to the disruption and to the defeat of the global terror network.

This war will not be like the war against Iraq a decade ago, with a decisive liberation of territory and a swift conclusion. It will not look like the air war above Kosovo two years ago, where no ground troops were used and not a single American was lost in combat.

Our response involves far more than instant retaliation and isolated strikes. Americans should not expect one battle, but a lengthy campaign, unlike any other we have ever seen. It may include dramatic strikes, visible on TV, and covert operations, secret even in success. We will starve terrorists of funding, turn them one against another, drive them from place to place, until there is no refuge or no rest. And we will pursue nations that provide aid or safe haven to terrorism. Every nation, in every region, now has a decision to make. Either you are with us, or you are with the terrorists. From this day forward, any nation that continues to harbor or support terrorism will be regarded by the United States as a hostile regime.

Our nation has been put on notice: We are not immune from attack. We will take defensive measures against terrorism to protect Americans. Today, dozens of federal departments and agencies, as well as state and local governments, have responsibilities affecting homeland security. These efforts must be coordinated at the highest level. So tonight I announce the creation of a Cabinet-level position reporting directly to me—the Office of Homeland Security.

And tonight I also announce a distinguished American to lead this effort, to strengthen American security: a military veteran, an effective governor, a true patriot, a trusted friend—Pennsylvania's Tom Ridge. He will lead, oversee and coordinate a comprehensive national strategy to safeguard our country against terrorism, and respond to any attacks that may come.

These measures are essential. But the only way to defeat terrorism as a threat to our way of life is to stop it, eliminate it, and destroy it where it grows.

Many will be involved in this effort, from FBI agents to intelligence operatives to the reservists we have called to active duty. All deserve our thanks, and all have our prayers. And tonight, a few miles from the damaged Pentagon, I have a message for our military: Be ready. I've called the Armed Forces to alert, and there is a reason. The hour is coming when America will act, and you will make us proud.

This is not, however, just America's fight. And what is at stake is not just America's freedom. This is the world's fight. This is civilization's fight. This is the fight of all who believe in progress and pluralism, tolerance and freedom.

We ask every nation to join us. We will ask, and we will need, the help of police forces, intelligence services, and banking systems around the world. The United States is grateful that many nations and many international organizations have already responded—with sympathy and with support. Nations from Latin America, to Asia, to Africa, to Europe, to the Islamic world. Perhaps the NATO Charter reflects best the attitude of the world: An attack on one is an attack on all.

The civilized world is rallying to America's side. They understand that if this terror goes unpunished, their own cities, their own citizens may be next. Terror, unanswered, can not only bring down buildings, it can threaten the stability of legitimate governments. And you know what—we're not going to allow it.

Americans are asking: What is expected of us? I ask you to live your lives, and hug your children. I know many citizens have fears tonight, and I ask you to be calm and resolute, even in the face of a continuing threat.

I ask you to uphold the values of America, and remember why so many have come here. We are in a fight for our principles, and our first responsibility is to live by them. No one should be singled out for unfair treatment or unkind words because of their ethnic background or religious faith.

I ask you to continue to support the victims of this tragedy with your contributions. Those who want to give can go to a central source of information, *libertyunites .org,* to find the names of groups providing direct help in New York, Pennsylvania, and Virginia.

The thousands of FBI agents who are now at work in this investigation may need your cooperation, and I ask you to give it.

I ask for your patience, with the delays and inconveniences that may accompany tighter security; and for your patience in what will be a long struggle.

I ask your continued participation and confidence in the American economy. Terrorists attacked a symbol of American prosperity. They did not touch its source. America is successful because of the hard work, and creativity, and enterprise of our people. These were the true strengths of our economy before September 11th, and they are our strengths today.

And, finally, please continue praying for the victims of terror and their families, for those in uniform, and for our great country. Prayer has comforted us in sorrow, and will help strengthen us for the journey ahead. . . .

Tonight, we face new and sudden national challenges. We will come together to improve air safety, to dramatically expand the number of air marshals on domestic flights, and take new measures to prevent hijacking. We will come together to promote stability and keep our airlines flying, with direct assistance during this emergency.

We will come together to give law enforcement the additional tools it needs to track down terror here at home. We will come together to strengthen our intelligence capabilities to know the plans of terrorists before they act, and find them before they strike.

We will come together to take active steps that strengthen America's economy, and put our people back to work. . . .

After all that has just passed—all the lives taken, and all the possibilities and hopes that died with them—it is natural to wonder if America's future is one of fear. Some speak of an age of terror. I know there are struggles ahead, and dangers to face. But this country will define our times, not be defined by them. As long as the United States of America is determined and strong, this will not be an age of terror; this will be an age of liberty, here and across the world.

Great harm has been done to us. We have suffered great loss. And in our grief and anger we have found our mission and our moment. Freedom and fear are at war. The advance of human freedom—the great achievement of our time, and the great hope of every time—now depends on us. Our nation—this generation—will lift a dark threat of violence from our people and our future. We will rally the world to this cause by our efforts, by our courage. We will not tire, we will not falter, and we will not fail.

It is my hope that in the months and years ahead, life will return almost to normal. We'll go back to our lives and routines, and that is good. Even grief recedes with time and grace. But our resolve must not pass. Each of us will remember what happened that day, and to whom it happened. We'll remember the moment the news came— where we were and what we were doing. Some will remember an image of a fire, or a story of rescue. Some will carry memories of a face and a voice gone forever.

And I will carry this: It is the police shield of a man named George Howard, who died at the World Trade Center trying to save others. It was given to me by his mom, Arlene, as a proud memorial to her son. This is my reminder of lives that ended, and a task that does not end.

I will not forget this wound to our country or those who inflicted it. I will not yield; I will not rest; I will not relent in waging this struggle for freedom and security for the American people.

The course of this conflict is not known, yet its outcome is certain. Freedom and fear, justice and cruelty, have always been at war, and we know that God is not neutral between them.

Fellow citizens, we'll meet violence with patient justice—assured of the rightness of our cause, and confident of the victories to come. In all that lies before us, may God grant us wisdom, and may He watch over the United States of America.

Thank you.

❧ 53 ❧

The Bush Doctrine*

(2002)

THE SEPTEMBER 11, 2001, terrorist attacks on the United States created a climate of deference to presidential leadership in matters of national security not seen since the end of the Cold War. Three days after the attacks, a nearly unanimous Congress granted President George W. Bush's request for authorization "to use all necessary and appropriate force against the nations, organizations, or people that he determines planned, authorized, committed, or aided the terrorist attacks."

Fortified with Cold War–era powers, Bush adopted a much more forward-leaning (critics called it reckless) approach in exercising them than his predecessors had ever employed against the Soviet Union and its communist allies. Deterrence of Soviet aggression and containment of the Soviet empire had been the primary doctrines of American foreign policy during the Cold War. Bush believed that these doctrines would be ineffective against America's new foes in

*Go to *http://georgewbush-whitehouse.archives.gov/news/releases/2002/06/print/20020601-3.html.*

the war on terrorism: terrorist organizations of global reach, especially al Qaeda; weak governments that harbor terrorists, such as the Taliban regime in Afghanistan; and "rogue states" that brutalize their people, threaten other nations in their region, and ultimately may endanger the United States through their pursuit of chemical, biological, and nuclear weapons of mass destruction. In his January 29, 2002, State of the Union address, Bush singled out Iraq, Iran, and North Korea as rogue states in an "axis of evil."

On June 1, 2002, Bush used the occasion of a graduation address at the United States Military Academy at West Point to outline the deficiencies he saw in the Cold War policies of deterrence and containment and to announce a new foreign policy, which was quickly dubbed the "Bush Doctrine." "Deterrence—the promise of massive retaliation against nations—means nothing against shadowy terrorist networks with no nation or citizens to defend," the president declared. In a veiled reference to Iraqi leader Saddam Hussein, Bush said, "Containment is not possible when unbalanced dictators with weapons of mass destruction can deliver those weapons on missiles or secretly provide them to terrorist allies." The president added that, unlike the Cold War rivalry with the Soviet Union, the threat from terrorism was imminent: "If we wait for threats to fully materialize, we will have waited too long." Because "the war on terror will not be won on the defensive," Bush concluded, "[w]e must take the battle to the enemy, disrupt his plans, and confront the worst threats before they emerge."

Variously described as "preemptive war," "preventive war," and "anticipatory self-defense" (the administration's preferred term), the Bush Doctrine held that the United States was prepared to attack another country to prevent being attacked by it. The new policy was clearly designed to set the stage for the war against Iraq. In October 2002 Congress voted overwhelmingly to support the president in deploying American forces "as he determines to be necessary and appropriate" to end the "continuing threat posed by Iraq." Bush ordered an invasion against Iraq, which began on March 20, 2003. The immediate objective of the war was met less than a month later with the fall of the Saddam Hussein regime, but instability bordering on chaos ensued in the aftermath, as various groups of Iraqis fought for control.

Even before the president's policy toward Iraq became widely unpopular, critics objected to the Bush Doctrine's open-ended character, which allowed the president great discretion to start wars on the basis of claims about another country's intentions. They also questioned Bush's application of the doctrine to Iraq, which had no proven role in assisting al Qaeda or in continuing to produce weapons of mass destruction. Finally, they criticized the Bush administration for its lack of forethought concerning the aftermath of the Iraqi war. As the critics argued, winning the peace and reconstructing the country posed more difficult challenges than winning the war.

. . . In every corner of America, the words "West Point" command immediate respect. This place where the Hudson River bends is more than a fine institution of learning. The United States Military Academy is the guardian of values that have shaped the soldiers who have shaped the history of the world. . . .

History has also issued its call to your generation. In your last year, America was attacked by a ruthless and resourceful enemy. You graduate from this Academy in a time of war, taking your place in an American military that is powerful and is honorable. Our war on terror is only begun, but in Afghanistan it was begun well. . . .

This war will take many turns we cannot predict. Yet I am certain of this: Wherever we carry it, the American flag will stand not only for our power, but for freedom. Our nation's cause has always been larger than our nation's defense. We fight, as we always fight, for a just peace—a peace that favors human liberty. We will defend the peace against threats from terrorists and tyrants. We will preserve the peace by building good relations among the great powers. And we will extend the peace by encouraging free and open societies on every continent.

Building this just peace is America's opportunity, and America's duty. From this day forward, it is your challenge, as well, and we will meet this challenge together. You will wear the uniform of a great and unique country. America has no empire to extend or utopia to establish. We wish for others only what we wish for ourselves—safety from violence, the rewards of liberty, and the hope for a better life.

In defending the peace, we face a threat with no precedent. Enemies in the past needed great armies and great industrial capabilities to endanger the American people and our nation. The attacks of September the 11th required a few hundred thousand dollars in the hands of a few dozen evil and deluded men. All of the chaos and suffering they caused came at much less than the cost of a single tank. The dangers have not passed. This government and the American people are on watch, we are ready, because we know the terrorists have more money and more men and more plans.

The gravest danger to freedom lies at the perilous crossroads of radicalism and technology. When the spread of chemical and biological and nuclear weapons, along with ballistic missile technology—when that occurs, even weak states and small groups could attain a catastrophic power to strike great nations. Our enemies have declared this very intention, and have been caught seeking these terrible weapons. They want the capability to blackmail us, or to harm us, or to harm our friends—and we will oppose them with all our power.

For much of the last century, America's defense relied on the Cold War doctrines of deterrence and containment. In some cases, those strategies still apply. But new threats also require new thinking. Deterrence—the promise of massive retaliation against nations—means nothing against shadowy terrorist networks with no nation or citizens to defend. Containment is not possible when unbalanced dictators with weapons of mass destruction can deliver those weapons on missiles or secretly provide them to terrorist allies.

We cannot defend America and our friends by hoping for the best. We cannot put our faith in the word of tyrants, who solemnly sign non-proliferation treaties, and then systemically break them. If we wait for threats to fully materialize, we will have waited too long.

Homeland defense and missile defense are part of stronger security, and they're essential priorities for America. Yet the war on terror will not be won on the defensive. We must take the battle to the enemy, disrupt his plans, and confront the worst threats before they emerge. In the world we have entered, the only path to safety is the path of action. And this nation will act.

Our security will require the best intelligence, to reveal threats hidden in caves and growing in laboratories. Our security will require modernizing domestic agencies such as the FBI, so they're prepared to act, and act quickly, against danger. Our security will require transforming the military you will lead—a military that must be ready to strike at a moment's notice in any dark corner of the world. And our security will require all Americans to be forward-looking and resolute, to be ready for preemptive action when necessary to defend our liberty and to defend our lives.

The work ahead is difficult. The choices we will face are complex. We must uncover terror cells in 60 or more countries, using every tool of finance, intelligence and law enforcement. Along with our friends and allies, we must oppose proliferation and confront regimes that sponsor terror, as each case requires. Some nations need military training to fight terror, and we'll provide it. Other nations oppose terror, but tolerate the hatred that leads to terror—and that must change. We will send diplomats where they are needed, and we will send you, our soldiers, where you're needed.

All nations that decide for aggression and terror will pay a price. We will not leave the safety of America and the peace of the planet at the mercy of a few mad terrorists and tyrants. We will lift this dark threat from our country and from the world.

Because the war on terror will require resolve and patience, it will also require firm moral purpose. In this way our struggle is similar to the Cold War. Now, as then, our enemies are totalitarians, holding a creed of power with no place for human dignity. Now, as then, they seek to impose a joyless conformity, to control every life and all of life.

America confronted imperial communism in many different ways—diplomatic, economic, and military. Yet moral clarity was essential to our victory in the Cold War. When leaders like John F. Kennedy and Ronald Reagan refused to gloss over the brutality of tyrants, they gave hope to prisoners and dissidents and exiles, and rallied free nations to a great cause.

Some worry that it is somehow undiplomatic or impolite to speak the language of right and wrong. I disagree. Different circumstances require different methods, but not different moralities. Moral truth is the same in every culture, in every time, and in every place. Targeting innocent civilians for murder is always and everywhere wrong. Brutality against women is always and everywhere wrong. There can be no neutrality between justice and cruelty, between the innocent and the guilty. We are in a conflict between good and evil, and America will call evil by its name. By confronting evil and lawless regimes, we do not create a problem, we reveal a problem. And we will lead the world in opposing it.

As we defend the peace, we also have an historic opportunity to preserve the peace. We have our best chance since the rise of the nation state in the 17th century to build a world where the great powers compete in peace instead of prepare for war.

The history of the last century, in particular, was dominated by a series of destructive national rivalries that left battlefields and graveyards across the Earth. Germany fought France, the Axis fought the Allies, and then the East fought the West, in proxy wars and tense standoffs, against a backdrop of nuclear Armageddon.

Competition between great nations is inevitable, but armed conflict in our world is not. More and more, civilized nations find ourselves on the same side—united by common dangers of terrorist violence and chaos. . . . In the past, great power rivals took sides in difficult regional problems, making divisions deeper and more complicated. Today, from the Middle East to South Asia, we are gathering broad international coalitions to increase the pressure for peace. We must build strong and great power relations when times are good; to help manage crisis when times are bad. America needs partners to preserve the peace, and we will work with every nation that shares this noble goal.

And finally, America stands for more than the absence of war. We have a great opportunity to extend a just peace, by replacing poverty, repression, and resentment around the world with hope of a better day. Through most of history, poverty was persistent, inescapable, and almost universal. In the last few decades, we've seen nations from Chile to South Korea build modern economies and freer societies, lifting millions of people out of despair and want. And there's no mystery to this achievement.

The 20th century ended with a single surviving model of human progress, based on non-negotiable demands of human dignity, the rule of law, limits on the power of the state, respect for women and private property and free speech and equal justice and religious tolerance. America cannot impose this vision—yet we can support and reward governments that make the right choices for their own people. In our development aid, in our diplomatic efforts, in our international broadcasting, and in our educational assistance, the United States will promote moderation and tolerance and human rights. And we will defend the peace that makes all progress possible.

When it comes to the common rights and needs of men and women, there is no clash of civilizations. The requirements of freedom apply fully to Africa and Latin America and the entire Islamic world. The peoples of the Islamic nations want and deserve the same freedoms and opportunities as people in every nation. And their governments should listen to their hopes.

A truly strong nation will permit legal avenues of dissent for all groups that pursue their aspirations without violence. An advancing nation will pursue economic reform, to unleash the great entrepreneurial energy of its people. A thriving nation will respect the rights of women, because no society can prosper while denying opportunity to half its citizens. Mothers and fathers and children across the Islamic world, and all the world, share the same fears and aspirations. In poverty, they struggle. In tyranny, they suffer. And as we saw in Afghanistan, in liberation they celebrate.

America has a greater objective than controlling threats and containing resentment. We will work for a just and peaceful world beyond the war on terror. . . .

❧ 54 ❧

George W. Bush's Signing Statement for the Defense Supplemental Appropriations Act*

(2005)

SIGNING STATEMENTS—THAT IS, statements that the president issues when signing a bill into law—are not a new tool of presidential power. Presidents as far back as James Monroe and Andrew Jackson occasionally used signing statements to declare their refusal to enforce one or more provisions of a bill because they regarded them as unconstitutional encroachments on executive authority. In the modern era, presidents starting with Ronald Reagan have employed such statements with growing frequency. None did so more avidly than George W. Bush, who challenged about twelve hundred provisions of bills as he signed them, about twice as many as all previous presidents combined. Nor has any president issued a more controversial signing statement than Bush did on December 30, 2005, when he signed a measure unwieldily called the Department of Defense, Emergency Supplemental Appropriations to Address Hurricanes in the Gulf of Mexico, and the Pandemic Influenza Act, 2006.

Spurred by Republican senator John McCain of Arizona, Congress had included in Title X of the act a provision barring the use of torture (defined as "cruel, inhuman and degrading" treatment) in the interrogation of detainees held in American facilities at home and abroad. Bush initially threatened to veto the measure as a burdensome restriction on intelligence gathering for the war on terrorism, but when Congress passed it with veto-proof majorities of 90–9 in the Senate and 308–122 in the House, the president signed the bill and issued a signing statement.

In the eighth paragraph of the statement, Bush made clear that he did not regard the ban on torture as binding the president. Instead, he wrote, "The executive branch shall construe Title X . . . , relating to detainees, in a manner consistent with the constitutional authority of the President to supervise the unitary executive branch and as Commander in Chief and consistent with the constitutional limitations on the judicial branch." The phrase "unitary executive branch" referred to the Bush administration's theory that neither the legislative nor judicial branch may restrict the president's authority to tell employees and agencies of the executive branch how to do their jobs. A corollary of the unitary executive

*Go to *http://www.presidency.ucsb.edu/ws/index.php?pid=65259*.

theory accounts for the reference to "constitutional limitations on the judicial branch." It was a warning to the Supreme Court not to interfere with how the Central Intelligence Agency and other executive agencies question detainees.

Additional paragraphs in the signing statement referred to other provisions of the wide-ranging defense appropriations act that Bush believed violate the Constitution. They include alleged infringements on "the President's constitutional authority to require the opinions of the heads of departments . . . and to recommend for congressional consideration such measures as the President shall judge necessary and expedient" (paragraph 4); "the Due Process Clause of the Constitution's Fifth Amendment" (paragraph 7); and the "presentment requirements of the Constitution for the making of a law" (paragraph 10).

The last of these—the reference to the presentment clause in Article I—was regarded by critics as especially ironic because that clause figured so heavily in the Supreme Court's ruling in *Clinton v. New York City* that the Line Item Veto Act of 1996 was unconstitutional because it allowed the president to approve some but not all parts of a bill presented for signature by Congress (see Document 49, p. 234). The irony is that signing statements constitute a de facto line-item veto—that is, a decision by the president to instruct the executive branch that certain items in a bill should not be enforced.

※ ※ ※

Today, I have signed into law H.R. 2863, the "Department of Defense, Emergency Supplemental Appropriations to Address Hurricanes in the Gulf of Mexico, and Pandemic Influenza Act, 2006." The Act provides resources needed to fight the war on terror, help citizens of the Gulf States recover from devastating hurricanes, and protect Americans from a potential influenza pandemic.

Sections 8007, 8011, and 8093 of the Act prohibit the use of funds to initiate a special access program, a new overseas installation, or a new start program, unless the congressional defense committees receive advance notice. The Supreme Court of the United States has stated that the President's authority to classify and control access to information bearing on the national security flows from the Constitution and does not depend upon a legislative grant of authority. Although the advance notice contemplated by sections 8007, 8011, and 8093 can be provided in most situations as a matter of comity, situations may arise, especially in wartime, in which the President must act promptly under his constitutional grants of executive power and authority as Commander in Chief of the Armed Forces while protecting certain extraordinarily sensitive national security information. The executive branch shall construe these sections in a manner consistent with the constitutional authority of the President.

Section 8059 of the Act provides that, notwithstanding any other provision of law, no funds available to the Department of Defense for fiscal year 2006 may be used to transfer defense articles or services, other than intelligence services, to another nation or an international organization for international peacekeeping, peace enforcement, or humanitarian assistance operations, until 15 days after the executive branch notifies six committees of the Congress of the planned transfer. To the extent that protection of the U.S. Armed Forces deployed for international peacekeeping, peace enforcement, or humanitarian assistance operations might require action of a kind covered by section 8059 sooner than 15 days after notification, the executive branch shall construe the section in a manner consistent with the President's constitutional authority as Commander in Chief.

A proviso in the Act's appropriation for "Operation and Maintenance, Defense-Wide" purports to prohibit planning for consolidation of certain offices within the Department of Defense. Also, sections 8010(b), 8032, 8037(b), and 8100 purport to specify the content of portions of future budget requests to the Congress. The executive branch shall construe these provisions relating to planning and making of budget recommendations in a manner consistent with the President's constitutional authority to require the opinions of the heads of departments, to supervise the unitary executive branch, and to recommend for congressional consideration such measures as the President shall judge necessary and expedient.

Section 8005 of the Act, relating to requests to congressional committees for reprogramming of funds, shall be construed as calling solely for notification, as any other construction would be inconsistent with the constitutional principles enunciated by the Supreme Court of the United States in *INS v. Chadha.*

The executive branch shall construe section 8104, relating to integration of foreign intelligence information, in a manner consistent with the President's constitutional authority as Commander in Chief, including for the conduct of intelligence operations, and to supervise the unitary executive branch. Also, the executive branch shall construe sections 8106 and 8119 of the Act, which purport to prohibit the President from altering command and control relationships within the Armed Forces, as advisory, as any other construction would be inconsistent with the constitutional grant to the President of the authority of Commander in Chief.

The executive branch shall construe provisions of the Act relating to race, ethnicity, gender, and State residency, such as sections 8014, 8020 and 8057, in a manner consistent with the requirement to afford equal protection of the laws under the Due Process Clause of the Constitution's Fifth Amendment.

The executive branch shall construe Title X in Division A of the Act, relating to detainees, in a manner consistent with the constitutional authority of the President to supervise the unitary executive branch and as Commander in Chief and consistent with the constitutional limitations on the judicial power, which will assist in achieving the shared objective of the Congress and the President, evidenced in Title X, of protecting the American people from further terrorist attacks. Further, in light of the principles enunciated by the Supreme Court of the United States in 2001 in Alexander v. Sandoval, and noting that the text and structure of Title X do not create a private right of action to enforce Title X, the executive branch shall construe Title X not to create a private right of action. Finally, given the decision of the Congress reflected in subsections 1005(e) and 1005(h) that the amendments made to section 2241 of title 28, United States Code, shall apply to past, present, and future actions, including applications for writs of habeas corpus, described in that section, and noting that section 1005 does not confer any constitutional right upon an alien detained abroad as an enemy combatant, the executive branch shall construe section 1005 to preclude the Federal courts from exercising subject matter jurisdiction over any existing or future action, including applications for writs of habeas corpus, described in section 1005.

Language in Division B of the Act, under the heading "Office of Justice Programs, State and Local Law Enforcement Assistance," purports to require the Attorney General to consult congressional committees prior to allocating appropriations for expenditure to execute the law. Because the President's constitutional authority to supervise the unitary executive branch and take care that the laws be faithfully executed cannot be made by law subject to a requirement to consult with congressional committees or to involve them in executive decision-making, the executive branch shall construe the provision to require only notification. At the same time, the Attorney General shall, as a matter of comity between the executive and legislative branches, seek and consider the views of appropriate committees in this matter as the Attorney General deems appropriate.

Certain provisions in the Act purport to allocate funds for specified purposes as set forth in the joint explanatory statement of managers that accompanied the Act or other Acts; to make changes in statements of managers that accompanied various appropriations bills reported from conferences in the past; or to direct compliance with a committee report. Such provisions include section 8044 in Division A, and sections 5022, 5023, and 5024 and language under the heading "Natural Resources Conservation Service, Conservation Operations" in Division B, of the Act. Other provisions of the Act, such as sections 8073 and 8082 in Division A, purport to give binding effect to legislative documents not presented to the President. The executive branch shall construe all these provisions in a manner consistent with the bicameral passage and presentment requirements of the Constitution for the making of a law.

⊰ 55 ⊱

*Hamdan v. Rumsfeld**

(2006)

WARTIME PRESIDENTS have sometimes turned to military courts that operate outside the normal rules of the judicial process as a way of dealing with captured, non-uniformed enemy combatants. During the Civil War, Abraham Lincoln became the first president to authorize the use of military "tribunals" or "commissions." In 1862 Lincoln issued an executive order declaring that all persons engaged in disloyal practices were subject to martial law and to trial by

*Go to *http://www.law.cornell.edu/supct/html/05-184.ZS.html.*
For oral arguments, go to *http://www.oyez.org/cases/2000-2009/2005/2005_05_184.*

military tribunals. In *Ex parte Milligan,* which was decided in 1866, after the war was over, the Supreme Court declared unconstitutional Lincoln's use of such commissions to try citizens in districts remote from the fighting (see Document 19, p. 95). Lambdin P. Milligan, who was arrested in 1864 on charges of conspiracy to free captured Confederate prisoners so they could rejoin the rebel army, was tried by a military commission and sentenced to be hanged. The Court ruled that the constitutional right to a fair trial cannot be set aside unless conditions are so grave as to close the civil courts.

In the World War II case of *Ex parte Quirin,* which was decided during rather than after the war, the Court took a different approach. The justices approved Franklin D. Roosevelt's use of a military tribunal to try eight Germans who came to the United States to commit acts of sabotage. Right after the saboteurs were captured in June 1942, Roosevelt convened a secret commission, which sentenced the eight men to death. Writing for the Court, Chief Justice Harlan Fiske Stone distinguished *Quirin* from *Milligan* by arguing that Milligan, a civilian, was not "part of or associated with the armed forces of the enemy." Moreover, Stone wrote, the conditions of modern warfare made acts of enemy sabotage on American soil more likely than in the past, which justified the use of military tribunals. "The law of war cannot rightly treat those agents of enemy armies who enter our territory, armed with explosives intended for the destruction of war industries and supplies, as any the less belligerent enemies than are agents similarly entering for the purpose of destroying fortified places or our Armed Forces," Stone concluded.

Roosevelt's decision to use military tribunals and the Supreme Court's ratification of his decision in *Quirin* took on new relevance after the September 11, 2001, terrorist attacks on New York and Washington. George W. Bush's authorization of military commissions to punish those who helped the terrorists assault the United States closely followed the language of Roosevelt's 1942 executive order on the German saboteurs. But whether that language would pass constitutional muster with a different court in a different era and a different kind of war was unclear.

On June 29, 2006, in *Hamdan v. Rumsfeld,* a five-member majority of the Court strongly limited the president's power to create military tribunals to try suspected terrorists imprisoned at the American naval base in Guantánamo Bay, Cuba. (Secretary of Defense Donald Rumsfeld was named in the lawsuit because the president assigned the tribunals to his department.) Brushing aside the administration's pleas not to second-guess the commander in chief during wartime, Justice John Paul Stevens ruled that the commissions were neither authorized by law or the Constitution nor justified by military necessity. Consequently, the Court ordered, no military tribunal could try either the former aide to al Qaeda leader Osama bin Laden, Salam Ahmed Hamdan, whose case was before the justices, or anyone else unless the president did one of two things that he had steadfastly refused to do: operate the commissions by the established laws governing regular military courts martial or ask Congress for specific permission to proceed differently.

Responding to *Hamdan,* Bush had little choice but to ask Congress for legislation authorizing the military tribunals. The Military Commissions Act, which Bush signed into law on October 18, 2006, authorized the use of tribunals and declared their rulings nonappealable in court. (The latter provision of the act was voided by the Supreme Court in the 2008 case of *Boumediene v. Bush.*) The act also granted defendants the right to be present at their hearings, a right not guaranteed under Bush's original plan and one whose omission the Court found particularly obnoxious.

　　　　　🐾 🐾 🐾

JUSTICE STEVENS announced the judgment of the Court. . . .

On September 11, 2001, agents of the al Qaeda terrorist organization hijacked commercial airplanes and attacked the World Trade Center in New York City and the national headquarters of the Department of Defense in Arlington, Virginia. Americans will never forget the devastation wrought by these acts. Nearly 3,000 civilians were killed.

Congress responded by adopting a joint resolution authorizing the President to "use all necessary and appropriate force against those nations, organizations, or persons he determines planned, authorized, committed, or aided the terrorist attacks . . . in order to prevent any future acts of international terrorism against the United States by such nations, organizations, or persons." Acting pursuant to the AUMF [Authorization for Use of Military Force], and having determined that the Taliban regime had supported al Qaeda, the President ordered the Armed Forces of the United States to invade Afghanistan. In the ensuing hostilities, hundreds of individuals, Hamdan among them, were captured and eventually detained at Guantanamo Bay.

On November 13, 2001, while the United States was still engaged in active combat with the Taliban, the President issued a comprehensive military order intended to govern the "Detention, Treatment, and Trial of Certain Non-Citizens in the War Against Terrorism" (hereinafter November 13 Order or Order). Those subject to the November 13 Order include any noncitizen for whom the President determines "there is reason to believe" that he or she (1) "is or was" a member of al Qaeda or (2) has engaged or participated in terrorist aimed at or harmful to the United States. Any such individuals "shall, when tried, be tried by military commission for any and all offenses triable by military commission that such individual is alleged to have committed, and may be punished in accordance with the penalties provided under applicable law, including imprisonment or death." The November 13 Order vested in the Secretary of Defense the power to appoint military commissions to try individuals subject to the Order, but that power has since been delegated to . . . [the] "Appointing Authority for Military Commissions."

On July 3, 2003, the President announced his determination that Hamdan and five other detainees at Guantanamo Bay were subject to the November 13 Order and thus triable by military commission. . . .

IV

The military commission, a tribunal neither mentioned in the Constitution nor created by statute, was born of military necessity. . . .

Exigency alone, of course, will not justify the establishment and use of penal tribunals not contemplated by Article I, §8 and Article III, §1 of the Constitution unless some other part of that document authorizes a response to the felt need. See *Ex parte Milligan* (1866). And that authority, if it exists, can derive only from the powers granted jointly to the President and Congress in time of war.

The Constitution makes the President the "Commander in Chief" of the Armed Forces, but vests in Congress the powers to "declare War . . . and make Rules concerning Captures on Land and Water," to "raise and support Armies," to "define and punish . . . Offences against the Law of Nations," and "To make Rules for the Government and Regulation of the land and naval Forces." The interplay between these powers was described by Chief Justice Chase in the seminal case of *Ex parte Milligan*:

"The power to make the necessary laws is in Congress; the power to execute in the President. Both powers imply many auxiliary and subordinate powers. . . . But neither the President, in war more than in peace, intrude upon the proper authority of Congress, nor Congress upon the proper authority of the President. . . . Congress cannot direct the conduct of campaigns, nor can the President, or any commander under him, without the sanction of Congress, institute tribunals for the trial and punishment of offences, either of soldiers or civilians, unless in cases of a controlling necessity. . . ."

Whether Chief Justice Chase was correct in suggesting that the President may constitutionally convene military commissions "without the sanction of Congress" in cases of "controlling necessity" is a question this Court has not answered definitively, and need not answer today. For we held in [*Ex parte*] *Quirin* [1942] that Congress had, through Article of War 15, sanctioned the use of military commissions in such circumstances. . . .

We have no occasion to revisit *Quirin*'s controversial characterization of Article of War 15 as congressional authorization for military commissions. Contrary to the Government's assertion, however, even *Quirin* did not view the authorization as a sweeping mandate for the President to "invoke military commissions when he deems them necessary." Rather, the *Quirin* Court recognized that Congress had simply preserved what power, under the Constitution and the common law of war, the President had had before 1916 to convene military commissions—with the express condition that the President and those under his command comply with the law of war. . . .

V

The charge against Hamdan . . . alleges a conspiracy extending over a number of years, from 1996 to November 2001. . . .

The charge's shortcomings are not merely formal, but are indicative of a broader inability on the Executive's part here to satisfy the most basic precondition—at least in the absence of specific congressional authorization—for establishment of military commissions: military necessity. Hamdan's tribunal was appointed not by a military commander in the field of battle, but by a retired major general stationed away from any active hostilities. Hamdan is charged not with an overt act for which he was caught redhanded in a theater of war and which military efficiency demands be tried expeditiously, but with an agreement the inception of which long predated the attacks of September 11, 2001 and the AUMF. That may well be a crime, but it is not an offense that "by the law of war may be tried by military commissio[n]." None of the overt acts alleged to have been committed in furtherance of the agreement is itself a war crime, or even necessarily occurred during time of, or in a theater of, war. Any urgent need for imposition or execution of judgment is utterly belied by the record; Hamdan was arrested in November 2001 and he was not charged until mid-2004. These simply are not the circumstances in which, by any stretch of the historical evidence or this Court's precedents, a military commission established by Executive Order under the authority of Article 21 of the UCMJ may lawfully try a person and subject him to punishment. . . .

JUSTIVE BREYER, with whom JUSTICE KENNEDY, JUSTICE SOUTER, and JUSTICE GINSBURG join, concurring.

The Court's conclusion ultimately rests upon a single ground: Congress has not issued the Executive a "blank check." . . . Nothing prevents the President from returning to Congress to seek the authority he believes necessary.

Where, as here, no emergency prevents consultation with Congress, judicial insistence upon that consultation does not weaken our Nation's ability to deal with danger. To the contrary, that insistence strengthens the Nation's ability to determine— through democratic means—how best to do so. The Constitution places its faith in those democratic means. Our Court today simply does the same.

JUSTICE THOMAS, with whom JUSTICE SCALIA joins, and with whom JUSTICE ALITO joins . . . , dissenting.

. . . [I]t is appropriate to respond to the Court's resolution of the merits of petitioner's claims because its opinion openly flouts our well-established duty to respect the Executive's judgment in matters of military operations and foreign affairs. The Court's evident belief that it is qualified to pass on the "[m]ilitary necessity," of the Commander in Chief's decision to employ a particular form of force against our enemies is so antithetical to our constitutional structure that it simply cannot go unanswered. I respectfully dissent. . . .

We are not engaged in a traditional battle with a nation-state, but with a worldwide, hydra-headed enemy, who lurks in the shadows conspiring to reproduce the atrocities of September 11, 2001, and who has boasted of sending suicide bombers into civilian gatherings, has proudly distributed videotapes of beheadings of civilian workers, and has tortured and dismembered captured American soldiers. But according to the plurality, when our Armed Forces capture those who are plotting terrorist atrocities like the bombing of the Khobar Towers, the bombing of the U.S.S. *Cole,* and the attacks of September 11—even if their plots are advanced to the very brink of fulfillment—our military cannot charge those criminals with any offense against the laws of war. Instead, our troops must catch the terrorists "redhanded" in the midst of the attack itself, in order to bring them to justice. Not only is this conclusion fundamentally inconsistent with the cardinal principle of the law of war, namely protecting non-combatants, but it would sorely hamper the President's ability to confront and defeat a new and deadly enemy. . . .

The plurality's willingness to second-guess the determination of the political branches that these conspirators must be brought to justice is both unprecedented and dangerous.

❧ 56 ❧

Barack Obama's Campaign Speech
on Race in America

(2008)

T HE 2008 ELECTION was marked by a dramatic diversification of the presidential talent pool. Sen. Barack Obama of Illinois and Sen. Hillary Rodham Clinton of New York battled for the Democratic nomination, guaranteeing that the Democrats would become the first party in history to nominate either an African American or a woman for president. Republican presidential nominee John McCain, a seventy-two-year-old senator from Arizona, would have become the oldest person ever elected president. He chose as his vice-presidential running mate the first woman ever nominated for national office by the Republican Party, Gov. Sarah Palin of Alaska. Every previous president and vice president had been a white male, and every president had been younger than seventy at the time of his election.

Barriers to the presidency other than race and gender had fallen in previous elections. In a book published on the eve of the 1960 election, presidential scholar Clinton Rossiter offered a list of "oughts" and "almost certainly musts" for would-be presidents that he gleaned from the historical record. They included: "northerner" or "westerner," "lawyer," "more than forty-five years old" but "less than sixty-five years old," "Protestant," "a small-town boy," and "a self-made man." John F. Kennedy, a rich (not self-made), urban (not small town), forty-three years old (not more than forty-five), Roman Catholic (not Protestant) with no law degree, was elected president. Four years later Lyndon B. Johnson of Texas, the first in a series of five presidential southerners (not northerners or westerners) who were elected from 1964 to 2004, won the election.

Polls showed that in 2008 voters were ready to elect a president with a non-traditional profile. In the 1930s the percentage of Americans surveyed by the Gallup Poll who said they were willing to vote for a "generally well-qualified" woman for president was the same percentage as said they would consider voting for a "generally well-qualified" African American—33 percent. By 2008, 88 percent said they were open to voting for a woman, and 94 percent for a black candidate. Offsetting those voters who still refused to vote for a female or African American nominee were those who were eager to do so.

Obama based his campaign on issues that transcended race, such as tax cuts for the middle class, expanded health care, and opposition to the war in Iraq. He downplayed issues that white voters tended to associate with black political leaders, including poverty, urban blight, and affirmative action. Although he defined himself as an African American, Obama often mentioned being raised by his white mother and her parents.

Despite Obama's best efforts, race became an issue on March 13, 2008, when videos surfaced of some of his Chicago pastor's incendiary sermons. Rev. Jeremiah Wright's declaration on the Sunday after September 11, 2001, that "the stuff we have done overseas is now brought right back into our own front yards. America's chickens are coming home to roost" was shown endlessly on broadcast and cable news programs and on the Internet.

Overriding his campaign advisers' judgment, Obama chose the path Kennedy had taken in 1960 to address voters' concerns about his Roman Catholic religion: he faced the issue directly in a nationally televised speech. Speaking at the National Constitution Center in Philadelphia on March 18, Obama declared that Wright had "expressed a profoundly distorted view of this country—a view that sees white racism as endemic, and that elevates what is wrong with America above all that we know is right with America." In contrast, Obama said, "we may have different stories, but we hold common hopes; we may not look the same and we may not have come from the same place, but we all want to move in the same direction—towards a better future for our children and our grandchildren." Obama also called for further progress in overcoming "legalized discrimination," "a lack of economic opportunity among black men," and other civil rights issues. His appeal to white working-class voters suffered as a result of the Wright controversy, but not as badly as it would have had he not addressed the issue. Meanwhile, Obama's support among young and college-educated whites soared.

In the fall campaign, Senator McCain consistently rejected supporters' advice to run attack ads linking Obama with Reverend Wright and publicly rebuked a voter at a town hall meeting who said she "can't trust Obama" because "he's an Arab." On election day, Obama won 44 percent of the white vote (54 percent among whites under thirty) and 95 percent of the black vote—both figures well above average for Democratic presidential candidates in recent decades. He defeated McCain in the Electoral College by a margin of 365–173.

"We the people, in order to form a more perfect union."

Two hundred and twenty one years ago, in a hall that still stands across the street, a group of men gathered and, with these simple words, launched America's improbable experiment in democracy. Farmers and scholars; statesmen and patriots who had traveled across an ocean to escape tyranny and persecution finally made real their declaration of independence at a Philadelphia convention that lasted through the spring of 1787.

The document they produced was eventually signed but ultimately unfinished. It was stained by this nation's original sin of slavery, a question that divided the colonies and brought the convention to a stalemate until the founders chose to allow the slave trade to continue for at least twenty more years, and to leave any final resolution to future generations.

Of course, the answer to the slavery question was already embedded within our Constitution—a Constitution that had at its very core the ideal of equal citizenship under the law; a Constitution that promised its people liberty, and justice, and a union that could be and should be perfected over time.

And yet words on a parchment would not be enough to deliver slaves from bondage, or provide men and women of every color and creed their full rights and obligations as citizens of the United States. What would be needed were Americans in successive generations who were willing to do their part—through protests and struggle, on the streets and in the courts, through a civil war and civil disobedience and always at great risk—to narrow that gap between the promise of our ideals and the reality of their time.

This was one of the tasks we set forth at the beginning of this campaign—to continue the long march of those who came before us, a march for a more just, more equal, more free, more caring and more prosperous America. I chose to run for the presidency at this moment in history because I believe deeply that we cannot solve the challenges of our time unless we solve them together—unless we perfect our union by understanding that we may have different stories, but we hold common hopes; that we may not look the same and we may not have come from the same place, but we all want to move in the same direction—towards a better future for our children and our grandchildren.

This belief comes from my unyielding faith in the decency and generosity of the American people. But it also comes from my own American story.

I am the son of a black man from Kenya and a white woman from Kansas. I was raised with the help of a white grandfather who survived a Depression to serve in Patton's Army during World War II and a white grandmother who worked on a bomber assembly line at Fort Leavenworth while he was overseas. I've gone to some of the best schools in America and lived in one of the world's poorest nations. I am married to a black American who carries within her the blood of slaves and slaveowners—an inheritance we pass on to our two precious daughters. I have brothers, sisters, nieces, nephews, uncles and cousins, of every race and every hue, scattered across three continents, and for as long as I live, I will never forget that in no other country on Earth is my story even possible.

It's a story that hasn't made me the most conventional candidate. But it is a story that has seared into my genetic makeup the idea that this nation is more than the sum of its parts—that out of many, we are truly one.

Throughout the first year of this campaign, against all predictions to the contrary, we saw how hungry the American people were for this message of unity. Despite the temptation to view my candidacy through a purely racial lens, we won commanding victories in states with some of the whitest populations in the country. In South Carolina, where the Confederate Flag still flies, we built a powerful coalition of African Americans and white Americans.

This is not to say that race has not been an issue in the campaign. At various stages in the campaign, some commentators have deemed me either "too black" or "not black enough." We saw racial tensions bubble to the surface during the week before the South Carolina primary. The press has scoured every exit poll for the latest evidence of racial polarization, not just in terms of white and black, but black and brown as well.

And yet, it has only been in the last couple of weeks that the discussion of race in this campaign has taken a particularly divisive turn.

On one end of the spectrum, we've heard the implication that my candidacy is somehow an exercise in affirmative action; that it's based solely on the desire of wide-eyed liberals to purchase racial reconciliation on the cheap. On the other end, we've heard my former pastor, Reverend Jeremiah Wright, use incendiary language to express views that have the potential not only to widen the racial divide, but views that denigrate both the greatness and the goodness of our nation; that rightly offend white and black alike.

I have already condemned, in unequivocal terms, the statements of Reverend Wright that have caused such controversy. For some, nagging questions remain. Did I know him to be an occasionally fierce critic of American domestic and foreign policy? Of course. Did I ever hear him make remarks that could be considered controversial while I sat in church? Yes. Did I strongly disagree with many of his political views? Absolutely—just as I'm sure many of you have heard remarks from your pastors, priests, or rabbis with which you strongly disagreed.

But the remarks that have caused this recent firestorm weren't simply controversial. They weren't simply a religious leader's effort to speak out against perceived injustice. Instead, they expressed a profoundly distorted view of this country—a view that sees white racism as endemic, and that elevates what is wrong with America above all that we know is right with America; a view that sees the conflicts in the Middle East as rooted primarily in the actions of stalwart allies like Israel, instead of emanating from the perverse and hateful ideologies of radical Islam.

As such, Reverend Wright's comments were not only wrong but divisive, divisive at a time when we need unity; racially charged at a time when we need to come together to solve a set of monumental problems—two wars, a terrorist threat, a falling economy, a chronic health care crisis and potentially devastating climate change; problems that are neither black or white or Latino or Asian, but rather problems that confront us all.

Given my background, my politics, and my professed values and ideals, there will no doubt be those for whom my statements of condemnation are not enough. Why associate myself with Reverend Wright in the first place, they may ask? Why not join another church? And I confess that if all that I knew of Reverend Wright were the snippets of those sermons that have run in an endless loop on the television and You Tube, or if Trinity United Church of Christ conformed to the caricatures being peddled by some commentators, there is no doubt that I would react in much the same way.

But the truth is, that isn't all that I know of the man. The man I met more than twenty years ago is a man who helped introduce me to my Christian faith, a man who spoke to me about our obligations to love one another; to care for the sick and lift up the poor. He is a man who served his country as a U.S. Marine; who has studied and lectured at some of the finest universities and seminaries in the country, and who for over thirty years led a church that serves the community by doing God's work here on Earth—by housing the homeless, ministering to the needy, providing day care services and scholarships and prison ministries, and reaching out to those suffering from HIV/AIDS.

In my first book, *Dreams From My Father*, I described the experience of my first service at Trinity:

People began to shout, to rise from their seats and clap and cry out, a forceful wind carrying the reverend's voice up into the rafters.... And in that single note—hope!—I heard something else; at the foot of that cross, inside the thousands of churches across the city, I imagined the stories of ordinary black people merging with the stories of David and Goliath, Moses and Pharaoh, the Christians in the lion's den, Ezekiel's field of dry bones. Those stories—of survival, and freedom, and hope—became our story, my story; the blood that had spilled was our blood, the tears our tears; until this black church, on this bright day, seemed once more a vessel carrying the story of a people into future generations and into a larger world. Our trials and triumphs became at once unique and universal, black and more than black; in chronicling our journey, the stories and songs gave us a means to reclaim memories that we didn't need to feel shame about ... memories that all people might study and cherish—and with which we could start to rebuild.

That has been my experience at Trinity. Like other predominantly black churches across the country, Trinity embodies the black community in its entirety—the doctor and the welfare mom, the model student and the former gang-banger. Like other black churches, Trinity's services are full of raucous laughter and sometimes bawdy humor. They are full of dancing, clapping, screaming and shouting that may seem jarring to the untrained ear. The church contains in full the kindness and cruelty, the fierce intelligence and the shocking ignorance, the struggles and successes, the love and yes, the bitterness and bias that make up the black experience in America.

And this helps explain, perhaps, my relationship with Reverend Wright. As imperfect as he may be, he has been like family to me. He strengthened my faith, officiated my wedding, and baptized my children. Not once in my conversations with him have I heard him talk about any ethnic group in derogatory terms, or treat whites with whom he interacted with anything but courtesy and respect. He contains within him the contradictions—the good and the bad—of the community that he has served diligently for so many years.

I can no more disown him than I can disown the black community. I can no more disown him than I can my white grandmother—a woman who helped raise me, a woman who sacrificed again and again for me, a woman who loves me as much as she loves anything in this world, but a woman who once confessed her fear of black men who passed by her on the street, and who on more than one occasion has uttered racial or ethnic stereotypes that made me cringe.

These people are a part of me. And they are a part of America, this country that I love.

Some will see this as an attempt to justify or excuse comments that are simply inexcusable. I can assure you it is not. I suppose the politically safe thing would be to move on from this episode and just hope that it fades into the woodwork. We can dismiss Reverend Wright as a crank or a demagogue, just as some have dismissed Geraldine Ferraro, in the aftermath of her recent statements, as harboring some deep-seated racial bias.

But race is an issue that I believe this nation cannot afford to ignore right now. We would be making the same mistake that Reverend Wright made in his offending sermons about America—to simplify and stereotype and amplify the negative to the point that it distorts reality.

The fact is that the comments that have been made and the issues that have surfaced over the last few weeks reflect the complexities of race in this country that we've never really worked through—a part of our union that we have yet to perfect. And if we walk away now, if we simply retreat into our respective corners, we will never be able to come together and solve challenges like health care, or education, or the need to find good jobs for every American.

Understanding this reality requires a reminder of how we arrived at this point. As William Faulkner once wrote, "The past isn't dead and buried. In fact, it isn't even past." We do not need to recite here the history of racial injustice in this country. But we do need to remind ourselves that so many of the disparities that exist in the African-American community today can be directly traced to inequalities passed on from an earlier generation that suffered under the brutal legacy of slavery and Jim Crow.

Segregated schools were, and are, inferior schools; we still haven't fixed them, fifty years after *Brown v. Board of Education,* and the inferior education they provided, then and now, helps explain the pervasive achievement gap between today's black and white students.

Legalized discrimination—where blacks were prevented, often through violence, from owning property, or loans were not granted to African-American business owners, or black homeowners could not access FHA mortgages, or blacks were excluded from unions, or the police force, or fire departments—meant that black families could not amass any meaningful wealth to bequeath to future generations. That history helps explain the wealth and income gap between black and white, and the concentrated pockets of poverty that persists in so many of today's urban and rural communities.

A lack of economic opportunity among black men, and the shame and frustration that came from not being able to provide for one's family, contributed to the erosion of black families—a problem that welfare policies for many years may have worsened. And the lack of basic services in so many urban black neighborhoods—parks for kids to play in, police walking the beat, regular garbage pick-up and building code enforcement—all helped create a cycle of violence, blight and neglect that continue to haunt us.

This is the reality in which Reverend Wright and other African-Americans of his generation grew up. They came of age in the late fifties and early sixties, a time when segregation was still the law of the land and opportunity was systematically constricted. What's remarkable is not how many failed in the face of discrimination, but rather how many men and women overcame the odds; how many were able to make a way out of no way for those like me who would come after them.

But for all those who scratched and clawed their way to get a piece of the American Dream, there were many who didn't make it—those who were ultimately defeated, in one way or another, by discrimination. That legacy of defeat was passed on to future generations—those young men and increasingly young women who we see standing on street corners or languishing in our prisons, without hope or prospects for the future. Even for those blacks who did make it, questions of race, and racism, continue to define their worldview in fundamental ways. For the men and women of Reverend Wright's generation, the memories of humiliation and doubt and fear have not gone away; nor has the anger and the bitterness of those years. That anger may not get expressed in public, in front of white co-workers or white friends. But it does find voice in the barbershop or around the kitchen table. At times, that anger is exploited by politicians, to gin up votes along racial lines, or to make up for a politician's own failings.

And occasionally it finds voice in the church on Sunday morning, in the pulpit and in the pews. The fact that so many people are surprised to hear that anger in some of Reverend Wright's sermons simply reminds us of the old truism that the most segregated hour in American life occurs on Sunday morning. That anger is not always productive; indeed, all too often it distracts attention from solving real problems; it keeps us from squarely facing our own complicity in our condition, and prevents the African-American community from forging the alliances it needs to bring about real change. But the anger is real; it is powerful; and to simply wish it away, to condemn it without understanding its roots, only serves to widen the chasm of misunderstanding that exists between the races.

In fact, a similar anger exists within segments of the white community. Most working- and middle-class white Americans don't feel that they have been particularly privileged by their race. Their experience is the immigrant experience—as far as they're concerned, no one's handed them anything, they've built it from scratch. They've worked hard all their lives, many times only to see their jobs shipped overseas or their pension dumped after a lifetime of labor. They are anxious about their futures, and feel their dreams slipping away; in an era of stagnant wages and global competition, opportunity comes to be seen as a zero sum game, in which your dreams come at my expense. So when they are told to bus their children to a school across town; when they hear that an African American is getting an advantage in landing a good job or a spot in a good college because of an injustice that they themselves never committed; when they're told that their fears about crime in urban neighborhoods are somehow prejudiced, resentment builds over time.

Like the anger within the black community, these resentments aren't always expressed in polite company. But they have helped shape the political landscape for at least a generation. Anger over welfare and affirmative action helped forge the Reagan

Coalition. Politicians routinely exploited fears of crime for their own electoral ends. Talk show hosts and conservative commentators built entire careers unmasking bogus claims of racism while dismissing legitimate discussions of racial injustice and inequality as mere political correctness or reverse racism.

Just as black anger often proved counterproductive, so have these white resentments distracted attention from the real culprits of the middle class squeeze—a corporate culture rife with inside dealing, questionable accounting practices, and short-term greed; a Washington dominated by lobbyists and special interests; economic policies that favor the few over the many. And yet, to wish away the resentments of white Americans, to label them as misguided or even racist, without recognizing they are grounded in legitimate concerns—this too widens the racial divide, and blocks the path to understanding.

This is where we are right now. It's a racial stalemate we've been stuck in for years. Contrary to the claims of some of my critics, black and white, I have never been so naïve as to believe that we can get beyond our racial divisions in a single election cycle, or with a single candidacy—particularly a candidacy as imperfect as my own.

But I have asserted a firm conviction—a conviction rooted in my faith in God and my faith in the American people—that working together we can move beyond some of our old racial wounds, and that in fact we have no choice if we are to continue on the path of a more perfect union.

For the African-American community, that path means embracing the burdens of our past without becoming victims of our past. It means continuing to insist on a full measure of justice in every aspect of American life. But it also means binding our particular grievances—for better health care, and better schools, and better jobs—to the larger aspirations of all Americans—the white woman struggling to break the glass ceiling, the white man who's been laid off, the immigrant trying to feed his family. And it means taking full responsibility for own lives—by demanding more from our fathers, and spending more time with our children, and reading to them, and teaching them that while they may face challenges and discrimination in their own lives, they must never succumb to despair or cynicism; they must always believe that they can write their own destiny.

Ironically, this quintessentially American—and yes, conservative—notion of self-help found frequent expression in Reverend Wright's sermons. But what my former pastor too often failed to understand is that embarking on a program of self-help also requires a belief that society can change.

The profound mistake of Reverend Wright's sermons is not that he spoke about racism in our society. It's that he spoke as if our society was static; as if no progress has been made; as if this country—a country that has made it possible for one of his own members to run for the highest office in the land and build a coalition of white and black; Latino and Asian, rich and poor, young and old—is still irrevocably bound to a tragic past. But what we know—what we have seen—is that America can change. That is true genius of this nation. What we have already achieved gives us hope—the audacity to hope—for what we can and must achieve tomorrow.

In the white community, the path to a more perfect union means acknowledging that what ails the African-American community does not just exist in the minds of black people; that the legacy of discrimination—and current incidents of discrimination, while less overt than in the past—are real and must be addressed. Not just with words, but with deeds—by investing in our schools and our communities; by enforcing our civil rights laws and ensuring fairness in our criminal justice system; by providing this generation with ladders of opportunity that were unavailable for previous generations. It requires all Americans to realize that your dreams do not have to come at the expense of my dreams; that investing in the health, welfare, and education of black and brown and white children will ultimately help all of America prosper.

In the end, then, what is called for is nothing more, and nothing less, than what all the world's great religions demand—that we do unto others as we would have them do unto us. Let us be our brother's keeper, Scripture tells us. Let us be our sister's keeper. Let us find that common stake we all have in one another, and let our politics reflect that spirit as well.

For we have a choice in this country. We can accept a politics that breeds division, and conflict, and cynicism. We can tackle race only as spectacle—as we did in the OJ trial—or in the wake of tragedy, as we did in the aftermath of Katrina—or as fodder for the nightly news. We can play Reverend Wright's sermons on every channel, every day and talk about them from now until the election, and make the only question in this campaign whether or not the American people think that I somehow believe or sympathize with his most offensive words. We can pounce on some gaffe by a Hillary supporter as evidence that she's playing the race card, or we can speculate on whether white men will all flock to John McCain in the general election regardless of his policies.

We can do that.

But if we do, I can tell you that in the next election, we'll be talking about some other distraction. And then another one. And then another one. And nothing will change.

That is one option. Or, at this moment, in this election, we can come together and say, "Not this time." This time we want to talk about the crumbling schools that are stealing the future of black children and white children and Asian children and Hispanic children and Native American children. This time we want to reject the cynicism that tells us that these kids can't learn; that those kids who don't look like us are somebody else's problem. The children of America are not those kids, they are our kids, and we will not let them fall behind in a 21st century economy. Not this time.

This time we want to talk about how the lines in the Emergency Room are filled with whites and blacks and Hispanics who do not have health care; who don't have the power on their own to overcome the special interests in Washington, but who can take them on if we do it together.

This time we want to talk about the shuttered mills that once provided a decent life for men and women of every race, and the homes for sale that once belonged to Americans from every religion, every region, every walk of life. This time we want to talk about the fact that the real problem is not that someone who doesn't look like you might take your job; it's that the corporation you work for will ship it overseas for nothing more than a profit.

This time we want to talk about the men and women of every color and creed who serve together, and fight together, and bleed together under the same proud flag. We want to talk about how to bring them home from a war that never should've been authorized and never should've been waged, and we want to talk about how we'll show our patriotism by caring for them, and their families, and giving them the benefits they have earned.

I would not be running for President if I didn't believe with all my heart that this is what the vast majority of Americans want for this country. This union may never be perfect, but generation after generation has shown that it can always be perfected. And today, whenever I find myself feeling doubtful or cynical about this possibility, what gives me the most hope is the next generation—the young people whose attitudes and beliefs and openness to change have already made history in this election.

There is one story in particularly that I'd like to leave you with today—a story I told when I had the great honor of speaking on Dr. King's birthday at his home church, Ebenezer Baptist, in Atlanta.

There is a young, twenty-three year old white woman named Ashley Baia who organized for our campaign in Florence, South Carolina. She had been working to organize a mostly African-American community since the beginning of this campaign, and one day she was at a roundtable discussion where everyone went around telling their story and why they were there.

And Ashley said that when she was nine years old, her mother got cancer. And because she had to miss days of work, she was let go and lost her health care. They had to file for bankruptcy, and that's when Ashley decided that she had to do something to help her mom.

She knew that food was one of their most expensive costs, and so Ashley convinced her mother that what she really liked and really wanted to eat more than anything else was mustard and relish sandwiches. Because that was the cheapest way to eat.

She did this for a year until her mom got better, and she told everyone at the roundtable that the reason she joined our campaign was so that she could help the millions of other children in the country who want and need to help their parents too.

Now Ashley might have made a different choice. Perhaps somebody told her along the way that the source of her mother's problems were blacks who were on welfare and too lazy to work, or Hispanics who were coming into the country illegally. But she didn't. She sought out allies in her fight against injustice.

Anyway, Ashley finishes her story and then goes around the room and asks everyone else why they're supporting the campaign. They all have different stories and reasons. Many bring up a specific issue. And finally they come to this elderly black man who's been sitting there quietly the entire time. And Ashley asks him why he's there. And he does not bring up a specific issue. He does not say health care or the economy. He does not say education or the war. He does not say that he was there because of Barack Obama. He simply says to everyone in the room, "I am here because of Ashley."

"I'm here because of Ashley." By itself, that single moment of recognition between that young white girl and that old black man is not enough. It is not enough to give health care to the sick, or jobs to the jobless, or education to our children.

But it is where we start. It is where our union grows stronger. And as so many generations have come to realize over the course of the two-hundred and twenty one years since a band of patriots signed that document in Philadelphia, that is where the perfection begins.

Barack Obama's Health Care Address

(2009)

N O SOONER WAS BARACK OBAMA inaugurated as president on January 20, 2009, than he was forced to deal with a pair of crises inherited from the outgoing administration of his predecessor, George W. Bush. One was the deteriorating military situation in Afghanistan, where the United States had been at war since 2001. Obama dealt with this crisis by deploying two waves of troops, the first in 2009 and the next in early 2010, totaling more than fifty thousand additional soldiers. The other crisis was the massive meltdown of the nation's financial system, which had sent the unemployment rate soaring to nearly 10 percent and jeopardized the existence of numerous large Wall Street firms and several major manufacturers, including General Motors. Obama persuaded Congress to pass an $814 billion economic stimulus bill in hopes of arresting the nation's economic free fall and placing it on the road to prosperity.

But Obama wanted to do more as president than put out fires. He also sought to enact a major reform of the nation's health care system. Health care reform had been a leading Democratic Party goal since the presidency of Harry S. Truman. In 1965 Lyndon B. Johnson secured the enactment of Medicare for older Americans and Medicaid for the poor. The next two Democratic presidents, Jimmy Carter and Bill Clinton, each failed to persuade Congress to pass legislation to guarantee health care coverage for everyone else. But neither Carter nor Clinton enjoyed Obama's combination of a strong popular vote majority in the election that brought him to power (53 percent) and long coattails in the accompanying congressional elections, in which the Democrats gained twenty-one seats in the House of Representatives and eight in the Senate.

Obama faced major hurdles in achieving his goal. Democrats in Congress, although united in support of health care reform, were divided about what form it should take, with some insisting that the federal government offer a "public-option" (that is, government-run) plan and others urging that private coverage be extended to those who lack it. More than three-fourths of Americans had private health insurance in some form, and, despite the steeply rising costs of health care, many of them worried that changing the system might make their own situation worse and add to the annual federal budget deficit that Obama's economic stimulus bill had already sent soaring above $1 trillion.

In the face of these obstacles, Obama resolved that any reform proposal would have to be budget-neutral—that is, save as much money as it spent. He accommodated the interests of the pharmaceutical and hospital industries, both of which had helped to sink Clinton's health care bill through massive advertising and extensive lobbying. He invited Congress to share in developing the bill, in contrast to the secret process of legislative formulation that Clinton employed.

These efforts alone were not enough to secure passage, especially when members of Congress encountered angry opposition to "Obamacare" in a series of August 2009 town-hall meetings in their home states and districts. The president, frustrated that he was not getting through to the American people, decided to speak to Congress and the nation in a prime-time address on September 9, 2009.

"The plan I'm announcing tonight would meet three basic goals," Obama declared. "It will provide more security and stability to those who have health insurance. It will provide insurance to those who don't. And it will slow the growth of health care costs." Specifically, "individuals will be required to carry basic health insurance—just as most states require you to carry auto insurance. Likewise, businesses will be required to either offer their workers health care, or chip in to help cover the costs of their workers."

Obama's argument was overshadowed to some degree when, in response to his declaration that the "claim . . . that our reform effort will insure illegal immigrants . . . is false," South Carolina Republican Joe Wilson shouted, "You lie!" from his seat in the House chamber. But the speech succeeded in arresting the months-long decline in public and congressional support for reform. In this altered political environment, the president launched a successful campaign to persuade members of Congress in face-to-face meetings. By year's end both houses of Congress had passed different versions of health care reform legislation. On March 23, 2010, after some elaborate legislative wrangling to get the House to pass the Senate bill, Obama signed the Patient Protection and Affordable Care Act into law. One week later he signed the Health Care and Education Reconciliation Act, which restored some of the House's preferred features.

⁂ ⁂ ⁂

Madame Speaker, Vice President Biden, Members of Congress, and the American people:

When I spoke here last winter, this nation was facing the worst economic crisis since the Great Depression. We were losing an average of 700,000 jobs per month. Credit was frozen. And our financial system was on the verge of collapse.

As any American who is still looking for work or a way to pay their bills will tell you, we are by no means out of the woods. A full and vibrant recovery is many months away. And I will not let up until those Americans who seek jobs can find them; until those businesses that seek capital and credit can thrive; until all responsible homeowners can stay in their homes. That is our ultimate goal. But thanks to the bold and decisive action we have taken since January, I can stand here with confidence and say that we have pulled this economy back from the brink.

I want to thank the members of this body for your efforts and your support in these last several months, and especially those who have taken the difficult votes that have put us on a path to recovery. I also want to thank the American people for their patience and resolve during this trying time for our nation.

But we did not come here just to clean up crises. We came to build a future. So tonight, I return to speak to all of you about an issue that is central to that future—and that is the issue of health care.

I am not the first President to take up this cause, but I am determined to be the last. It has now been nearly a century since Theodore Roosevelt first called for health care reform. And ever since, nearly every President and Congress, whether Democrat or Republican, has attempted to meet this challenge in some way. A bill for comprehensive health reform was first introduced by John Dingell Sr. in 1943. Sixty-five years later, his son continues to introduce that same bill at the beginning of each session.

Our collective failure to meet this challenge—year after year, decade after decade—has led us to a breaking point. Everyone understands the extraordinary hardships that are placed on the uninsured, who live every day just one accident or illness away from bankruptcy. These are not primarily people on welfare. These are middle-class Americans. Some can't get insurance on the job. Others are self-employed, and can't afford it, since buying insurance on your own costs you three times as much as the coverage you get from your employer. Many other Americans who are willing and able to pay are still denied insurance due to previous illnesses or conditions that insurance companies decide are too risky or expensive to cover.

We are the only advanced democracy on Earth—the only wealthy nation—that allows such hardships for millions of its people. There are now more than thirty million American citizens who cannot get coverage. In just a two year period, one in every three Americans goes without health care coverage at some point. And every day, 14,000 Americans lose their coverage. In other words, it can happen to anyone.

But the problem that plagues the health care system is not just a problem of the uninsured. Those who do have insurance have never had less security and stability than they do today. More and more Americans worry that if you move, lose your job, or change your job, you'll lose your health insurance too. More and more Americans pay their premiums, only to discover that their insurance company has dropped their coverage when they get sick, or won't pay the full cost of care. It happens every day.

One man from Illinois lost his coverage in the middle of chemotherapy because his insurer found that he hadn't reported gallstones that he didn't even know about. They delayed his treatment, and he died because of it. Another woman from Texas was about to get a double mastectomy when her insurance company canceled her policy because she forgot to declare a case of acne. By the time she had her insurance reinstated, her breast cancer more than doubled in size. That is heart-breaking, it is wrong, and no one should be treated that way in the United States of America.

Then there's the problem of rising costs. We spend one-and-a-half times more per person on health care than any other country, but we aren't any healthier for it. This is one of the reasons that insurance premiums have gone up three times faster than wages. It's why so many employers—especially small businesses—are forcing their employees to pay more for insurance, or are dropping their coverage entirely. It's why so many aspiring entrepreneurs cannot afford to open a business in the first place, and why American businesses that compete internationally—like our automakers—are at a huge disadvantage. And it's why those of us with health insurance are also paying a hidden and growing tax for those without it—about $1000 per year that pays for somebody else's emergency room and charitable care.

Finally, our health care system is placing an unsustainable burden on taxpayers. When health care costs grow at the rate they have, it puts greater pressure on programs like Medicare and Medicaid. If we do nothing to slow these skyrocketing costs, we will eventually be spending more on Medicare and Medicaid than every other government program combined. Put simply, our health care problem is our deficit problem. Nothing else even comes close.

These are the facts. Nobody disputes them. We know we must reform this system. The question is how.

There are those on the left who believe that the only way to fix the system is through a single-payer system like Canada's, where we would severely restrict the private insurance market and have the government provide coverage for everyone. On the right, there are those who argue that we should end the employer-based system and leave individuals to buy health insurance on their own.

I have to say that there are arguments to be made for both approaches. But either one would represent a radical shift that would disrupt the health care most people currently have. Since health care represents one-sixth of our economy, I believe it makes more sense to build on what works and fix what doesn't, rather than try to build an entirely new system from scratch. And that is precisely what those of you in Congress have tried to do over the past several months.

During that time, we have seen Washington at its best and its worst.

We have seen many in this chamber work tirelessly for the better part of this year to offer thoughtful ideas about how to achieve reform. Of the five committees asked to develop bills, four have completed their work, and the Senate Finance Committee announced today that it will move forward next week. That has never happened before. Our overall efforts have been supported by an unprecedented coalition of doctors and nurses; hospitals, seniors' groups and even drug companies—many of whom opposed reform in the past. And there is agreement in this chamber on about eighty percent of what needs to be done, putting us closer to the goal of reform than we have ever been.

But what we have also seen in these last months is the same partisan spectacle that only hardens the disdain many Americans have toward their own government. Instead of honest debate, we have seen scare tactics. Some have dug into unyielding ideological camps that offer no hope of compromise. Too many have used this as an opportunity to score short-term political points, even if it robs the country of our opportunity to solve a long-term challenge. And out of this blizzard of charges and counter-charges, confusion has reigned.

Well the time for bickering is over. The time for games has passed. Now is the season for action. Now is when we must bring the best ideas of both parties together, and show the American people that we can still do what we were sent here to do. Now is the time to deliver on health care.

The plan I'm announcing tonight would meet three basic goals:

It will provide more security and stability to those who have health insurance. It will provide insurance to those who don't. And it will slow the growth of health care costs for our families, our businesses, and our government. It's a plan that asks everyone to take responsibility for meeting this challenge—not just government and insurance companies, but employers and individuals. And it's a plan that incorporates ideas from Senators and Congressmen; from Democrats and Republicans—and yes, from some of my opponents in both the primary and general election.

Here are the details that every American needs to know about this plan:

First, if you are among the hundreds of millions of Americans who already have health insurance through your job, Medicare, Medicaid, or the VA, nothing in this plan will require you or your employer to change the coverage or the doctor you have. Let me repeat this: nothing in our plan requires you to change what you have.

What this plan will do is to make the insurance you have work better for you. Under this plan, it will be against the law for insurance companies to deny you coverage because of a pre-existing condition. As soon as I sign this bill, it will be against the law for insurance companies to drop your coverage when you get sick or water it down when you need it most. They will no longer be able to place some arbitrary cap on the amount of coverage you can receive in a given year or a lifetime. We will place a limit on how much you can be charged for out-of-pocket expenses, because in the United States of America, no one should go broke because they get sick. And insurance companies will be required to cover, with no extra charge, routine checkups and preventive care, like mammograms and colonoscopies—because there's no reason we shouldn't be catching diseases like breast cancer and colon cancer before they get worse. That makes sense, it saves money, and it saves lives.

That's what Americans who have health insurance can expect from this plan—more security and stability.

Now, if you're one of the tens of millions of Americans who don't currently have health insurance, the second part of this plan will finally offer you quality, affordable choices. If you lose your job or change your job, you will be able to get coverage. If you strike out on your own and start a small business, you will be able to get coverage. We will do this by creating a new insurance exchange—a marketplace where individuals and small businesses will be able to shop for health insurance at competitive prices. Insurance companies will have an incentive to participate in this exchange because it lets them compete for millions of new customers. As one big group, these customers will have greater leverage to bargain with the insurance companies for better prices and quality coverage. This is how large companies and government employees get affordable insurance. It's how everyone in this Congress gets affordable insurance. And it's time to give every American the same opportunity that we've given ourselves.

For those individuals and small businesses who still cannot afford the lower-priced insurance available in the exchange, we will provide tax credits, the size of which will be based on your need. And all insurance companies that want access to this new marketplace will have to abide by the consumer protections I already mentioned. This exchange will take effect in four years, which will give us time to do it right. In the meantime, for those Americans who can't get insurance today because they have pre-existing medical conditions, we will immediately offer low-cost coverage that will protect you against financial ruin if you become seriously ill. This was a good idea when Senator John McCain proposed it in the campaign, it's a good idea now, and we should embrace it.

Now, even if we provide these affordable options, there may be those—particularly the young and healthy—who still want to take the risk and go without coverage. There may still be companies that refuse to do right by their workers. The problem is, such irresponsible behavior costs all the rest of us money. If there are affordable options and people still don't sign up for health insurance, it means we pay for those people's expensive emergency room visits. If some businesses don't provide workers health care, it forces the rest of us to pick up the tab when their workers get sick, and gives those businesses an unfair advantage over their competitors. And unless everybody does their part, many of the insurance reforms we seek—especially requiring insurance companies to cover pre-existing conditions—just can't be achieved.

That's why under my plan, individuals will be required to carry basic health insurance—just as most states require you to carry auto insurance. Likewise, businesses will be required to either offer their workers health care, or chip in to help cover the cost of their workers. There will be a hardship waiver for those individuals who still cannot afford coverage, and 95% of all small businesses, because of their size and narrow profit margin, would be exempt from these requirements. But we cannot have large businesses and individuals who can afford coverage game the system by avoiding responsibility to themselves or their employees. Improving our health care system only works if everybody does their part.

While there remain some significant details to be ironed out, I believe a broad consensus exists for the aspects of the plan I just outlined: consumer protections for those with insurance, an exchange that allows individuals and small businesses to purchase affordable coverage, and a requirement that people who can afford insurance get insurance.

And I have no doubt that these reforms would greatly benefit Americans from all walks of life, as well as the economy as a whole. Still, given all the misinformation that's been spread over the past few months, I realize that many Americans have grown nervous about reform. So tonight I'd like to address some of the key controversies that are still out there.

Some of people's concerns have grown out of bogus claims spread by those whose only agenda is to kill reform at any cost. The best example is the claim, made not just by radio and cable talk show hosts, but prominent politicians, that we plan to set up panels of bureaucrats with the power to kill off senior citizens. Such a charge would be laughable if it weren't so cynical and irresponsible. It is a lie, plain and simple.

There are also those who claim that our reform effort will insure illegal immigrants. This, too, is false—the reforms I'm proposing would not apply to those who are here illegally. And one more misunderstanding I want to clear up—under our plan, no federal dollars will be used to fund abortions, and federal conscience laws will remain in place.

My health care proposal has also been attacked by some who oppose reform as a "government takeover" of the entire health care system. As proof, critics point to a provision in our plan that allows the uninsured and small businesses to choose a publicly-sponsored insurance option, administered by the government just like Medicaid or Medicare.

So let me set the record straight. My guiding principle is, and always has been, that consumers do better when there is choice and competition. Unfortunately, in 34 states, 75% of the insurance market is controlled by five or fewer companies. In Alabama, almost 90% is controlled by just one company. Without competition, the price of insurance goes up and the quality goes down. And it makes it easier for insurance companies to treat their customers badly—by cherry-picking the healthiest individuals and trying to drop the sickest; by overcharging small businesses who have no leverage; and by jacking up rates.

Insurance executives don't do this because they are bad people. They do it because it's profitable. As one former insurance executive testified before Congress, insurance companies are not only encouraged to find reasons to drop the seriously ill; they are rewarded for it. All of this is in service of meeting what this former executive called "Wall Street's relentless profit expectations."

Now, I have no interest in putting insurance companies out of business. They provide a legitimate service, and employ a lot of our friends and neighbors. I just want to hold them accountable. The insurance reforms that I've already mentioned would do just that. But an additional step we can take to keep insurance companies honest is by making a not-for-profit public option available in the insurance exchange. Let me be clear—it would only be an option for those who don't have insurance. No one would be forced to choose it, and it would not impact those of you who already have insurance. In fact, based on Congressional Budget Office estimates, we believe that less than 5% of Americans would sign up.

Despite all this, the insurance companies and their allies don't like this idea. They argue that these private companies can't fairly compete with the government. And they'd be right if taxpayers were subsidizing this public insurance option. But they won't be. I have insisted that like any private insurance company, the public insurance option would have to be self- sufficient and rely on the premiums it collects. But by avoiding some of the overhead that gets eaten up at private companies by profits, excessive administrative costs and executive salaries, it could provide a good deal for consumers. It would also keep pressure on private insurers to keep their policies affordable and treat their customers better, the same way public colleges and universities provide additional choice and competition to students without in any way inhibiting a vibrant system of private colleges and universities.

It's worth noting that a strong majority of Americans still favor a public insurance option of the sort I've proposed tonight. But its impact shouldn't be exaggerated—by the left, the right, or the media. It is only one part of my plan, and should not be used as a handy excuse for the usual Washington ideological battles. To my progressive friends, I would remind you that for decades, the driving idea behind reform has been to end insurance company abuses and make coverage affordable for those without it. The public option is only a means to that end—and we should remain open to other ideas that accomplish our ultimate goal. And to my Republican friends, I say that rather than making wild claims about a government takeover of health care, we should work together to address any legitimate concerns you may have.

For example, some have suggested that that the public option go into effect only in those markets where insurance companies are not providing affordable policies. Others propose a co-op or another non-profit entity to administer the plan. These are all constructive ideas worth exploring. But I will not back down on the basic principle that if Americans can't find affordable coverage, we will provide you with a choice. And I will make sure that no government bureaucrat or insurance company bureaucrat gets between you and the care that you need.

Finally, let me discuss an issue that is a great concern to me, to members of this chamber, and to the public—and that is how we pay for this plan.

Here's what you need to know. First, I will not sign a plan that adds one dime to our deficits—either now or in the future. Period. And to prove that I'm serious, there will be a provision in this plan that requires us to come forward with more spending cuts if the savings we promised don't materialize. Part of the reason I faced a trillion dollar deficit when I walked in the door of the White House is because too many initiatives over the last decade were not paid for—from the Iraq War to tax breaks for the wealthy. I will not make that same mistake with health care.

Second, we've estimated that most of this plan can be paid for by finding savings within the existing health care system—a system that is currently full of waste and abuse. Right now, too much of the hard-earned savings and tax dollars we spend on health care doesn't make us healthier. That's not my judgment—it's the judgment of medical professionals across this country. And this is also true when it comes to Medicare and Medicaid.

In fact, I want to speak directly to America's seniors for a moment, because Medicare is another issue that's been subjected to demagoguery and distortion during the course of this debate.

More than four decades ago, this nation stood up for the principle that after a lifetime of hard work, our seniors should not be left to struggle with a pile of medical bills in their later years. That is how Medicare was born. And it remains a sacred trust that must be passed down from one generation to the next. That is why not a dollar of the Medicare trust fund will be used to pay for this plan.

The only thing this plan would eliminate is the hundreds of billions of dollars in waste and fraud, as well as unwarranted subsidies in Medicare that go to insurance companies—subsidies that do everything to pad their profits and nothing to improve your care. And we will also create an independent commission of doctors and medical experts charged with identifying more waste in the years ahead.

These steps will ensure that you—America's seniors—get the benefits you've been promised. They will ensure that Medicare is there for future generations. And we can use some of the savings to fill the gap in coverage that forces too many seniors to pay thousands of dollars a year out of their own pocket for prescription drugs. That's what this plan will do for you. So don't pay attention to those scary stories about how your benefits will be cut—especially since some of the same folks who are spreading these tall tales have fought against Medicare in the past, and just this year supported a budget that would have essentially turned Medicare into a privatized voucher program. That will never happen on my watch. I will protect Medicare.

Now, because Medicare is such a big part of the health care system, making the program more efficient can help usher in changes in the way we deliver health care that can reduce costs for everybody. We have long known that some places, like the Intermountain Healthcare in Utah or the Geisinger Health System in rural Pennsylvania, offer high-quality care at costs below average. The commission can help encourage the adoption of these common-sense best practices by doctors and medical professionals throughout the system—everything from reducing hospital infection rates to encouraging better coordination between teams of doctors.

Reducing the waste and inefficiency in Medicare and Medicaid will pay for most of this plan. Much of the rest would be paid for with revenues from the very same drug and insurance companies that stand to benefit from tens of millions of new customers. This reform will charge insurance companies a fee for their most expensive policies, which will encourage them to provide greater value for the money—an idea which has the support of Democratic and Republican experts. And according to these same experts, this modest change could help hold down the cost of health care for all of us in the long-run.

Finally, many in this chamber—particularly on the Republican side of the aisle—have long insisted that reforming our medical malpractice laws can help bring down the cost of health care. I don't believe malpractice reform is a silver bullet, but I have talked to enough doctors to know that defensive medicine may be contributing to unnecessary costs. So I am proposing that we move forward on a range of ideas about how to put patient safety first and let doctors focus on practicing medicine. I know that the Bush Administration considered authorizing demonstration projects in individual states to test these issues. It's a good idea, and I am directing my Secretary of Health and Human Services to move forward on this initiative today.

Add it all up, and the plan I'm proposing will cost around $900 billion over ten years—less than we have spent on the Iraq and Afghanistan wars, and less than the tax cuts for the wealthiest few Americans that Congress passed at the beginning of the previous administration. Most of these costs will be paid for with money already being spent—but spent badly—in the existing health care system. The plan will not add to our deficit. The middle-class will realize greater security, not higher taxes. And if we are able to slow the growth of health care costs by just one-tenth of one percent each year, it will actually reduce the deficit by $4 trillion over the long term.

This is the plan I'm proposing. It's a plan that incorporates ideas from many of the people in this room tonight—Democrats and Republicans. And I will continue to seek common ground in the weeks ahead. If you come to me with a serious set of proposals, I will be there to listen. My door is always open.

But know this: I will not waste time with those who have made the calculation that it's better politics to kill this plan than improve it. I will not stand by while the special interests use the same old tactics to keep things exactly the way they are. If you misrepresent what's in the plan, we will call you out. And I will not accept the status quo as a solution. Not this time. Not now.

Everyone in this room knows what will happen if we do nothing. Our deficit will grow. More families will go bankrupt. More businesses will close. More Americans will lose their coverage when they are sick and need it most. And more will die as a result. We know these things to be true.

That is why we cannot fail. Because there are too many Americans counting on us to succeed—the ones who suffer silently, and the ones who shared their stories with us at town hall meetings, in emails, and in letters.

I received one of those letters a few days ago. It was from our beloved friend and colleague, Ted Kennedy. He had written it back in May, shortly after he was told that his illness was terminal. He asked that it be delivered upon his death.

In it, he spoke about what a happy time his last months were, thanks to the love and support of family and friends, his wife, Vicki, and his children, who are here tonight. And he expressed confidence that this would be the year that health care reform—"that great unfinished business of our society," he called it—would finally pass. He repeated the truth that health care is decisive for our future prosperity, but he also reminded me that "it concerns more than material things." "What we face," he wrote, "is above all a moral issue; at stake are not just the details of policy, but fundamental principles of social justice and the character of our country."

I've thought about that phrase quite a bit in recent days—the character of our country. One of the unique and wonderful things about America has always been our self-reliance, our rugged individualism, our fierce defense of freedom and our healthy skepticism of government. And figuring out the appropriate size and role of government has always been a source of rigorous and sometimes angry debate.

For some of Ted Kennedy's critics, his brand of liberalism represented an affront to American liberty. In their mind, his passion for universal health care was nothing more than a passion for big government.

But those of us who knew Teddy and worked with him here—people of both parties—know that what drove him was something more. His friend, Orrin Hatch, knows that. They worked together to provide children with health insurance. His friend John McCain knows that. They worked together on a Patient's Bill of Rights. His friend Chuck Grassley knows that. They worked together to provide health care to children with disabilities.

On issues like these, Ted Kennedy's passion was born not of some rigid ideology, but of his own experience. It was the experience of having two children stricken with cancer. He never forgot the sheer terror and helplessness that any parent feels when a child is badly sick; and he was able to imagine what it must be like for those without insurance; what it would be like to have to say to a wife or a child or an aging parent—there is something that could make you better, but I just can't afford it.

That large-heartedness—that concern and regard for the plight of others—is not a partisan feeling. It is not a Republican or a Democratic feeling. It, too, is part of the American character. Our ability to stand in other people's shoes. A recognition that we are all in this together; that when fortune turns against one of us, others are there to lend a helping hand. A belief that in this country, hard work and responsibility should be rewarded by some measure of security and fair play; and an acknowledgement that sometimes government has to step in to help deliver on that promise.

This has always been the history of our progress. In 1933, when over half of our seniors could not support themselves and millions had seen their savings wiped away, there were those who argued that Social Security would lead to socialism. But the men and women of Congress stood fast, and we are all the better for it. In 1965, when some argued that Medicare represented a government takeover of health care, members of Congress, Democrats and Republicans, did not back down. They joined together so that all of us could enter our golden years with some basic peace of mind.

You see, our predecessors understood that government could not, and should not, solve every problem. They understood that there are instances when the gains in security from government action are not worth the added constraints on our freedom. But they also understood that the danger of too much government is matched by the perils of too little; that without the leavening hand of wise policy, markets can crash, monopolies can stifle competition, and the vulnerable can be exploited. And they knew that when any government measure, no matter how carefully crafted or beneficial, is subject to scorn; when any efforts to help people in need are attacked as un-American; when facts and reason are thrown overboard and only timidity passes for wisdom, and we can no longer even engage in a civil conversation with each other over the things that truly matter—that at that point we don't merely lose our capacity to solve big challenges. We lose something essential about ourselves.

What was true then remains true today. I understand how difficult this health care debate has been. I know that many in this country are deeply skeptical that government is looking out for them. I understand that the politically safe move would be to kick the can further down the road—to defer reform one more year, or one more election, or one more term.

But that's not what the moment calls for. That's not what we came here to do. We did not come to fear the future. We came here to shape it. I still believe we can act even when it's hard. I still believe we can replace acrimony with civility, and gridlock with progress. I still believe we can do great things, and that here and now we will meet history's test.

Because that is who we are. That is our calling. That is our character. Thank you, God Bless You, and may God Bless the United States of America.

◄§ 58 §►

National Labor Relations Board v. Noel Canning et al.

(2014)

AS SEVERAL earlier documents in this volume have shown, arguments about the appointment power, both political and constitutional, have been a recurring theme in the history of the presidency. In 1789 Rep. James Madison of Virginia prevailed on the First Congress to recognize the president's unilateral power to remove appointees from positions in the executive branch. In 1829 President Andrew Jackson fiercely defended the practice of using appointments to reward his political support-ers. In 1868 President Andrew Johnson was impeached for attempting to exercise the removal power, which Congress had claimed to take back the year before by passing the Tenure of Office Act. Fifteen years later Congress passed the Pendleton Act, designed to replace Jackson's "spoils system" with merit-based executive appoint-ments. In 1926 the Supreme Court affirmed the president's executive removal power in *Myers v. United States,* only to restrict it somewhat nine years later in *Humphrey's Executor v. United States.*

All of these presidential actions, congressional statutes, and Supreme Court cases involved ordinary appointments—that is, those covered by the president's constitutional "Power, by and with the Advice and Consent of the Senate, . . . [to] appoint Ambassadors, other public Ministers and Consuls, Justices of the Supreme Court, and all other Officers of the United States, whose Appointments are not otherwise herein provided for." But Article II, section 2 of the Constitu-tion also includes a related provision dealing with appointments when the Senate is not in session. Concerning so-called recess appointments it says: "The President shall have Power to fill up all Vacancies that may happen during the Recess of the Senate" with temporary appointments, "which shall expire at the End of their next Session."

The recess appointments clause was fraught with ambiguities. Does "the Recess of the Senate" mean only the biennial "inter-session" recess that occurs at the end of each two-year Congress or does it also apply to "intra-session" recesses within a Congress? If the latter, how long does an intra-session break have to be to count as an actual recess? And does the phrase "may happen during" apply only to vacancies that occur when the Senate is in recess or also to vacancies that occur before the recess but remain unfilled after it begins?

These ambiguities in the recess appointments clause came before the Supreme Court in *National Labor Relations Board v. Noel Canning et al.* Frustrated by the Senate's unwillingness to confirm his nominees to the five-member National Labor Relations Board, President Barack Obama had granted recess appointments to three individuals. He claimed that the Senate was in recess when he did so, but the Senate claimed that it was in session. The stakes were high: without Obama's three recess appointees, the five-member NLRB lacked a quorum and could not make any legally binding decisions.

Claiming after Obama's recess appointments that it did have a quorum, the NLRB made numerous rulings in disputes between companies and their work-ers, including one that went against Noel Canning, a bottler and distributor of Pepsi Cola products. Canning appealed, arguing that the vacancies on the board that Obama filled had not occurred while the Senate was in recess and that, in any event, the Senate was not in recess when Obama made them. In a 5–4 ruling, the Supreme Court agreed with the president that he can make recess appoint-ments to fill any vacancies that exist while the Senate is in recess no matter when the vacancies occur. It also agreed that the phrase "the recess" applied to intra-session as well as inter-session recesses. But the Court ruled for Canning on the narrow grounds that a valid intra-session recess has to be at least ten days—longer than the three-day recesses during which Obama made his appointments to the NLRB. Justice Stephen Breyer wrote the opinion of the Court, joined by the other three liberal justices and by the moderate conservative Justice Anthony Kennedy. The other conservatives united behind Justice Antonin Scalia, who wrote a blistering dissent.

※ ※ ※

BREYER, J., delivered the opinion of the Court, in which KENNEDY, GINSBURG, SOTOMAYOR, and KAGAN, JJ., joined. SCALIA, J., filed an opinion concurring in the judgment, in which ROBERTS, C. J., and THOMAS and ALITO, JJ., joined. . . .

Justice Breyer delivered the opinion of the Court.

Ordinarily the President must obtain "the Advice and Consent of the Senate" before appointing an "Office[r] of the United States." But the Recess Appointments Clause creates an exception. It gives the President alone the power "to fill up all Vacancies that may happen during the Recess of the Senate, by granting Commissions which shall expire at the End of their next Session." We here consider three questions about the application of this Clause.

The first concerns the scope of the words "recess of the Senate." Does that phrase refer only to an inter-session recess (i.e., a break between formal sessions of Congress), or does it also include an intra-session recess, such as a summer recess in the midst of a session? We conclude that the Clause applies to both kinds of recess.

The second question concerns the scope of the words "vacancies that may happen." Does that phrase refer only to vacancies that first come into existence during a recess, or does it also include vacancies that arise prior to a recess but continue to exist during the recess? We conclude that the Clause applies to both kinds of vacancy.

The third question concerns calculation of the length of a "recess." The President made the appointments here at issue on January 4, 2012. At that time the Senate was in recess pursuant to a December 17, 2011, resolution providing for a series of brief recesses punctuated by "pro forma session[s]," with "no business . . . transacted," every Tuesday and Friday through January 20, 2012. In calculating the length of a recess are we to ignore the pro forma sessions, thereby treating the series of brief recesses as a single, month-long recess? We conclude that we cannot ignore these pro forma sessions.

Our answer to the third question means that, when the appointments before us took place, the Senate was in the midst of a 3-day recess. Three days is too short a time to bring a recess within the scope of the Clause. Thus we conclude that the President lacked the power to make the recess appointments here at issue. . . .

The first question concerns the scope of the phrase "*the recess* of the Senate" (emphasis added). The Constitution provides for congressional elections every two years. And the 2-year life of each elected Congress typically consists of two formal 1-year sessions, each separated from the next by an "inter-session recess." The Senate or the House of Representatives announces an inter-session recess by approving a resolution stating that it will "adjourn sine die," i.e., without specifying a date to return (in which case Congress will reconvene when the next formal session is scheduled to begin).

The Senate and the House also take breaks in the midst of a session. The Senate or the House announces any such "intra-session recess" by adopting a resolution stating that it will "adjourn" to a fixed date, a few days or weeks or even months later. All agree that the phrase "the recess of the Senate" covers inter-session recesses. The question is whether it includes intra-session recesses as well.

In our view, the phrase "the recess" includes an intra-session recess of substantial length. . . .

We recognize that the word "the" in "the recess" might suggest that the phrase refers to the single break separating formal sessions of Congress. That is because the word "the" frequently (but not always) indicates "a particular thing." But the word can also refer "to a term used generically or universally." The Constitution, for example, directs the Senate to choose a President *pro tempore* "in *the* Absence of the Vice-President." (emphasis added). . . .

The constitutional text is thus ambiguous. And we believe the Clause's purpose demands the broader interpretation. The Clause gives the President authority to make appointments during "the recess of the Senate" so that the President can ensure the continued functioning of the Federal Government when the Senate is away. The Senate is equally away during both an inter-session and an intra-session recess, and its capacity to participate in the appointments process has nothing to do with the words it uses to signal its departure.

History also offers strong support for the broad interpretation. . . .

[B]etween the founding and the Great Depression, Congress took substantial intra-session breaks (other than holiday breaks) in four years: 1867, 1868, 1921, and 1929. And in each of those years the President made intra-session recess appointments.

Since 1929, and particularly since the end of World War II, Congress has shortened its inter-session breaks as it has taken longer and more frequent intra-session breaks; Presidents have correspondingly made more intra-session recess appointments. . . .

The Senate as a body has done nothing to deny the validity of this practice for at least three-quarters of a century. And three-quarters of a century of settled practice is long enough to entitle a practice to "great weight in a proper interpretation" of the constitutional provision. . . .

That is not to say that the President may make recess appointments during any recess that is "more than three days." The Recess Appointments Clause seeks to permit the Executive Branch to function smoothly when Congress is unavailable. And though Congress has taken short breaks for almost 200 years, and there have been many thousands of recess appointments in that time, we have not found a single example of a recess appointment made during an intra-session recess that was shorter than 10 days. . . .

We therefore conclude, in light of historical practice, that a recess of more than 3 days but less than 10 days is presumptively too short to fall within the Clause. We add the word "presumptively" to leave open the possibility that some very unusual circumstance—a national catastrophe, for instance, that renders the Senate unavailable but calls for an urgent response—could demand the exercise of the recess-appointment power during a shorter break. . . .

The second question concerns the scope of the phrase "vacancies *that may happen* during the recess of the Senate." (emphasis added). All agree that the phrase applies to vacancies that initially occur during a recess. But does it also apply to vacancies that initially occur before a recess and continue to exist during the recess? In our view the phrase applies to both kinds of vacancy.

We believe that the Clause's language, read literally, permits, though it does not naturally favor, our broader interpretation. We concede that the most natural meaning of "happens" as applied to a "vacancy" (at least to a modern ear) is that the vacancy "happens" when it initially occurs. See 1 Johnson 913 (defining "happen" in relevant part as meaning "[t]o fall out; to chance; to come to pass"). But that is not the only possible way to use the word.

Thomas Jefferson wrote that the Clause is "certainly susceptible of [two] constructions." It "may mean 'vacancies that may happen to be' or 'may happen to fall'" during a recess. . . .

A statute that gives the President authority to act in respect to "any financial crisis that may happen during his term" can easily be interpreted to include crises that arise before, and continue during, that term. . . .

The Clause's purpose strongly supports the broader interpretation. That purpose is to permit the President to obtain the assistance of subordinate officers when the Senate, due to its recess, cannot confirm them. . . .

While we concede that both interpretations carry with them some risk of undesirable consequences, we believe the narrower interpretation risks undermining constitutionally conferred powers more seriously and more often. It would prevent the President from making any recess appointment that arose before a recess, no matter who the official, no matter how dire the need, no matter how uncontroversial the appointment, and no matter how late in the session the office fell vacant. Overall, like [President James Monroe's] Attorney General [William] Wirt, we believe the broader interpretation more consistent with the Constitution's "reason and spirit."

Historical practice over the past 200 years strongly favors the broader interpretation. The tradition of applying the Clause to pre-recess vacancies dates at least to President James Madison . . .

Thus, it is not surprising that the Congressional Research Service, after examining the vacancy dates associated with a random sample of 24 inter-session recess appointments since 1981, concluded that "[i]n most of the 24 cases, the preponderance of evidence indicated that the vacancy arose prior to the recess during which the appointment was made. . . ."

The upshot is that the President has consistently and frequently interpreted the Recess Appointments Clause to apply to vacancies that initially occur before, but continue to exist during, a recess of the Senate. The Senate as a body has not countered this practice for nearly three-quarters of a century, perhaps longer. . . . In light of some linguistic ambiguity, the basic purpose of the Clause, and the historical practice we have described, we conclude that the phrase "all vacancies" includes vacancies that come into existence while the Senate is in session.

The third question concerns the calculation of the length of the Senate's "recess." On December 17, 2011, the Senate by unanimous consent adopted a resolution to convene "pro forma session[s]" only, with "no business . . . transacted," on every Tuesday and Friday from December 20, 2011, through January 20, 2012. At the end of each pro forma session, the Senate would "adjourn until" the following pro forma session. During that period, the Senate convened and adjourned as agreed. It held pro forma sessions on December 20, 23, 27, and 30, and on January 3, 6, 10, 13, 17, and 20; and at the end of each pro forma session, it adjourned until the time and date of the next.

The President made the recess appointments before us on January 4, 2012, in between the January 3 and the January 6 pro forma sessions. We must determine the significance of these sessions—that is, whether, for purposes of the Clause, we should treat them as periods when the Senate was in session or as periods when it was in recess. If the former, the period between January 3 and January 6 was a 3-day recess, which is too short to trigger the President's recess-appointment power. If the latter, however, then the 3-day period was part of a much longer recess during which the President did have the power to make recess appointments.

The Solicitor General argues that we must treat the pro forma sessions as periods of recess. He says that these "sessions" were sessions in name only because the Senate was in recess as a functional matter. The Senate, he contends, remained in a single, unbroken recess from January 3, when the second session of the 112th Congress began by operation of the Twentieth Amendment, until January 23, when the Senate reconvened to do regular business.

In our view, however, the pro forma sessions count as sessions, not as periods of recess. We hold that, for purposes of the Recess Appointments Clause, the Senate is in session when it says it is, provided that, under its own rules, it retains the capacity to transact Senate business. The Senate met that standard here.

The standard we apply is consistent with the Constitution's broad delegation of authority to the Senate to determine how and when to conduct its business. The Constitution explicitly empowers the Senate to "determine the Rules of its Proceedings." . . .

The Recess Appointments Clause responds to a structural difference between the Executive and Legislative Branches: The Executive Branch is perpetually in operation, while the Legislature only acts in intervals separated by recesses. The purpose of the Clause is to allow the Executive to continue operating while the Senate is unavailable. We believe that the Clause's text, standing alone, is ambiguous. It does not resolve whether the President may make appointments during intra-session recesses, or whether he may fill pre-recess vacancies. But the broader reading better serves the Clause's structural function. Moreover, that broader reading is reinforced by centuries of history, which we are hesitant to disturb. We thus hold that the Constitution empowers the President to fill any existing vacancy during any recess—intra-session or inter-session—of sufficient length.

Justice Scalia would render illegitimate thousands of recess appointments reaching all the way back to the founding era. More than that: Calling the Clause an "anachronism," he would basically read it out of the Constitution. He performs this act of judicial excision in the name of liberty. We fail to see how excising the Recess Appointments Clause preserves freedom. In fact, Alexander Hamilton observed in the very first Federalist Paper that "the vigour of government is essential to the security of liberty." And the Framers included the Recess Appointments Clause to preserve the "vigour of government" at times when an important organ of Government, the United States Senate, is in recess. Justice Scalia's interpretation of the Clause would defeat the power of the Clause to achieve that objective.

The foregoing discussion should refute Justice Scalia's claim that we have "embrace[d]" an "adverse-possession theory of executive power." Post, at 48. Instead, as in all cases, we interpret the Constitution in light of its text, purposes, and "our whole experience" as a Nation. And we look to the actual practice of Government to inform our interpretation.

Given our answer to the last question before us, we conclude that the Recess Appointments Clause does not give the President the constitutional authority to make the appointments here at issue. Because the Court of Appeals reached the same ultimate conclusion (though for reasons we reject), its judgment is affirmed.

It is so ordered. . . .

JUSTICE SCALIA, with whom THE CHIEF JUSTICE, JUSTICE THOMAS, and JUSTICE ALITO join, concurring in the judgment. . . .

To prevent the President's recess-appointment power from nullifying the Senate's role in the appointment process, the Constitution cabins that power in two significant ways. First, it may be exercised only in "the Recess of the Senate," that is, the intermission between two formal legislative sessions. Second, it may be used to fill only those vacancies that "happen during the Recess," that is, offices that become vacant during that intermission. Both conditions are clear from the Constitution's text and structure, and both were well understood at the founding. . . .

Today's Court agrees that the appointments were invalid, but for the far narrower reason that they were made during a 3-day break in the Senate's session. On its way to that result, the majority sweeps away the key textual limitations on the recess-appointment power. It holds, first, that the President can make appointments without the Senate's participation even during short breaks in the middle of the Senate's session, and second, that those appointments can fill offices that became vacant long before the break in which they were filled. The majority justifies those atextual results on an adverse-possession theory of executive authority: Presidents have long claimed the powers in question, and the Senate has not disputed those claims with sufficient vigor, so the Court should not "upset the compromises and working arrangements that the elected branches of Government themselves have reached."

The Court's decision transforms the recess-appointment power from a tool carefully designed to fill a narrow and specific need into a weapon to be wielded by future Presidents against future Senates. To reach that result, the majority casts aside the plain, original meaning of the constitutional text in deference to late-arising historical practices that are ambiguous at best. The majority's insistence on deferring to the Executive's untenably broad interpretation of the power is in clear conflict with our precedent and forebodes a diminution of this Court's role in controversies involving the separation of powers and the structure of government. I concur in the judgment only. . . .

The first question presented is whether "the Recess of the Senate," during which the President's recess-appointment power is active, is (a) the period between two of the Senate's formal sessions, or (b) any break in the Senate's proceedings. I would hold that "the Recess" is the gap between sessions and that the appointments at issue here are invalid because they undisputedly were made during the Senate's session. The Court's contrary conclusion—that "the Recess" includes "breaks in the midst of a session"—is inconsistent with the Constitution's text and structure, and it requires judicial fabrication of vague, unadministrable limits on the recess-appointment power (thus defined) that overstep the judicial role. And although the majority relies heavily on "historical practice," no practice worthy of our deference supports the majority's conclusion on this issue.

Intra-session recess appointments were virtually unheard of for the first 130 years of the Republic, were deemed unconstitutional by the first Attorney General to address them, were not openly defended by the Executive until 1921, were not made in significant numbers until after World War II, and have been repeatedly criticized as unconstitutional by Senators of both parties. It is astonishing for the majority to assert that this history lends "strong support," ante, at 11, to its interpretation of the Recess Appointments Clause. And the majority's contention that recent executive practice in this area merits deference because the Senate has not done more to oppose it is utterly divorced from our precedent. "The structural interests protected by the Appointments Clause are not those of any one branch of Government but of the entire Republic," and the Senate could not give away those protections even if it wanted to. . . .

The second question presented is whether vacancies that "happen during the Recess of the Senate," which the President is empowered to fill with recess appointments, are (a) vacancies that arise during the recess, or (b) all vacancies that exist during the recess, regardless of when they arose. I would hold that the recess-appointment power is limited to vacancies that arise during the recess in which they are filled, and I would hold that the appointments at issue here—which undisputedly filled pre-recess vacancies— are invalid for that reason as well as for the reason that they were made during the session. The Court's contrary conclusion is inconsistent with the Constitution's text and structure, and it further undermines the balance the Framers struck between Presidential and Senatorial power. Historical practice also fails to support the majority's conclusion on this issue. . . .

Washington's and Adams' Attorneys General read the Constitution to restrict recess appointments to vacancies arising during the recess, and there is no evidence that any of the first four Presidents consciously departed from that reading. The contrary reading was first defended by an executive official in 1823, was vehemently rejected by the Senate in 1863, was vigorously resisted by legislation in place from 1863 until 1940, and is arguably inconsistent with legislation in place from 1940 to the present. . . .

What the majority needs to sustain its judgment is an ambiguous text and a clear historical practice. What it has is a clear text and an at-best-ambiguous historical practice. Even if the Executive could accumulate power through adverse possession by engaging in a consistent and unchallenged practice over a long period of time, the oft-disputed practices at issue here would not meet that standard. . . .

The real tragedy of today's decision is not simply the abolition of the Constitution's limits on the recess-appointment power and the substitution of a novel framework invented by this Court. It is the damage done to our separation-of-powers jurisprudence more generally. It is not every day that we encounter a proper case or controversy requiring interpretation of the Constitution's structural provisions. Most of the time, the interpretation of those provisions is left to the political branches—which, in deciding how much respect to afford the constitutional text, often take their cues from this Court. We should therefore take every opportunity to affirm the primacy of the Constitution's enduring principles over the politics of the moment. Our failure to do so today will resonate well beyond the particular dispute at hand. Sad, but true: The Court's embrace of the adverse-possession theory of executive power (a characterization the majority resists but does not refute) will be cited in diverse contexts, including those presently unimagined, and will have the effect of aggrandizing the Presidency beyond its constitutional bounds and undermining respect for the separation of powers.

I concur in the judgment only.

❦ 59 ❦

Barack Obama's State of the Union Address

(2015)

T HE CONSTITUTION requires that the president "shall from time to time give to the Congress Information of the State of the Union, and recommend to their Consideration such Measures as he shall judge necessary and expedient." Nothing is said concerning the form, frequency, or setting in which the president is to fulfill these responsibilities. In practice, the first two presidents, George Washington and John Adams, and every president since Woodrow Wilson has reported on the state of the union annually in the form of a speech to Congress delivered in the chamber of the House of Representatives. But for more than a century, presidents from Thomas Jefferson to William Howard Taft did so in writing, in an annual message.

Nor does the Constitution give any guidance about the weight properly assigned to "report" and "recommend." In truth, presidents do some of both but nearly always devote much more time and attention in the state of the union address to recommending than to reporting. On January 20, 2015, for example, Barack Obama's state of the union address was filled with legislative recommendations concerning taxation, education, child care, and numerous other issues.

The modern state of the union is the most important annual speech the president gives. Visually, it is almost as rich as the inaugural address in symbolism that affirms the president's unifying role as chief of state. The president enters the House chamber to a prolonged bipartisan ovation and proceeds up a center aisle bordered by legislators of both parties clamoring for handshakes and autographs. The audience includes not just senators and representatives but also cabinet members, justices of the Supreme Court, members of the Joint Chiefs of Staff, foreign ambassadors and, in an innovation introduced by Ronald Reagan and emulated by all of his successors, admirable figures whose stories the president recounts in the speech. In 2015 these ranged from Rebekah Erler, a working mother, to astronaut Scott Kelly. Watching a state of the union address on television with the sound off, one might readily conclude that the president is the government and that everyone else works for him.

In contrast to the setting, however, the address itself shines the national spotlight on the president as chief of government—the leader of the victorious political party in the most recent presidential election. The words the president speaks from the well of the House consist largely of legislative recommendations that he wants Congress to enact, most of them politically controversial. Sometimes, as in Obama's 2015 address, veto threats may be included as warnings to legislators that certain measures should not be passed. Members of the president's party invariably cheer these recommendations and threats, while members of the opposition party cross their arms, look bored, and occasionally boo or hiss.

Like all of the reelected presidents of the post–World War II era, Obama faced an opposition party–controlled Congress at the start of his penultimate year in office. The tensions inherent in a divided government were on dramatic display toward the end of the speech, when sarcastic applause from congressional Republicans greeted his statement that "I have no more campaigns to run." In response, Obama ignited cheers from the Democrats by ad-libbing, "I know, because I won both of them."

⁂ ⁂ ⁂

Mr. Speaker, Mr. Vice President, Members of Congress, my fellow Americans:

We are fifteen years into this new century. Fifteen years that dawned with terror touching our shores; that unfolded with a new generation fighting two long and costly wars; that saw a vicious recession spread across our nation and the world. It has been, and still is, a hard time for many.

But tonight, we turn the page.

Tonight, after a breakthrough year for America, our economy is growing and creating jobs at the fastest pace since 1999. Our unemployment rate is now lower than it was before the financial crisis. More of our kids are graduating than ever before; more of our people are insured than ever before; we are as free from the grip of foreign oil as we've been in almost 30 years.

Tonight, for the first time since 9/11, our combat mission in Afghanistan is over. Six years ago, nearly 180,000 American troops served in Iraq and Afghanistan. Today, fewer than 15,000 remain. And we salute the courage and sacrifice of every man and woman in this 9/11 Generation who has served to keep us safe. We are humbled and grateful for your service.

America, for all that we've endured; for all the grit and hard work required to come back; for all the tasks that lie ahead, know this:

The shadow of crisis has passed, and the State of the Union is strong.

At this moment—with a growing economy, shrinking deficits, bustling industry, and booming energy production—we have risen from recession freer to write our own future than any other nation on Earth. It's now up to us to choose who we want to be over the next fifteen years, and for decades to come.

Will we accept an economy where only a few of us do spectacularly well? Or will we commit ourselves to an economy that generates rising incomes and chances for everyone who makes the effort?

Will we approach the world fearful and reactive, dragged into costly conflicts that strain our military and set back our standing? Or will we lead wisely, using all elements of our power to defeat new threats and protect our planet?

Will we allow ourselves to be sorted into factions and turned against one another—or will we recapture the sense of common purpose that has always propelled America forward?

In two weeks, I will send this Congress a budget filled with ideas that are practical, not partisan. And in the months ahead, I'll crisscross the country making a case for those ideas.

So tonight, I want to focus less on a checklist of proposals, and focus more on the values at stake in the choices before us.

It begins with our economy.

Seven years ago, Rebekah and Ben Erler of Minneapolis were newlyweds. She waited tables. He worked construction. Their first child, Jack, was on the way.

They were young and in love in America, and it doesn't get much better than that.

"If only we had known," Rebekah wrote to me last spring, "what was about to happen to the housing and construction market."

As the crisis worsened, Ben's business dried up, so he took what jobs he could find, even if they kept him on the road for long stretches of time. Rebekah took out student loans, enrolled in community college, and retrained for a new career. They sacrificed for each other. And slowly, it paid off. They bought their first home. They had a second son, Henry. Rebekah got a better job, and then a raise. Ben is back in construction—and home for dinner every night.

"It is amazing," Rebekah wrote, "what you can bounce back from when you have to . . . we are a strong, tight-knit family who has made it through some very, very hard times."

We are a strong, tight-knit family who has made it through some very, very hard times.

America, Rebekah and Ben's story is our story. They represent the millions who have worked hard, and scrimped, and sacrificed, and retooled. You are the reason I ran for this office. You're the people I was thinking of six years ago today, in the darkest months of the crisis, when I stood on the steps of this Capitol and promised we would rebuild our economy on a new foundation. And it's been your effort and resilience that has made it possible for our country to emerge stronger.

We believed we could reverse the tide of outsourcing, and draw new jobs to our shores. And over the past five years, our businesses have created more than 11 million new jobs.

We believed we could reduce our dependence on foreign oil and protect our planet. And today, America is number one in oil and gas. America is number one in wind power. Every three weeks, we bring online as much solar power as we did in all of 2008. And thanks to lower gas prices and higher fuel standards, the typical family this year should save $750 at the pump.

We believed we could prepare our kids for a more competitive world. And today, our younger students have earned the highest math and reading scores on record. Our high school graduation rate has hit an all-time high. And more Americans finish college than ever before.

We believed that sensible regulations could prevent another crisis, shield families from ruin, and encourage fair competition. Today, we have new tools to stop taxpayer-funded bailouts, and a new consumer watchdog to protect us from predatory lending and abusive credit card practices. And in the past year alone, about ten million uninsured Americans finally gained the security of health coverage.

At every step, we were told our goals were misguided or too ambitious; that we would crush jobs and explode deficits. Instead, we've seen the fastest economic growth in over a decade, our deficits cut by two-thirds, a stock market that has doubled, and health care inflation at its lowest rate in fifty years.

So the verdict is clear. Middle-class economics works. Expanding opportunity works. And these policies will continue to work, as long as politics don't get in the way. We can't slow down businesses or put our economy at risk with government shutdowns or fiscal showdowns. We can't put the security of families at risk by taking away their health insurance, or unraveling the new rules on Wall Street, or refighting past battles on immigration when we've got a system to fix. And if a bill comes to my desk that tries to do any of these things, it will earn my veto.

Today, thanks to a growing economy, the recovery is touching more and more lives. Wages are finally starting to rise again. We know that more small business owners plan to raise their employees' pay than at any time since 2007. But here's the thing—those of us here tonight, we need to set our sights higher than just making sure government doesn't halt the progress we're making. We need to do more than just do no harm. Tonight, together, let's do more to restore the link between hard work and growing opportunity for every American.

Because families like Rebekah's still need our help. She and Ben are working as hard as ever, but have to forego vacations and a new car so they can pay off student loans and save for retirement. Basic childcare for Jack and Henry costs more than their mortgage, and almost as much as a year at the University of Minnesota. Like millions of hardworking Americans, Rebekah isn't asking for a handout, but she is asking that we look for more ways to help families get ahead.

In fact, at every moment of economic change throughout our history, this country has taken bold action to adapt to new circumstances, and to make sure everyone gets a fair shot. We set up worker protections, Social Security, Medicare, and Medicaid to protect ourselves from the harshest adversity. We gave our citizens schools and colleges, infrastructure and the internet—tools they needed to go as far as their effort will take them.

That's what middle-class economics is—the idea that this country does best when everyone gets their fair shot, everyone does their fair share, and everyone plays by the same set of rules. We don't just want everyone to share in America's success—we want everyone to contribute to our success.

So what does middle-class economics require in our time?

First—middle-class economics means helping working families feel more secure in a world of constant change. That means helping folks afford childcare, college, health care, a home, retirement—and my budget will address each of these issues, lowering the taxes of working families and putting thousands of dollars back into their pockets each year.

Here's one example. During World War II, when men like my grandfather went off to war, having women like my grandmother in the workforce was a national security priority—so this country provided universal childcare. In today's economy, when having both parents in the workforce is an economic necessity for many families, we need affordable, high-quality childcare more than ever. It's not a nice-to-have—it's a must-have. It's time we stop treating childcare as a side issue, or a women's issue, and treat it like the national economic priority that it is for all of us. And that's why my plan will make quality childcare more available, and more affordable, for every middle-class and low-income family with young children in America—by creating more slots and a new tax cut of up to $3,000 per child, per year.

Here's another example. Today, we're the only advanced country on Earth that doesn't guarantee paid sick leave or paid maternity leave to our workers. Forty-three million workers have no paid sick leave. Forty-three million. Think about that. And that forces too many parents to make the gut-wrenching choice between a paycheck and a sick kid at home. So I'll be taking new action to help states adopt paid leave laws of their own. And since paid sick leave won where it was on the ballot last November, let's put it to a vote right here in Washington. Send me a bill that gives every worker in America the opportunity to earn seven days of paid sick leave. It's the right thing to do.

Of course, nothing helps families make ends meet like higher wages. That's why this Congress still needs to pass a law that makes sure a woman is paid the same as a man for doing the same work. Really. It's 2015. It's time. We still need to make sure employees get the overtime they've earned. And to everyone in this Congress who still refuses to raise the minimum wage, I say this: If you truly believe you could work full-time and support a family on less than $15,000 a year, go try it. If not, vote to give millions of the hardest-working people in America a raise.

These ideas won't make everybody rich, or relieve every hardship. That's not the job of government. To give working families a fair shot, we'll still need more employers to see beyond next quarter's earnings and recognize that investing in their workforce is in their company's long-term interest. We still need laws that strengthen rather than weaken unions, and give American workers a voice. But things like child care and sick leave and equal pay; things like lower mortgage premiums and a higher minimum wage—these ideas will make a meaningful difference in the lives of millions of families. That is a fact. And that's what all of us—Republicans and Democrats alike—were sent here to do.

Second, to make sure folks keep earning higher wages down the road, we have to do more to help Americans upgrade their skills.

America thrived in the 20th century because we made high school free, sent a generation of GIs to college, and trained the best workforce in the world. But in a 21st century economy that rewards knowledge like never before, we need to do more.

By the end of this decade, two in three job openings will require some higher education. Two in three. And yet, we still live in a country where too many bright, striving Americans are priced out of the education they need. It's not fair to them, and it's not smart for our future.

That's why I am sending this Congress a bold new plan to lower the cost of community college—to zero.

Forty percent of our college students choose community college. Some are young and starting out. Some are older and looking for a better job. Some are veterans and single parents trying to transition back into the job market. Whoever you are, this plan is your chance to graduate ready for the new economy, without a load of debt. Understand, you've got to earn it—you've got to keep your grades up and graduate on time. Tennessee, a state with Republican leadership, and Chicago, a city with Democratic leadership, are showing that free community college is possible. I want to spread that idea all across America, so that two years of college becomes as free and universal in America as high school is today. And I want to work with this Congress, to make sure Americans already burdened with student loans can reduce their monthly payments, so that student debt doesn't derail anyone's dreams.

Thanks to Vice President Biden's great work to update our job training system, we're connecting community colleges with local employers to train workers to fill high-paying jobs like coding, and nursing, and robotics. Tonight, I'm also asking more businesses to follow the lead of companies like CVS and UPS, and offer more educational benefits and paid apprenticeships—opportunities that give workers the chance to earn higher-paying jobs even if they don't have a higher education.

And as a new generation of veterans comes home, we owe them every opportunity to live the American Dream they helped defend. Already, we've made strides towards ensuring that every veteran has access to the highest quality care. We're slashing the backlog that had too many veterans waiting years to get the benefits they need, and we're making it easier for vets to translate their training and experience into civilian jobs. Joining Forces, the national campaign launched by Michelle and Jill Biden, has helped nearly 700,000 veterans and military spouses get new jobs. So to every CEO in America, let me repeat: If you want somebody who's going to get the job done, hire a veteran.

Finally, as we better train our workers, we need the new economy to keep churning out high-wage jobs for our workers to fill.

Since 2010, America has put more people back to work than Europe, Japan, and all advanced economies combined. Our manufacturers have added almost 800,000 new jobs. Some of our bedrock sectors, like our auto industry, are booming. But there are also millions of Americans who work in jobs that didn't even exist ten or twenty years ago—jobs at companies like Google, and eBay, and Tesla.

So no one knows for certain which industries will generate the jobs of the future. But we do know we want them here in America. That's why the third part of middle-class economics is about building the most competitive economy anywhere, the place where businesses want to locate and hire.

21st century businesses need 21st century infrastructure—modern ports, stronger bridges, faster trains and the fastest internet. Democrats and Republicans used to agree on this. So let's set our sights higher than a single oil pipeline. Let's pass a bipartisan infrastructure plan that could create more than thirty times as many jobs per year, and make this country stronger for decades to come.

21st century businesses, including small businesses, need to sell more American products overseas. Today, our businesses export more than ever, and exporters tend to pay their workers higher wages. But as we speak, China wants to write the rules for the world's fastest-growing region. That would put our workers and businesses at a disadvantage. Why would we let that happen? We should write those rules. We should level the playing field. That's why I'm asking both parties to give me trade promotion authority to protect American workers, with strong new trade deals from Asia to Europe that aren't just free, but fair.

Look, I'm the first one to admit that past trade deals haven't always lived up to the hype, and that's why we've gone after countries that break the rules at our expense. But ninety-five percent of the world's customers live outside our borders, and we can't close ourselves off from those opportunities. More than half of manufacturing executives have said they're actively looking at bringing jobs back from China. Let's give them one more reason to get it done.

21st century businesses will rely on American science, technology, research and development. I want the country that eliminated polio and mapped the human genome to lead a new era of medicine—one that delivers the right treatment at the right time. In some patients with cystic fibrosis, this approach has reversed a disease once thought unstoppable. Tonight, I'm launching a new Precision Medicine Initiative to bring us closer to curing diseases like cancer and diabetes—and to give all of us access to the personalized information we need to keep ourselves and our families healthier.

I intend to protect a free and open internet, extend its reach to every classroom, and every community, and help folks build the fastest networks, so that the next generation of digital innovators and entrepreneurs have the platform to keep reshaping our world.

I want Americans to win the race for the kinds of discoveries that unleash new jobs—converting sunlight into liquid fuel; creating revolutionary prosthetics, so that a veteran who gave his arms for his country can play catch with his kid; pushing out into the Solar System not just to visit, but to stay. Last month, we launched a new spacecraft as part of a re-energized space program that will send American astronauts to Mars. In two months, to prepare us for those missions, Scott Kelly will begin a year-long stay in space. Good luck, Captain—and make sure to Instagram it.

Now, the truth is, when it comes to issues like infrastructure and basic research, I know there's bipartisan support in this chamber. Members of both parties have told me so. Where we too often run onto the rocks is how to pay for these investments. As Americans, we don't mind paying our fair share of taxes, as long as everybody else does, too. But for far too long, lobbyists have rigged the tax code with loopholes that let some corporations pay nothing while others pay full freight. They've riddled it with giveaways the superrich don't need, denying a break to middle class families who do.

This year, we have an opportunity to change that. Let's close loopholes so we stop rewarding companies that keep profits abroad, and reward those that invest in America. Let's use those savings to rebuild our infrastructure and make it more attractive for companies to bring jobs home. Let's simplify the system and let a small business owner file based on her actual bank statement, instead of the number of accountants she can afford. And let's close the loopholes that lead to inequality by allowing the top one percent to avoid paying taxes on their accumulated wealth. We can use that money to help more families pay for childcare and send their kids to college. We need a tax code that truly helps working Americans trying to get a leg up in the new economy, and we can achieve that together.

Helping hardworking families make ends meet. Giving them the tools they need for good-paying jobs in this new economy. Maintaining the conditions for growth and competitiveness. This is where America needs to go. I believe it's where the American people want to go. It will make our economy stronger a year from now, fifteen years from now, and deep into the century ahead.

Of course, if there's one thing this new century has taught us, it's that we cannot separate our work at home from challenges beyond our shores.

My first duty as Commander-in-Chief is to defend the United States of America. In doing so, the question is not whether America leads in the world, but how. When we make rash decisions, reacting to the headlines instead of using our heads; when the first response to a challenge is to send in our military—then we risk getting drawn into unnecessary conflicts, and neglect the broader strategy we need for a safer, more prosperous world. That's what our enemies want us to do.

I believe in a smarter kind of American leadership. We lead best when we combine military power with strong diplomacy; when we leverage our power with coalition building; when we don't let our fears blind us to the opportunities that this new century presents. That's exactly what we're doing right now—and around the globe, it is making a difference.

First, we stand united with people around the world who've been targeted by terrorists—from a school in Pakistan to the streets of Paris. We will continue to hunt down terrorists and dismantle their networks, and we reserve the right to act unilaterally, as we've done relentlessly since I took office to take out terrorists who pose a direct threat to us and our allies.

At the same time, we've learned some costly lessons over the last thirteen years.

Instead of Americans patrolling the valleys of Afghanistan, we've trained their security forces, who've now taken the lead, and we've honored our troops' sacrifice by supporting that country's first democratic transition. Instead of sending large ground forces overseas, we're partnering with nations from South Asia to North Africa to deny safe haven to terrorists who threaten America. In Iraq and Syria, American leadership—including our military power—is stopping ISIL's advance. Instead of getting dragged into another ground war in the Middle East, we are leading a broad coalition, including Arab nations, to degrade and ultimately destroy this terrorist group. We're also supporting a moderate opposition in Syria that can help us in this effort, and assisting people everywhere who stand up to the bankrupt ideology of violent extremism. This effort will take time. It will require focus. But we will succeed. And tonight, I call on this Congress to show the world that we are united in this mission by passing a resolution to authorize the use of force against ISIL.

Second, we are demonstrating the power of American strength and diplomacy. We're upholding the principle that bigger nations can't bully the small—by opposing Russian aggression, supporting Ukraine's democracy, and reassuring our NATO allies. Last year, as we were doing the hard work of imposing sanctions along with our allies, some suggested that Mr. Putin's aggression was a masterful display of strategy and strength. Well, today, it is America that stands strong and united with our allies, while Russia is isolated, with its economy in tatters.

That's how America leads—not with bluster, but with persistent, steady resolve.

In Cuba, we are ending a policy that was long past its expiration date. When what you're doing doesn't work for fifty years, it's time to try something new. Our shift in Cuba policy has the potential to end a legacy of mistrust in our hemisphere; removes a phony excuse for restrictions in Cuba; stands up for democratic values; and extends the hand of friendship to the Cuban people. And this year, Congress should begin the work of ending the embargo. As His Holiness, Pope Francis, has said, diplomacy is the work of "small steps." These small steps have added up to new hope for the future in Cuba. And after years in prison, we're overjoyed that Alan Gross is back where he belongs. Welcome home, Alan.

Our diplomacy is at work with respect to Iran, where, for the first time in a decade, we've halted the progress of its nuclear program and reduced its stockpile of nuclear material. Between now and this spring, we have a chance to negotiate a comprehensive agreement that prevents a nuclear-armed Iran; secures America and our allies—including Israel; while avoiding yet another Middle East conflict. There are no guarantees that negotiations will succeed, and I keep all options on the table to prevent a nuclear Iran. But new sanctions passed by this Congress, at this moment in time, will all but guarantee that diplomacy fails—alienating America from its allies; and ensuring that Iran starts up its nuclear program again. It doesn't make sense. That is why I will veto any new sanctions bill that threatens to undo this progress. The American people expect us to only go to war as a last resort, and I intend to stay true to that wisdom.

Third, we're looking beyond the issues that have consumed us in the past to shape the coming century.

No foreign nation, no hacker, should be able to shut down our networks, steal our trade secrets, or invade the privacy of American families, especially our kids. We are making sure our government integrates intelligence to combat cyber threats, just as we have done to combat terrorism. And tonight, I urge this Congress to finally pass the legislation we need to better meet the evolving threat of cyber-attacks, combat identity theft, and protect our children's information. If we don't act, we'll leave our nation and our economy vulnerable. If we do, we can continue to protect the technologies that have unleashed untold opportunities for people around the globe.

In West Africa, our troops, our scientists, our doctors, our nurses and healthcare workers are rolling back Ebola—saving countless lives and stopping the spread of disease. I couldn't be prouder of them, and I thank this Congress for your bipartisan support of their efforts. But the job is not yet done—and the world needs to use this lesson to build a more effective global effort to prevent the spread of future pandemics, invest in smart development, and eradicate extreme poverty.

In the Asia Pacific, we are modernizing alliances while making sure that other nations play by the rules—in how they trade, how they resolve maritime disputes, and how they participate in meeting common international challenges like nonproliferation and disaster relief. And no challenge—no challenge—poses a greater threat to future generations than climate change.

2014 was the planet's warmest year on record. Now, one year doesn't make a trend, but this does—14 of the 15 warmest years on record have all fallen in the first 15 years of this century.

I've heard some folks try to dodge the evidence by saying they're not scientists; that we don't have enough information to act. Well, I'm not a scientist, either. But you know what—I know a lot of really good scientists at NASA, and NOAA, and at our major universities. The best scientists in the world are all telling us that our activities are changing the climate, and if we do not act forcefully, we'll continue to see rising oceans, longer, hotter heat waves, dangerous droughts and floods, and massive disruptions that can trigger greater migration, conflict, and hunger around the globe. The Pentagon says that climate change poses immediate risks to our national security. We should act like it.

That's why, over the past six years, we've done more than ever before to combat climate change, from the way we produce energy, to the way we use it. That's why we've set aside more public lands and waters than any administration in history. And that's why I will not let this Congress endanger the health of our children by turning back the clock on our efforts. I am determined to make sure American leadership drives international action. In Beijing, we made an historic announcement—the United States will double the pace at which we cut carbon pollution, and China committed, for the first time, to limiting their emissions. And because the world's two largest economies came together, other nations are now stepping up, and offering hope that, this year, the world will finally reach an agreement to protect the one planet we've got.

There's one last pillar to our leadership—and that's the example of our values.

As Americans, we respect human dignity, even when we're threatened, which is why I've prohibited torture, and worked to make sure our use of new technology like drones is properly constrained. It's why we speak out against the deplorable anti-Semitism that has resurfaced in certain parts of the world. It's why we continue to reject offensive stereotypes of Muslims—the vast majority of whom share our commitment to peace. That's why we defend free speech, and advocate for political prisoners, and condemn the persecution of women, or religious minorities, or people who are lesbian, gay, bisexual, or transgender. We do these things not only because they're right, but because they make us safer.

As Americans, we have a profound commitment to justice—so it makes no sense to spend three million dollars per prisoner to keep open a prison that the world condemns and terrorists use to recruit. Since I've been President, we've worked responsibly to cut the population of GTMO in half. Now it's time to finish the job. And I will not relent in my determination to shut it down. It's not who we are.

As Americans, we cherish our civil liberties—and we need to uphold that commitment if we want maximum cooperation from other countries and industry in our fight against terrorist networks. So while some have moved on from the debates over our surveillance programs, I haven't. As promised, our intelligence agencies have worked hard, with the recommendations of privacy advocates, to increase transparency and build more safeguards against potential abuse. And next month, we'll issue a report on how we're keeping our promise to keep our country safe while strengthening privacy.

Looking to the future instead of the past. Making sure we match our power with diplomacy, and use force wisely. Building coalitions to meet new challenges and opportunities. Leading—always—with the example of our values. That's what makes us exceptional. That's what keeps us strong. And that's why we must keep striving to hold ourselves to the highest of standards—our own.

You know, just over a decade ago, I gave a speech in Boston where I said there wasn't a liberal America, or a conservative America; a black America or a white America—but a United States of America. I said this because I had seen it in my own life, in a nation that gave someone like me a chance; because I grew up in Hawaii, a melting pot of races and customs; because I made Illinois my home—a state of small towns, rich farmland, and one of the world's great cities; a microcosm of the country where Democrats and Republicans and Independents, good people of every ethnicity and every faith, share certain bedrock values.

Over the past six years, the pundits have pointed out more than once that my presidency hasn't delivered on this vision. How ironic, they say, that our politics seems more divided than ever. It's held up as proof not just of my own flaws—of which there are many—but also as proof that the vision itself is misguided, and naïve, and that there are too many people in this town who actually benefit from partisanship and gridlock for us to ever do anything about it.

I know how tempting such cynicism may be. But I still think the cynics are wrong.

I still believe that we are one people. I still believe that together, we can do great things, even when the odds are long. I believe this because over and over in my six years in office, I have seen America at its best. I've seen the hopeful faces of young graduates from New York to California; and our newest officers at West Point, Annapolis, Colorado Springs, and New London. I've mourned with grieving families in Tucson and Newtown; in Boston, West Texas, and West Virginia. I've watched

Americans beat back adversity from the Gulf Coast to the Great Plains; from Midwest assembly lines to the Mid-Atlantic seaboard. I've seen something like gay marriage go from a wedge issue used to drive us apart to a story of freedom across our country, a civil right now legal in states that seven in ten Americans call home.

So I know the good, and optimistic, and big-hearted generosity of the American people who, every day, live the idea that we are our brother's keeper, and our sister's keeper. And I know they expect those of us who serve here to set a better example.

So the question for those of us here tonight is how we, all of us, can better reflect America's hopes. I've served in Congress with many of you. I know many of you well. There are a lot of good people here, on both sides of the aisle. And many of you have told me that this isn't what you signed up for—arguing past each other on cable shows, the constant fundraising, always looking over your shoulder at how the base will react to every decision.

Imagine if we broke out of these tired old patterns. Imagine if we did something different.

Understand—a better politics isn't one where Democrats abandon their agenda or Republicans simply embrace mine.

A better politics is one where we appeal to each other's basic decency instead of our basest fears.

A better politics is one where we debate without demonizing each other; where we talk issues, and values, and principles, and facts, rather than "gotcha" moments, or trivial gaffes, or fake controversies that have nothing to do with people's daily lives.

A better politics is one where we spend less time drowning in dark money for ads that pull us into the gutter, and spend more time lifting young people up, with a sense of purpose and possibility, and asking them to join in the great mission of building America.

If we're going to have arguments, let's have arguments—but let's make them debates worthy of this body and worthy of this country.

We still may not agree on a woman's right to choose, but surely we can agree it's a good thing that teen pregnancies and abortions are nearing all-time lows, and that every woman should have access to the health care she needs.

Yes, passions still fly on immigration, but surely we can all see something of ourselves in the striving young student, and agree that no one benefits when a hardworking mom is taken from her child, and that it's possible to shape a law that upholds our tradition as a nation of laws and a nation of immigrants.

We may go at it in campaign season, but surely we can agree that the right to vote is sacred; that it's being denied to too many; and that, on this 50th anniversary of the great march from Selma to Montgomery and the passage of the Voting Rights Act, we can come together, Democrats and Republicans, to make voting easier for every single American.

We may have different takes on the events of Ferguson and New York. But surely we can understand a father who fears his son can't walk home without being harassed. Surely we can understand the wife who won't rest until the police officer she married walks through the front door at the end of his shift. Surely we can agree it's a good thing that for the first time in 40 years, the crime rate and the incarceration rate have come down together, and use that as a starting point for Democrats and Republicans, community leaders and law enforcement, to reform America's criminal justice system so that it protects and serves us all.

That's a better politics. That's how we start rebuilding trust. That's how we move this country forward. That's what the American people want. That's what they deserve.

I have no more campaigns to run. My only agenda for the next two years is the same as the one I've had since the day I swore an oath on the steps of this Capitol—to do what I believe is best for America. If you share the broad vision I outlined tonight, join me in the work at hand. If you disagree with parts of it, I hope you'll at least work with me where you do agree. And I commit to every Republican here tonight that I will not only seek out your ideas, I will seek to work with you to make this country stronger.

Because I want this chamber, this city, to reflect the truth—that for all our blind spots and shortcomings, we are a people with the strength and generosity of spirit to bridge divides, to unite in common effort, and help our neighbors, whether down the street or on the other side of the world.

I want our actions to tell every child, in every neighborhood: your life matters, and we are as committed to improving your life chances as we are for our own kids.

I want future generations to know that we are a people who see our differences as a great gift, that we are a people who value the dignity and worth of every citizen—man and woman, young and old, black and white, Latino and Asian, immigrant and Native American, gay and straight, Americans with mental illness or physical disability.

I want them to grow up in a country that shows the world what we still know to be true: that we are still more than a collection of red states and blue states; that we are the United States of America.

I want them to grow up in a country where a young mom like Rebekah can sit down and write a letter to her President with a story to sum up these past six years:

"It is amazing what you can bounce back from when you have to . . . we are a strong, tight-knit family who has made it through some very, very hard times."

My fellow Americans, we too are a strong, tight-knit family. We, too, have made it through some hard times. Fifteen years into this new century, we have picked ourselves up, dusted ourselves off, and begun again the work of remaking America. We've laid a new foundation. A brighter future is ours to write. Let's begin this new chapter—together—and let's start the work right now.

Thank you, God bless you, and God bless this country we love.